Palgrave Studies in Young People and Politics

Series Editors
James Sloam
Royal Holloway, University of London
Dept of Politics and International Relations
Egham, United Kingdom

Constance Flanagan
School of Human Ecology
University of Wisconsin–Madison
Madison, Wisconsin, USA

Bronwyn Hayward
University of Canterbury
School of Social and Political Sciences
Christchurch, New Zealand

Over the past few decades, many democracies have experienced low or falling voter turnout and a sharp decline in the members of mainstream political parties. These trends are most striking amongst young people, who have become alienated from mainstream electoral politics in many countries across the world. Young people are today faced by a particularly tough environment. From worsening levels of child poverty, to large increases in youth unemployment, to cuts in youth services and education budgets, public policy responses to the financial crisis have placed a disproportionate burden on the young.

This book series will provide an in-depth investigation of the changing nature of youth civic and political engagement. We particularly welcome contributions looking at:

- Youth political participation: for example, voting, demonstrations, and consumer politics.
- The engagement of young people in civic and political institutions, such as political parties, NGOs and new social movements.
- The influence of technology, the news media and social media on young people's politics.
- How democratic innovations, such as social institutions, electoral reform, civic education, can rejuvenate democracy.
- The civic and political development of young people during their transition from childhood to adulthood (political socialisation).
- Young people's diverse civic and political identities, as defined by issues of gender, class and ethnicity.
- Key themes in public policy affecting younger citizens – e.g. youth (un)employment and education.
- Cross-cutting themes such as intergenerational inequality, social mobility, and participation in policy-making – e.g. school councils, youth parliaments and youth wings of political parties.

The series will incorporate a mixture of pivot publications (25,000–50,000 words), full-length monographs and edited volumes that will analyse these issues within individual countries, comparatively, and/or through the lenses of different case studies.

More information about this series at
http://www.springer.com/series/15478

Sarah Pickard • Judith Bessant
Editors

Young People Re-Generating Politics in Times of Crises

palgrave
macmillan

Editors
Sarah Pickard
Université Sorbonne Nouvelle
Paris, France

Judith Bessant
RMIT University
Melbourne, Australia

Palgrave Studies in Young People and Politics
ISBN 978-3-319-86359-7   ISBN 978-3-319-58250-4   (eBook)
DOI 10.1007/978-3-319-58250-4

© The Editor(s) (if applicable) and The Author(s) 2018
Softcover reprint of the hardcover 1st edition 2017
This work is subject to copyright. All rights are solely and exclusively licensed by the Publisher, whether the whole or part of the material is concerned, specifically the rights of translation, reprinting, reuse of illustrations, recitation, broadcasting, reproduction on microfilms or in any other physical way, and transmission or information storage and retrieval, electronic adaptation, computer software, or by similar or dissimilar methodology now known or hereafter developed.
The use of general descriptive names, registered names, trademarks, service marks, etc. in this publication does not imply, even in the absence of a specific statement, that such names are exempt from the relevant protective laws and regulations and therefore free for general use.
The publisher, the authors and the editors are safe to assume that the advice and information in this book are believed to be true and accurate at the date of publication. Neither the publisher nor the authors or the editors give a warranty, express or implied, with respect to the material contained herein or for any errors or omissions that may have been made. The publisher remains neutral with regard to jurisdictional claims in published maps and institutional affiliations.

Printed on acid-free paper

This Palgrave Macmillan imprint is published by Springer Nature
The registered company is Springer International Publishing AG
The registered company address is: Gewerbestrasse 11, 6330 Cham, Switzerland

This book is dedicated to the memory of Professor Andy Furlong who did so much for Youth Studies and young people.

Acknowledgements

We would like to thank all the contributors for their valuable insights into the diverse and rich ways young people are engaging politically.

Thanks also go to the young people around the world involved in projects like those documented in this book who give hope for our future.

We are grateful to Ambra Finotello and Imogen Gordon Clark at Palgrave Macmillan for their enthusiasm and support.

We are also most grateful for the constructive observations and comments made by the anonymous peer reviewers.

Lastly, we are indebted to our respective universities for providing the institutional support that allowed us to develop this project: Université Sorbonne Nouvelle, France and RMIT University, Australia.

Sarah Pickard and *Judith Bessant*
Paris and Melbourne, March 2017

Also by Sarah Pickard

Pickard, S. (2018). *Politics, protest and young people. Political participation and dissent in Britain in the 21st century.* London: Palgrave Macmillan.

Pickard, S. (2017). *Civilisation Britannique-British Civilisation* (bilingual). 12th revised edition. Paris: Pocket.

Pickard, S. (Ed.). (2014). *Anti-social behaviour in Britain: Victorian and contemporary perspectives.* Basingstoke: Palgrave Macmillan.

Pickard, S. (Ed.). (2014). *Higher education in the UK and the US: Converging university models in a global academic world?* Leiden and Boston: Brill.

Pickard, S., Nativel, C., & Portier, F. (Eds.). (2012). *Les Politiques de Jeunesse au Royaume-Uni et en France: Désaffection, Répression et Accompagnement à la Citoyenneté.* Paris: Presses de la Sorbonne Nouvelle (PSN).

Pickard, S. (2009). *Phénomènes Sociaux en Grande-Bretagne Aujourd'hui.* Paris: Ellipses.

Pickard, S. (2007). *Les Anglais.* Paris: Cavalier Bleu.

Also by Judith Bessant

Bessant, J. (2018). *The great transformation, politics, labour and learning in the digital age.* London and New York: Routledge.

Grasso, M., & Bessant, J. (Eds.). (2018). *Governing youth politics in the age of surveillance.* London and New York: Routledge.

Bessant, J., Farthing, R., & Watts, R. (2017). *The precarious generation: A political economy of young people.* London and New York: Routledge.

Bessant, J. (2014). *Democracy bytes: New media and new politics and generational change.* London: Palgrave Macmillan.

General Editor for Book Series: 'Criminalization of political dissent.' London and New York: Routledge.

Contents

1 Introduction   1
Sarah Pickard and Judith Bessant

Part I   Young People and Student Activism   17

2 Young People and the #Hashtags That Broke the Rainbow Nation   19
Rekgotsofetse Chikane

3 Students Taking Action in Los Angeles Schools: An Ethnographic Case Study of Student Activism in the United States   41
Analicia Mejia Mesinas

4 'Professional Students Do Not Play Politics': How Kenyan Students Professionalise Environmental Activism and Produce Neoliberal Subjectivities   59
Grace Muthoni Mwaura

5 The 'Good,' the 'Bad' and the 'Useless': Young People's
   Political Action Repertoires in Quebec   77
   Nicole Gallant

Part II Young People and Online Political Action   95

6 The Crisis of Democracy in Hong Kong: Young People's
   Online Politics and the Umbrella Movement   97
   Rob Watts

7 Momentum and the Movementist 'Corbynistas': Young
   People Regenerating the Labour Party in Britain   115
   Sarah Pickard

8 Right-Wing Populism and Young 'Stormers': Conflict
   in Democratic Politics   139
   Judith Bessant

9 'How Not to Be a Terrorist': Radicalisation and Young
   Western Muslims' Digital Discourses   161
   Andrew Hope and Julie Matthews

10 Young People's Political Participation in Europe in
   Times of Crisis   179
   Maria Grasso

Part III Young People, Collective Identity and Community
          Building   197

11 The Gezi Resistance of Turkey as Young People's
   Counter-Conduct   199
   Nilay Çabuk Kaya and Haktan Ural

12	Off the Radar Democracy: Young People's Alternative Acts of Citizenship in Australia Lucas Walsh and Rosalyn Black	217
13	(Re)Politicising Young People: From Scotland's Indyref to Hong Kong's Umbrella Movement Susan Batchelor, Alistair Fraser, Leona Li Ngai Ling, and Lisa Whittaker	233
14	New Forms of Solidarity and Young People: An Ethnography of Youth Participation in Italy Nicola De Luigi, Alessandro Martelli, and Ilaria Pitti	253
15	Youth Heteropolitics in Crisis-Ridden Greece Alexandros Kioupkiolis and Yannis Pechtelidis	273

Part IV Young People and Protest as Politics 295

16	Youth-Led Struggles Against Racialized Crime Control in the United States Tim Goddard and Randolph R. Myers	297
17	Youth Work, Agonistic Democracy and Transgressive Enjoyment in England Graham Bright, Carole Pugh, and Matthew Clarke	315
18	Political Participation and Activism in the Post-15m Era: Young People's Political Identifications in Lleida, Catalonia Eduard Ballesté Isern and José Sánchez García	333

19 New Modes of Youth Political Action and Democracy in the Americas: From the Chilean Spring to the Maple Spring in Quebec 349
Ricardo Peñafiel and Marie-Christine Doran

20 Youth Participation in Eastern Europe in the Age of Austerity 375
Marko Kovacic and Danijela Dolenec

Index 395

List of Abbreviations and Acronyms

ABC	Australian Broadcasting Commission
ABS	Australian Bureau of Statistics
ANC	African National Congress
ANCYL	African National Congress Youth League
AYF	Australian Youth Forum
BBC	British Broadcasting Corporation
BES	British Election Study
BOE	Board of Education of the City of Los Angeles
CODESA	Convention for a Democratic South Africa
CRC	Community Rights Campaign
DDS	Distributed Denial of Service
DoH	Department of Health
EDL	English Defence League
EFF	Economic Freedom Fighters
EU	European Union
FMF	FeesMustFall
GDP	Gross Domestic Product
GFC	Global Financial Crisis
IER	Individual Electoral Registration
ILO	International Labour Organization
IMF	International Monetary Fund
ISSP	International Social Science Programme
JDP	Justice and Development Party
LASPD	Los Angeles School Police Department
LAUSD	Los Angeles Unified School District
LCSC	The Labor Community Strategy Center
LGBTQ	Lesbian, Gay, Bisexual, Transgender and Queer

LSX	London Stock Exchange
MEP	Member of the European Parliament
MP	Member of Parliament
NCAFC	National Campaign Against Fees and Cuts
NCG	National Coordinating Group
NCIT	New Communication and Information Technologies
NCS	National Citizenship Service
NEC	National Executive Committee
NEET	Not in Education, Employment or Training
NGO	Non-Governmental Organisation
NHS	National Health Service
NVRD	National Voter Registration Day
NYPD	New York Police Department
OECD	Organisation for Economic Cooperative Development
OMOV	One Member One Vote
PAH	*Plataforma de Afectados por las Hipotecas*
PaTH	Prepare, Trial, Hire
PLP	Parliamentary Labour Party
PRC	People's Republic of China
RMF	RhodesMustFall
SAPA	South Africa Press Association
SNP	Scottish National Party
SONA	State of the Nation Address
SRC	Student Representative Council
SSA	Statistics South Africa
SWP	Socialist Workers Party
TUSC	Trade Union and Socialist Coalition
UCEN	Central University of Chile
UKIP	United Kingdom Independence Party
UNICEF	United Nations International Children's Fund
YCC	Youth Citizenship Commission
YOTP	Youth Organizer Training Programs

List of Illustrations

Fig. 20.1	Total expenditure on social protection, per inhabitant, Europe	380
Table 7.1	Results of the Labour Party leadership election, Britain, 2015	119
Table 10.1	Age group differences in political activism	183
Table 10.2	Age group differences in political activism, by country	185
Table 10.3	Levels of political activism by generations	188
Table 10.4	Class differences in political activism	191
Table 13.1	Focus group sample, Glasgow	239
Table 13.2	Focus group sample, Hong Kong	239
Table 20.1	Austerity in the core and peripheral EU member states, 2014	383
Table 20.2	Conventional youth participation, EU member states, 2014	385
Table 20.3	Unconventional youth political participation, EU member states, 2014	387

CHAPTER 1

Introduction

Sarah Pickard and Judith Bessant

This book counters the widespread negative stereotypes from the media and elsewhere that portray young people today as apolitical. The authors contest claims that young people constitute a passive, narcissistic, self-motivated and individualistic 'me generation,' which is just one negative generalisation among a plethora of simplistic and negative catch phrases and clichés used to claim young people today form 'a generation' who have no interest or involvement in politics and public affairs. The book also counters the claim that young people's alleged civic disengagement threatens the legitimacy of democratic political systems, thereby creating a looming 'crisis of democracy.' We argue that rather than being responsible for 'the end of democracy,' there are significant numbers of young people assuming political responsibility and in doing so they are regenerating democracy. They do this by participating politically in numerous creative ways that address directly and indirectly the multifarious socio-economic,

S. Pickard (✉)
British Studies and Youth Studies, Université Sorbonne Nouvelle, Paris, France

J. Bessant
School of Global, Urban and Social Studies, Royal Melbourne Institute of Technology (RMIT) University, Melbourne, VIC, Australia

© The Author(s) 2018
S. Pickard, J. Bessant (eds.), *Young People Re-Generating Politics in Times of Crises*, Palgrave Studies in Young People and Politics, DOI 10.1007/978-3-319-58250-4_1

political, democratic, constitutional and environmental crises that have shaped and are shaping the world in which they live today.

In this introduction to *Young People Re-Generating Politics in Times of Crises*, we first examine the main features of these crises that many young people face in different ways. Next, we identify some of the means by which young people are exercising their political agency to regenerate politics around the globe. We then introduce each of the 20 chapters by 34 contributors who document the many and varied ways young people are regenerating politics in time of crisis in Africa, Asia, Australia, Central and South America, Europe and North America. Evidence drawn on in this book provides the basis for an optimistic outlook on young people and politics in the early twenty-first century.

Young People Facing Manifold Crises

This book was written as we head into the third decade of the third millennium. Previous centuries saw the Age of Enlightenment and the Industrial Revolution, as well as democratic revolutions in France and the United States of America. Added to this were processes of colonisation, which together contributed to transforming the western world to begin with and in time most other parts of the world, in ways that seemed to hold out the promise of progress. It was a promise based on technological rationalisation, unprecedented wealth creation and democratic politics, as well as liberal rights and freedoms.

This faith in fundamental concepts such as progress, liberalism, democracy and social justice remains potent. For many young people, these ideas inform their expectations that guides their hopes and dreams for a better future. However, for too many young people, the reality of their (everyday) lives differs quite radically from that expectation of a decent future. Too many young people confront minimal employment prospects, inadequate basic public services, high levels of debt, shortages of affordable adequate housing, a lack of access to (affordable) education, poor provision of physical and mental health care, non-existent or under-funded youth services, poor policing, prejudices, and considerable intergenerational inequalities.

This context that can be explained largely in terms of the dominant neoliberal worldview that policy-makers adopted as they drove waves of reforms from the late 1970s across the global north and the globe south (Bessant, Farthing, & Watts, 2017; Howker & Malik, 2013[2010];

Jones, 2017; Mizen, 2003; Sukarieh & Tannock, 2014). While acknowledging the different ways neoliberalism has been expressed and how it has been variously experienced by young people, the decisions taken by governments and other power elites contributed to a sense of insecurity, precarity and fear among many young people about their future (Furlong, 2009, 2014; Standing, 2011).

The neoliberal policy regime brought about the deregulation of the financial and labour markets, reneging on commitments to full employment and reductions in many key state welfare programs, accompanied by 'a punitive turn' and new forms of authoritarianism in youth justice and welfare. The new policy rhetoric spoke of the morality of 'user pays,' 'reciprocal obligation' and an 'active society.' In addition, many countries saw the progressive privatisation, marketisation and contracting out of public activities, hitherto critical to the lives of large numbers of young people without the means to pay for basic civic goods. These policies in conjunction with a commitment to free trade policies led to the demise of many industries where young people had historically began their working lives and careers. It produced the near complete collapse of the full-time youth labour market, as youth unemployment and underemployment became the new norm.

In parallel with this development, increasing numbers of young people have been encouraged by governments to remain in some form of education or training. One consequence of this has been the dramatic growth of higher education enrolments against the backdrop of its marketisation (Ward, 2014). It was, in part, a policy attempt to reduce youth unemployment and under-employment that increased significantly under the reign of neoliberalism (Côté, 2014). Moreover, as enrolments grew the value of young people's formal academic qualifications declined due to credential inflation (Furlong, 2009). Additionally, in many countries cuts to public spending on higher education and the rise in tuition fees shifted the cost of education onto young people and their families. For many, and particularly those from middle class and lower socio-economic backgrounds, this meant having to combine full or part-time work with full or part-time study, and carrying significant student debt (Pickard, 2014). This is a situation in which many young graduates find themselves as they struggle to secure a decent job and pursue some semblance of income security.

Many young people interpret these conditions as the result of a failure on the part of governments and other power elites to do their job; namely, to develop a political agenda and policies that are supportive of young people's aspirations to live a good life. This is why so many young people say they are taking action into their own hands by engaging in politics themselves.

Technology and particularly the increasing use of information and communication technology in the labour market has exacerbated existing tensions and conflicts in the economy, while amplifying inequality. Whilst these innovations initially affected manual, unskilled and low-skilled workers (i.e., traditional working-class jobs), more recently, they have begun affecting high skilled, well credentialed professional workers, in clerical, administrative and professional fields. It is now 'disrupting' the lives of many who hoped their costly investment in 'human capital investment' (education) and steadfast commitment to the work ethic would protect them from the threat of technological unemployment that had shadowed the lives of their working-class peers (Streeck, 2016; Wallerstein, Collins, Mann, Derluguian, & Calhoun, 2013). The creation of new jobs, however, will not replace those lost to technological displacement, while increasingly most new jobs that are created tend to be typically precarious and part-time (Ford, 2015).

The lives of young people are also influenced by current and persistent national and global crises. The twenty-first century began with the 9/11 attacks on New York and Washington in the United States of America, which segued into US-led wars in Afghanistan and Iraq. These were military and humanitarian disasters that in turn ignited war in Syria, and unleashed one of the cruellest refugee and humanitarian crisis in modern times with 65 million refugees seeking sanctuary in early 2017. International relations are now shaped by on-going armed conflicts in Syria, Libya, Ukraine and elsewhere around the globe, each of which are linked to growing xenophobic nationalism, religion, and populism.

Liberal states across the globe now claim they are fighting a 'war on terror' mandating assaults on their own long-cherished liberal rights and freedoms. In many cases, it has seen the criminalisation of journalists reporting news and penalisation of citizens engaging in political dissent. It is a development that has triggered concern about the chilling effect the prevailing preoccupation with security and 'threat' of terror is having on the social and political life of our communities.

The 'triumph of free markets' culminated in the Great Recession of 2008 the most serious economic crisis since the 1930s depression. The consequence of a series of disasters in the banking, credit and finance sectors, it was kick-started by the deregulation of the financial markets in the late 1990s, which culminated in 'the crash' that saw the bankruptcy of major banks and financial houses, and the drying up of the supply of credit. To address these problems, governments used taxpayers' money to fund bank bailouts and other major financial institutions responsible for bringing on the crisis. All this drew attention to the ways governments and the finance sector—informed by a neoliberal worldview—were creating a degree of social inequality not seen since the 1890s. It also drew attention to the risky, irresponsible and even criminal conduct of many players in the banking sector and financial sector generally.

Added to this is the environmental challenge posed by climate warming underscoring the fact we live on a small and fragile planet. Climate change is so challenging that many are now asking whether the dominant socio-economic worldview premised on a commitment to constant growth of productivity, energy and consumerism is viable. If the past half-century has been a time of unparalleled economic growth and development, it is now haunted by what Žižek (2011) calls the 'horsemen of the apocalypse,' his metaphor for the threat posed by war, climate catastrophe, famine and insufficient drinking water.

Nor can we ignore the recent history of repeated economic crises, involving a series of governance and ethical failures resulting in 'banking panics,' debt defaults and currency crises. These led to austerity policies ostensibly designed to address the economic problems, but which placed a disproportionate burden on the more vulnerable (the young, the aged and the poor). Importantly, they are austerity regimes that provoked popular protest and widespread uncertainty about the value of the dominant neoclassical model of economics that encourages pursuit of never ending economic growth and increasing social inequality (Piketty, 2014). Today, young people live in a world marked by unprecedented levels of economic inequality and uncertainty.

Following the global financial crisis in 2008, numerous countries across the globe fell into deep recession. In a bid to reach recovery, many governments responded by cutting public spending to reduce government budget deficits imposing harsh 'austerity policies' that further exacerbated poverty and unemployment across western societies. This crisis was experienced differently across the world. While countries such as Australia and Germany were relatively unaffected, the impact on others such as Brazil, Greece, Pakistan, South Africa, Spain and the United States of America were seriously detrimental. Common to all, however, was the disproportionate impact on particular demographic groups and specifically young people.

In a globalised world, that some people say has homogenised cultures, we have witnessed a significant revival of parochial politics centring on local issues of racial, religious and nationalist identity and sentiment. In 2016, for example, the referendum on whether the United Kingdom should remain in or leave the European Union (EU) was enveloped by 'little Englander' and national-centric anti-immigration discourses emanating from toxic populists like Nigel Farage, then-leader of the United Kingdom Independence Party (UKIP) and other politicians. The result was a victory for those advocating 'Brexit,' although a clear majority of young people voted to remain in the EU. Similarly, Donald Trump's victory in the 2016 Presidential elections in the United States signified an equivalent shift toward xenophobic nationalism and isolationism, while the more liberal views of Bernie Sanders made him popular amongst many younger voters.

In many countries around the world, political issues related to race, ethnicity, religion and culture have animated social movements. The 'Black Lives Matters' social movement highlights how in the United States, like in Australia, South Africa and many other countries still carry a significant white racist legacy. In South Africa, the legacy of apartheid combined with high levels of unemployment and poverty manifests in new forms, continuing to plague the lives of its population. Across the globe, from France, to the Netherlands, to Germany, to the USA and Australia, we see the resurgence of ultra-right extremism and conservatism reshaping the political right and attracting the hearts and minds of many young people via new media.

Meanwhile, struggles to establish basic democratic practices continue, such as free and democratic elections and civic rights, freedom of the press, freedom of speech, freedom of academics and freedom from arbitrary arrest continue, in countries including Chile, China, Hong Kong, Malaysia, Myanmar, Russia, South Africa and Turkey. Far from assuming there is one inevitable model these countries will take, the question of what paths they pursue remains a matter of political contest to be determined politically with no guarantee 'the solutions' will be liberal or democratic. This is why the intervention by young people will prove critical to these countries.

All of this points to a pattern of on-going crisis. However, any popular concern about a 'politics of fear' (Furedi, 2007), a loss of political alternatives and a crisis of democracy manifest in disengagement with politics on the part of young people is radically misplaced. As the contributors to this book argue politics is very much alive, and at the centre of it are young people.

Young People Exercising Their Political Agency and Regenerating Politics

Young people around the world are responding to these local, national and global crises in a variety of ways. It is action that occurs against a background that began emerging in the 1990s characterised by popular accounts of young people as politically apathetic, lazy and politically disengaged due to their excessive preoccupation with material and leisure pursuits. This view evolved into pejorative suggestions that young people are self-absorbed and living their lives through superficial social media experiences. This has proved to be a pervasive and resilient portrayal, perpetrated through mainstream media, politics and through mainstream media and politics, and to some extent in academia (for example, Twenge, 2014[2007]).

There has been growing interest on the part of some social and political scientists in refuting these negative claims and pointing to the ways many young people are engaging politically and creating new kinds of politics. However, it has tended to rely on relatively small scale studies or confined to a few regions of the globe (Bessant, 2014; Manning, 2015; Pickard, 2018).

This edited collection builds on this more constructive literature by documenting how young people from different parts of the world are engaging in redemptive actions that are regenerating politics. The volume also explores some of the many and varied ways young people are experiencing a sense of felt crisis and injustice, which move them to engage politically and enact change. The authors provide a rich body of evidence that illustrates the imaginative and creative engagement of young people in politics today. Each chapter reveals how young people are indeed participating in old and new forms of political action locally, nationally and globally. This is a process that is reclaiming the public sphere, while opening up new sites for deliberative practice, community building, critique and mobilisation.

In most cases, young people's actions are born out of the distinct fabric of their own political experience, whether that be those of young Muslims in Adelaide, Australia living with deep-seated prejudices, or English university students concerned about rising tuition fees and graduate under/unemployment. In the ways documented in this book, young people are giving a renewed immediacy to the political through their voices and through their actions. The chapters in this volume document how young people are developing ways of speaking and being heard that recognise the conditions of public life, including the value of their own political autonomy and agency. In these ways, young people's actions help mitigate the erosion of the public sphere.

Importantly, the cases in this book directly challenge conventional understandings of the 'political' and the narrow and restrictive nature of those definitions of what counts as politics, which tend to exclude many of the actions described in this book. These conventional accounts of political participation are framed in ways that emphasise disengagement from 'real politics' namely party-based parliamentary and electoral systems (being a member of a political party and voting in elections). As the chapters in this book reveal, these restrictive accounts are often abstractions that are remote from the ways so many young people actually think about and do politics. We believe this regeneration that is richly illustrated in the chapters in this book, will help to reorient the practice of academic research on young people and political participation.

The Chapters: Political Regeneration Around the World in 20 Chapters

The 20 chapters in this book by 34 authors are based on original research carried out by scholars and activists, combining young and more experienced academic talents in their respective fields of expertise. Chapters document a rich variety of ways young people now are responding to 'situated injustice' and crisis, by acting to renew our political cultures. Each chapter also contributes to the relevant scholarly literature and informs popular understandings of politics.

Young people's (political) lives cannot be neatly compartmentalised and inevitably the different parts of this edited volume overlap and complement each other. All the chapters address the overarching theme of how young people are regenerating politics within the context of diverse crises, often through new and creative forms of political participation. Nonetheless, four specific themes stand out: first, 'Young People and Student Activism,' second 'Young People and Online Political Action,' third 'Young People, Collective Identity and Community Building,' and fourth, 'Young People and Protests as Politics.' These themes provide the structure for this edited volume.

The first part of the book is entitled **'Young People and Student Activism.'** It opens with a vivid account from Rekgotsofetse Chikane, a young South African man, describing his arrest in Cape Town in October

2015 during university student protests that were taking place across his country. His chapter 'Young people and the #hashtags that broke the Rainbow Nation' documents how the global financial crisis of 2008 exacerbated the already existing problems of youth unemployment and inter-racial inequality, thereby creating the impetus for emergence of three different student-led movements: The Economic Freedom Fighters (EFF), #RhodesMustFall and #FeesMustFall. The chapter then examines how young people, especially university students, have altered the way they engage in political discourse and how social media and a new discourse of defiance have changed the way they engage in politics.

The next chapter by Analicia Mejia Mesinas is entitled 'Students taking action in Los Angeles schools: An ethnographic case study of student activism in the United States.' She provides an ethnographic case study of the political activism by secondary school students challenging the crisis surrounding the criminalisation of school discipline and the militarisation of school police, in public-funded schools in Los Angeles, California. Through participant observations, the author shows how sustained student activism has been energetic, imaginative and ultimately successful. In this way, political actions of students have been crucial to the reforming of zero tolerance school policies and practices.

The chapter 'Professional students do not play politics: How Kenyan students professionalise environmental activism and produce neoliberal subjectivities' is by Grace Muthoni Mwaura. She shows the ways contemporary Kenyan university students engage in environmentalism in a context shaped by socio-economic, political, and environmental crises. Through student environmental activism, the author examines how some students disengage from traditional student politics, while simultaneously generating new ways of responding to situated injustices such as environmental degradation and unemployment. By interrogating what politics means for such students in the context of neoliberalism, she challenges and critiques claims that Kenyan student environmentalists are non-political and demonstrates how their actions promote change without significantly challenging the very neoliberal context generating the social problems they seek to address.

The last chapter in this first part is by Nicole Gallant and is called 'The good, the bad and the useless: Young people's political action repertoires in Quebec.' She reveals that many young people, especially students, are increasingly politically active, but in less institutionalised ways. Using a definition of the political that encompasses what many young people themselves consider political, and drawing primarily on 20 in-depth qualitative interviews with young activists in Quebec, this chapter provides a relational framework to distinguish among the variety of forms that young people's political action may take. By analysing participants' discourses about their political concerns and the types of actions undertaken, it distinguishes four political stances, which take into account the relationship to State authorities: associative participation, underground protest, politicized artwork, and personal lifestyle.

The second part of the book is entitled '**Young People and Online Political Action**.' It starts with a chapter by Rob Watts called 'The crisis of democracy in Hong Kong: Young people's online politics and the Umbrella Movement.' He addresses the role of young people as pro-democracy activists who created the Umbrella Movement, in 2014, in the on-going crisis of democracy in Hong Kong. The chapter highlights young activists use of online sites, such as Hong Kong Golden and 4chan. The author argues that the Umbrella Movement is a mix of new and old forms of democratic politics, which segue into civil disobedience. Framing Hong Kong Golden and 4chan as political thus requires a reframing of how we think about the political and about how young people now engage in the political.

Next comes the chapter 'Momentum and the movementist 'Corbynistas': young people regenerating the Labour Party in Britain' by Sarah Pickard. The chapter discusses how the Momentum project provided the political awakening for many young people and a sense of political community for young movementists against a backdrop of political crisis. Young people have used their political agency, especially through social media to campaign energetically within this grassroots organisation founded in 2015. The chapter also addresses extremism and entryism in Momentum, as well as resulting changes in governance and organisation.

Judith Bessant's chapter is called 'Right-wing populism and young 'Stormers': Conflict in democratic politics.' She highlights the diversity of young people's politics by providing a case study of ultra-right populism amid the crisis of the rise of extremist populist politics. Attention is given to the ways digital media is used variously to recruit, to persuade and to mobilise young people and why so many are attracted to ultra-right populist groups. She also observes how many young people are drawn to extremism for political-emotional reasons that are commonly shared within the broader community. Finally, it is argued that urgent attention is needed to engage better with the politics of the kind examined here.

"How not to be a terrorist': radicalisation and young Western Muslims' digital discourses' is the title of the next chapter by Andrew Hope and Julie Matthews. They deal with how some young Muslims online react to perceived 'threats of terrorism' that has reached crisis point in many Western countries. They document how many of the policies and practices intended to combat these alleged dangers often result in the harassment, isolation, victimisation and invasive surveillance of 'suspect communities.' The chapter explores the harmful practices of anti-radicalisation strategies and the online response of young Muslims in Western democracies. The authors document how the use of humour by some young Muslims online works as powerful political tool, engendering resistance, while nurturing a shared sense of identity.

The second part closes with a chapter by Maria Grasso entitled 'Young people's political participation in Europe in times of crisis.' She presents comparative evidence on young people's political participation during the economic crisis based on survey data from across Europe collected in 2015 to analyse patterns of youth participation. The results show that while young people are less engaged than older citizens via conventional means, they are engaged in politics through more confrontational modes of unconventional politics and online activism. The author argues that young people's regeneration of politics is likely to come through social media and other forms of technological advances for the practice of political engagement.

The third part of the book is entitled '**Young People, Collective Identity and Community Building**.' It starts with 'The Gezi Resistance of Turkey as young people's counter-conduct' by Nilay Çabuk Kaya and Haktan Ural. The chapter examines the Gezi Resistance as a counter-conduct led by young people in Turkey. The authors demonstrate how young protesters counteract multiple crises such as the promotion of consumerist lifestyles, conservative and family-based social policies, and the silencing of the media by the ruling JDP party. The authors argue that young people invent and perform political subjectivity known as 'the Gezi Spirit' that give priority to openness, inclusiveness, autonomy and freedom over consumerism, conservatism and authoritarianism. Through this community-building, young protesters transform the image of youth depicted as individualist, consumerist and cynical subjects.

In Lucas Walsh and Rosalyn Black's 'Off the radar democracy: Young people's alternate acts of citizenship in Australia' chapter, they argue that many young people in Australia are serious about their citizenship and engage in politics in ways that are not captured by current measures or analyses. The chapter explores the growth of youth social enterprise and volunteering as alternative spaces for youth citizenship. It draws on field research conducted to consider young people's attitudes to power, influence and democratic change-making, as well as implications for conventional notions and practices of politics.

The chapter entitled '(Re)Politicising young people: From Scotland's Indyref to Hong Kong's Umbrella Movement' is by Susan Batchelor, Alistair Fraser, Leona Li Ngai Ling and Lisa Whittaker. The authors analyse the two independence movements involving young people that emerged in two very different settings in 2014. Drawing on a wider study of young people and social change, the chapter explores the rise of nationalist politics in Scotland and Hong Kong, as well as independence in times of crisis, highlighting similarities and differences in young people's political participation in these two distinctive contexts.

The following chapter is 'New forms of solidarity and young people: An ethnography of youth participation in Italy' by Nicola de Luigi, Alessandro Martelli and Ilaria Pitti. Drawing from the findings of the European project 'Partispace,' the authors analyse three solidarity initiatives promoted by youth leftist groups in Bologna through an ethnographic study. The chapter highlights the connections between the initiatives, objectives and practices of the youth-led groups, in the context of the global financial crisis. The projects emerge as 'laboratories of political resistance' where strategies for collective action based on mutual help and self-empowerment are experimented with and enacted.

The last chapter in this part is entitled 'Youth heteropolitics in crisis-ridden Greece' and was written by Alexandros Kioupkiolis and Yannis Pechtelidis. The authors enquire into alternative modes of self-organised youth political engagement in contemporary Greece. Young people are engaging in hetero-politics, namely in practices of alternative community organisation in response to the crises of social dislocation, the failures and the pressures of the market and the state. It is argued that they belong to a politicised generational unit, which develops a common heteropolitical habitus by participating in various alternative social and cultural sites, displaying a common political dynamic despite their differences.

The fourth and last part of the book is entitled '**Young People and Protest as Politics.**' Tim Goddard and Randolph Myers take us to North America in their chapter entitled 'Youth-led struggles against racialized crime control in the United States.' Their chapter details the work of youth-led grassroots organisations in the United States that create counter-movements against the crisis of the criminalisation of school discipline, racialised policing and mass incarceration. The authors argue that although their victories are often small in scale, the work of these organisations should not be overlooked, as they help to bring together young people to mobilise for criminal justice reform, thus introducing them to the world of politics and collective action.

Graham Bright, Carole Pugh and Matthew Clarke author the next chapter 'Youth work, agonistic democracy and transgressive enjoyment in England.' The chapter shares the narratives of active engagement with politics on the part of a number of young people, as part of their efforts to resist the crisis brought about threats to youth services posed by neoliberal policies and austerity policies in particular. The analysis in the chapter links the young people's engagement to the tenets of agonistic models of democracy, namely pluralism, contestation and tragedy. The authors conclude by considering the implications of participants' experiences for future studies of politics and political engagement.

The following chapter, 'Political participation and activism in the Post15m Era: Young people's political identifications in Lleida, Catalonia' was written by Eduard Ballesté Isern and José Sánchez García. They discuss new spaces for political participation since the beginning of the Los Indignados 15M movement, in 2011. Drawing on an ethnographic inquiry into youth activism in Lleida, Catalonia, they identify and analyse new forms of political participation. The authors focus on the discursive construction around the actors' own accounts of what they call 'new political activism,' and consider how it differs from more conventional understandings of political participation. In this way, they analyse two post-15M movements, including their evolution and how the involvement of the young activists has changed them.

The next chapter is a case study by Ricardo Peñafiel and Marie-Christine Doran called 'New modes of youth political action and democracy in the Americas: From the Chilean Spring to the Maple Spring in Quebec.' Through their analysis of the Chilean and Quebecois cases of student protest in 2011 and 2012 with reference to Mexico, the authors show how young people created new oppositional public spaces, despite accusations of violence or political apathy intended to undermine their status as legitimate political subjects. Using innovative forms of political participation, young people in contexts marked by on-going crises have been able to challenge their exclusion from the political scene, and achieve changes in the public culture. While these youth-led protest movements are often opposed to neoliberal austerity policies, their main interest was to challenge restricted forms of representative democracy, inventing new forms of political subjectivation based on a fundamental principle of democracy: *isonomy*, i.e. equality of political rights.

The last chapter of this volume, is by Marko Kovacic and Danijela Dolenec is 'Youth participation in the age of austerity in Eastern Europe.' The chapter explores ways in which austerity policies have influenced patterns of youth political participation between the core and periphery of the European Union (EU), focusing on Eastern Europe. They examine the varied impact of austerity across the EU and young people's conventional and unconventional modes of political participation.

Thus, the richness and scope of the chapters considered collectively indicates why this book will be of interest to scholars and students in the disciplines of: politics, sociology, youth and childhood studies, social studies, political sociology, and social policy, as well as professional-vocational fields like journalism, youth work, and social work. It will also be a valuable text for practitioners of human rights and in the fields of human services, socio-legal services and education.

Young people are taking action themselves due to a sense that many of their political and business leaders are ineffective and acting in ways that are detrimental to their interests. Indeed, through the chapters in the book, we hear the voices of many young people who express how they have been moved to act due to their concerns about corruption, wayward governance and the general failure of power elites to address the major socio-economic and political problems. Concerns of the young people in this book include unparalleled economic growth, social inequality, environmental threats, unemployment and what they see as meagre prospects for a decent future. In short, the reasons they give for their political action often include a righteous sense of outrage and anger regarding injustice and abuses of public trust It is a sense of anger over ethical failures of the kind mentioned above that galvanised them to action. In short, it is concern about the capacity of the elite, i.e. their leaders of government, key institutions and business to govern well that provoked popular disenchantment and protest.

In this way, many of the young people included in this book say it is not they who have disengaged from politics or selfishly retreated into their private world, rather, it is their elders, our leaders who have disengaged from them and from taking politics seriously. The power elite have disengaged from their job and too often failed to exercise good judgment and to work out what the intrinsic purpose of politics is: to govern fairly and wisely in the public interest.

To conclude, the research on which these chapters are based clearly demonstrates the numerous, varied creative ways many young people are playing a key role in renewing the political life of their communities. From 'communal meals' and the 'woman in the red dress' in Istanbul, to Anarchopanda and naked demonstrations (maNufestations) in Quebec, through school pupils in Los Angeles bringing about changes to policing methods to new kinds of environmentalism in Kenya, we see how young people are actively and creatively reshaping politics. As the authors in this edited collection reveal, young people are revitalising the life of our political communities and enhancing prospects for viable alternative political practices and institutional arrangements. Contributors to this edited collection explore the political lives of young in Africa, Asia, Australia, Central and South America, Europe and North America. This political voyage around the world underlines points to the ways we are witnessing a significant global development propelled by young people's interest in regenerating politics in times of crises.

REFERENCES

Bessant, J. (2014). *Democracy bytes: New media and new politics and generational change*. Basingstoke: Palgrave Macmillan.
Bessant, J., Farthing, R., & Watts, R. (2017). *The precarious generation: A political economy of young people*. London and New York: Routledge.
Côté, J. (2014). *Youth studies. Fundamental issues and debates*. Basingstoke: Palgrave Macmillan.
Ford, M. (2015). *The rise of the robots: Technology and the threat of mass unemployment*. London: One World.
Furedi, F. (2007). *Invitation to terror: The expanding empire of the unknown*. London: Continuum.
Furlong, A. (2009). *Handbook of youth studies. New perspectives and agendas*. London and New York: Routledge.
Furlong, A. (2014). *Youth studies. An introduction*. London and New York: Routledge.
Furlong, A., & Cartmel, F. (1997). *Young people and social change*. Buckingham: Open University Press.
Howker, E., & Malik, S. (2013[2010]). *The jilted generation. How Britain has bankrupted its youth*. London: Icons Books.

Jones, O. (2017, January 12). The Tory policy for young people in Britain is victimisation by design. *The Guardian*. Retrieved from https://www.theguardian.com/commentisfree/2017/jan/12/tory-policy-young-people-britain-wellbeing

Manning, N. (Ed.). (2015). *Political disengagement: The changing nature of the 'political'*. Bristol: Policy Press.

Mizen, P. (2003). *Changing state of youth*. Basingstoke: Palgrave Macmillan.

Pickard, S. (2014). Widening participation in English universities: Accessing social justice? In S. Pickard (Ed.), *Higher education in the UK and the US. Converging models in a global academic world?* (pp. 113–138). Leiden and Boston, MA: Brill.

Pickard, S. (2018). *Politics, protest and young people. Political participation and dissent in Britain in the 21st century*. London: Palgrave Macmillan. [forthcoming]

Piketty, T. (2014). *Capital in the twenty-first century* (A. Goldhammer, Trans.). Cambridge, MA: The Belknap Press.

Standing, G. (2011). *The precariat: The new dangerous class*. London and New York: Bloomsbury Academic.

Streeck, W. (2016). *How will capitalism end?* London: Verso.

Sukarieh, M., & Tannock, S. (2014). *Youth rising? The politics of youth in the global economy*. London and New York: Routledge.

Twenge, J. (2014[2007]). *Generation me: Why today's young Americans are more confident, assertive, entitled – And more miserable than ever before*. New York, NY: Simon and Schuster. Revised and updated.

Wallerstein, I., Collins, R., Mann, M., Derluguian, G., & Calhoun, C. (Eds.). (2013). *Does capitalism have a future?* Oxford: Oxford University Press.

Ward, S. (2014). Creating the enterprising student: The moral projects of neoliberalism and higher education reform in the UK and the US. In S. Pickard (Ed.), *Higher education in the UK and the US. Converging models in a global academic world?* (pp. 11–34). Leiden and Boston, MA: Brill.

Žižek, S. (2011). *Living in the end times*. London: Verso Books.

Sarah Pickard is Senior Lecturer at the Université Sorbonne Nouvelle, Paris, France. Her research in contemporary Youth Studies focuses on the interaction between youth policy and youth politics. She is publishing *Politics, Protest and Young People. Political Participation and Dissent in Britain in the 21st Century* with Palgrave Macmillan in 2018.

Judith Bessant is Professor in the School of Global, Urban and Social Studies at the Royal Melbourne Institute of Technology (RMIT) University, Melbourne, Australia. She publishes in the areas of sociology, youth studies, politics, policy and history, and has worked as an advisor to governments and to non-government organisations.

PART I

Young People and Student Activism

CHAPTER 2

Young People and the #Hashtags That Broke the Rainbow Nation

Rekgotsofetse Chikane

Introduction

I never thought that 30 years after my own father was charged with treason against the state for anti-apartheid activism that I would be sitting in the Cape Town office of the Directorate for Priority Crime Investigation being charged with the same crime. I remember feeling a deep sense of abandonment during the day leading up to my arrest in 2015. While the South African President (Jacob Zuma) and his entire ministerial Cabinet listened to the Minister of Finance's Medium Term Budget Report within Parliament, students sang songs along the streets outside. The songs recalled the struggle against the apartheid[1] regime that many within the current Parliament fought against. Even with the ringing of stun grenades around us, we sang to remind those who ran the state that by not listening to the concerns of students, they were no better than the old regime. While I was sitting in the back of the police van with no idea of where they were taking me, I remember thinking that this country had lost its mind and it was our responsibility to bring it back to its senses; to remind our

---

R. Chikane (✉)
Mandela-Rhodes Scholar, Cape Town, South Africa

parents that to demand economic freedom in our lifetime was simply an extension of their call during apartheid for democratic freedom in their lifetime.

The current generation of young people in South Africa has been instilled with the belief that we live in a country united in our racial diversity and should be the proud torchbearers of its future. But during the nationwide protests of 2015, I, alongside thousands of young South Africans, found the courage and belief to break the myth of the Rainbow Nation and embark on a programme of civil disobedience, which would change the role that young people played in the politics of South Africa. We sought to bring South Africa closer to what Achille Mbembe describes as our Fanonian Moment: a moment in which a critical mass of disenfranchised people who feel that they are being treated as "foreigners" on their own land and are convinced that the doors of opportunity are closing on them. He further states that under these conditions, members of this grouping will believe that if they are unable to take advantage of the available opportunities in the present, they will be excluded for generations to come. This creates a social stampede and a willingness to risk a fight because waiting for opportunities to arise is no longer a viable option (Mbembe, 2015).

The youth-led protests that have gripped South Africa since the beginning of 2015 have challenged the country's false consciousness regarding democracy. Marx and Engels in *The German Ideology* explain how our consciousness of reality is not of our own, but rather it is formed by the world around us, thus creating a false sense of consciousness (Marx & Friedrich, 1965). In fact, Marx would later go on to crystallise this notion by stating "it is not the consciousness of men that determines their existence, but their social existence that determines their consciousness" (Marx, 1977). In a similar sense, the social existence within South Africa has been so deeply embedded in the notion of the Rainbow Nation that it has formed a false consciousness, which hides and disguises the real relationship people have with the racially exploitative nature of the South African economy.

This chapter explores how a critical mass of young people within universities in South Africa have begun to shift away from the pacification of the Rainbow Nation project, towards a more politically active youth who are increasingly questioning the socio-economic structural inequalities in our country. The dearth of formal political engagement from young people has resulted in a lack of understanding from both policy makers and young people regarding the role they play within the economy. Thus, the political crisis in the country is a result of young people seeking political expression in a manner, not foreign to policy makers, but unseen since the defiance campaigns during apartheid.

The chapter begins by exploring the concept of the Rainbow Nation and dominance of the two-nation economic state of the country. It then discusses the role the 2008 global financial crisis (GFC) had on South Africa's real economy (goods and services) and the subsequent effects on youth unemployment. The chapter then examines how young people (in particular university students) have changed the way they engage in political discourse, which was precipitated by the phrase "Economic Freedom in Our Lifetime." The last part of the chapter seeks to understand how the Economic Freedom Fighters (EFF), #RhodesMustFall (#RMF) and #FeesMustFall (#FMF) have used social media and a newly equipped discourse of defiance to change the way we have engaged in politics.

The Rainbow Nation: A Case of Two-Nations

The term 'Rainbow Nation' has become ubiquitous within South Africa. The term represents a dominant consciousness in which all races, genders, ethnicities, and religions—through their diversity—have overcome the storm of apartheid and forged a democratic society. However, as Mottiar & Bond (2012, p. 283) explain: "Rapidly rising unemployment, inequality and ecological degradation, along with sustained violence against women, criminality and persistent xenophobia, mean that the 'Rainbow Nation' did not live up to the expectations of the majority of its citizens, nor were those citizens passive." Through the convergence of social media and social activism, young people in South Africa have used both social movements and political parties to help remove the veil of ignorance used to manufacture democracy in the country.

The false consciousness within South Africa is the maintenance of what Mahmood Mamdani and Thabo Mbeki both describe as the 'two nations' of South Africa. For Mamdani, South Africa lived in two different political worlds, divided by a Chinese wall that separates the world of the natives from that of the settler (cited in Letseka, Visser, & Breier, 2010, p. 25). Mbeki, gives a fuller account of the 'settler-native' divide by amplifying the importance of race in the country's economic organisation and utilising it as his differentiator:

> One of these nations is white, relatively prosperous, regardless of gender or geographic dispersal. It has ready access to a developed economic,

physical, educational, communication and other infrastructure. This enables it to argue that, except for the persistence of gender discrimination against women, all members of this nation have the possibility to exercise their right to equal opportunity, the development opportunities to which the Constitution of '93 committed our country.

The second and larger nation of South Africa is black and poor, with the worst affected being women in the rural areas, the black rural population in general and the disabled. This nation lives under conditions of a grossly underdeveloped economic, physical, educational, communication and other infrastructure.

It has virtually no possibility to exercise what in reality amounts to a theoretical right to equal opportunity, with that right being equal within this black nation only to the extent that it is equally incapable of realisation. This reality of two nations, underwritten by the perpetuation of the racial, gender and spatial disparities born of a very long period of colonial and apartheid white minority domination, constitutes the material base which reinforces the notion that, indeed, we are not one nation, but two nations. And neither are we becoming one nation. Consequently, also, the objective of national reconciliation is not being realized. (Mbeki, 1998)

In a study attempting to understand the growing economic and income inequalities in South Africa, Leibbrandt, Finn, & Woolard (2012, p. 33) explain that in spite of intra-race inequality growing in its importance as a policy concern in South Africa, especially amongst the African population group. Inter-race inequality remains a central indicator of the lingering effects of apartheid and further adds credence to the argument that South Africa exists as a two-nation state (Finn & Woolard, 2012, p. 33). In fact, inter-race inequality is the leading contributor to increasing inequality in South Africa. In addition to income-related inequality, non-income related inequality, as measured by an index of private and public assets in South Africa after the end of apartheid, decreased (Bhorat, Van der Westhuizen, & Jacobs, 2009, p. 57). However, while non-income inequality decreased generally, this was not the case for low-income African families, who predominately remained without access to basic services such as running water, sanitation and electricity (Bhorat et al., 2009, pp. 57–58).

The youth-led protests in 2015 and 2016 were spurred on by an apparent social amnesia about the effects that apartheid has on the present and its continued influence on growing inequality. I characterise it as the perception that South Africa is a post-apartheid society, rather than understanding South Africa as a post-1994 society. Understanding South

Africa as a post-apartheid society is at the core of understanding the predominance of the Rainbow Nation motif. South Africa is a democracy that revels in what prominent South African intellectual Netshitenzhe (2015) describes as the festival of negatives: non-racialism, non-sexism, anti-colonialism, anti-apartheid. The Born-Free generation[2] have become disenchanted with the lack of economic, racial, and cultural transformation in South Africa and have begun to dismiss many of the apparent achievements made by the post-1994 government in South Africa as merely cosmetic changes to a system with deep structural problems. The global financial crisis caused a change in the approach taken by young people with regards to participation in policy decisions, in order to give them a more active role in determining their own futures. The change involved a return to the civil disobedience of past defiance campaigns[3] that helped end apartheid.

The shift in youth politics in South Africa can be attributed to the change from the dominant narrative of a Rainbow Nation, towards a narrative that acknowledges that the compromises made to create a racially unified country came at the expense of human restitution and economic redistribution linked to Apartheid's past injustice. It is an economic divide that continues to marginalise black and coloured racial groups in the country. This is not to say that young people are looking to renege on the post-apartheid settlement or to rewrite history; instead, we are seeking to create a space to negotiate a post-settlement settlement.

The Convention for a Democratic South Africa (CODESA), through a negotiated settlement, achieved a multi-racial, multi-cultural and multi-party democratic dispensation enshrined by Constitution. However, as Sisk (1994, p. 72)—commenting on South Africa's democratic transition—warned: "without economic and social change the underlying societal base for elite-negotiated institutions will not exist." Students believe that our realisation of a truly democratic South Africa requires a change in politics that previously sought democratic freedom, towards politics that seek economic freedom. For students, the post-settlement settlement would require another CODESA focused on the economy, rather than simply the democratic system. The desire to create a space such as this has created an action-orientated approach towards disruptive politics focused on economic and racial inequality.

Whether within the halls of South Africa's parliament—the National Assembly—through the emergence of political parties such as the Economic Freedom Fighters (EFF), or through the 2015–2016 civil disobedience movements and campaigns seen throughout universities in the country such as #RhodesMustFall and #FeesMustFall, students are armed with the belief that they stand on the right side of history. The emergence of the EFF, #RMF, and #FMF has created new spaces and platforms for renegotiating the terms and conditions of a youth social contract.

Youth Inequality in South Africa and the Global Financial Crisis

In his analysis of the structural causes of the global financial crisis (GFC) between 2007 and 2009, Ramskogler (2015, p. 48) believes that the serious repercussions of the crisis are still keenly felt throughout the global economy. The GFC had an adverse effect on rich and poor countries and a significant negative impact on South Africa (Reinhart & Rogoff, 2009, p. 161). During the crisis, global trade volumes collapsed and the value of South Africa's real exports of goods and services fell by 19.5% in 2009. Inflation breached its controlled upper limit of 6%, the mining sector recorded its largest decrease on record shrinking 33% and the property market decreased due to the declining demand caused by the depressed labour market and decreased expected household incomes (Kganyago, 2012; Marais, 2009; Padayachee, 2012). The key distinction between South Africa and most other countries experiences of the GFC was the large extent of job destruction in the South African economy. Though net employment increased by 1.6 million between 2003 and 2007, over the course of the GFC (2008–2010) net unemployment decreased by approximately 800,000, with the heaviest job losses in construction, retail and financial services (Kganyago, 2012).

The GFC opened up many of the cracks within various sectors in South Africa still suffering from the long-lasting effects of apartheid. Apartheid's segregationist policies resulted in low levels of education and large socio-economic inequalities, especially amongst the African population. Thus, even though the legislative bedrock of apartheid was dismantled in 1994, the county is still influenced by its historical legacy (Verick, 2012, p. 374). The repercussions of the GFC affected South Africa's real economy of goods and services and exacerbated the damage caused by apartheid affecting marginalised and vulnerable groups.

South Africa defines youth as 18–34 years (Statistics South Africa, 2015, 2016), which is longer than the definition used by the International Labour Organization (ILO) that defines youth as 18–24. In a report on vulnerable young people in South Africa by Statistics South Africa (SSA),

70% of the country's 5.1 million unemployed individuals were between the ages of 18 and 34 (Statistics South Africa, 2015, 2016). Between 2008 and 2010, during the country's first economic recession since 1994, the unemployment rate for 18- to 24-year-olds increased by 20% (National Treasury, 2011, p. 9). This number accounted for 40% of the job losses during that same period and can be primarily attributed to the global economic slowdown (National Treasury, 2011, p. 12).

The youth unemployment rate in South Africa is often comparable to other emerging countries; however, during the financial crisis, the magnitude of the unemployment set us apart (National Treasury, 2011, p. 12). Youth unemployment is often associated with low levels of education, low skills in literacy, numeracy and communication and little to no work experience (Cassim & Oosthuizen, 2014; National Treasury, 2011, p. 9). It is this constellation of traits among young unemployed South Africans that has been exacerbated by issues like high levels of inequality in the educational sector, low quality of healthcare services and social welfare dependence (Hill, Baxen, Craig, & Namakula, 2012; Mayosi & Benatar, 2014; Spaull, 2013).

During the protests, I would often hear how being young means having to choose either a life of crime and unemployment or a succession of meaningless jobs; meaningless, not in the sense that the jobs provide no meaning to life—though one could argue this point—but rather in that the jobs obtained did not commensurate with their own qualification. As Beukes, et al. explain: "individuals who have no choice but to accept employment associated with a level below his or her qualification as well as skill level and experience" (Beukes, Fransman, Murozvi, & Yu, 2016, p. 4). Jobs and job opportunities available to young people do not provide training or up skilling that allows one to take advantage of future opportunities. They function as placeholders for young people; they are jobs that placate and keep the mind busy, while the soul remains restless. The financial crisis changed the manner in which young people engaged in politics and their discourse about freedom.

Economic Freedom in Our Lifetime

In August 2010, the African National Congress's (ANC) youth wing, the ANC Youth League (ANCYL), presented a discussion document at its National General Council meeting. Headed by its then President, Julius Malema, the document (which was both presented and adopted) declared that the political programme of young activists across the country would be to achieve "Youth Action for Economic Freedom in Our Lifetime" (African National Congress Youth League, 2010, p. 16). The declaration was in response to the economic slowdown that occurred over the previous three years, due to the financial crisis. Having understood themselves as the militant wing of the ruling party, Malema and the ANCYL began a programme of action that sowed the seeds for youthful dissent in the country. Since the declaration, 'Economic Freedom in Our Lifetime' has become synonymous with youth-focused political discourse and action. It gave young people their raison d'être to argue for structural changes to the economy of South Africa. It spoke of actively seeking to change one's circumstances from what the status quo would have one believe was a democratic and progressive country towards an economy that is truly reflective of the goals and ambitions of the Freedom Charter.

The declaration resonated with many young people because it helped re-orientate the manner in which they viewed upward social mobility within society and allowed them to think differently about youth politics. It allowed for the emergence of a discourse focused on the re-conceptualisation of freedom in South Africa. The phrase, 'Economic Freedom in Our Lifetime,' allowed young activists in South Africa to take the first step towards re-engaging other young people and the population at large with the aims of the Freedom Charter.

The Freedom Charter, written in 1955, functioned as a symbolic statement of the core principles of the type of state South Africa hoped to transform into once apartheid had been abolished. Malema was attempting to renegotiate how we understand the terms and conditions that were placed on democracy after the election in 1994. For him and the ANCYL, economic freedom in our lifetime entailed realising all the economic principles of the Freedom Charter, namely:

1. The people shall share in the wealth of the country;
2. The national wealth of our country, the heritage of South Africans, should be restored to the people;
3. The mineral wealth beneath the soil, the Banks, the monopoly industry shall be transferred to the ownership of the people as a whole;
4. All other industry and trade should be controlled to assist the well-being of the people; and

5. All people should have equal rights to trade where they choose, to manufacture and enter all trades, crafts, and professions (ANCYL, 2010, p. 16).

By echoing the Freedom Charter, Malema helped create the rationale that the current participation in civil disobedience is equivalent to anti-apartheid disobedience.

Policy makers often see young people in South Africa as a social liability and as presenting various policy challenges (Oyedemi & Mahlatji, 2016, p. 314). Civic competence and participation refers to "understanding of how government functions, and the acquisition of behaviours that allow citizens to participate in government and permit individuals to meet, discuss and collaborate to promote their interests within a framework of democratic principles" (Youniss et al., 2002, p. 124). The lack of formal civic competence and participation amongst young people in policy discussions further reinforces the negative perspective amongst policy makers regarding the role of young people within policy-making.

Hofmeyr (cited in Oyedemi & Mahlatji, 2016, p. 314) argues that young people deliberately dissociate themselves from formal political processes due to a sense of alienation and marginalisation from their socio-political environment. The combination of being labelled as a social liability and lacking the required civic competence to adequately influence policy creates the conditions for the emergence of a group that is apathetic towards its own advancement. Asking young people to reclaim their economic freedom, so that they can truly experience democratic freedom within their lifetime, is an attempt to make them feel empowered and more responsible rather than alienated from their environment.

I often advocate that young people should not be seen as apathetic or alienated, but rather that policy makers have failed to encourage them to have an interest in policy change. Representing young people as apathetic places the responsibility for their alleged lack of policy engagement on the shoulders of young people. It frames them as the problem and further blames them for their subsequent disengagement, rather than describing it as a problem with the political milieu that alienates them. This latter understanding of the problem would produce different remedies in the form of incentives designed to encourage their participation and by removing obstacles to their engagement. Furthermore, representing young people as apathetic represents them as inept to change and devoid of agency.

During the protests of 2015 and 2016, I realised students in South Africa are willing to mobilise themselves, but never had the incentives that would encourage them to do so. New forms of information technology and increased access to the internet has made traditional forms of political participation such as public meetings, town hall discussions, public participatory budgeting ill-equipped mechanisms to communicate with young people.

The rallying call for economic freedom, at the expense of the older Rainbow Nation call, has become synonymous with change in South African, especially with regards to youth-orientated activism. More importantly, it is a call that speaks directly to many young people who have begun to think about their social and economic position within society, especially after the GFC. 'Economic Freedom in our Lifetime' gave life to three different social movements who all used the call differently and for different reasons in organising and mobilising young people. The Economic Freedom Fighters, #RhodesMustFall and #FeesMustFall all used to varying degrees the GFC's impact on South Africa and the growing interest in changing the political discourse away from viewing South Africa as a post-apartheid society to seeing it as a post-1994 society. The following section details how each group has gone about successfully mobilising young people.

Breaking the Rainbow Nation: The Rise of the Economic Freedom Fighters and #MustFall Movements

Julius Malema established the Economic Freedom Fighters (EFF) in 2013 after he was ousted from the ANCYL by its mother body, the ANC. The formation of the party came out of the growing democratic crisis in South Africa, which peaked when 34 striking miners were shot and killed by the South African Police Service in August 2012 during a wage dispute, an event described as the Marikana Massacre. Through its populist rhetoric, the party immediately captured the political imagination and was perceived to be transforming the political landscape of the country (Mbete, 2015, p. 35). The EFF sought to constantly engage outside the traditional ambit of parliament by symbolically associating themselves with the working class of society (Mbete, 2015, p. 44). Utilising political regalia within parliament such as red berets, stereotypical attire of associated with domestic workers and miners; the EFF believed they could defy the status quo of parliament.

The EFF fulfils Moffitt and Tormey's three attributes that make a populist political style. It appeals to the people by rejecting the political and economic elite in the country, it takes advantage of the economic crisis in the country caused by the global slowdown and most importantly it has disregarded the appropriate forms of behaviour within the political realm (Moffitt & Tormey, 2014, pp. 391–392). The party believes that it is the best representative for poor, marginalised mass social groupings who have been and continue to be exploited by white monopoly capital[4] and those with political power. The EFF has taken on the role left vacant over the preceding decade by a lack of institutional and political arrangements for youth participation in South Africa. However, it was not the creation of the party that saw a change in youth politics in South Africa; rather it was the way it engaged with young people.

In the lead up to the 2015 State of the Nation Address (SONA)—the official opening of Parliament—the EFF began to engage in a form of politics that leveraged social media as a means of distributing a political message to young people: #PayBacktheMoney. This slogan sought to hold President Zuma accountable for using state finances for the personal upgrades to his personal home in Nkandla, KwaZulu-Natal. The hashtag was created after the EFF was removed from Parliament on 18 June due to their insistence that the President account for when he would act on the recommendation of the Public Protector that he repays the taxpayer for the upgrades made to his private residence. The chanting of "Pay Back the Money" while leaving Parliament led to the creation of the hashtag that became synonymous with corruption and with the president. Utilising the popularity of the hashtag, the EFF created a 10-day countdown to the 2015 State of the Nation Address, which was linked to a vow by the EFF to disrupt the President's opening of Parliament unless a special sitting of the National Assembly was organised to discuss the upgrades to his private home in Nkandla (SAPA, 2015).

Since the initial protest action in 2014 and its subsequent formalisation in 2015, the EFF successfully continued its campaign of parliamentary defiance that culminated with the party successfully taking the President and the Speaker of the National Assembly (and thus Parliament) to the Constitutional Court. The hashtag #PayBacktheMoney helped to create a form of politics the country has never utilised before. Through online political pressure focused on a single-issue campaign, #PayBacktheMoney successfully allowed for a new method of online engagement through social media platforms that helped create a shift away from hashtag activism towards hashtag movements in South Africa.

The Growth of #MustFall Politics

#RhodesMustFall (#RMF) and #FeesMustFall (#FMF) redefined the way students engaged in political discourse in South Africa. Both movements are reactions to the socio-economic crisis that currently grips the young black youth of the country. Mottiar & Bond (2012, p. 309) allude to the idea that increased levels of popular demonstrations—under the guise of service delivery protests—indicate that a growing amount of social discontent within society. Reporting on the nature of protests after 2009, Alexander (2010, p. 33) explains that there was a growth in the importance of unemployment within protests, which is reflected by the predominance in the participation of young adults particularly the unemployed and/or underemployed. However, Mottiar & Bond (2012, p. 309) stop short of associating the protests during that time as a movement with norms, values, strategies, tactics or a transformational political agenda meant to unify seemingly disparate groups. However, movements such as #RhodesMustFall and #FeesMustFall have shown that Mottiar and Bond's hesitation was premature.

What made these protest movements different from previous mass action protests in the country pertaining to service delivery was the use of the internet and social media generally. Castell (cited in Luescher, Loader, & Mugume, 2016, p. 3) explains that protests in the internet age open new forms of space that allow localised territorial movements to share and amplify their experiences through virtual flows of information. This form of virtual communication created permanent forums of solidarity, debate, and strategic planning. Through the use of the internet, these movements are characterised by "spontaneity, a lack of clearly defined leadership and an attempt at a new active democratic practice" (Castell cited in Luescher et al., 2016, p. 3). Furthermore, Castell argues that networked social movements such as these can reconstruct the public sphere. #RhodesMustFall and #FeesMustFall are such movements.

#RMF is a university student-led movement whose roots are found in the actions of Chumani Maxwele, a young man who on the 9 March 2015 threw a bucket of faeces at a statue of Cecil John Rhodes at the

University of Cape Town. Maxwele believed that the statue was symbolic of the oppression of the black child in South Africa's colonial, apartheid and democratic periods. Though the movement originally focused on the removal of the Rhodes statue it quickly evolved into a multi-faceted protest focused on decolonising the university curriculum and highlighting various forms of institutionalised discrimination. The protest spoke to how the country had effectively failed to address the central issues that face the black African in the country; how the Rainbow Nation was simply a façade that masked the deeper issues faced by black young people.

#RMF understood that the best means for achieving mass mobilisation was to ensure that the protest action trended on social media, with a clear and concise message that would mobilise those who were willing and able to participate. Social movement theorists assert that through the use of social media as information hubs, individuals are able to exchange updates regarding their activities with other as well share their own interests (Valenzuela, Arriagada, & Scherman, 2012, p. 302). #RhodesMustFall, more than just a social movement, was a virtual and physical informational hub that worked as an arbiter of intellectual exchange regarding its underlying ideological frameworks. The name #RhodesMustFall not only became the moniker of the movement, but also a social media trend that allowed for individuals to build relationships along similar ideological views and receive mobilising information one could not receive elsewhere.

Although the name #RMF suggests that the removal of the Rhodes statue was a key priority, this was never the case. The key to the movement and why it distinguished itself from other #hashtag activism campaigns across the globe was due to its ability to evolve from a single-issue campaign to a movement that found its protest action informed by long-standing ideological frameworks such as Black Consciousness, Decolonial Thought, Radical Black Feminism and Pan-Africanism. #RMF viewed itself as a vehicle for young people on campus to organise themselves under a combination of the above frameworks describing its own ideology as Fallism. It shifted away from the dominance of #hashtag activism because it grounded itself in the pre-existing ontological understanding of society. It took a commonly understood concept in South Africa such as "Transformation"[5] and rejected it due to its failure to be used to facilitate change in South Africa, replacing it with decolonisation. #RMF as an ontological movement based its support on the opting-out of dominant narratives, rather than the opt-in nature of other #social media campaigns.

The statue of Rhodes became a symbol of changing conceptions of the nature of being a young black person in South Africa. As Mitchell (2003, p. 448) explains, in situations such as these—historical disjuncture's and in this case the changing of youth politics—monuments of memory become subject to three possible fates: co-optation and glorification, disavowal, or contestation. In this instance, the latter has become the modus operandi of many of the political movements that have formed in solidarity with Rhodes Must Fall.

These movements mushroomed across South African university campuses as localised diffusions of #RhodesMustFall: #BlackStudentMovement (at the University currently known as Rhodes), #OpenStellenbosch (University of Stellenbosch), #AfrikaansMustFall (University of Pretoria), #BlackStudentsStokvel (Nelson Mandela Metropolitan University), #PatriarchyMustFall (University of Cape Town), #TheTransCollective (University of Cape Town), and #SteynMustFall (University of the Free State). The movements, although all territorially contained, are connected through virtual spaces. The strategies and tactics of each organisation were to dispel the Rainbow Nation myth by changing the discourse within the public sphere and bringing to the forefront questions of race, class, gender, and disability.

By rejecting many previously accepted methods of engagement, #RMF, and other Fallist movements worked to conscientise university students towards a form of political engagement that sought to move away from engagement/negotiations that led to small incremental changes, to switching focus to systemic issues. Mbembe (2015) described this as a shift from the old politics of waiting towards "a new politics of impatience and, if necessary, of disruption." The movements forced authorities to make concessions that had previously been deemed to be impossible. The movements no longer allowed the university to be a space for open debate on issues the university deemed appropriate. The argument made by participants in the movements was based on the belief that such debates inevitably favoured the powerful over the 'vulnerable black youth' within the university and were never open.

The movements took on the unapologetic stance of freedom in their lifetime—in this case, their time at university. In the same way that the call for Economic Freedom in Our Lifetime sought to create a radical re-imagining of the South African society within a young person's lifetime, Fallist movements seek to unapologetically re-imagine university spaces within their time at the university rather than accepting incremental changes made over subsequent generations of student leaders.

From #RhodesMustFall to #FeesMustFall

On the 14 October 2015, student leaders at the University of Witwatersrand, in Johannesburg, brought a long-standing debate within the Higher Education sector in South Africa to the forefront of the public imagination (The Daily Vox, 2015). Using the proposed 10.5% tuition fee increment for the 2016 academic year as its lightning rod, student leaders at the university combined Higher Education sector issues such as, but not limited to, transformation, accessibility, fee increases and the 'black tax,' as a means of generating support for the advocacy for free-decolonial university education. Using one another as human shields to barricade the campus' three main entrances, students argued that the proposed fee increment would be detrimental to black students' accessibility to the University. The Student Representative Council (SRC) described the fee increment as a "deliberate and anti-progressive decision to once more entrench the financial exclusion of poor students" (The Daily Vox, 2015).

What started out as a handful of students attempting to shut down the university, turned into a nationally coordinated protest to shut down the entire higher education sector of South Africa until students were granted free, decolonial education. The urgency of the demand was directly informed by the changing nature of youth politics (argued earlier in this chapter) with regards to defiance and the eradication of the two-nation state in South Africa. Although the demand for free, decolonial education was seen as a call for free education for all, #FeesMustFall understood it as an attempt to create a level playing field for young people between the two nations in South Africa.

#FeesMustFall is the latest example of how young people are no longer accepting the outcomes of processes to determine whether their claims to economic freedom are justified. #FeesMustFall in 2015 and 2016 has been emblematic of an interest group fighting to escape the cost of fiscal adjustment within the state and amongst its universities caused by of the financial crisis on the government budget (Calitz & Fourie, 2016, p. 152). The #FeesMustFall protests have arguably been the largest mass mobilisation of young people across the country to hold the state accountable since the 1976 Soweto Uprising. The 16 June 1976 Soweto student uprising that involved thousands of students across townships in

South Africa was a response by high school students to the introduction of Afrikaans as the medium of instruction in Black African schools. Like the 1976 Soweto Uprising, #FeesMustFall evolved into a national protest movement after the repressive response by the state police on the first day to quell the protest.

The attention of #FMF as a movement at this point in 2015 shifted from the university towards the political elite and the State, with marches planned for the ANC's headquarters in Johannesburg, Parliament in Cape Town and the Union Buildings (the President's Executive Office) in Pretoria. Besides the protest at the ANC headquarters, the other two protests were met with violence by police officers that attempted to clear the protestors from the government premises. The reaction by the police towards the protest at the gates of Parliament was critically important to the movement because it shifted the narrative of the protests away from the dominant view that the students were hooligans, towards a narrative that they had a justified cause. The scenes of the day were eerily akin the aggression used against students in 1976, an event many of the parents of the current student protesters lived through themselves. For the first time since 2010, defiance and civil disobedience in the name of Economic Freedom in Our Lifetime and the dismantling of the two-nation state were celebrated rather than dismissed.

Seen as the spiritual successor of #RhodesMustFall, #FeesMustFall utilised tactics similar to that of by #RMF in order to create a single-issue movement with a wide array of supporters. The movement addressed issues such as youth unemployment, outsourcing of labour in university, intersectionality, identity politics, and socio-economic inequality. #FeesMustFall became a movement for students who believed that the status quo of society should be forcibly changed by threatening the collapse and entire sector of society. Like #RMF, #FMF engaged in a radical form of protest that achieved a previously inconceivable concession from the state of a national zero per cent fee increment after only one week of nationally coordinated protest.

Conclusion

The Economic Freedom Fighters, #RhodesMustFall and #FeesMustFall find their political action informed by a commitment to achieve "Economic Freedom in Our Lifetime." Considering that current challenges facing young people would most likely have "far-reaching, over-arching socio-economic consequences" (Statistics South Africa, 2016, p. vii). These movements are spurred on by the need to redefine what it means to be born-free and to live in a Rainbow Nation; the movements have been direct responses by young people to their confinement in pre-defined modes of political engagement, and a rejection of the saccharine Rainbow Nation. The Economic Freedom Fighters, through its use of populism and social media, sparked a new interest in democratic institutions such as Parliament and the South African Constitutional Court. By challenging the 'rules of the game' defined by the Constitutional Court and rejecting the agreed conventions of political conduct, the EFF attempted to establish itself as a party of the people (Mbete, 2015, p. 50). #RhodesMustFall and #FeesMustFall have brought into action our Fanonian moment and changed the way the young people have engaged in identity politics.

The youth crisis in South Africa, as seen by the rise in the various youth-focused social movements in the country, is predicated on the belief that the Rainbow Nation discourse simply masked the on-going legacy of apartheid. The impact of the global financial crisis amplified this belief by increasing the already unacceptably high levels of youth unemployment in the country and by further exacerbating inter and intra-racial inequality. This allowed for the legacy of apartheid to be seen more clearly by many young South Africans. Many chose to express their anger through a form of radical political engagement that harkens back to earlier apartheid political engagement against the state. However, given the radical nature of this protest, the student movements have begun to unravel. Previous protest tactics have been replaced with activities such as arson and vandalism, leaving many students and broader society disenchanted with the movements' respective futures.

For the crisis to be resolved from the perspective of young people, a plan of action or roadmap would be needed. A roadmap designed to achieve their economic freedom within their lifetime. In a similar way that CODESA was utilised to facilitate post-apartheid *political* settlement, an 'economic convention' for a democratic South Africa is proposed by young people as a post-settlement settlement.

The current unrest in the country shows no signs of being curtailed by any state intervention because of the rationales for the protest action and because of the energy behind it. The shift towards social media as a means of organising and engaging young citizens means that traditional forms of engagement made available by the state to resolve the impasse are often left underutilised or rejected. For many student leaders in South Africa, including myself, the two-nation state of South Africa provide us with the rationale to mobilise students and continue our Fanonian moment.

Notes

1. Apartheid was a legislated form of racial discrimination in South Africa that begun with the election of the National Party in 1948 and its subsequent implementation of the Population Registration Act of 1950 that required that all citizens classify themselves under a racial grouping. The Reservation of the Separate Amenities Act of 1953 created racially segregated Group Areas, Amenities, differing educational, sexual and land tenure. The system officially ended in 1994 when the first democratic election.
2. The 'Born-Free Generation' is a term used in South Africa to denote the generation of young people born after the end of apartheid in 1994 or those who have no real recollection of the effects of apartheid.
3. Though many campaigns took place against the Apartheid regime the following are attributed to have been important to the end of Apartheid: The 1952 Defiance Campaign, 1973 Trade Union Strikes in Durban, he 1976 Soweto Uprising, 1983 End Conscription Campaign and the work by the United Democratic Front during the 1980s.
4. White Monopoly Capital is a slogan utilised in South Africa to describe the racially structured economy of the country of which the white people—a minority racial group—own the majority of capital in the country.
5. Transformation was often considered a word the captured the social, economic and political imperatives and aspirations of South Africa after the fall of apartheid (Wangenge-Ouma, 2010, p. 482).

References

African National Congress Youth League. (2010). *ANCYL report of the first national general council – Youth action for economic freedom in our lifetime*. Midrand, Johannesburg: African National Congress (ANC).

Alexander, P. (2010). Rebellion of the poor: South Africa's service delivery protests – A preliminary analysis. *Review of African Political Economy, 37*(123), 25–40. Retrieved from http://www.tandfonline.com/doi/full/10.1080/03056241003637870

Beukes, R., Fransman, T., Murozvi, S., & Yu, D. (2016). Underemployment in South Africa. *Economic Research Southern Africa*. Retrieved from http://www.econrsa.org/system/files/publications/working_papers/working_paper_575.pdf

Bhorat, H., Van der Westhuizen, C., & Jacobs, T. (2009). *Income and non-income inequality in post-apartheid South Africa.* Social Science Research Network. Retrieved from https://papers.ssrn.com/sol3/papers.cfm?abstract_id=1474271

Calitz, E., & Fourie, J. (2016). The historically high cost of tertiary education in South Africa. *Politikon, 43*(1), 149–154. Retrieved from http://www.tandfonline.com/doi/full/10.1080/02589346.2016.1155790

Cassim, A., & Oosthuizen, M. (2014). *The state of youth unemployment in South Africa – Brookings Institute.* Brookings Institute. Retrieved December 7, 2016, from https://www.brookings.edu/blog/africa-in-focus/2014/08/15/the-state-of-youth-unemployment-in-south-africa

The Daily Vox. (2015). Students shut down wits in fee protest. *The Daily Vox.* Retrieved December 10, 2016, from http://www.thedailyvox.co.za/students-shut-down-wits-in-fee-protest

Hill, L., Baxen, J., Craig, A., & Namakula, H. (2012). Citizenship, social justice, and evolving conceptions of access to education in South Africa: Implications for research. *Implications for Research, 36*(1), 239–260. Retrieved from http://journals.sagepub.com/doi/abs/10.3102/0091732X11421461

Kganyago, L. (2012). *The impact of the Eurozone and global financial crisis on South Africa.* South African Reserve Bank. Retrieved from https://www.resbank.co.za/lists/speeches/attachments/337/speech_lesetja%20kganyago.pdf

Leibbrandt, M., Finn, A., & Woolard, I. (2012). Describing and decomposing post-apartheid income inequality in South Africa. *Development South Africa, 29*(1), 19–34. Retrieved from http://www.tandfonline.com/doi/abs/10.1080/0376835X.2012.645639

Letseka, M., Visser, M., & Breier, M. (2010). Poverty, race and student achievement in seven higher education institutions. In M. Letseka, M. Cosser, M. Breier, & M. Visser (Eds.), *Student retention and graduate destination. Higher education and labour market access and success.* Cape Town: Human Science Research Council Press.

Luescher, T., Loader, L., & Mugume, T. (2016). #FeesMustFall: An internet – Age student movement in South Africa and the case of the University of the Free State. *Politikon, 44*(2), 1–15. Retrieved from http://www.tandfonline.com/doi/full/10.1080/02589346.2016.1238644?scroll=top&needAccess=true

Marais, H. (2009, September 23). The impact of the global recession on South Africa. *Elcano Newsletter,* 58. Retrieved from http://biblioteca.ribei.org/1716

Marx, K. (1977). *A contribution to the critique of political economy.* Moscow: Progress Publishers.

Marx, K., & Friedrich, E. (1965). *The German ideology* (Trans. German; Ed. S. Ryazanskaya). London: Lawrence & Wishart.

Mayosi, B., & Benatar, S. (2014). Health and health care in South Africa – 20 years after Mandela. *New England Journal of Medicine, 371*(14), 1344–1353. Retrieved December 9, 2016, from http://www.nejm.org/doi/full/10.1056/NEJMsr1405012

Mbeki, T. (1998, May 29). *Statement of deputy President Thabo Mbeki at the opening of the debate in the National Assembly, on "Reconciliation and Nation Building," National Assembly Cape Town*. Retrieved December 10, 2016, from http://www.dirco.gov.za/docs/speeches/1998/mbek0529.html

Mbembe, A. (2015, September 15). Achille Mbembe on the state of South African political life. *Africa is a country*. Retrieved from http://africasacountry.com/2015/09/achille-mbembe-on-the-state-of-south-african-politics

Mbete, S. (2015). *The economic freedom fighters – South Africa's turn towards populism?*. Retrieved from http://www.repository.up.ac.za/handle/2263/51821

Mitchell, K. (2003). Monuments, memorials, and the politics of memory. *Urban Geography*, 24(5), 442–459. Retrieved from http://www.tandfonline.com/doi/pdf/10.1080/02589346.2016.1238644?needAccess=true

Moffitt, B., & Tormey, S. (2014). Rethinking populism: Politics, mediatisation and political style. *Political Studies*, 62(2), 381–397. Retrieved December 8, 2016, from http://onlinelibrary.wiley.com/doi/10.1111/1467-9248.12032/abstract

Mottiar, S., & Bond, P. (2012). The politics of discontent and social protest in Durban. *Politikon*, 39(3), 309–330. Retrieved from http://www.tandfonline.com/doi/abs/10.1080/02589346.2012.746183

National Treasury. (2011). *Confronting youth unemployment: Policy options for South Africa*. Pretoria: National Treasury. Retrieved from http://www.treasury.gov.za/documents/national%20budget/2011/Confronting%20youth%20unemployment%20-%20Policy%20options.pdf

Netshitenzhe, J. (2015). Interrogating the concept and dynamics of race in public policy. In X. Mangcu (Ed.), *The colour of our future: Does race matter in post-apartheid South Africa?*. Johannesburg: Wits University Press.

Oyedemi, T., & Mahlatji, D. (2016). The 'born-free' non-voting youth: A study of voter apathy among a selected cohort of South African youth. *Politikon*, 43(3), 311–323. Retrieved from http://www.tandfonline.com/doi/full/10.1080/02589346.2016.1160857

Padayachee, V. (2012). *Global economic recession: Effects and implication for South Africa at a time of political challenges*. Claves de la Economia Mundial. Retrieved December 6, 2016, from http://www.lse.ac.uk/internationalDevelopment/20thAnniversaryConference/ImpactoftheGlobalFC.pdf

Ramskogler, P. (2015). Tracing the origins of the financial crisis. *OECD Journal: Financial Market Trends 2014*, 8(2), 47–61. Retrieved from http://www.oecd-ilibrary.org/finance-and-investment/tracing-the-origins-of-the-financial-crisis_fmt-2014-5js3dqmsl4br

Reinhart, C., & Rogoff, K. (2009). *This time is different: Eight centuries of financial folly*. Princeton, NJ: Princeton University Press.

SAPA. (2015, February 2). EFF counting down to Sona, "Zuma #paybackthemoney". *Times LIVE*. Retrieved from http://www.timeslive.co.za/politics/2015/02/02/EFF-counting-down-to-Sona-Zuma-paybackthemoney1

Sisk, T. (1994). Review article: Perspectives on South Africa's transition implications for democratic consolidation. *Politikon, 21*(1), 66–75. Retrieved from http://www.tandfonline.com/doi/abs/10.1080/02589349408705002

Spaull, N. (2013, October). *South Africa's education crisis: The quality of education in South Africa 1994–2011.* Report commissioned by Centre for Development and Enterprise. Johannesburg: Centre for Development and Enterprise. Retrieved December 9, 2016, from http://www.section27.org.za/wp-content/uploads/2013/10/Spaull-2013-CDE-report-South-Africas-Education-Crisis.pdf

Statistics South Africa. (2015). *Labour market dynamics in South Africa.* Pretoria: Statistics South Africa. Retrieved from http://www.statssa.gov.za/?page_id=1861&PPN=Report-02-11-02&SCH=6307

Statistics South Africa. (2016). *Vulnerable groups series 1: The social profile of youth.* Vulnerable Group Series. Pretoria: Statistics South Africa. Retrieved from http://www.statssa.gov.za/?page_id=1861&PPN=Report-03-19-01&SCH=6659

Valenzuela, S., Arriagada, A., & Scherman, A. (2012). The social media basis of youth protest behaviour: The case of Chile. *Journal of Communication, 62*(2), 299–314. Retrieved from http://onlinelibrary.wiley.com/doi/10.1111/j.1460-2466.2012.01635.x/abstract

Verick, S. (2012). Giving up job search during a recession: The impact of the global financial crisis on the South African labour market. *Journal of African Economies, 21*(3), 373–408. Retrieved from http://jae.oxfordjournals.org/content/21/3/373

Wangenge-Ouma, G. (2010). Funding and the attainment of transformation goals in South Africa's higher education. *Oxford Review of Education, 36*(4), 481–497. Retrieved from http://www.tandfonline.com/doi/abs/10.1080/03054985.2010.491181

Youniss, J., Bales, S., Christmas-Best, V., Diversi, M., McLaughlin, M., & Silbereisen, R. (2002). Youth civic engagement in twenty-first century. *Journal of Research on Adolescence, 12*(1), 121–148. Retrieved from http://onlinelibrary.wiley.com/doi/10.1111/1532-7795.00027/abstract

Rekgotsofetse Chikane is a Mandela-Rhodes Scholar, a Mandela-Washington Fellow and alum of the South Africa-Washington International Programme. He was the National President of InkuluFreeHeid, a youth-led non-partisan social movement to enhance social cohesion, deepen democracy and create solutions to socio-economic problems amongst young people in South Africa.

CHAPTER 3

Students Taking Action in Los Angeles Schools: An Ethnographic Case Study of Student Activism in the United States

Analicia Mejia Mesinas

INTRODUCTION

I was standing silently in my high school cafeteria: the location designated for On Campus Suspension, where students are sent when they show up late to class.[1] The year was 2003; I was 15 years old. I was wearing my school uniform and picture identification card around my neck, both of which were required to enter the school. The campus administrator who took my attendance ordered me to remain standing silent in the cafeteria until the class period ended, because going into class late would be a disruption to my classmates. He warned me that if I continued to be 'tardy,' I would receive a legal citation from a police officer for truancy.[2] As I stood in the cafeteria, school officers slowly brought in additional students found outside of a classroom after the class bell rung—some of whom were given citations for "chronic truancy." Standing there, in silence,

A. Mejia Mesinas (✉)
Department of Criminology, Law and Society, University of California, Irvine, CA, USA

I had mixed emotions. Mad, upset and frustrated, I could not help but think, "What is the point of this?" I just wanted to get to class.

I begin with this personal account to give an example of the now common disciplinary policies and practices used in public government schools in the United States to monitor student behavior.[3] Fueled by important concerns for school safety, contemporary school disciplinary policies in the United States rest on the idea that students should be punished for the violation of specific school rules; that students should be provided with no leniency in the delivery of punishment; and that punishment should involve law enforcement officials (Kafka, 2011). However, critical examinations of contemporary school discipline do not support the conclusion that these policies and practices significantly contribute to safer school environments (Skiba & Rausch, 2006). Instead, these policies and practices have contributed to a crisis in public government schools across the United States.

Contemporary school disciplinary policies subjugate students to degrading experiences that symbolically, and overtly, treat them like suspicious criminals (Hirschfield, 2008). Student misbehavior commonly triggers contact with police officers, often resulting in a citation and/or arrest (Na & Gottfredson, 2011). In addition to police, use of security cameras, random searches, metal detectors, and identification cards are largely unquestioned common practices of public schools (Kupchik & Monahan, 2006; Skiba, 2000). While social control and discipline have always been a cornerstone of American schools (Hirschfield, 2008; Noguera, 2003), the growth of these practices has sparked a new area of research on the criminalization of school discipline (Hirschfield & Celinska, 2011). Although the experiences of students are a key focus of this work, the ways in which students are actively resisting and challenging these policies are too often overlooked (Monahan & Torres, 2010).

This chapter provides an ethnographic case study of the political activism of students who are challenging the criminalization of school discipline. I draw on one year of participant observation research that I conducted with the Labor Community Strategy Center (LCSC). The LCSC is a social movement organization located in Los Angeles, California. Over the last ten years, the LCSC has organized high school student activists, aged 14–18, and built a youth-led movement challenging the criminalization of students in Los Angeles. I focus on the efforts of LCSC student activists, and detail the ways student activists have confronted zero tolerance policies, and the increased use of police. I argue, that over the last decade, student activism has been vigorous, and critical to reforming school policies and practices in Los Angeles public schools.

Los Angeles Public Government Schools

The Los Angeles Unified School District (LAUSD) is the second largest public government school district in the United States (LAUSD, 2016a). Currently, the district enrolls more than 640,000 students across kindergarten through 12th grade (LAUSD, 2016b). Latino students make up the vast majority of the student population (74 percent), and approximately 75 percent of students within the district qualify for free or reduced price meals. LAUSD is also home to one of the largest independent school police departments in the nation (LASPD, 2016). The Los Angeles Schools Police Department (LASPD) is the primary law enforcement agency operating within LAUSD, dedicated to providing a safe and crime-free school environment.

LAUSD also has a long history of serving as national leader in the development and implementation of zero tolerance policies (Kafka, 2011).[4] These policies mandate the delivery of strict punishments, often in the form of suspension, expulsion, and legal citations for students' violations of school rules (Skiba & Rausch, 2006). The ongoing enforcement of zero tolerance policies transformed LAUSD schools into highly policed and punitive environments, which consistently subjugated students to intensified scrutiny and surveillance, essentially treating students as criminals (CRC, 2013). LAUSD students regularly encountered police officers within their schools, and some schools began to use metal detectors. Additionally, it was not uncommon for police officers to issue legal citations, or tickets, to students for the violation of school policies (CRC, 2013). An investigation of student and parent experiences with LAUSD policies conducted in 2007 revealed that students often felt intimidated and threatened by heavy police presence in their schools (Sullivan, 2007). Parents and students reported that police officers often used excessive force during minor disciplinary encounters with the students, including slamming them onto the ground or into the wall and, in some cases, spraying them with mace (Sullivan, 2007).[5]

Organizing for Reform

In 2007, the LAUSD governing board acknowledged the disparate rates of punishment within LAUSD schools, and passed the Resolution to Support Equal Protection and Civil Rights for all Students in all Los Angeles Unified School District Schools (BOE, 2007). In the resolution, the school board declared LAUSD's commitment to social justice, and pledged to remedy the inequitable treatment of students.[6] The resolution ordered all LAUSD officials to take immediate action to identify and reform inequitable school practices, including collaborating with parents and community organizations to develop fair and just policies and practices that protect the civil rights of its students.

Over the last decade, student and community activists have called attention to the criminalization of schools and the policing of students. Activists have emphasized the need to end the aggressive enforcement of zero tolerance policies. However, the LAUSD governing board has focused on the need to maintain safe school environments—through strict discipline and law enforcement. In the section that follows, I narrow my focus to the work of the Labor Community Strategy Center (LCSC), the organization where I conducted my participant observations. While many organizations in Los Angeles are dedicated to reforming LAUSD school practices, the LCSC's long term campaign allows for a historically rich case study of student activism.

Youth Led Movement to Reform LAUSD Schools

The LCSC was founded in the late 1980s and operates as a "think tank/act tank for regional, national and international movement building" (LCSC, 2016a). Previous projects of the LCSC revealed a related set of problems that specifically affected high school students, who used public transportation to get to and from school. These issues included: an unreliable public transportation system, challenges in accessing affordable student bus passes, and a growing number of police citations for tardiness and truancy. The identification of these issues catalyzed the need for a new campaign targeting the experiences of students with police, and the culture of criminalization across Los Angeles public schools. In 2007, the LCSC launched its long-term campaign to "challenge suppressive, pre-prison conditions in Los Angeles Public Schools" (CRC, 2013). The goal of the campaign was to build a youth-led local movement for school reform in Los Angeles. The work focused on LAUSD school disciplinary practices and the experiences of students in schools. The campaign identified LAUSD high schools as critical sites for student activism. To organize high school students within their schools, the campaign established school clubs called "Taking Action." These high school clubs generated a space for students to examine their experiences within their schools, connect school disciplinary practices to broader issues of punishment, and develop strategies for change. The campaign also developed Youth Organizer Training Programs to provide its high school student activists with more formalized training in community organizing and social movement building tactics.[7]

Students Take Action: Sharing Personal Narratives

I was introduced to the work of the LCSC in the year 2013, at a School Criminalization information session at the University of California. During this event, LCSC high school student activists shared their experiences at their schools. I remember the story told by a Latino high school student named Tony, who explained that he felt harassed by officers at his school.[8] He told us that when he was a freshman [15 years of age], he was given three or four "truancy tickets" that required him to pay a lot of money in fines.[9] He eventually dropped out of his high school because "it was easier to avoid tickets that way," but had recently started attending a new school in order to earn his high school diploma. At his new school, he learned about the LCSC and joined their project.

Tony's presentation deeply moved me. At the end of his talk, I greeted Tony and talked with him for some time about my interest in school criminalization. Tony explained that he was part of a movement against the criminalization of students and had shared his story at a number of community presentations—a tactic developed by the student activists to raise awareness about the aggressive policing practices that were criminalizing students in LAUSD schools. He wanted others to see that he was not a criminal, but his school was treating him like one. Part of his activism was to share his personal narrative in order to reveal the problematic nature of LAUSD school policies. For Tony, and the LCSC group of student activists, personal narratives were a key tactic for change.

Following the launch of LCSC's campaign in 2007, students identified, and targeted, the wide range of aggressive policing tactics used by Los Angeles School Police officers. However, students did more than identify these issues. They began to develop an account of what it was like to be a student in LAUSD. To do this, students developed an online blog that narrated individualized experiences (LCSC, 2009). These stories publicly shared student narratives and LAUSD practices to a wide audience (Hing, 2009). For example, the blog told the story of Nancy, a Latina, LAUSD high school sophomore (16 years of age) who was arrested on her way to school. Nancy used public transportation to get to school each morning, and was handcuffed by a police officer one block away from school. The officer told her that she was being arrested because she was breaking daytime curfew laws and needed to be in school.[10] Nancy's blog post explained that she tried to tell the officer that she was on her way to school but was running late. She also revealed the fear she experienced the day she encountered the police officer, and the disappointment she felt when the officer cuffed her hands behind her back. Blog posts with narratives like Nancy's documented the intimidating nature of interactions between LAUSD students and police officers.

To build on the blog posts, LCSC student activists conducted a number student surveys asking participants about their experiences of school discipline, including zero tolerance policies and interactions with police officers in their schools. Student surveys were consistent with the online blog posts, and revealed a culture of criminalization largely stemming from the constant ticketing and arrest of students. Indeed, surveys revealed that the number one cause of student referrals to the juvenile courts was for violations of municipal daytime curfew and school truancy (CRC, 2013).[11]

Demanding Change

While daytime curfew and school truancy laws were originally established to encourage school attendance and reduce school truancy, students' narratives revealed that the aggressive enforcement of these policies more often had the opposite effect; these policies harshly punished and criminalized students, especially low income, Black and Latino students. Building on these personalized narratives, LCSC student activists targeted the LAUSD governing school board and local elected officials to demand changes in the policies and practices that negatively impacted LAUSD students. Student activists attended and presented at a number of LAUSD school board meetings and Los Angeles City Government Meetings. In their presentations, student activists shared their stories and revealed results from their student surveys. At the end of their presentations they explicitly called for changes; they called on officials to protect students from aggressive policing and repeal the aggressive truancy and curfew laws.

In 2011, LAUSD officials began to meet some of the demands of student activists and adopted strategies for new approaches to school discipline. The Los Angeles School Police Department adopted new restrictions for the enforcement of truancy and daytime curfew laws (Hing, 2011). More specifically, the department announced that it would no longer give out tickets to students within the first 90 minutes of the school day, in order to eliminate the ticketing of students on their way to school and encourage school attendance (Ferris, 2012). LCSC student advocates celebrated this new practice, but argued that more comprehensive policies were needed to limit aggressive policing practices (CRC, 2013). To call attention to this demand, the students published a policy report comparing LAUSD school police data from the 2012–2013 to the 2011–2012 school years. The report revealed that although school police tickets and citations were reduced by 50 percent, Latino and Black students were still much more likely to be ticketed and/or arrested than White students (CRC, 2013).[12]

Following continued collaborations with students and organizations, in 2013, LAUSD adopted the School Discipline Policy and School Climate Bill of Rights (LAUSD, 2016c). This resolution was developed by a coalition of community organizations in Los Angeles, and championed by LAUSD school board members as a means to minimize the use of zero tolerance policies and implement the use of positive behavior interventions. On the day that LAUSD board members were scheduled to discuss and vote on this plan, youth activists across Los Angeles held a rally outside of LAUSD headquarters to encourage the successful adoption of the plan. Almost 300 students, parents, and community partners attended the rally to show their support (LCSC, 2016b).

MILITARY WEAPONS IN LAUSD SCHOOLS

In 2014, the Los Angeles School Police Department (LASPD) also adopted new protocols for enforcement, citations, and arrests on LAUSD school campuses (Watanabe, 2014; Zipperman, 2014).[13] However, only a month after the LASPD announced their new policies, news reports also revealed official data showing police participation in a military program that provided surplus weapons to local police departments—including departments affiliated with schools (Musgrave, 2014; Pamer & Romero, 2014). Through the Department of Defense Excess Military Equipment Program, more commonly referred to as the 1033 program, the LASPD received 61 M-16 assault rifles, three grenade launchers, and a mine-resistant protective vehicle (Chokshi, 2014).[14] The unexpected discovery of LASPD's possession of these weapons created serious concerns for activists about the prospect that weapons would be used to arm police in schools (LDF, 2014). To ease public concern both the LASPD Chief of Police and LAUSD superintendent explained that the weapons would only be used in extraordinary cases of armed threats presenting life-threatening circumstances (Associated Press, 2014). Unconvinced by this response, LCSC student demanded an immediate end to this program in LAUSD schools and called for the removal of all military weapons.[15]

Building a Critique of the 1033 Program

To focus their efforts on the militarization of school police, students examined the history of LAUSD school policies and practices and developed critical analyses of school discipline, student criminalization, and the role of police in schools. Following this work, students engaged in close readings and discussions of a number of news articles and reports providing information about the 1033 program. During my observations, I sat quietly listening to the dialogue between students. Manuel, an 18-year-old high school student expressed his concerns about police violence in schools to the group:

> I just don't understand why they have these military weapons. Here we are reading stories about students who were punished by police officers, and I know what that's like. I've been thrown on the ground and told to obey orders. And, I am glad. I feel good to know that they [LAUSD] changed their policies, but I can't say that it never happens anymore. It still happens, and I know that, for real. So now, really, a gun is supposed to make me feel safe? Where is the logic in that? (Fieldnotes, July 15, 2015)

Manuel's interrogation of LAUSD's participation in the '1033 program' reveals the contradictory nature between new school policies, like the Student Bill of Rights, and police possession of military weapons. He questions school police officer's use for these weapons and the purpose of these weapons in schools. He emphasized that these weapons that are normally used by the US military during times of war. In addition, he challenges conventional notions of safety to justify the possession of these weapons, and he questions how he can be expected to feel safe given his experiences and the militarization of school police. After Manuel presented his thoughts, Britney shared her views with the group:

> Schools are not warzones, why do they [LAUSD] think they need these weapons? I know they are gonna tell us that it's to protect us from school shootings, but that kind of stuff doesn't happen at my school. Giving the

police weapons doesn't fix the problem from the root. And when White kids go and shoot up schools, they respond and say that they were sick, it's because they didn't have enough counseling. So why not give us counselors instead of weapons? (Fieldnotes, July 15, 2015)

Britney's response reinforces Manuel's confusion. Both Manuel and Britney are not convinced that the militarization of school police will contribute to more safety. Britney, however, identifies racial differences in police responses to acts of violence. She points to the lack of treatment-based resources offered to members in her community, like counseling—resources that she believes are immediately offered to White students who may engage in acts of violence. This comment provides an additional layer of analysis; for Britney, race plays a critical role in the range of police responses to violent behavior. She demands more resources are provided to her school, rather than weapons.

The comments of Manuel and Britney demonstrate many of the grave concerns shared by the student activists when discussing the 1033 program, including disappointment, fear, and outrage. Fueled by these emptions, student activists prepared for a day of activism at the LAUSD headquarters that would be held during the final week of the Youth Organizer Training Program. Students wanted to hold a rally outside of LAUSD headquarters to publicly demonstrate their disapproval of the 1033 program. They wanted to inform LAUSD officials they had become aware of the 1033 program, and notify LAUSD officials of their plans to actively resist the program until the program was terminated.

Planning for Action

To prepare for the rally, students developed posters and large signs demanding an end to the 1033 program. As students engaged in this work, Jessica, a 15-year-old high school student, expressed her concerns to me:

> These are military weapons. They [the Los Angeles School Police Department] have these weapons, so they [LAUSD officials] got to see them. I haven't seen the weapons, and just because I might not see them doesn't mean they are not there. When people finally see the weapons, I think it will scare them. That's why we are making pictures of these weapons; they got to see them. (Fieldnotes, July 21, 2015)

Jessica reflected a general concern within the student body about the firearms and the need to demand their removal. For Jessica and others, abstract discussions of these weapons did not lead to sufficient understandings of students' concerns and fears. Rather, student activists also had to utilize visual images to call attention to their concerns; visual images provided a powerful tool to communicate concerns and challenge political arguments that defended the 1033 program. To leverage visual imagery, students drew pictures of military tanks, grenades, and M-16 assault rifles on the posters and signs that they planned to carry during their rally. Students also included drawings police officers with the weapons, and included sketches of young people standing in front of a school, with their hands up.

In addition to this artwork, LCSC organizers planned to wear costume, bulletproof vests during their demonstration. "We are not bulletproof" a student declared, "LAUSD school officials need to know that these weapons can actually paralyze me and kill me" (Fieldnotes, July 17, 2015). The costume, bulletproof vest, was a prop that could demonstrate the violent nature of military weapons; military weapons are used to kill people, and students needed protection. Students planned to used props to challenge frameworks held by LAUSD officials, and used to defend policies for student safety. Students hoped the props would invoke strong emotional reactions, including notions of discomfort and fear.

Students Demonstrate at LAUSD Headquarters

On the final day of the Youth Organizer Training Program, students arrived at LAUSD headquarters and took action. Wearing their costume bulletproof vests, students organized themselves into groups of three to four people and passed out fliers outside of the LAUSD headquarters building. The fliers provided a brief overview of the 1033 program and outlined the student demands to end this program. As people passed by the LAUSD building, students approached people asking, "Have you heard about the 1033 program?" For about 30 minutes, students organized to educate others about the program and gather support for their demands. Then, just before the start of the board meeting, students came together as a large group and began to demonstrate. They marched up and down the street chanting in protest of the 1033 program. In their bulletproof vests, students held up large signs that said "END 1033" and "My school is not a war zone," and chanted phrases like, "Back to school, no weapons" and "Students ain't bullet proof" (Fieldnotes, July 30, 2015).

After about an hour of chanting, students made their way into the board meeting. During the meeting, LCSC staff members testified to the LAUSD board and presented their concerns. As the LCSC staff members made their way up to the front of the room, all the student activists stood up in solidarity. Following the testimony of the LCSC staff members, students locked arms and began to chant. As students chanted "Back to school, no weapons," police officers slowly approached the students. However, the school board president stopped the officers and said, "You can let them go on." Students stood together and chanted for about fifteen minutes before they were interrupted by comments from the LAUSD board members.

One board member defended the use of the weapons in schools. The board member explained that he has been an educator since the 1960s, and has worked in very tough neighborhoods characterized by high rates of poverty and gang violence. He argued that he had yet to see the use of the weapons, but has personally witnessed gang violence. He welcomed the concerns of students, but told students that in the end, he believed that in the case of 'an emergency,' he wanted school police officers to be prepared. Not pleased by this response, as soon as the board member finished his comments the students resumed in their chants. Another board member then tried to work with the students by taking a quite different approach. She began by applauding their efforts, explaining that their work demonstrated much bravery. She also referenced the district's dramatic decrease in punishment, and affirmed that it was their actions that were directly responsible for that fact. She concluded by declaring she was unaware of this program, and pledged to look into the matter and take up the issue. As she spoke, she stood up and walked over to the group of students. She then shouted, "You all have much to be proud of, and I will continue to work with you students to ensure your safety. Thank you for being here." One of the LCSC staff organizers approached her, thanked her for her comments, and announced to the group, "Well, looks like we have to continue to fight for this."

A month after the demonstration at the LAUSD school board meeting, students began the new academic school year. Over the course of the academic year, student activists continued to organize within their schools. LCSC student activists met weekly to organize strategies to increase public awareness of the 1033 program, and demand its termination. This included delivering presentations in schools and encouraging teachers and students to discuss the 1033 program. In addition, student activists met with LAUSD Board Officials to maintain a constructive dialogue around this issue.

Student activists also incorporated the use of social media. Social media provided young activists with a fun way to document their actions, communicate their concerns, and continue their momentum in their fight against the 1033 program. Using a variety of social media platforms, like Facebook and Instagram, LCSC student activists developed individualized accounts dedicated to the campaign against the 1033 program. Once the accounts were established, they used the social media pages to announce upcoming events and actions, share pictures of student activism, and convey concerns with the 1033 program. Through the use of social media, students were able to encourage a continued political dialogue amongst their peers around the existence of the 1033 program. Students viewed social media as a resourceful tool to further communicate their concerns, build support for their cause, and ultimately, continue to put pressure on school officials.

In the final months of the 2016 academic school year, the LCSC students energetically cheered as they read a letter sent from the Los Angeles Unified School District (LAUSD) Board of Education President. The letter officially reported the termination of LAUSD participation with the 1033 program. In addition, the letter acknowledged the efforts of LCSC student activists, and provided an apology for the district's participation with the 1033 program. The Los Angeles School Police Chief also provided a letter to the LCSC to clarify information regarding the department's possession of military weapons. In the letter the Police Chief also acknowledged the department's lack of consideration for important concerns during the initial development of the program. Most importantly, the police department provided an official inventory of all the weapons received and then returned the arms to the Department of Defense.

Conclusion

Contemporary investigations of schools in the United States point to a crisis in education. With the adoption of zero tolerance policies police officers have come to play pivotal roles in the enforcement of school policy, and schools have become increasingly punitive. However, this work typically focuses on school policies and practices, including implementation by school officials, and outcomes for students. While these inquiries have contributed to important insights for school discipline, the political efforts of student activists have too often been overlooked. Over the last decade, community organizations and youth activists have worked to actively challenge and reform problematic, contemporary school policies.

As research on school practices and the criminalization of schools continues to develop, the actions of young people must also play a key role in our analyses.

Indeed, student activists have played a critical role in the transformation of LAUSD policies and practices throughout the last decade; the actions of these students cannot be ignored. This chapter relied on a year of participant observations with LCSC student activists to explicitly illustrate the political actions of student activists seeking reform in LAUSD schools. Often fuelled by their personal experiences in schools, LCSC high school student activists have built a youth-led movement that challenges the criminalization of students, including zero tolerance policies, aggressive policing practices in LAUSD schools, and the militarization of school police. In demanding change, students have shared personal narratives, developed an online blog, challenged LAUSD school officials, and incorporated to use of social media to produce change. These new and existing forms of political actions have generated new politics around contemporary school policies, and provided useful insights about possibilities for social change in public schools in the United States.

Notes

1. The education system in the United States can be organized into primary, secondary, and higher education. Primary education is typically referred to as elementary school, secondary education is referred to as high school, and higher education is referred to as college or university. In this chapter, I focus on students in high school (secondary school). High school consists of four years of education after primary school. Students typically attend from about age 14 to 18.
2. In the state of California, education is compulsory until 18 years of age. A student is truant if he or she misses more than thirty minutes of class instruction three times during the academic year. Students who are in violation of truancy laws are issued legal tickets, or citations, for their violations.
3. In the United States, public school refers to elementary and high schools that are funded by State and Federal governments; what some countries call state schools. For clarity, in this chapter I will refer to US public schools, as public government schools.
4. The zero tolerance approach emphasizes that students will be immediately punished for misbehavior, usually through suspension and expulsion. These laws send the message that certain behaviors, no matter how minor, will not be tolerated in schools (Skiba, 2000).

5. Mace refers to a chemical aerosol spray with a chemical makeup similar to tear gas. The spray severely irritates skin, and is used to incapacitate individuals.
6. The LAUSD board of education is the governing body of LAUSD. These elected officials make policy decisions for LAUSD.
7. Youth Organizer Training Programs are held twice a year, during the spring and summer school breaks, each bringing together anywhere from 20 to 30 high school students. Since students most often organize within their respective high schools during the academic school year, the training programs also provide opportunities for students who attend different schools to come together and build collectively.
8. Pseudonyms are used for all individuals mentioned in this chapter.
9. Tickets, or citations, typically require students to appear in court. In addition, these tickets often resulted in up to US$250 in student fines, up to US$1000 in court fees, and mandatory court appearances that threatened the possibility of incarceration.
10. Los Angeles municipal curfew laws legally prohibited students under the age of 18 to be in any public place during school hours. Minors found in public areas without parental supervision were ticketed by police officers.
11. In the United States, juvenile courts are the courts of law for individuals under the age of 18.
12. The report revealed that Latino students were twice as likely to be ticketed and arrested, than a White student. Black students were almost six times more likely to be ticketed and arrested, than a White student (CRC, 2013).
13. These protocols placed limits on the use of official arrests and legal citations in schools, in an effort to align police practices with the School Discipline Policy and School Climate Bill of Rights (2013).
14. This program is also known as the 1033 program because it was authorized in Section 1033 of the National Defense Authorization Act 1997.
15. As LCSC activists began to strategize their new campaign to end the 1033 program, I also began my participant observation research with the LCSC. This work began in June 2015, at the commencement of the organization's summer Youth Organizer Training Program. I participated in the training program alongside the LAUSD high school activists. The program was held at the office of the LCSC, and hosted about 25 Black and Latino high school student activists. The program was held three times a week, with two days of each week dedicated to seminar-style student workshops and one day each week dedicated to organizing across Los Angeles to inform community members about the LCSC's current project targeting the militarization of police.

REFERENCES

Associated Press. (2014, September 18). US school districts given free machine guns and grenade launchers. *The Guardian*. Retrieved November 17, 2016, from https://www.theguardian.com/world/2014/sep/18/us-school-districts-given-free-machine-guns-and-grenade-launchers

Board of Education (BOE). (2007, October 23). *Special meeting minutes*. Retrieved December 1, 2016, from http://laschoolboard.org/sites/default/files/10-23-07CSMinutes.pdf

Chokshi, N. (2014, September 16). School police across the country receive excess military weapons and gear. *The Washington Post*. Retrieved November 1, 2016, from https://www.washingtonpost.com/blogs/govbeat/wp/2014/09/16/school-police-across-the-country-receive-excess-military-weapons-and-gear/?utm_term=.769a262f44f9

Community Rights Campaign (CRC). (2013). *Black, brown and over-policed in L.A. Schools: Structural proposals to end the school to prison pipeline in Los Angeles Unified School District and to build a national movement to stop the mass incarceration of Black and Latino communities*. Community Rights Campaign of the Labor/Community Strategy Center. Policy report.

Equal Protection and Civil Rights for all Students. (2007). *Los Angeles Unified School Board resolution*, adopted 2007.

Ferris, S. (2012, June 14). *L.A. school police, district agree to rethink court citations of students*. Juvenile Justice Information Exchange. Retrieved November 12, 2016, from http://jjie.org/2012/06/14/la-school-police-district-agree-rethink-court-citations-of-students

Hing, J. (2009, September 2). Young, brown—And charged with truancy. *Colorlines*. Retrieved November 15, 2016, from https://www.colorlines.com/articles/young-brown—and-charged-truancy

Hing, J. (2011, October 24). Why Los Angeles police can't ticket students on their way to school. *Colorlines*. Retrieved November 15, 2016, from http://www.colorlines.com/articles/why-los-angeles-police-cant-ticket-students-their-way-school

Hirschfield, P. J. (2008). Preparing for prison: The criminalization of school discipline in the USA. *Theoretical Criminology, 12*(1), 79–101.

Hirschfield, P. J., & Celinska, K. (2011). Beyond fear: Sociological perspectives on the criminalization of school discipline. *Sociology Compass, 5*(1), 1–12.

Kafka, J. (2011). *The history of "zero tolerance" in American public schooling*. New York, NY: Palgrave Macmillan.

Kupchik, A., & Monahan, T. (2006). The new American school: Preparation for post-industrial discipline. *British Journal of Sociology of Education, 27*(5), 617–631.

Labor Community Strategy Center (LCSC). (2009, March 19). *Ticketing towards prisons: LAUSD's truancy tickets and the pre-prisoning of our youth*. The Labor Community Strategy Center. Retrieved November 10, 2016, from http://www.thestrategycenter.org/blog/2009/03/19/ticketing-towards-prisons-lausd's-truancy-tickets-and-pre-prisoning-our-youth

Labor Community Strategy Center (LCSC). (2016a). *The Labor Community Strategy Center*. Retrieved November 10, 2016, from http://www.thestrategy-center.org/about

Labor Community Strategy Center (LCSC). (2016b). *The Labor Community Strategy Center*. Retrieved January 12, 2016, from http://www.thestrategy-center.org/blog/2013/05/16/making-history-school-climate-bill-rights-passes-5-2-lausd-board

Legal Defense Fund (LDF). (2014, September 15). *Newly discovered 1033 military surplus records show school districts around the country are receiving advanced military equipment*. NAACP Legal Defense and Educational Fund. Retrieved November 10, 2016, from http://www.naacpldf.org/press-release/newly-discovered-1033-military-surplus-records-show-school-districts-around-country

Los Angeles School Police Department (LASPD). (2016). *Los Angeles School Police Department*. Retrieved October 23, 2016, from http://laspd.com/about.html

Los Angeles Unified School District (LAUSD). (2016a). *Los Angeles Unified School District*. Retrieved November 30, 2016, from http://achieve.lausd.net/about

Los Angeles Unified School District (LAUSD). (2016b). *Los Angeles Unified School District*. Retrieved November 2, 2016, from http://achieve.lausd.net/cms/lib08/CA01000043/Centricity/Domain/32/Fingertip%20Facts2016-17_FINAL.pdf

Los Angeles Unified School District (LAUSD). (2016c). *Fingertip facts*. Los Angeles Unified School District. Retrieved November 30, 2016, from http://home.lausd.net/pdf/Toolkits/SCBOR/MessagePoints.pdf

Monahan, T., & Torres, R. D. (Eds.). (2010). *Schools under surveillance: Cultures of control in public education*. New Brunswick: Rutgers University Press.

Musgrave, S. (2014, September 8). California releases its 1033 program data. *Muckrock*. Retrieved November 30, 2016, from https://www.muckrock.com/news/archives/2014/sep/08/california-releases-1033-program-data

Na, C., & Gottfredson, D. C. (2011). Police officers in schools: Effects on school crime and the processing of offending behaviors. *Justice Quarterly, 30*(4), 619–650.

National Defense Authorization Act for Fiscal Year 1997, § 1033, Pub. L. No. 104–201, 110 Stat. 2422, 2639 (1996).

Noguera, P. A. (2003). The trouble with Black boys: The role and influence of environmental and cultural factors on the academic performance of African American males. *Urban Education, 38*(4), 431–459.

Pamer, M., & Romero, L. (2014, September 15). LAUSD police arsenal includes armored vehicle, grenade launchers, chief confirms. *KTLA*. Retrieved November 30, 2016, from http://ktla.com/2014/09/15/lausd-police-arsenal-includes-armored-vehicle-grenade-launchers-chief-confirms

School Discipline Policy and School Climate Bill of Rights. (2013). *Los Angeles School Board of Education*, adopted May 2013.

Skiba, R. J. (2000). *Zero tolerance, zero evidence: An analysis of school disciplinary practice*. Indiana Education Policy Center (Policy research report #SRS2).

Skiba, R. J., & Rausch, M. K. (2006). Zero tolerance, suspension, and expulsion: Questions of equity and effectiveness. In C. Evertson & C. Weinstein (Eds.), *Handbook of classroom management: Research, practice, and contemporary issues*. Mahwah, NJ: Lawrence Erlbaum Associates, Publishers.

Sullivan, E. (2007). *Deprived of dignity: Degrading treatment and abusive discipline in New York City and Los Angeles public schools*. National Economic and Social Rights Initiative (NESRI). Policy research report. Retrieved November 15, 2016, from https://www.nesri.org/sites/default/files/deprived_of_dignity_07.pdf

Watanabe, T. (2014, August 19). L.A. Unified School Police to stop citing students for minor offenses. *LA Times*. Retrieved November 10, 2016, from http://www.latimes.com/local/education/la-me-lausd-discipline-20140820-story.html

Zipperman, S. K. (2014, August 15). *Los Angeles School Police Department roles and responsibilities for: Enforcement, citation and arrest protocols on school campus and safe passages*. Los Angeles School Police Department. Retrieved November 12, 2016, from http://fixschooldiscipline.org/wp-content/uploads/2014/10/LASPD-Arrest-and-Citation-Reform-Policy.-8-15-14.pdf

Analicia Mejia Mesinas is a PhD candidate and a National Science Foundation Graduate Research Fellow in the Department of Criminology, Law and Society at the University of California, Irvine, US. Her interdisciplinary research focuses on experiences of young people, and examines school criminalization and the use of police in schools.

CHAPTER 4

'Professional Students Do Not Play Politics': How Kenyan Students Professionalise Environmental Activism and Produce Neoliberal Subjectivities

Grace Muthoni Mwaura

Introduction

While conducting research in 2012 and 2014 on students' participation in environmental clubs in six public universities in Kenya (Mwaura, 2015), I came across a new form of political engagement among these students who identified as environmentalists and distanced themselves from the more traditional forms of student and national politics. Through the environmental clubs, the students engaged in both nature-based activities (such as tree planting, clean-ups and camping), and social organising activities (such as conferences, seminars, campaigns and dialogues). Although the overall study focused on the changing aspirations of educated young people, it was apparent that these students were not only working towards

---

G. Muthoni Mwaura (✉)
African Centre for Technology Studies, Nairobi, Kenya

Institute of Development Studies, Nairobi, Kenya

© The Author(s) 2018
S. Pickard, J. Bessant (eds.), *Young People Re-Generating Politics in Times of Crises*, Palgrave Studies in Young People and Politics,
DOI 10.1007/978-3-319-58250-4_4

gaining experience and joining new social networks that would open up future occupational opportunities; they were also consciously disengaging from traditional styles of student politics. Particularly, they argued that this model of politics no longer represented a way to achieve respectable status in society and that student environmentalism offered them a new way of self-making and identity.

The chapter interrogates how these students perceived their kind of environmental activism. I conducted focus group discussions with 15 members of each of the six environmental clubs, attended events organised by the clubs, and interviewed leaders as well as members to get a deeper sense of their understanding of environmental activism. I aim to show that their claim to be involved in non-political environmental activism is not a mere romanticism of nature; rather, it is a disengagement from confrontational politics and a search for new interventions that still challenge the existing systems of power for failing to adequately respond both to the looming environmental crises and to youth employment uncertainties in Kenya. Hence, students' environmental activism remains deeply embedded in the national neoliberal politics that they desire to change.

I broadly define environmentalism as the ways in which relationships between people and their environment are understood and acted upon (Carter, 2004). I situate student environmentalism, also referred here as student environmental activism, as a kind of new social movement within environmentalism, which is characteristically different in the actors' (students') ability to express hybrid identities, produce multiple subjectivities, and exploit non-conventional political channels and tactics to achieve desired goals (Carter, 2004). Throughout out the chapter, I bring out how students claim to be non-political, or disengaged from politics, implying their lack of interest to engage in traditional student and national politics, but not necessarily a lack of awareness of the Kenyan political system. Their pursuit of student environmentalism as a non-political identity is a factor of neoliberalism in Kenya, here understood as the International Monetary Fund (IMF) and World Bank-led liberal economic changes since the 1970s that resulted in the shrinking of the State and the expansion of the private sector. Importantly, I am concerned with the neoliberal reforms that promoted self-governing technologies that aim to make autonomous and self-reliant individuals who take on their responsibilities instead of relying on the State. I show how my respondents were socialised in a society undergoing neoliberal changes and, therefore, are emerging with neoliberal subjectivities reflected in their self-identification as professional environmentalists.

The chapter is organised as follows. I first review some of the global literature addressing ideas of youth disengagement and identify how neoliberal ideologies manifest in new forms of engagement. The second section discusses the divergence from student politics to student environmentalism as a result of globalisation and situated injustices resulting from Kenya's experience of neoliberalism in the early 1990s. The third section presents findings on how student environmentalism provides a space for students to generate local political practices and their emerging neoliberal subjectivities embedded in their self-making efforts and hybrid identities.

The Claim on Political Disengagement

While young people are conventionally understood to be a critical indicator of a nation's politics, economy, and socio-cultural life (Honwana, 2012), the society also accuses them of disengaging from the very issues that shape their identity, either out of their own choice, or because of hegemonic identities that the society has given them (Farthing, 2010). However, many studies have challenged this claim. Indeed, in a context of ever-changing national politics and the complex dynamics set loose by globalisation, urbanisation, migration, new labour markets, and connectivity offered by technology (Beck, 1992; Furlong, 2009), young people continually create new identities and produce new forms of politics. As a result, many are disengaging from 'normal' or conventional politics, such as voting in elections or being members of political parties, while simultaneously engaging in new forms of political action (Pickard, 2018).

Young people's new forms of action are grounded on their need for a livelihood and self-identification. Farthing (2010, p. 12) advances a 'politics of fun' implying that youth disengagement from normative politics is deliberate because it provides the young people a space to devise and explore their own questions about the political processes. These politics of fun exhibit three key features: a transformative agenda, which is self-actualisation; a radically revised target, reflected in the individualised goals; and new forms of participation. I argue that the politics of fun are a true reflection of 'youth waithood'—a period of uncertain labour market opportunities when young people continually embody multiple identities in an attempt to secure the capitals that mark their attainment of independent adulthood (Honwana, 2012). This being the case, young people are continually navigating systems of power, authority and political inadequacies, while also seeking self-making opportunities in rather uncertain contexts (Mwaura, Pradhan, & Gitahi, 2017).

Several studies have shown how environmental activism relates to prevailing political regimes, the changing socio-economic space, and anxiety about uncertain life opportunities (Nagel & Staeheli, 2016; Tsing, 2011). Tsing's (2011) account of the cosmopolitanism of Indonesian students in the wake of environmental degradation, economic 'miracles' and political upheavals in neoliberal Indonesia in the late 1980s and 1990s illustrates how some young people have responded to a context of environmental degradation and political crisis. At a time of political turmoil, when Indonesian university students were generally seen as opponents of the ruling government, the proliferating self-declared 'nature-lovers clubs' in that country became generative spaces that fashioned new student identities that reflected new kinds of political choices. It also enabled the 'nature-lovers' to accumulate various kinds of social and intellectual capital, which they could draw on in the future (Tsing, 2011). Adventure hikes, mountaineering and camping, activities previously associated with foreign tourists, became "a process of identity formation and an avenue for passion and growth" for some Indonesian students (Tsing, 2011, p. 153). In short, these students both influenced and were influenced by the changing physical and political landscape of Indonesia.

In post-civil war Lebanon, civil society organisations generate a discourse of environmentalism as a way of seeking national cohesion between otherwise hostile groups (Nagel & Staeheli, 2016). Their environmental activities provide the divided Lebanese community with an alternative political vision and a form of dissent against the political status quo in Lebanon. Since the 1980s, non-governmental organisations have organised youth camps "to remove young people from their increasingly 'ghettoized' existence and mix them together in order to bring down 'the walls of prejudice' between them" (p. 2). Nagel and Staeheli argue that as young people engage in these activities, particular understandings of nature are deployed to reconstitute their citizenship and re-imagine Lebanon as a unified nation-state. The organisations frame these environmental activities as 'non-political,' treating the environmental issues and activism, as somehow disconnected from the country's prevailing contentious politics. However, this does not mean that the environmental activities are not political; on the contrary, they create new forms of political activity where actions are directed towards contesting the prevailing power relations in ways that are more sensitive to the local ecology (Agrawal, 2005).

Historically, different actors have used nature as sites, both real and imagined, for producing self-made subjects. For instance, since its establishment, the Scouting movement organises nature camps to build "tough and self-sufficient young men," to indoctrinate them with a collective sense of duty, while also instilling patriotism and national greatness (Cupers, 2008). Likewise, the 1970s community gardening movement in the United States transitioned from a protest against consumerism and corporate power to an instrument of neoliberal governmentality, promoting personal changes in attitude and behaviour. As a result, individuals were encouraged to become 'self-sufficient' in order to overcome social marginalisation (Pudup, 2008, cf.: Nagel & Staeheli, 2016).

We see something of a similar process underway in Kenya where university students have variously engaged and disengaged from national politics in three ways. First, some students remain disengaged and show no interest in either conventional or new forms of politics. Second, some students engage in Student Union[1] politics (here referred to as student politics) with most student leaders eventually becoming active in national political parties. Finally, some students disassociate from conventional forms of student politics, while simultaneously choosing to participate in politics of specific issues that involve new forms of engagement such as professional clubs.[2] In the ensuing sections, I demonstrate how student environmentalism is a form of politics of fun, which manifests neoliberal strategies centred on an individuals' contact with nature and their circumstantial socio-economic and political realities.

The Divergence from Student Politics

In the mid-1960s, the post-independence Kenyan university students were less engaged politically because of a buoyant economy, the provision of free university education and student allowances, and the assurance of employment upon graduation[3] (Amutabi, 2002). However, as socio-economic and political disjunctures started to grow,[4] many students were motivated to engage in confrontational protests in order to oppose government policies seen to be causing the problems (Amutabi, 2002; Chege, 2009; Hughes, 1987; Klopp & Orina, 2002; Savage & Taylor, 1991). Generally, students' discontent was provoked by socio-economic policies, which lowered the quality of education, overcrowded universities, increased graduate unemployment, and reduced access to social welfare (Hughes, 1987; Munene & Otieno, 2008). In the absence of an official opposition during the presidencies of Jomo Kenyatta (1963–1978) and Daniel Moi (1978–2002), students also imagined themselves as part of the opposition and expressed their opinions through the Student Unions which then coordinated nationwide students' protests (Klopp & Orina, 2002). These protests were marked by destruction of public property and fierce confrontations with the police often resulting in closure of universities and eventually vilifying university students as dissidents.

The disengagement of some students from this kind of confrontational politics started in early 1990s, following major reforms in university education, which adversely affected graduate educational aspirations and employment prospects. After the withdrawal of student allowances, introduction of university fees in 1991, and the lack of guaranteed jobs upon graduating, students became increasingly concerned with their individual economic prospects and hopes for social mobility. In this context, student political goals shifted from a more collective political orientation to economic and individualistic expressions. As a result, some students lost faith in the student unions believing that these organisations no longer provided the best the platform for expressing their grievances.[5]

Concurrently, ongoing democratisation struggles in the country led to the passing of civil society legislation in 1992, which opened up new spaces for civic participation. Globalisation and access to new media further introduced university students to a new world of multiple sources of knowledge and identity formation. These developments prepared the ground for the emergence of new forms of student action, including environmental activism.

The Rationale for Professional Student Environmentalism

Students' first documented participation in environmental activism was during the 1992 protests by Kenyan environmental activists against development of Uhuru Park led by the Late Professor Wangari Maathai (Maathai, 2009). The establishment of student environmental clubs was motivated in part by the need to understand emerging environmental issues, partly by the campaigns responding to environmental crises in the country, and partly by the need to develop individualised and specialised skills as environmentalists. The clubs embodied a professional outlook that enabled members to reconfigure significantly their life aspirations by manifesting their political views in professionalised settings. In doing so, the clubs disengaged from both national and student politics and chose to engage in mundane nature-based activities (such as tree planting, clean-ups and camping), and social organising activities (such as conferences, seminars and dialogues), that generated active spaces for neoliberal identity formation.

The focus of this chapter is on the reorientation of student activism away from traditional forms of protest against state policies and towards a politics of environment. Like Student Unions, professional groups played a significant role in enabling students to self-actualise; develop a sense of occupational identity; and provided the basis for the formation of environmental subjects that were neoliberal and hybrid in nature (Mwaura, 2015). It is possible then to think that professionalisation and politicisation are different and indeed somewhat antithetical modes of action but as I argue here, professionalisation offered a new way to engage with environmental and social issues. Professionalising student environmental clubs enabled these young Kenyans to shape and choose identities that are claimed, desired, and mainly associated with the norms and values of those at the margins (Bottrell, 2007). Student environmentalists were on the one hand resisting being associated with student politics that were now seen as denigrating, while on the other hand, they were resourcefully positioning themselves as environmentalists who would actively participate in future environmental politics. Their resistance gave them a sense of belonging as respectable 'professionals' enabling them to anticipate being able to cope with the adversities of graduate unemployment. At the same time, they were also able to develop competences as members of these clubs, join social networks, and remain optimistic about their ability to take responsibility in society despite the apparent uncertainties.

The next section draws on conversations with student environmentalists in which they illuminate their new political identities that incorporate aspects of neoliberal worldviews expressed in terms of their self-making strategies combined with the professionalisation of their commitment to environmental politics.

PROFESSIONAL AND NEOLIBERAL STUDENT ENVIRONMENTALISM

The main argument here is that university students professionalised their environmental activism meaning that, they avoided confronting those actors whom they thought needed to address environmental challenges, and instead, regenerated spaces for equipping themselves with skills and other capitals that positioned them as 'professional environmentalists' obligated to safeguard the environment. They did this because they wanted an identity that reflected their commitments to environmental politics, but also one that was clearly distinct and differentiated them from earlier forms of university student activism.

Disengaging from traditional forms of student politics did not however always imply a lack of interest in politics. Rather students chose 'professional' identities that involved assuming some aspects of neoliberal subjectivities. The environmental clubs were used as fields in which particular kinds of social and cultural capital were accumulated as personal skills were developed, new identities were formed and new relations formed. Despite having been disillusioned by the State, students were able to reconfigure their environmental politics framing it as a broader set of concerns that included arguments for protecting the environment for its own sake, as spaces for actualising occupational aspirations, and for accumulating symbolic capitals, which they believed would enhance their 'transition into adulthood.' In what follows, I explore these hybrid identities that straddled commitments to two seemingly incongruous positions: a commitment to a neoliberal agenda of self-making and a commitment to environmental politics.

Neoliberal Subjectivities

As young people are exposed to a world of liberal opportunities and economic uncertainties, they are forced to explore mechanisms that continually improve their selves and enable them to attain social adulthood. For a majority, it means becoming autonomous individuals who are competitive and embrace multiple identities, here understood as neoliberal subjectivities (Mwaura, 2015). It also means that the individuals prioritise their role over that of the State in addressing their social welfare. It is in this context that Kenyan university students produce their neoliberal-environmental subjectivities that shift the burden of environmental politics and of graduate employment from the State to the individual.

Most students perceived environmental stewardship as a responsibility that needed to be assumed by every citizen. They framed the role of the State, in terms of environmental stewardship, as having declined because of insufficient resources and linked this with the need for individuals to take on environmental leadership:

> For the environment to be green and clean you don't rely on someone, or think the government should do this, collect this garbage, recycle this waste; they don't have the funds to do this. It's our responsibility, but this is lacking. Right now you produce a lot of waste, and just let it go, you are not responsible, yet you are the one who has produced it. You take this burden to someone else; you don't want to be responsible. (Camilla, third year female student)[6]

State failure to take environmental action was emphasised by most students. For instance, Echitwa framed the government as detached from the local environmental problems that citizens were experiencing:

> We should not wait for the government to implement anything. At the end of the day, the people who feel the effects of what is done to the environment are the common people. […] But, those people in government have air conditioners in their offices and homes. Maybe they use cars to travel, they never feel the heat. They never get to experience hunger because they never lack the food. It is therefore upon us to take the initiative and protect the environment. (Echitwa, fourth year male student)

Students did not limit their responsibility to becoming members of environmental clubs. Rather, their everyday actions and behaviours were viewed as part of a bigger project of contributing to national development. This was despite the fact that their mundane club activities seemed insignificant in relation to the magnitude of environmental challenges in the country. Belonging to clubs and engaging in environmental activities (such as bird watching, tree planting, camping, and debates) allowed students to shape their identities as productive citizens who played a role in nation-building:

> If we plant trees, it means we are going to have more land under tree cover. Among the things the government is trying to get is the 10 per cent tree cover. When I go back to my home, I see that I have participated towards the national goal of achieving Vision 2030 and the government master plan. I have a hand in the development of our country. (Wambugu, fourth year male student)

Students were also able to link their local actions to prevailing global environmental narratives through which they claimed to learn new skills:

> Through [the club], I have been able to gain more skills on issues beyond tree planting. I have been able to do a lot all over the country. It also opens me up to learn many new things and new environmental aspects. It's not

just about planting trees, there are policies and regulations for the conservation of environment, education, green economy; it's actually how we govern the environment. (Catherine, fourth year female student)

Camilla, Echitwa, Wambugu, and Catherine represent the views of many other students who perceived the environment as an individualised project obligating every citizen to take some responsibility for safeguarding. We see here a classic expression of neoliberalism with calls to reduce the role of state while increasing the responsibility of the individual, hence manifesting neoliberal subjectivity. In effect, the students used the clubs as spaces of expression, of mobilisation, and for empowering the self, other students, and local communities in what were horizontal processes of environmental action, thus enhancing their agency in environmental governance.

Protesting and Professionalising

Student environmentalists strongly resisted any identification with, or having any interest in traditional student politics. All the environmental clubs I visited identified as professional groups, and students identified as professional environmentalists. In our conversations, they claimed not to engage with the politics of Student Unions or with national politics. These students pointed to the difference between peaceful environmental demonstrations that environmental clubs organised in collaboration with environmental organisations and compared these with the highly vibrant student protests organised by Student Unions that often provoked police intervention sometimes resulting in the destruction of public property and the closure of universities. Ndiguna, the legal affairs secretary of one of the clubs explained the differences between the political and professional student bodies:

[The club], unlike other university clubs, is professional and not political. Leaders undergo professional elections. Due to that, we came to a point; we should be vetting leaders and interview those who are vying for the positions in leadership to get professionals and not politicians. [...] Politics goes with sycophants. I may have numbers to vote me in, but I may fail to deliver along the line of service. But a professional like myself, I believe in myself. I didn't have the mass, but being professional in nature made me go through. I got vetted; expressed myself and I made it. I am now able to deliver. If I was political, I would not have made it. (Ndiguna, third year male student)

We see here how students developed a narrative that distinguished between politics and professionalism. For example, Ndiguna's account of "professional elections" emphasised how prospective student leaders were vetted using rigorous interviews, which assessed their skills and competence to lead environmental clubs. He claimed that in the Student Unions, prospective leaders relied on sycophancy and their ability to mobilise majority votes during elections. Ndiguna further emphasised the difference between the environmental clubs and traditional politics, wherein he said that prospective leaders in the clubs needed to exhibit certain leadership skills, confidence, and demonstrate that they would deliver on their responsibilities and remain competitive in the environmental space. In traditional political systems, there was no guarantee that elected student leaders would deliver on their assigned responsibilities or on their promises to the voters.

Professionalising environmental clubs positioned a section of university students as distinct professional actors—environmentalists—while denigrating older and more traditional forms of student activism that faces intense resistance by university administration and the government because it is disruptive, involving destruction of public property and fierce confrontations with the police. While Student Unions have continually protested against national and university issues, such activism has not addressed the fundamental challenge of graduate unemployment and poor quality education. Thus, student environmentalism thrives as some students regenerate a new space where they identify as "professional environmentalists" committed to environmental stewardship and self-actualisation expressed through what they say and through their actions.

Ochieng, a first year student explained in his account of how club members do not engage in conventional forms of national politics. For once they do "[…] they forget the core issues of serving the people and […] we find that the environmental agenda is side-lined" (Ochieng, first year student). Ochieng argued that conventional politics failed to address the needs of the people, and in that context, environmental issues were deemed less significant politically. Other students defended moves to professionalise environmental clubs, arguing it gives credibility to 'environmental experts' and the capacity to effect change in society. As Fuchaka, a second year student argued:

> Most environmental issues get politicised. For example, if there is a hot subject, politicians take the opportunity to politicise the issue. […] [But] first

they should organise, put money into the programme, organise for education, and call on environmental experts to come and talk to the community on how they can get involved and protect the environment for their benefit. They should give them the knowledge that protecting the environment is not for anyone else's benefit, but for the individual's benefit.

According to Fuchaka, to ensure that environmental concerns were addressed, they needed to be taken seriously as factual matters that require proper planning, financing, education, and implementation, best managed by experts. He explained how the students were becoming environment experts who were already helping communities to address local environmental issues.

Disengaging and Re-engaging

Even when students knew the State and institutions such as the university and local governments were failing to adequately address environmental issues, they were keen to align themselves with those institutions because they recognised them as potential future employers.

For instance, in one of the universities, instead of the environmental club confronting the local government for its failure to manage solid waste in the community neighbouring the university, the club framed the problem as one requiring a public-private partnership. They engaged the local government, the university, several environmental organisations, and local politicians who financed the club to carry out clean-up activities in this area. The clean-up event also involved a public gathering where the local government and politicians commended the students for their good work in waste management and urged the local community to seek ways of managing their own waste. Such collaborative activities provided a safe space for both the students and the local government. On one hand, the local governments were increasingly under pressure to deliver public services, so assistance from students who offered free labour and mounted public awareness campaigns was welcome. On the other hand, the students' approach to addressing waste management highlighted their preference to stress their 'responsibility': it tacitly pointed to their hybrid character of a neoliberal political style, in which they played down an overtly oppositional style of environmental concern in order to lobby the local government to take action while emphasising the need for individuals to take action, rather than simply insisting that the State take action by itself.

We see related instances of simultaneously disengaging and re-engaging in politics in the ways students responded to a range of local environmental issues including climate change, land degradation, population growth. In one respect, the mention of these issues resulted quite intense and often heated debates amongst the students. Debate about environmental issues was escalated to a national level, when one environmental organisation hosted an annual Mazingira Challenge, in which university environmental clubs engaged in competitive debates on key environmental issues. In the course of these debates, students' views were reconstructed and personalised by the way the best performing individuals and clubs were judged on their debating skills and by how well the issues were articulated in the debates, while any substance of confrontational politics was filtered out.

Yet it was not always possible to completely blank out the politics that was operating. This was especially so with the way students responded to the 2011 government decision to evict communities from the Mau Forest. In all the clubs I visited, members disagreed with that decision. The Mau Forest evictions had started with illegal land allocations in the 1980s and 1990s; something exposed by the 2004 Amnesty International Report of the Commission of Inquiry into the Illegal/Irregular Allocation of Public Land. These evictions then became an international human rights issue when an estimated 100,000 people were left homeless as a result of forced evictions between 2004 and 2006 (Amnesty International, 2007). This generated international concern about the extent of loss of the forest, which adversely affected the ecological systems in the region. From 2005, the Kenyan government embarked on a plan to stop further degradation, relocate the 'illegal' settlers, and restore the Mau Forest (Government of Kenya, 2009), a move opposed by some politicians. This controversy was also reflected in the environmental clubs and students attempted to redefine the Mau Forest case as less a case involving global issues and more as one requiring individuals to understand and develop local and individual solutions. Equally, while some clubs responded by inviting state and non-state actors to dialogue with the students on forest conservation issues, others organised regular tree-planting activities in the Mau Forest, and others volunteered to fundraise and build houses for evictees.

Hybrid Identities

As it is the case with the environmental movement in Kenya, students simultaneously operated in a range of political identities allowing them to experiment with new forms of action that suited their individual and collective goals. In everyday life, their experiences of political and professional action were virtually indistinguishable: a convergence that produces what can be called a hybrid identity. Arguably, this was a deliberate strategy that enabled the individuals to believe that they were advancing their personal professional interests, even as the clubs found new ways of engaging in national politics:

> Whenever the government tries to propose something that is contrary to environmental conservation, we will automatically go against it, because that is our role as an environmental club, to advocate for environmental conservation. [...] But at the same time, we have to work with them, because without their support we cannot do much. We need jobs and recommendations after university. (Lumumba, second year male student)

As Lumumba argued, while students wanted to hold the government accountable for environmental injustices in the country, they also needed to avoid any actions that would frame them as 'dissidents.' They were compelled to present themselves as 'responsible graduates' capable of contributing to environmental conservation efforts without protests and confrontations traditionally associated with student activism. For instance, Wambugu who had earlier referred to tree planting as an indicator of students' contribution to national development, further explained how these activities translated into future environmental and social (personal) benefits:

> So, if you consider the activities we are doing in [the club], I don't think there is any way we get immediate benefit. [...] What we do, we are looking in ten years' time or beyond. If you plant a tree today, you don't expect to benefit immediately in two years, maybe after a long period of time. We are focusing on the future. Not short terms benefits. That's what we want to build into young people. (Wambugu, fourth year male student)

Clearly, Wambugu perceived club activities as shaping his identity, while providing an avenue to promote future aspirations. This view was widespread among the students who often emphasised being recognised through certificates for their environmental stewardship that they would eventually use when job-seeking.

Essentially, hybridity was an effective way for the students to thrive in contingent and often extreme economic and political landscapes, where they believed that assuming this identity led to immediate benefits such as knowledge, skills, and social networks that would propel them as social change-makers in the future. It was a new form of politics inspired by changing career aspirations, individual and collective environmental actions, and the broader national socio-economic and political context. It confirms that when students claimed to be 'non-political,' they were not necessarily disengaged from national politics so much as withdrawing from traditional political styles and practices while cultivating a neoliberal politics emphasising private self-development and self-responsibility.

Conclusion

This chapter demonstrates that there is nothing non-political about student environmentalism in Kenya. On the contrary, students' alertness to socio-economic and political changes motivates their navigations in a risk society, as they seek new identities towards transitioning into respectable adulthood. I have articulated how everyday actions of university students can be interpreted to explain their non-political engagements, their politics of fun, that are deeply embedded in an individuals' desire to continually develop self-governing technologies, while at the same time, remaining deeply embedded in national politics.

The main argument made in this chapter is that student environmentalists were performing three things: romanticising the environment through their environmental subjectivities; professionalising activism to attain 'respectable' identities; and governing the environment through their hybrid identities. I also showed that student environmental clubs are embedded in the broader Kenyan political economy and indeed respond to pertinent issues of youth aspirations and participation. They are consciously positioned as professional clubs distinct from the political identities associated with the Student Unions. However, professionalisation must not be viewed as indicating a depoliticised environmental space in Kenya; rather, it portrays the hybrid positions that some university students occupy so as to attain certain recognitions and accumulate certain cultural and social capitals. Kenya's environmental space remains highly political and university students are actively engaged.

Although students' environmental concerns are largely shaped by a mix of global environmental narratives and local experiences, they are also deeply inspired by every possible imagination of change that educated youth hold of themselves, the environment, and the society. The clubs provide an enabling environment for the students to actively wait, as well as a generative space for accumulating the necessary capitals to carve out a living in uncertain economic times.

Just as the economy is precarious, student environmentalists remain unsure if their engagement in these new spaces will be any different. Their actions remain flexible, hybrid and open to change, and indeed a form of resilience in the face of persistent crises. Their identities do not publicly resist the failing developmental state or challenge the hegemonic powers; instead, most are strategies for navigating their precarity and resourceful pathways of producing new subjectivities. In a world of socio-economic crisis and dynamic political environments, student environmentalists might then help us gain a deeper understanding into the diverse ways that young people respond to these transformations and indeed regenerate national politics into politics of specific issues.

Notes

1. Upon joining university, all students become members of the Student Union and are obliged to pay an annual membership fee often included in the university fees. However, membership through registration does not imply that all students actively participate in the daily activities of the Union.
2. An alternative to Student Unions, there were dozens of these clubs in the universities I visited, ranging from human rights, business, gender, adventure, Scouting, and science clubs. Students could freely join a club of their choice.
3. After independence in 1963, President Jomo Kenyatta's government prioritised education as a way of building the human capital to support nation-building.
4. Resulting from declining government resources and changing political dynamics.
5. Particularly, the withdrawal of student allowances affected the ability of students from poor backgrounds to provide for their families back home, and thus their need to find a platform where such individualised concerns for responsibility and financial independence could be addressed.
6. Names have been changed for confidentiality.

References

Agrawal, A. (2005). Environmentality: Community, intimate government, and the making of environmental subjects in Kumaon, India. *Current Anthropology, 46*(2), 161–190.

Amnesty International. (2007). *Nowhere to go: Forced evictions in Mau forest* (Briefing Paper No. AFR/32/006/2007). London: Amnesty International.

Amutabi, M. (2002). Crisis and student protest in universities in Kenya: Examining the role of students in national leadership and the democratization process. *African Studies Review, 45*(2), 157–177.

Beck, U. (1992). *Risk society: Towards a new modernity* (M. Ritter, Trans.). London: Sage.

Bottrell, D. (2007). Resistance, resilience and social identities: Reframing "problem youth" and the problem of schooling. *Journal of Youth Studies, 10*(5), 597–616.

Carter, N. (2004). *The politics of the environment: Ideals, activism, policy.* Cambridge: Cambridge University Press.

Chege, A. (2009). Post-Moi era discourse patterns in Kenyan universities: A nation crying for "organic" intellectuals. *Kenya Studies Review, 1*(1), 31–53.

Cupers, K. (2008). Governing through nature: Camps and youth movements in interwar Germany and the United States. *Cultural Geographies, 15*(2), 173–205.

Farthing, R. (2010). The politics of youthful antipolitics: Representing the "issue" of youth participation in politics. *Journal of Youth Studies, 13*(2), 181–195.

Furlong, A. (Ed.). (2009). *Handbook of youth and young adulthood.* London: Routledge.

Government of Kenya. (2009). *Report of the Prime Minister's Task Force on the conservation of the Mau Forest complex.* Nairobi: Office of the Prime Minister.

Honwana, A. (2012). *The time of youth: Work, social change and politics in Africa.* Sterling, VA: Kumarian Press.

Hughes, R. (1987). Revisiting the fortunate few: University graduates in the Kenyan labor market. *Comparative Education Review, 31*(4), 583–601.

Klopp, J., & Orina, J. (2002). University crisis, student activism, and the contemporary struggle for democracy in Kenya. *African Studies Review, 45*(1), 43–76.

Maathai, W. (2009). *The challenge for Africa.* New York, NY: Anchor Books.

Munene, I., & Otieno, W. (2008). Changing the course: Equity effects and institutional risk amid policy shift in higher education financing in Kenya. *Higher Education, 55*(4), 461–479.

Mwaura, G. (2015). *Educated youth in Kenya: Negotiating waithood by greening livelihoods.* DPhil Thesis, Oxford: University of Oxford, Social Sciences Division; School of Geography and the Environment.

Mwaura, G., Pradhan, M., & Gitahi, K. (2017). Envisioning youth futures through university students' education for sustainability initiatives. In P. B. Corcoran, J. Weakland, & A. Wals (Eds.), *Envisioning futures for environmental and sustainability education.* Wageningen: Wageningen Academic Publishers.

Nagel, C., & Staeheli, L. (2016). Nature, environmentalism, and the politics of citizenship in post-civil war Lebanon. *Cultural Geographies, 23*(2), 247–263.

Pickard, S. (2018). *Politics, protest and young people. Political participation and dissent in Britain in the 21st century.* London: Palgrave Macmillan. [Forthcoming].

Pudup, M. (2008). It takes a garden: Cultivating citizen. Subjects in organized garden projects. *Geoforum, 39*(3), 1228–1240.

Savage, D., & Taylor, C. (1991). Academic freedom in Kenya. *Canadian Journal of African Studies, 25*(2), 308–321.

Tsing, A. (2011). *Friction: An ethnography of global connection.* Princeton, NJ: Princeton University Press.

Grace Muthoni Mwaura is a Non-residential Research Fellow at the African Centre for Technology Studies in the Gender, Youth, and Inclusive Development programme, Kenya, and a Matasa Fellow at the Institute of Development Studies. She publishes on youth unemployment in Africa. Her PhD at the University of Oxford focused on alternative livelihoods for educated youth in contemporary Kenya.

CHAPTER 5

The 'Good,' the 'Bad' and the 'Useless': Young People's Political Action Repertoires in Quebec

Nicole Gallant

INTRODUCTION

Over the past few decades, much attention has been focused on the decline of the participation of young people in democratic structures. Voter turnout has been declining in all groups, especially among young people and the gap between electoral participation of different age groups is widening in many developed democracies. This is perceived as a crisis in democratic participation by many political science scholars, election-directorates, and policy makers alike. Most frame this as signifying a general disinterest in politics and the political process among young people (Henn & Foard, 2014), resulting in a "democratic deficit" (Norris, 2011).

But decline in *participation in democratic institutions* should not be mistaken for decline of political *action* in a broader sense. Indeed, recent work points to so-called 'new' forms of political participation. To grasp these emerging forms of political action, research has moved away from

N. Gallant (✉)
INRS University (Institut national de la recherche scientifique),
Quebec, Canada

the notion of 'participation,' to better encompass forms of political action that fall outside the realm of formally organised politics.

This chapter aims to contribute to a better understanding of the variety uncovered by this broader understanding of politics. Specifically, I seek to portray a diverse array of political actions deployed by young people, in Quebec,[1] in the 2010s. Drawing primarily on in-depth interviews with 20 young people actively defending social justice issues in the face of neoliberal policies, this portrayal will document their discourses regarding issues they deem most significant, and map out the manifold collective and individual actions they undertake online and offline to defend them.

As political action is not monolithic, I offer a framework to organise a diversity of political actions, especially with regards to young people's relationship to the State and how they are perceived by the State. By contrasting young people's political actions to conventional expectations of traditional representative democracy, I distinguish four overlapping modes of conduct delineating broader stances regarding politics: organisational participation, underground protest, artistic creativity, and personal lifestyle choices. The first type is most favoured by democratic institutions, while the others are generally disregarded by the State as either inappropriate and undemocratic, or useless. I also seek to unravel some of the processes by which young people navigate from one mode to another. Indeed, the four types of stances are often combined and intertwined in young people's lived experience of counteracting neoliberalism and austerity measures.

The focus of this chapter is the relationship between young people's repertoire of political actions and the State, and the ways they are perceived and treated by State authorities. This relational approach helps take into account social and State representations of what is considered legitimate action.

The chapter begins with a brief review of the literature which focuses on the broad definition of politics required to understand young people's current political activity. After a description of the inductive, qualitative methodology used, I delineate four types of stances that young people can have regarding political action and the state, as well as some of the processes by which one person may move from one stance to another. I then discuss how neoliberalism and austerity could have fostered a deeper antagonism toward the State among young people today.

Recognising Youth Political Action

Traditional concepts of political participation focus on measurable accounts of 'democratic participation.' This approach rests on a definition of politics as the struggle for power among formal political parties to gain control over state decision-making institutions, therefore placing elections (and participation in political parties) at the core of political life (Verba & Nie, 1972). According to this view, the paramount indicator of political interest or politicisation is the act of voting in democratic state elections. Other traditional indicators of political interest focus on actions mediated through institutionalised organisations, including formal participation in political parties, but also in trade unions (Cultiaux & Vendramin, 2011), and diverse associations and community groups (Ekman & Amnå, 2012; Jones, 2000; Paré, Pelletier, & Vigeant, 2008). Some political participation surveys (such as those of the International Social Statistics Programme— ISSP) also ask respondents about peaceful demonstrations, and individual and collective acts of formal communication with elected officials, such as signing petitions and writing to state representatives. These dominant narrow definitions led to the assumption that young people are now less politicised than previous generations at the same age.

As many young people today recoil from participation within formal, organised institutions (Pickard, Nativel, & Portier, 2012, p. 23), a more comprehensive conceptualisation of politics is needed to understand a vaster array of political activity than that captured by empirical work on political participation (Gauthier, 2003; O'Toole, Lister, Marsh, Jones, & McDonagh, 2003). Indeed, young people's expression and action seem stronger when it takes other, less institutionalised forms (Gallant & Garneau, 2016; Loncle, Cuconato, Muniglia, & Walther, 2012), especially those that channel dissent (Roudet, 2012) and/or individuality (Pastinelli, 2013). These include innovative forms of demonstrations (such as flash mobs or the Occupy and Indignados movements), political citizenship expressed through cultural practices (Poirier, 2017), or even unplanned riots (Bertho, 2016; Newburn et al., 2016). Young people's online participatory experience (Caron, 2014) also takes many shapes: the use of Facebook and other social media to organise various political action, political expression on blogs, Twitter and YouTube (Caron, 2014; Jenkins & Carpentier, 2013; Millette, 2015). As political topics also crop up on entertainment-driven forums and on other social media such as Twitter

(Fuchs, 2014), research has also looked into online political conversation (Latzko-Toth, Gallant, & Pastinelli, 2017).

These contributions confirm the value of broadening the definition of what constitutes the political, instead of jumping to the conclusion that young people are politically apathetic (Gallant & Garneau, 2016; O'Toole et al., 2003). Indeed, "[t]hose with the most restrictive and conventional conceptions of political participation identify a strong and consistent pattern of declining political participation and engagement over time, whilst those with a more inclusive conception discern instead a change in the mode of political participation" (Hay, 2007, p. 23, in Pickard, 2016).

To grasp the everyday experiences of politics among 'ordinary' citizens (Dryzek, 1990), i.e., people who are not part of the decision-making elite, I adopt a more encompassing approach, based on a definition of politics centred on an interest for social issues (Gaxie, 2003), or for the betterment of the collective world (Arendt, 1995). This approach allows us to encompass both traditional political participation and what Beck calls sub-politics, i.e., everyday political activity taking place beneath visible institutional politics (Beck, 1997). By keeping the State in the analysis, while enlarging the definition of political action, we can better assess the extent to which politicisation remains a dynamic, relational process.

Data and Methodology: An Inductive, Qualitative Design

The analysis presented in this chapter is based on original empirical data, with additional information drawn from empirical literature, and day-to-day observation of public actions as reported in the media or through direct observation on the street or online. The original data consists of 20 semi-structured qualitative interviews with young people aged 18–30[2] who were actively defending global social justice issues in the face of neoliberal policies and austerity measures.[3] The interviews were carried out in 2011, i.e., a year prior to the student protest following post-secondary tuition hikes in 2012 (see Doran and Peñafiel in this volume).

While acknowledging that this data is culturally and socially situated in Quebec, I use it as a stepping-stone for a broad conceptual analysis. Quebec being politically and socially at a crossroads between North American influences, British parliamentary institutions and a French republican tradition, it seems likely that phenomena observed there could be relevant elsewhere.

The qualitative sample was not intended to be representative of the general population of young people in Quebec, because I was specifically seeking young people active in some form of global issues. Nonetheless, the goal was to set up a diverse sample within this specific subgroup comprising engaged and active young people. To create variety within the sample, I relied on individual socio-demographic characteristics, such as age (respondents ranged from 19 to 30, with the mean and median age both 24 years), gender (11 young men and nine young women), and visible ethnicity (three respondents were Black—from Africa or Haiti—and four others had middle-Eastern origins and traits). Moreover, because local contexts have some bearing on opportunities for associative participation and for the collective expression of dissident, we met young activists in Montreal, in smaller cities and in small towns in rural areas. More importantly, I was looking for young people whose political concerns covered a board range of issues, rather than those involved in (and recruited within) the same social movement.

Together with four graduate students, I identified these respondents through an innovative array of open recruitment techniques. The two principal methods were the 'address book' (Duchesne, 2000), whereby one asks people one knows to help identify other people who meet the research criteria, and 'direct recruitment,' which consists in hanging about in places where one believes one might see people who fit the research criteria (in this project: protest rallies and peaceful demonstrations, pubs with an openly ideological stance, concerts from bands carrying a political message, etc.), in order to present them with the research project. In smaller geographical locations, my research assistants and I also needed to use the more traditional approach of asking associations to refer people, but specifically asking not to meet official representatives or the central figures in the organisation. All of these methods were complemented by so-called 'snowball sampling.' The overall goal was to introduce a wide variety of entry points, so as not to study a specific, somewhat homogeneous subgroup of activists working together on the same issues. By moving away from the case-study approach, we are able to identify a cross section of diverse *types* of engagement or participation within the broad field of global activism.

During the interviews, we first asked what were the issues or concerns the respondents cared about. Then, we introduced the subject of actions, by asking 'what do you *do* about these issues?' This detour helped to go beyond the boundaries of what respondents might consider to be 'political' (or what they would think we as academics would count as political activity).

Results: Making Sense of a Diverse Repertoire of Actions

Framing the Issues: Working for Justice ... or Fighting Against Injustice?

The activists we met each had multiple issues which they considered significant. Yet, at the core of these young people's global action lays a coherent narrative challenging neoliberal values and articulating a discourse on human solidarity. Depending on the individual, this narrative may take one of two overarching stances. When asked about the issues that they care about, some young people frame their responses mostly positively, stating they are working *for* or *toward* a cause (such as social justice, human rights, etc.). Yet, about the very same concerns, others take a more antagonistic stance: they state that they are fighting *against* a situation (such as inequality or discrimination). Some mingling of the two rhetorical stances does occur (especially, several respondents say that they are 'fighting for' something), and thus this variation in rhetoric should not be construed as a clear-cut analytical tool to characterise and distinguish types of individuals. Nonetheless, the next section shows how this difference in overall stance may be embodied in their political action repertoire, as it translates into somewhat different types of actions, or rather into differing overall political stances.

This core issue of human solidarity encompasses diverse scales. Some young people we interviewed focus their actions mostly on international solidarity. This is framed either in a discourse about fighting against capitalist globalisation, or about working toward '*altermondialisme*,' an alternative world order very much inspired by the Porto Alegre Conference. Concretely, many of these young people get involved regarding specific local situations that embody those values, such as protesting at the 2010 G20 summit in Toronto, Canada. In other cases, the focus may be on specific situations occurring at a micro level, either locally, or elsewhere around the globe. They either emphasise working for the 'rights' of specific peoples who are deemed oppressed (Tibetans, Palestinians, or Aboriginals), or, conversely, call for the 'fight against' discrimination of specific subsets of the population (ethnic groups, women or homosexuals). Some participants also focus their energy and contribution on the struggle against police brutality, especially since the death of Fredy Villanueva (an innocent young man killed by Montreal police in 2008).

Whatever their focus(es), all these young participants frame their discourse on these issues at a larger, more universal level of values of solidarity. They claim to devote their time either *for* social justice, equity and respect for human rights, or—depending on their overall stance—*against* racism, inequality and poverty.

Secondly, more than half our participants were involved in the student movement. This topic dovetails with part of the literature on political socialisation, which identifies post-secondary education—and the exposure to people from different backgrounds and diverse points of view it often provides—as a primary factor in interest for politics (Flanagan, 2009). The concern for the student movement in my sample is also relevant to the specific context that was to unfold a year later in Quebec, which deeply divided Québécois society. The prevalence of this issue in our sample also partially results from our sampling methods in rural areas, which relied in part on suggestions from student associations. Some respondents imbed the student issue as part of a more comprehensive, symbolic rhetoric regarding concerns such as (free) public access to knowledge and culture.

The third most often mentioned group of concerns are a range of issues relating to the environment. These first three topics each garnered the attention of more than half of the sample. Other themes were mentioned by more than a few respondents, such as defending Quebec's autonomy and independence, or fighting for the preservation of the French language (as part of the defence of oppressed peoples).

Action Repertoires and Overarching Political Stance

The open-ended approach to grasping young people's individual political activity yielded data about a plethora of actions undertaken by our interviewees. To find some order within this diversity, the data was inductively categorised through an iterative process, which yielded four types. This typology's coherence was reiterated when we noticed that the types happened to also be articulated, not to the issues themselves, but to the rhetoric in which they are discussed by the participant ('working for' or 'fighting against,' as outlined above).

The most prevalent mode of action that we observed in our non-representative small sample (just over half the respondents) is a very straightforward and rather traditional one, in which action or participation is mediated through associations or organisations. Such associative action may hinge on political parties, but in the sample, it was mostly structured by non-profit and non-governmental organisations: student associations or activist groups (such as Amnesty International or Solidarity for Palestinian Human Rights), or small social economy companies (for instance the 'Reboiseurs du monde'). Most of the respondents who included the student movement among their primary concerns also chiefly engage through this organised, associative mode of action, especially with relation to this issue.

Most organisations in which our participants were involved were highly structured. In many cases, the participant was active in a local selection of larger (provincial or international) structures, which often seemed to have a centralised decision process. This mode of action is the type most often assessed in studies of political participation, which tend focus on traditional forms of action. Such organised actions are also somewhat easy to measure and quantify, and they are readily, openly discussed. Indeed, this is the 'good' form of participation in the eyes of established powers. In this mode, the individual works 'with' the institutional system, through a range of 'positive' actions. Discontent is thus channelled into forms of expression and interactions which are deemed legitimate by official institutions: writing to elected officials and encouraging other people to do so; sending letters to the media; marching in a peaceful, announced demonstration, in cooperation with police of other security forces; starting or signing a petition—online or offline.

Conversely, some protest marches appear to be more spontaneous, and are clearly more antagonistic than others. This form of political expression is presented as the 'bad' one, often decried, criticised, ridiculed or demonised by established powers and the media alike. Among the four participants who engaged in this type of activity, this organic form of political action is deeply rooted in engagement within what we may call an *underground sub-culture* infused with a rhetoric of underground resistance. Depending on the person, it is entrenched in different cultural movements: punk/skinheads, anarchists, or a combination thereof (i.e. RASH, red anarchist skin heads), as well as hip-hop.

Within these underground movements, participation seems to be more diffuse and less formalised than in formal organisations, but it is not less tangible in respondents' everyday life. Quite the contrary, they seem constantly and intensely steeped in both the cultural aspects and in the (local) community of people sharing their passion. Politics is intertwined with a coherent, overall outlook on life, in such a way that political action is sometimes indistinguishable form more cultural activities (e.g. organising or attending concerts where the bands share a political message). But some actions are more clearly political. These actions are often antagonistic and seldom solitary. The collectivity seems based on a very close bond: when talking about actions, these respondents use first person plural pronouns 'we' and 'us,' far more than respondents who are in more formal organisations (and who either talk of the organisation in third person or about some specific actions in the first person singular, i.e. 'I went to this march that they organised,' rather than 'we marched'). Moreover, they do not make clear distinctions between organising a protest event or participating in it. Several specify that the collectivity bases its activities on the principles of self-management. Although more organic than formal, there is a (loose and somewhat blurry) collective structure, made of multiple entangled informal networks (some of which are called 'local chapters,' making it fleetingly sound almost like a formal organised association).

But it is not because of its loose structure that this overall stance is perceived as the 'bad' one by authorities and the media. This perception is due both to the nature of the actions undertaken (disruptive and sometimes illegal) and the overall discourse, which emphasises resistance and protest. Thus, rather than participating in the social conversation about the greater good and about the best ways for the State to implement it, their stance challenges the very legitimacy of established powers.

But several more of our participants who were deeply involved in hip-hop culture do not engage in such antagonistic action. They represent a third overall mode of action, which is more expressive or artistic, and which may be broadly defined as the production of activist artwork. Of course, many more of our participants infuse art—especially music and visual arts—within their political action (such as using songs in a street demonstration, or placing striking images or visual symbols on posters for events or on pamphlets for their organisation). In that way, they use art to further their causes. But for four respondents, the use of art rests at the core of their political action. Thus, when asked what they do with regards to the issues they hold dear, these young people immediately highlight art production (e.g. 'Well, I do political graffiti' or 'I make activist artwork' ('*art engagé*' in French)). This art production is not merely used to enhance another action by making it more resonant; it is, in itself, the political action. Examples of such art production in our sample include writing lyrics to a song and writing a blog or articles, as well as making documentary videos and short films. Their overall outlook can be participatory (e.g. a state funded documentary about the plight of aboriginal people), or more antagonistic (e.g. illegal graffiti with a political message).

Thus, with exceptions such as illegal graffiti (seldom performed by any of the four people we interviewed, including the one who is a celebrated graffiti artist), this artistic creativity and production is largely perceived as positive by State authorities, who may even subsidise some types of political artwork (such as documentaries). But the State and mainstream media mostly seem to see this as an uncanny and somewhat pointless 'new' form of civic engagement of young people, i.e., as generally 'useless.'

These participants are typically not affiliated to any network of activists, however informal. Although some among them do organise some forms of collective political activities, this is the only mode of action where we met people who never did. However, because activist art production is ultimately and intrinsically geared toward a collective audience whose worldviews it aims to influence, their solitary political work is oriented differently from the form best circumscribed in Quéniart's (2008) seminal work on personal lifestyle choices.

Quéniart shows that one of the changing modes of political expression favoured by young people today revolves around personal lifestyle choices which embody their view of the collective good. This constitutes a fourth mode of action. The structure of our recruitment efforts could not have led us to meet young people whose only form of political activism would take this isolated form, but many among our participants—while also being active in one of the other three modes—did make sure that their lifestyle was in accordance with their political values. They cycle to work or buy local food; they make compost from their organic waste and carefully recycle the rest. One punk skinhead respondent is also vegan. Many others insisted that they would only take work that is in conformity with their worldview, or manage to transform their activism into a job, for instance by creating a not-for-profit organisation. Some of these actions are set in a slightly more dissenting fashion, for instance boycotting a particular product, store or event. Most of these activities are experienced not so much as contributions to the civic conversation about the collective good, but as an intrinsic contribution to the collective good itself. For example, being mindful of one's own individual 'ecological footprint' is experienced as a direct contribution to diminishing the collective ecological footprint of society.

These personal lifestyle choices are partly encouraged by the explicit injunctions of Quebec's broader youth policy (which promotes 'environmental responsibility,' etc.). However, they are usually not interpreted as political actions, and, as such, would be broadly considered 'good' (or even 'cute'), but 'useless' in terms of the value of their contribution to politics. My participants would probably partly agree. Although many do express that it is relevant to practice what you preach and thus to live in a way that implements one's worldview, none of them are satisfied with only that. Several clearly articulate that these personal actions alone are not enough to progress toward the better world they seek; thus, they speak disapprovingly of those who think it might be. Therefore, their repertoire of action is broader than these personal lifestyle choices, as it seeks to bring about more substantial and collective changes in society.

The Dynamics Between Forms of Action

We have seen a wide range of actions undertaken by young activists which can be loosely grouped into four broad categories. These categories distinguish between overall modes of action, which are steeped in specific narratives about politics and the meaning of involvement. Although built inductively through analysis of respondents' depiction of their actions and political beliefs, these broad categories remain abstract, in that they are not fully distinct, mutually-exclusive types. Indeed, several respondents combine two or more modes together. Although each individual participant can be classified according to a dominant mode of entry into the political arena,[4] this is not readily established in all cases. Especially, the distinction between underground protest and artistic production is not always clear, mostly because the people we met who were involved in underground action did so in relation to a more or less artistic subculture (for instance the hip-hop movement), rather than primarily political ones (such as anarchism). They also made use of artwork in their political activity far more than the respondents whose political involvement was primarily associative and organisational. Despite these shortcomings—which merely suggest that the modes ought to be thought of as a continuum rather than as ideal-types—this analytical exercise does show that it is relevant to attempt to distinguish subtypes in the otherwise fuzzy mass of 'new' forms of political activity among young people.

By taking into account the discourse through which young people frame the issues they care about, the results show that young activists' political values and political action are infused with a narrative that is either meant to be constructive of the political order with established powers, or set against the current order and the (partisan) forces that keep it in place. Generally, organisational or associative work is more participatory. In such a mode, the person works 'with' the system, whereas underground protest often intrinsically calls into question the established authorities themselves, not only their decisions. However, this cannot easily be deducted from the nature of the actions themselves. For instance, even a seemingly simple gesture such as cycling to work can be experienced as a physical act of ideological resistance and protest against the dominant use of common spaces in society. Similarly, in one single demonstration, some demonstrators may believe they are contributing to a peaceful march hoping to influence policy, while others may think they are protesting the very legitimacy of the societal order on which authorities govern. Thus, analysis ought to take into account how the individuals perceive their own actions, rather than deductions based on behaviour alone.

Demonstrations and marches are one of the situations where the continuum between forms is most apparent. Indeed, such 'social movement' activism can move back and forth between participatory or protest modes. Sometimes, the very same person may change his/her mind in the course of a single demonstration. For example, when a peaceful protest march is met by a strong police force expecting violence, the situation can send a signal to the protestors that their action is considered illegitimate from the onset, suggesting that the message will be entirely disregarded. Like a self-fulfilling prophecy, this anticipation can in return brace the demonstrators into a less participatory stance. It might not be so surprising, then, that some demonstrations *become* violent after having (sometimes repeatedly) been greeted by police arrogance and brutality, as well as disregard from the media and politicians.

This dynamic serves as a reminder that the overall mode of action of young individuals is largely relational. When participatory action is (repeatedly) met with disregard, this non-reciprocity can contribute to push away into protest mode. This is by no means a linear, chronological process; nonetheless, if political powers do not wish young people to express their anger through illegal or spectacular action, they ought to consider responding more efficiently when the issues young people care about are being voiced through channels the State deems legitimate.[5] This seems an important reminder, considering the current worldwide trend towards the 'criminalisation of protest' (Pickard, 2018).

Discussion: Protesting the Neoliberal World Order

Traditional representations of political participation remain the social benchmark for assessing the political engagement of young people (Pickard, 2016). Therefore, some forms of political mobilisations tend to be systematically disregarded, criticised or even automatically associated with violence by both the media and public officials (Muncie, 2009; Newburn et al., 2016; Pickard, 2009; Roudet, 2012). This rejection of their efforts to express a political message can be a source of cynicism (Cockburn & Cleaver, 2012; Roudet, 2012) or frustration (Benedicto & Luz Morán, 2016; Boire, 2015). As we have seen, by not recognising the new forms of political expression as legitimate political contributions to the civic conversation, State authorities may push them further away, sometimes toward illegal action or violence. This leads to a vicious circle, whereby rejection tends to produce or increase types of political action which are in essence, and unsurprisingly, disregarded and repudiated by established authorities. Similarly, Bertho (2016) analyses riots as a symptom of the failure of representative democracy to channel young people's discontents. Such non-traditional forms of expression are bound to grow in the future, considering both the current economic context (especially high levels of unemployment among young people) and the Western world's current tendency to respond with rampant austerity measures (including cuts in youth support programmes and increases in the individual costs of post-secondary education), while postponing (if not altogether denying) environmental concerns.

As there is also a widespread social perception that all political parties with a realistic chance of attaining power tend to favour similar measures, young people seem to increasingly feel powerless and angry (Van de Velde, 2017). This is one of the factors explaining lower electoral turnout among young people, because they doubt the efficiency of democratic elections as a means of conceding decision-making powers to political parties perceived as intrinsically flawed.

In this context, when, furthermore, political authorities use State institutions (such as police force) to counteract opposition and challenges arising from these looser, new forms of political expression, this increases the sense that the State itself (rather than just the existing government) embodies neoliberalism. It also reduces the impression that the State is meant to represent the people (rather than business interests). As a result, young people's political actions attacking neoliberalism challenge not only specific neoliberal policies, but may also defy neoliberalism as currently embodied in the State itself (a conundrum which may explain their somewhat counterintuitive emphasis on anarchism as a solution). In sum, if they perceive the State itself to almost intrinsically embody neoliberalism instead of the will of the people or nation, young people are lead to alternative modes of political expression in part because they feel that it is impossible to communicate their message in more participatory ways (which, by definition, recognise the State as a legitimate interlocutor for the political conversation). The fact that many of my participants mobilise a rhetoric of 'resistance' seems to comfort this interpretation.

Conclusion

This chapter aimed to depict and establish the diversity of political behaviour emerging among some young people today as they struggle to express their voice and values against the selling of their world, often by the (neoliberal) State itself, to private interests. Such bottom-up, inductive analysis of young people's modes of operation in times of crisis is required to deconstruct the notion that young people are inactive, by providing tools to assess levels of political action where it actually lays, rather than where established powers and classical North American political science have traditionally sought to find it.

In this perspective, I outlined three broad ways that people can relate to political power holders. The first, classic form—the 'good' one in the eyes of State institutions—, consists in participating in and with the 'system.' This includes voting, but also associative action aiming to bring a message to the State, recognised as a legitimate receiver. Secondly, some young people express their political views in more indirect, often artistic or humoristic ways, both online and offline. This is the chief mode of action for some activists in my sample. This form of expression is not particularly criticised by established authorities, in part because it goes largely unnoticed except among young people.[6] As such, it is often perceived as a 'nice but useless' form of political action, if it is regarded as political at all. Thirdly, political action can be structured around protest. Although not always violent or illegal (contrary to common media and social representations which present it as the 'bad' forms of political expression), protest fundamentally differs from participatory stances in that it challenges the very legitimacy of the State to enact appropriate policy in the name of the people. In my small sample, such underground protest is very much collective, and happens to be steeped in diverse more or less political (sub)cultures.

These three types are not fully distinct and do not constitute consistent packages that neatly structure everything else. They are neither mutually exclusive nor some sort of linear continuum ultimately building up to a 'good' or 'bad' form of political action. Moreover, one person may change action mode over time, or hover between more than one type at any given moment, depending on the situation and context.

Instead of conceiving demonstrations or alternative projects and art production as something to be controlled and managed (especially in a surveillance perspective) as is increasingly the case, the State could make a greater effort to listen to young people's less traditional types of actions, and ought perhaps to better understand that these represent a growing form of (legitimate) political expression for young people in Western democracies.

Notes

1. With a population of just over 8 million, Quebec is the core French-speaking part of Canada. As a province in the Canadian federation, it has its own parliament with governing powers on such matters as education, employment, health and immigration, among others. Commonly known as a "distinct society" (which is generally more left-leaning than the rest of Canada), Quebec periodically seeks independence. The result of the last referendum in 1995 was almost a tie, with 50.58% of votes against secession.
2. Public policy in Quebec defines youth as covering the period from ages 15 to 30.
3. This data collection was supported financially by the *Programme de soutien à la recherche en matière d'affaires intergouvernementales et d'identité québécoise* of Quebec government's Secrétariat aux affaires intergouvernementales canadiennes.
4. This mode may not have been chronologically the first, but it was the most significant at the time of the interview.
5. This situation calls to mind John Lennon's comment that "When it gets down to having to use violence, then you are playing the system's game. The Establishment will irritate you—pull your beard, flick your face—to make you fight! Because once they've got you violent, then they know how to handle you. The only thing they don't know how to handle is non-violence and humour" (1 June 1969, during the *Bed-In for Peace* in Montreal).
6. Some civil servants in Quebec's youth secretariat are a notable exception, as they are developing with researchers at the Observatoire Jeunes et Société (OJS) various experiments for bringing independent YouTubers' messages into the governmental sight (see Balleys & Gallant, 2017).

References

Arendt, H. (1995). *Qu'est-ce que la politique?* Paris: Seuil.
Balleys, C., & Gallant, N. (2017). *La participation citoyenne des jeunes à travers YouTube. Rapport de recherche.* Montréal: Institut national de la recherche scientifique (INRS).
Beck, U. (1997). Subpolitics. *Organization & Environment, 10*(1), 52.
Benedicto, J., & Luz Morán, M. (2016). Les chemins complexes de la politisation. Frustration, impuissance et engagement civique chez les jeunes Espagnols désavantagés. In N. Gallant & S. Garneau (Eds.), *Les jeunes et action politique: Participation, Contestation, Résistance* (pp. 167–188). Québec: Presses de l'Université Laval.
Bertho, A. (2016). Naissance d'une génération? In N. Gallant & S. Garneau (Eds.), *Les jeunes et action politique: Participation, contestation, résistance* (pp. 43–58). Québec: Presses de l'Université Laval. [forthcoming]
Boire, M. (2015). *Laboratoire vivant sur la participation politique des jeunes raccrocheurs au Québec.* Montréal: Institut national de la recherche scientifique (INRS).
Caron, C. (2014). Les jeunes et l'expérience participative en ligne. *Lien social et politiques, 71*, 13–30. doi:10.7202/1024736ar.
Cockburn, T., & Cleaver, F. (2012). Involving young people in democratic political structures in England. In S. Pickard et al. (Eds.), *Les politiques de jeunesse au Royaume-Uni et en France. Désaffection, répression et accompagnement à la citoyenneté* (pp. 185–199). Paris: Presses de la Sorbonne Nouvelle (PSN).
Cultiaux, J., & Vendramin, P. (2011). *Militer au quotidien. Regard prospectif sur le travail syndical de terrain.* Louvain-la-Neuve: Presses universitaires de Louvain.
Dryzek, J. S. (1990). *Discursive democracy: Politics, policy, and political science.* Cambridge: Cambridge University Press.
Duchesne, S. (2000). Pratique de l'entretien dit "non-directif". In Centre Universitaire de Recherches Administratives et Politiques de Picardie (CURAPP) (Ed.), *Les méthodes au concret* (pp. 9–30). Paris: Presses Universitaires de France.
Ekman, J., & Amnå, E. (2012). Political participation and civic engagement: Towards a new typology. *Human Affairs, 22*(3), 283–300.
Flanagan, C. (2009). Young people's civic engagement and political development. In A. Furlong (Ed.), *Handbook of youth and young adulthood* (pp. 293–300). London: Routledge.
Fuchs, C. (2014). Twitter and democracy: A new public sphere? In *Social media a critical introduction* (pp. 179–209). London: Sage. http://dx.doi.org/10.4135/9781446270066
Gallant, N., & Garneau, S. (Eds.). (2016). *Les jeunes et l'action politique: Participation, contestation, résistance.* Québec: Presses de l'Université Laval.

Gauthier, M. (2003). Inadequacy of concepts: The rise of youth interest for civic participation in Québec. *Journal of Youth Studies, 6*(3), 265–276.

Gaxie, D. (2003). *La Démocratie représentative* (4th ed.). Paris: Montchrestien.

Hay, C. (2007). *Why we hate politics*. Cambridge: Polity Press.

Henn, M., & Foard, N. (2014). Social differentiation in young people's political participation: The impact of social and educational factors on youth political engagement in Britain. *Journal of Youth Studies, 17*(3), 360–380.

Jenkins, H., & Carpentier, N. (2013). Theorizing participatory intensities: A conversation about participation and politics. *Convergence, 19*(3), 265–286.

Jones, F. (2000). Le bénévolat à la hausse chez les jeunes. *L'emploi et le revenu en perspective, 12*(1), 38–45.

Latzko-Toth, G., Gallant, N., & Pastinelli, M. (2017). Pratiques informationnelles des jeunes Québécois à l'ère des médias sociaux: le cas du Printemps érable. *Recherches sociographiques, LVIII*(1).

Loncle, P., Cuconato, M., Muniglia, V., & Walther, A. (2012). *Youth participation in Europe: Beyond discourses, practices and realities*. Chicago: The Policy Press/University of Chicago Press.

Millette, M. (2015). *L'usage des médias sociaux dans les luttes pour la visibilité: le cas des minorités francophones au Canada anglais*. Montréal: Université du Québec à Montréal.

Muncie, J. (2009). *Youth and crime* (3rd ed.). London: Sage.

Newburn, T., Deacon, R., Diski, B., Cooper, K., Grant, M., & Burch, A. (2016). "The best three days of my life": Pleasure, power and alienation in the 2011 riots. *Crime, Media, Culture*. doi:10.1177/1741659016667438.

Norris, P. (2011). *Democratic deficit: Critical citizens revisited*. Cambridge: Cambridge University Press.

O'Toole, T., Lister, M., Marsh, D., Jones, S., & McDonagh, A. (2003). Tuning out or left out? Participation and non-participation among young people. *Contemporary Politics, 9*(1), 45–61.

Paré, J.-L., Pelletier, C., & Vigeant, P. (2008). *Le bénévolat de participation citoyenne en CCL: Cinq 'points phares' pour réflexion et intervention*. Québec: Fédération québécoise des centres communautaires de loisir (FGCCL).

Pastinelli, M. (2013). Ressorts et enjeux de la vie publique 2.0: Que sont devenues les tyrannies de l'intimité? *Bulletin de l'Observatoire Jeunes et Société, 11*(1), 16–17.

Pickard, S. (2009). Blade Britain and broken Britain. Knife crime among young people in Great Britain. In J.-P. Fons, ed. *Regards sur la jeunesse britannique. Revue française de civilisation britannique, XV*(3), 65–78.

Pickard, S. (2016, June 15). *Finding the gaps, minding the gaps, filling the gaps: Cross-disciplinary studies of young people and political participation*. Keynote presentation. Minding the gaps between disciplines. Political engagement among youth. Institut National de la Recherche Scientifique (INRS), Montreal.

Pickard, S. (2018). Governing, monitoring and regulating youth protest in contemporary Britain. In M. Grasso & J. Bessant (Eds.), *Governing youth politics in the age of surveillance*. London and New York: Routledge.

Pickard, S., Nativel, C., & Portier, F. (2012). Introduction. In *Les politiques de jeunesse au Royaume-Uni et en France. Désaffection, répression et accompagnement à la citoyenneté* (pp. 15–25). Paris: Presses de la Sorbonne Nouvelle (PSN).

Poirier, C. (2017). La citoyenneté culturelle. Considérations théoriques et empiriques. In N. Casemajor (Ed.), *Expériences critiques de la médiation culturelle*. Québec: Presses de l'Université Laval.

Quéniart, A. (2008). The form and meaning of young people's involvement in community and political work. *Youth and Society, 40*(2), 224–244.

Roudet, B. (2012). Dépolitisation ou radicalisation? Les liens à la politique des jeunes Français à la lumière des enquêtes *Valeurs*. In S. Pickard et al. (Eds.), *Les politiques de jeunesse au Royaume-Uni et en France. Désaffection, répression et accompagnement à la citoyenneté* (pp. 29–43). Paris: Presses de la Sorbonne Nouvelle.

Van de Velde, C. (2017). Sous la colère, les épreuves du devenir adulte en monde néolibéral. *Informations sociales, 195*(7).

Verba, S., & Nie, N. H. (1972). *Participation in America: Political democracy and social equality*. New York, NY: Harper and Row.

Nicole Gallant is Professor in Social Sciences at INRS University (Institut national de la recherche scientifique) in Quebec. With a PhD in political science, she now specialises in youth studies and in minority studies. Her research interests focus on citizenship and identity. She was Director of the Observatory on Youth and Society 2010–2017.

PART II

Young People and Online Political Action

CHAPTER 6

The Crisis of Democracy in Hong Kong: Young People's Online Politics and the Umbrella Movement

Rob Watts

INTRODUCTION

In 1997, Britain ceded sovereignty over its Hong Kong colony to the People's Republic of China (PRC). China promised to leave Hong Kong's democratic polity intact. With evidence everywhere seeming to support Fukuyama's (1989) thesis about the triumph of democracy and capitalism, it was too easily assumed that China would abide by its promise and that Hong Kong would remain a democracy. Yet as Pepper argues, the Chinese Communist Party seemed determined "to confound assumptions about the inevitability of democracy's inevitable advance" (Pepper, 2007, p. 3). The evolution of a pro-democracy movement in Hong Kong that began 2013 as 'Occupy Central' (佔中), and morphed into the so-called 'Umbrella Movement,' is a clear sign of the space of persistent crisis that Hong Kong has become. As Serres reminds us, the word 'crisis' comes from the Greek κρίνω (*krínō,*) which means to "pick out, choose,

---

R. Watts (✉)
RMIT University, Melbourne, VIC, Australia

decide, judge" (2015, p. xi). In medical cases, a crisis is like a fork in the road, and as Serres insists, there is no going back from a crisis: "a crisis propels the body forward either towards death or to something new that it is forced to invent" (Serres, 2015, p. xii). That Hong Kong now faces such a crisis is due in no small measure to a political process driven largely by young people.

Though there was a long history prior to 2014 of pro-democratic activism in Hong Kong, I focus here on the pro-democracy movement that began with a strike by students from all major tertiary institutions in Hong Kong in September 2014 (Cai, 2017; Myan, 2014; Ortmann, 2015).[1] The strikes were in reaction to a decision taken by the PRC's Standing Committee of the National People's Congress on 31 August 2014 on electoral reform in Hong Kong that failed to guarantee universal suffrage for Hong Kong, and more importantly the right of Hong Kong voters to directly elect their own Chief Executive in 2017 (Martin, 2015).[2]

The leadership of Occupy Central had planned to start a process of civil disobedience involving occupation of streets and squares on China's National Day (1 October). However, students pre-empted this on Friday 26 September 2014, when up to 100 students occupied an area known as Civic Square and sat peacefully waiting to be arrested. Several key student leaders were arrested and released on 28 September. By then, Benny Tai, the acknowledged 'leader' of 'Occupy Central with Love and Peace' (和平佔) (2014) had no choice but to bring the formal start of protests forward. Thousands of protestors began to occupy key streets like Tim Mei Avenue, Connaught Road and Chater Road. That day also saw the police use CSR gas ('tear' gas or pepper spray) on protestors on Connaught Road, and as Myan (2014) reports, this led to the use of umbrellas as protection:

> People on the ground began to yell up to us on the raised walkway. "有遮俾遮!" ('If you have an umbrella, give it to us!'). The protesters were using umbrellas as shields against pepper spray on the front lines. People around me began to open their umbrellas and toss them down, gently floating into the waiting hands below. Protesters at the front of the lines turned the umbrellas inside-out so that when they were sprayed, the residue wouldn't hit or drip onto their neighbors but instead gather on the ground.

It was this action that prompted Adam Cotton in a Twitter post to call the pro-democracy movement the 'Umbrella Revolution.' Video images of tens of thousands of mostly young people, occupying key roads in protests that began on 26 September 2014 and lasted for months, soon achieved the same kind of iconic status that images from other pro-democracy protests like Tiananmen Square in Beijing (1989), Occupy Wall Street in New York (2009), or Tahrir Square in Cairo in 2012–2013. The street-based occupations lasted 80 days before police closed protests down, making it the most significant political movement in Hong Kong since 1997 (Cai, 2017, p. 1). Since then, the pro-democracy movement has adopted new tactics.

Two aspects of the Umbrella Revolution of 2014 intersect to provide the central problematic for this chapter. One is the ubiquitous presence of young people in the Hong Kong pro-democracy movement. The other is the role, still not properly understood or documented, played by online pro-democracy and free speech activists using sites like Hong Kong Golden and 4chan. The conjunction of these two aspects raises a question about how we are to make sense of young people's political activism, especially when it involves online processes. I briefly outline the way political science has dealt with young people's politics, and the way it has dealt with online activism. I then turn to the particular way political theory inspired by Habermas's (1989) account of the 'public sphere' has understood the internet before turning to some aspects of online politics in Hong Kong in 2014 to highlight the gap between 'theory and practice' and the prospects for (re)generating democracy in Hong Kong.

ONLINE POLITICS IN HONG KONG, 2014

The need to address what many call a 'crisis in democracy' is suggested by recent scholarly research and commentary. As is now acknowledged, research and commentary addressing young people's political participation since the 1980s has led some to insist that young people are the most apolitical generation ever, while others emphasise how young people are engaging in new kinds of political engagement. As writers like Bessant (2004, 2014), Farthing (2010) and Pickard (2018) argue, the contradictory stories about young people and politics point to important differences about how we conceptualise the political.

The point of this observation becomes even sharper when we turn to the online world and the role played by online activists using sites like Hong Kong Golden and 4chan. Though more will be said about 4chan and Hong Kong Golden later, these websites and activist networks like Anonymous played a major role in the Occupy Central movement.

4chan itself was created by a 15-year-old New Yorker initially known only as 'moot.' 4chan has achieved a mix of fame and notoriety as much for its Manga-style porn as for its politics (Coleman, 2014, p. 51). Since 2008, 4chan's bulletin board (called '/b/') has persistently hosted mass online interventions or 'raids,' orchestrated by 'Anonymous,' involving millions of online users flooding a targeted website effectively forcing it to close down. On 1 October 2014, Anonymous announced the start of 'Operation Hong Kong,' when it posted a message on News2Share:

> It has come to our attention that recent tactics used against peaceful protesters here in the United States have found their way to Hong Kong. To the protesters in Hong Kong, we have heard your plea for help. Take heart and take to your streets. You are not alone in this fight. Anonymous members all over the world stand with you, and will help in your fight for democracy. To the Hong Kong police and any others that are called to the protests, we are watching you very closely and have already begun to wage war on you for your inhumane actions against your own citizens. If you continue to abuse, harass or harm protesters, we will continue to deface and take every web-based asset of your government off line.
>
> That is not a threat. It is a promise ... Operation Hong Kong engaged. We are Anonymous. We are legion. We do not forgive. We do not forget. Government of Hong Kong, expect us. (Moyer, 2014)

Anonymous quickly instigated distributed denial of service actions, which targeted various official websites causing them to crash and left behind garbled homepages complete with loud music, the group's logo and a block of text which read: "We Are Sick And Tired Of your Bullshit! This is Operation Hong Kong. We Will Not Stop. We Will Not Give Up! You've Pissed All The Anons Off #SaveHongKong #OpHongKong #Anonymous #Hacked (4chan Archive, 2014)."

A local website called Hong Kong Golden played an even more conspicuous role in the evolution of the Umbrella Movement. Founded in 1999, Hong Kong Golden has been aptly described as the Umbrella Movement's "combative id," a mix of "attack dogs," and "merry pranksters" (Beam, 2014, p. 1). Like Anonymous, Hong Kong Golden relies on anonymity to mobilise large numbers of people (Beam, 2014, p. 1). For example, in the early evening of 11 October 2014, someone on Hong Kong Golden proposed that Occupy Central protesters 'seize Lung Wo

Road' running through Hong Kong's central business district. The user suggested demonstrators could 'coincidentally and accidentally walk onto the road.' Soon after 9 pm, a group of protestors swarmed into the street, halting traffic in both directions and provoking violent clashes with police. After midnight, someone posted a photo on Facebook showing protestors barricading a tunnel, with the title 'Brave Golden Forum, Suddenly Attacking Lung Wo Road.' Hong Kong Golden would play a role in sustaining the next two months of civil disobedience.

This brief description of mostly young people using 4chan and Hong Kong Golden to engage in digital politics, raises several important intellectual and practical problems which I want to address here.

The first is an extremely puzzling feature of contemporary political science. Mainstream political science has so far largely managed to avoid engaging online activism. A survey of a sample of eleven major American, British and Australian political science journals (2010–2015), tells us that these academic journals have yet to publish one research paper addressing either 4chan, Anonymous or related instances of digital activism.[3] Shedd (2015, p. 1) suggests that sites like 4chan and Hong Kong Golden have attracted relatively little interest from political scientists "because of the widespread use of politically incorrect language and images, the ephemerality of its content and its generally negative reputation." While these features may begin to explain the failure to engage with online activism, I suggest that political science sometimes, perhaps often, has trouble acknowledging the political. Other social sciences like sociology, media studies or anthropology seem to have had no such trouble: apart from Coleman (2011, 2014) see Fuchs (2013); Goode (2015) and Pickard (2016, 2018).

Rather than asking what does political science have to say about Hong Kong Golden, 4chan and Anonymous (the answer is nothing), we need to ask what does 4chan and Anonymous have to say about political science. As we have seen, this question has already been raised in regard to the way conventional political science pursues ideas like the claim that democracy is in crisis or that young people are politically disengaged.

POLITICAL SCIENCE AND THE POLITICAL

Conventional political scientists are having trouble dealing with online activity involving 4chan, Hong Kong Golden and Anonymous because it does not conform with various constructive schemes that define 'political science.'

Constructive schemes are those ideas or beliefs without which it is not possible to do the science or the discipline in question. People working in disciplines like political science, criminology, sociology, psychology, economics and so forth, establish over time certain basic discipline-defining narratives, 'theoretical' frames and ways of doing their discipline. Examining a discipline like political science suggests that far from being a simple 'reflection' of reality, we encounter as Sandywell (1996) has shown, a constructive process based on narrative schemes and constitutive metaphors that cohere into "constructive schemes." As Danziger stresses, "constructive schemes" "are not just cognitive frameworks for the *interpretation* of empirical data, but involve practical rules for the *production* of such data" (Danziger, 1990, p. 4).

If there is no single 'operational definition of politics' or constructive scheme shaping modern political science, there are certainly a number of leading traditions and approaches. Leftwich (2004, p. 4), for example, highlights the dominance of an 'institutionalist' approach, which focuses on formal political actors, institutions or government and implies that 'politics' is only found in certain societies possessing certain institutions like governments, parliaments and so forth. Running alongside that tradition has been a 'behaviourist' tradition which often privileges quantitative methods and is committed to scientism. Arguably, enthusiasm for this positivist 'science of politics' peaked in the 1950s and 1960s with the emergence, especially in the United States, of a form of behaviourist political analysis that led to institutionalism being marginalised during the 1960s and 1970s (Marsh & Stoker, 2010). From the 1980s, a 'new institutionalism' emerged. Political institutions were no longer equated with political organisations, which were treated instead as sets of 'rules' that guide or constrain the behaviour of individual actors. This understanding seems to underpin the idea that 'real politics' has nothing to do with what Srnicek and Williams (2015, p. 11) dismiss as 'folk politics' of the kind represented "by Occupy, Spain's 15M, student occupations, [...] Tiqqun and the Invisible Committee [...] the Zapatistas and contemporary anarchist-tinged politics".

An implicit understanding of what is properly political is operating in each of these 'traditions.' For any action to be 'political,' political science assumes there needs to be motivations capable of being expressed in political language, i.e., of being rationally articulated and of being expressed through legitimate, institutional means. As Akram (2014, p. 382) observes, the focus on rationality is especially telling because it points to the way a discipline like political science only acknowledges certain forms of activity as 'political,' by relying on tacit premises like the idea that 'rationality' is coterminous with conventional forms of political action.

This may explain why any emphasis on the 'non-rational' evident in sites like 4chan or Hong Kong Golden simply serves to strengthen the refusal by conventional political science to engage with these interventions. This point is if anything, reinforced when we turn to arguments that the internet has become a new kind of public sphere.

The Internet as New Public Sphere?

A good deal of the discussion about 'new politics' has relied heavily on links being drawn between Habermas's (1989) much admired, if often criticised, account of the 'public sphere,' and the idea that the internet now provides a new platform for a new politics. Habermas belongs to a venerable European tradition that is recognisably 'liberal.' Western liberalism has long insisted that constitutional norms undergird all political decisions and that the rule-of-law provides the state with its ultimate legitimacy. While Habermas works in this tradition, he offers a two-track account of democracy by adding the deliberative public opinion forming role of the public sphere to the role played by institutionalised procedures of constitutional and parliamentary decision-making.

Habermas's account of the 'public sphere' makes 'publicity' a source of reasoned consensus formation. This is plainly appealing to many liberal theorists like Tsekeris (2008, p. 12) who claims:

> The conception of the public sphere is most commonly employed to signify the open realm of rational public discourse and debate, a realm which is conceptually linked with the very democratic process and in which individuals can freely discuss everyday issues of common concern.

Even his severest critics like Fraser (1990, p. 77) have said that "something like Habermas's idea of the public sphere is indispensable to critical social theory and to democratic political practice."

Since the 1990s, Habermas's work has provided an 'obvious' interpretative framework for commentators eager to make sense of the digital technologies and practices associated with the internet. Many commentators have argued that the internet has regenerated the 'public sphere' and reinvigorated democratic politics. Deploying Habermas's discursive rationality framework has encouraged many to treat the internet as a 'new public sphere.' Westling (2007, p. 12) is typical when he argues that sites like Facebook "have the potential to actually exceed Habermas's expectations of a public sphere and become a major hub for political action among community members."

All this relies on Habermas's claim that all "communicative action" is oriented to understanding or agreement and is based on the "intersubjective redemption of validity claims" (Habermas, 1998, p. 12). At its most basic, this simply means mutual comprehension, i.e., that people are using the same words with the same meanings so as to achieve a degree of shared meanings and mutual comprehension. At its most elevated 'understanding' also means a shared consensus about the universal validity of claims people make to speak the truth or to know the good. This is why the characteristic discourse that constitutes the public sphere is austerely rational. This apparently means that collective rational deliberation creates a new space "where the authority of the better argument" can "be asserted against the established order," which in turn "holds out the possibility of reforming the asymmetrical relations of force" (sic) (Tsekeris, 2008, p. 13). Gimmler adds that "there is no plausible alternative model to rational and un-coerced discourse as the normative basis for democracy" (Gimmler, 2001, p. 23).

There are several problems with this. Firstly, Habermas has been reluctant to treat the internet as part of a 'public sphere' emphasising, e.g., the fragmenting effects of the internet:

> The internet has certainly reactivated the grassroots of an egalitarian public of writers and readers […]. In the context of liberal regimes, the rise of millions of fragmented chat rooms across the world tend instead to lead to the fragmentation of large but politically focused mass audiences into a huge number of isolated issue publics. (Habermas, 2006, p. 424)

Equally, it is not surprising that claims that by reasoning alone we might subvert the 'asymmetrical relations of force' has led critics to say that Habermas's public sphere treats politics as the kind of thing a professor running a seminar in logic does. The third problem is that there are simply too many discrepancies between sites like 4chan or Hong Kong Golden and Habermas's conception of public deliberation. There are several features which suggest that these websites transgress conventional conceptions of civility and/or what counts as 'proper,' i.e., Habermasian political communication.

4CHAN AND HONG KONG GOLDEN, 2014

4chan has been and remains a digital-discursive space with global reach. A simple site, spartan by contemporary Web 2.0 standards, it was originally designed for conversation and image sharing and the site still provides the basic tools for those functions. Though it started only with '/b/,' 4chan currently (November 2016) has 69 boards (with topics ranging from photography, papercraft, Pokémon the paranormal and pornography).[4] While users across the site remain anonymous, conversations in the boards with a specific theme are focused and threads on-topic, barring the occasional incursion of spam from /b/ users. 4chan is a highly transient website. Threads generally 404 (die) typically after an hour, and there are approximately 700,000 posts a day.

The commitment to anonymity is ensured because 4chan users are not required to register to post and people are not required to identify themselves. Indeed, as 4chan's Rule Number 4 says clearly "The posting of personal information […] is prohibited." In this respect, 4chan represents a counter-movement to the current preoccupation with personal identity that has come to characterise websites like Facebook and Twitter. The result is an exuberantly open-minded website where almost anything goes. The protection afforded by anonymity supporting freedom of expression is exemplified in 'trolling.' Trolling is a semiotically-rich term describing provocative posts on the internet. Trolling also referred to by 'Anonymous' as 'chemo,' seems to aim at being maximally offensive. In October 2014, one Anonymous post simply proclaimed:

> HK people don't want to be Chinese. We want to be Hong Kong. Sure, HK people are ethnically (Han) Chinese majority. But we do not like to associate as being a China 'country.' At least as British Colony, we can be a western government. But now we belong to China, we do not like. Want independent like Taiwan. You go up to any Hong Kong man and ask if they are from china, they say no and get angry. They say they are Hong Konger, not Chinese. We don't want to be communism. (4chan Archive: Anonymous 2014-10-02 12:47:37 Post No.36665280)

Among the replies came this:

Don't you know? It's not cool to be Chinese. I'm assuming you are from Hong Kong, or a Hong Konger outside of Hong Kong, so I won't say much. But considering how Mainland Chinese people literally shit on the streets and have bad manners, these are some of the reasons why HK people don't want to be categorized as 'China Chinese' people. In the eyes of China people, they think Hong Kong people want to suck British Dick. (4chan Archive Anonymous 2014-10-02 12:57:52 Post No.36665619)

The porousness of the internet has allowed not just new styles of 'civic discourse,' which are not all that civil, but it has also facilitated quite vigorous forms of direct political action. 4chan through '/b/' also hosts mass online interventions called raids or distributed denial of service actions, in which hundreds of thousands of internet-users flood a targeted website causing it to crash. Anonymous has used the very accessibility of the internet to launch political attacks which do not respect the conventions of political action directed at organisations deemed to be subverting the principle of freedom of speech.

Hong Kong Golden has used this affordance liberally. It was originally created in 1999 as a website for personal computer users to check the prices of hardware sold at the Golden Shopping Center, an electronics market in Kowloon. Within a few months, a discussion forum had been added which enabled users to start to talk politics. By mid-2014, there were more and more 'Golden brothers' using the site. (The users are referred to as 'Golden brothers' because the forum's users are mostly male who like 4chan users are attracted by the mix of politics and pornography). Before 28 September, the current affairs chat room of the website was logging about 300,000 hits a day. That increased dramatically after police fired 87 canisters of tear gas at protesters in Admiralty on 28 September 2014. The site began to get 2.9 million page views a day (Sui, 2014). The chat room ceased to be just a site for exchanging pornography or political views. The 'Golden brothers' began to dig up personal information on people who opposed the Umbrella Movement. They posted photos of the anti-Occupy thugs who harassed peaceful protesters. They created memes including parody songs mocking government figures, which protesters then posted on Facebook and WhatsApp. Given the fluid nature of the leadership structure of Occupy central leadership structure, the forum also become a staging ground where 'keyboard fighters' discussed strategy and floated plans to occupy key roads.

The mobilising role played by Hong Kong Golden became increasingly visible in mid-October 2014. On 17 October, police officers tore down street barricades in Mong Kok Road. A message appeared on Hong Kong Golden:

> Warriors on Lung Wo Road and Mong Kok, let's stand united. The battle this time will be the turning point of the revolution ... If we take back Mong Kok, this will enter a new stage. If we have to, we can block MTR stations and paralyse the MTR.

Soon after the message appeared on the forum, thousands of people flocked to Mong Kok, in case police tore down more barricades. Police used pepper spray and batons on the crowds to try to disperse the occupiers who finally dispersed in November 2014.

There is one other less-noticed aspect of the way the online activists worked in Hong Kong that is worthy of discussion.

The Politics of Language

It should come as no surprise that there has been a politics of language at play in the struggle over Hong Kong's future (Edwards, 2016). This again reminds us that Habermas's account of rational deliberation misses important aspects of real politics.

As part of its emphasis on political and cultural unity, the PRC has long insisted that Mandarin be the official language of China, though reference to the use of 'the Chinese language' in Hong Kong's Basic Law encouraged many in Hong Kong to think this protected the majority status of Cantonese. It therefore came as something of a surprise when in February 2014, Hong Kong's Education Bureau announced on its webpage that Cantonese was not an official language of Hong Kong. This directly affected the 97 per cent of the population of Hong Kong who speak Cantonese. The Education Bureau's e-learning portal also posted an anti-Cantonese video. To members of the Occupy Central movement both actions appeared to subvert the Basic Law and produced an immediate response on Hong Kong Golden. Ng Kap-chuen a young graphic designer and illustrator saw the Education Bureau's interventions as propaganda. Already active on Hong Kong Golden under the *nom de plume* Ah To, and committed to the idea that 'Cantonese make us "us"' Ng created the figures and text for a multi-media production he called *Great Canton and Hong Kong Proverbs* (Sin, 2014).

Soon there was evidence of a larger more intricate political contest at work in the way Mandarin and Cantonese (Yue) were put to work in the construction of Hong Kong identity that points to some of the less 'obvious,' less 'rational' ways political discourse works.

As Guilford (2014) shows us, the very name of the 'Umbrella Movement' provides a telling example of this. While members of the Hong Kong pro-democracy movement frequently wrote 'Umbrella Movement' and used the Mandarin character for 'umbrella' (雨傘), they also frequently wrote it using the Cantonese character (遮). Doing this meant that the meaning of the Cantonese phrase (遮打) would be lost on a Mandarin-only speaker (The discussion here and in the next few paragraphs depends very heavily on Gwynne 2014).

When a Mandarin-reader reads the Cantonese words for 'Umbrella Movement,' and if read as Mandarin rather than Cantonese, the characters 遮打 are pronounced *('juh da')*. Both are usually verbs. *'Juh'* means 'to obscure' or 'cover,' while *da* means 'to hit' or 'fight.' The Cantonese phrase does not make much sense: it's the 'Cover-Hit Movement.' The Mandarin-reader will see a fairly innocuous, even somewhat nonsensical phrase. However, those same two characters in Hong Kong Cantonese, while pronounced similarly to Mandarin *('juh daa')* mean something quite different: among other things they are the Cantonese characters for 'Chater Road' one of the key Hong Kong roads occupied by the Umbrella Movement. Yet the second character, (打) also means 'to fight' in both Cantonese and Mandarin, and so it carries yet another layer of meaning given that the character '打' to a Cantonese speaker means 'to attack' or 'knock down.' By implication, the target of such an attack would be C.Y. Leung, Hong Kong's chief executive widely understood to be pro-Beijing. In short, a Cantonese-reader reads the characters as a play on words meaning both 'Chater Road Movement' and, literally, 'Umbrella Fight Movement,' or, more abstractly, 'Umbrella Fight-Against-CY Leung Movement.'

The frequent and deliberate use of characters like 遮 and other Cantonese phrases in Umbrella Movement slogans therefore served expressively to denominate not just Hong Kong's resistance to the Communist Party's political values, but to persistently instantiate the defence of its own distinct cultural and linguistic identity, as well as the history of the autonomy the members of the Hong Kong Umbrella Movement are fighting to defend.

This has mattered given evidence of a strengthening of a Hong Kong identity, particularly among younger people. A recent poll on People's Ethnic Identity conducted by Hong Kong University's Public Opinion Programme in June 2015, for example, found that younger respondents (ages 18–29) were more likely to state they were 'Hong Kongers' (62.5%) and that this number had increased from 2014. In the 2015 poll, only 5.3% of this age group claimed a Chinese identity, a number that has been steadfastly decreasing over the last few years (People's Ethnic Identity, 2015).

Conclusion

Habermas may well be proposing some entirely worthy prescriptive intentions about how 'good' political speech should look and work. I have argued that framing 4chan and Anonymous as political requires a reframing of what 'the political' is and how people engage in politics.

What we see in Anonymous and 4chan is a challenge to the liberal idea foundational to mainstream political science that the political relies on rational and un-coerced public discourse and practices of public reasoning oriented to consensus. Writers like Habermas, Gimmler and Tsekeris insist on the link between rational deliberation, the public sphere and the democratic order. These claims notwithstanding, no particular reasons, however, have been advanced to say why we can believe that rational arguments will transform asymmetrical power relations or that rational deliberation can challenge a status quo, nor are we shown why there is some inherent relationship between rational deliberation, the public sphere and democratic order. This is the point first made by Carl Schmitt (1996) in the 1920s.

What we see firstly in the Umbrella Movement is a mix of new and old forms of civil disobedience. 4chan and Hong Kong Golden also look very little like a Habermasian digital public sphere. On the one hand, much of the posts going up on these websites are rude, vulgar, impolite and often uncivil. These sites can also switch quickly over to political activism. In the Occupy Movement, we saw cyber-activism inform the evolution of civil disobedience that made use of the affordances of digital information and networks in support the pro-democracy movement (Baase, 2008). Cyber activists used their considerable technical skills to cause variously economic, social or political disruption to their targets by hacking websites or to mobilise political support for more traditional forms of protest and civil disobedience.

What is found on Hong Kong Golden or 4chan is vulgar, emotional, exuberant, energetically disrespectful and prone to ridicule, rather than seeking to rationally persuade in the kind of hushed and respectful tones Habermas would have us adopt. In each case, we see an example of what Ono and Sloop (1995) called "outlaw discourses," which call into account dominant and conventional frames of judgment by appealing to powerful moral emotions tied up with identity, justice and freedom. As the discussion above of the politics of language also indicates, there are non-universal idiosyncratic and particularist aspects of language use, which do not conform to Habermas's universalising theory of discursive pragmatics. It also tends to edge into old/new forms of political activism including civil disobedience, carried out enthusiastically by young people.

Notes

1. I have relied on a website set up by an American Fulbright scholar (Myan, 2014), which provides daily eyewitness accounts and links to media reporting for each day after 26 September to the end of 2014. Cai (2017) provides a very good account of the Umbrella Movement in 2014.
2. The Chief Executive is the head of the Government of Hong Kong, a role established by the Basic Law in 1997 to replace the colony's Governor-General.
3. I surveyed all journal articles published between January 2010 and the end of 2015 in the *Journal of Political Science, Political Studies, Political Studies Review*, the *British Journal of Politics* and *International Relations, Political Science Quarterly, American Journal of Political Science*, the *American Political Science Review*, the *Australian Journal of Political Science, British Journal of Political Science, Journal of Politics*, and *Comparative Political Studies*. This is not to overlook the work of political scientists like Vromen who in Marsh and Vromen (2012) briefly addresses Anonymous.
4. This may explain the site's user demographics which 4chan says is aged 18–34, 70 per cent male and mostly college-educated (advertise@4chan.org).

References

4chan Archive. (2014). Retrieved from https://boards.fireden.net/
Akram, S. (2014). Recognizing the 2011 United Kingdom riots as political protest: A theoretical framework based on agency, habitus and the preconscious. *British Journal of Criminology, 54*(3), 375–392.

Baase, S. (2008). *A gift of fire: Social, legal and ethical issues for computing and the internet* (3rd ed.). New York: Prentice-Hall.

Beam, C. (2014). Hong Kong's own reddit is doing the protesters' dirty work—Sometimes too dirty. *New Republic*. Retrieved June 23, 2016, from https://newrepublic.com/article/119835/hong-kong-golden-website-doing-occupy-protesters-dirty-work

Bessant, J. (2004). Mixed messages: Youth participation and democratic practice. *Australian Journal of Political Science, 39*(2), 387–404.

Bessant, J. (2014). *Democracy bytes: New media and new politics and generational change*. Basingstoke: Palgrave Macmillan.

Cai, Y. (2017). *The Occupy movement in Hong Kong: Sustaining decentralized protest*. Abingdon: Routledge.

Coleman, G. (2011). Hacker politics and publics. *Public Culture, 23*(3), 511–516.

Coleman, G. (2014). *Hacker, hoaxer, whistleblower, spy: The many faces of anonymous*. London: Verso.

Danziger, K. (1990). *Constructing the subject: Historical origins of psychological research*. Cambridge: Cambridge University Press.

Edwards, J. (2016). The politics of language and identity: Attitudes towards Hong Kong English pre and post the Umbrella Movement. *Asian Englishes, 18*(2), 157–164.

Farthing, R. (2010). The politics of youthful antipolitics: Representing the "Issue" of youth participation in politics. *Journal of Youth Studies, 13*(2), 181–195.

Fraser, N. (1990). Rethinking the public sphere: A contribution to the critique of actually existing democracy. *Social Text, 25/26*, 56–80.

Fuchs, C. (2013). The Anonymous movement in the context of liberalism and socialism. *Interface, 5*(2), 345–376.

Fukuyama, F. (1989). The end of history? *The National Interest*, Summer. Retrieved from http://www.wesjones.com/eoh.htm

Gimmler, A. (2001). Deliberative democracy, the public sphere and the internet. *Philosophy & Social Criticism, 27*(4), 21–39.

Goode, L. (2015). Anonymous and the political ethos of hacktivism. *Popular Communication, 13*(1), 74–86.

Guilford, G. (2014). Here's why the name of Hong Kong's "Umbrella Movement" is so subversive. *QUARTZ*. http://qz.com/283395/how-hong-kongs-umbrella-movement-protesters-are-using-their-native-language-to-push-back-against-beijing

Habermas, J. (1989). *Structural transformation of the public sphere: An inquiry into a category of bourgeois, society* (T. Burger & F. Lawrence, Trans.). Cambridge: MIT Press.

Habermas, J. (1998). *The inclusion of the other. Studies in political theory.* Cambridge MA: MIT Press.
Habermas, J. (2006). Political communication in media society: Does democracy still enjoy an epistemic dimension? The impact of normative theory on empirical research. *Communication Theory, 16*(4), 411–426.
Leftwich, A. (2004). *What is politics? The activity and its study.* Cambridge: Polity.
Marsh, D., & Stoker, G. (2010). *Theory and methods in political science.* Basingstoke: Palgrave Macmillan.
Marsh, D., & Vromen, A. (2012). Everyday makers with a difference? Contemporary forms of political participation. TASA conference. Retrieved from https://www.tasa.org.au/wp-content/uploads/2012/11/Marsh-David-Vromen-Ariadne.pdf
Martin, M. (2015). Prospects for democracy in Hong Kong: The 2017 election reforms. *Congressional Research Service Report: R44031.* Washington: Congressional Research Service.
Moyer, J. (2014). Hacker collective anonymous joins Hong Kong's occupy central *Washington Post.* Retrieved October 2, from https://www.washingtonpost.com/news/morning-mix/wp/2014/10/02/report-anonymous-hacker-collective-joins-hong-kongs-occupy-central
Myan, V. (2014). *Fulbright* |富布賴特 *Ten months in beautiful Hong Kong.* Retrieved from https://vsmyanhk.wordpress.com/category/hk-blog
Occupy Central with Love and Peace. (2014). Retrieved from https://oclphkenglish.wordpress.com
Ono, K., & Sloop, J. (1995). The critique of vernacular discourses. *Communication Monographs, 62*(2), 19–46.
Ortmann, S. (2015). The Umbrella Movement and Hong Kong's protracted democratization process. *Asian Affairs, 46*(3), 32–50.
People's Ethnic Identity. (2015, June 23). Retrieved October 21, 2016, from https://www.hkupop.hku.hk/english/popexpress/ethnic
Pepper, S. (2007). *Keeping democracy at bay: Hong Kong and the challenge of Chinese political reform.* New York: Rowman and Littlefield.
Pickard, S. (2016, June 15). Finding the gaps, minding the gaps, filling the gaps: Cross-disciplinary studies of young people and political participation. Keynote presentation. *Minding the Gaps between Disciplines. Political Engagement among Youth.* Institut National de la Recherche Scientifique (INRS), Montreal.
Pickard, S. (2018). *Politics, protest and young people. Political participation and dissent in Britain in the 21st century.* London: Palgrave Macmillan. [Forthcoming].
Sandywell, B. (1996). *Logological investigations, (volume 1) reflexivity and the crisis of western reason.* London: Routledge.
Schmitt, C. (1996). *The concept of the political* (G. Schwab, Trans.). Chicago: University of Chicago Press.
Serres, M. (2015). *Times of crisis.* London: Bloomsbury.

Shedd, J. (2015). *Portrait of an anonymous image board: The board-tans of 4chan*. Unpublished Master's Thesis. Savannah: University of Georgia. Retrieved from http://hdl.handle.net/1853/53595

Sin, B. (2014, March 18). Is Cantonese in danger? Hongkongers take steps to protect their heritage. *South China Morning Post*. Retrieved from http://www.scmp.com/lifestyle/family-education/article/1450856/hongkongers-take-steps-preserve-their-language-and

Srnicek, N., & Williams, A. (2015). *Inventing the future: Postcapitalism and a world without work*. London: Verso.

Sui, P. (2014, October 31). How social media shapes occupy: Web Forum HKGolden.com Takes Off. *South China Morning Post*. Retrieved from http://www.scmp.com/news/hong-kong/article/1628549/how-social-media-shapes-occupy-web-forum-hkgoldencom-takes

Tsekeris, C. (2008). The public sphere in the context of media freedom and regulation. *Humanity & Social Sciences Journal, 3*(1), 12–17.

Westling, M. (2007). Expanding the public sphere: The impact of Facebook on political communication Madison: University of Wisconsin-Madison. Retrieved from http://www.bytec.co.uk/wp-content/uploads/bytec/manufacturers/pdfs/2012-08-18_afacebook_and_political_communication.pdf

Rob Watts is Professor of Social Policy at RMIT University, Melbourne, Australia and author most recently of *States of violence and the Civilising Process: On Criminology and State Crime* (2016) and *Public Universities, Managerialism and the Value of Higher Education* (2017).

CHAPTER 7

Momentum and the Movementist 'Corbynistas': Young People Regenerating the Labour Party in Britain

Sarah Pickard

INTRODUCTION

Young people's rates of traditional or conventional political participation in Britain have been increasing in the twenty-first century, contrary to many developed democracies (see other chapters in this volume). The proportion of 18–24-year-olds voting in general elections (who were registered to vote) has been going up,[1] and the proportion of young people being a member of a political party has grown. Indeed, the membership rates of young people in political parties and their youth wings went up markedly before and especially after the 2015 general election. This was the case for all the main political parties across the political spectrum (Green Party, Labour Party, Scottish National Party—SNP, the Liberal Democrats, Conservative Party and United Kingdom Independence Party—UKIP) (Pickard, 2015, 2018b).

There are several explanations for this bucking of the trend regarding institutional political participation of young people in recent years. First,

S. Pickard (✉)
Université Sorbonne Nouvelle, Paris, France

young people in Britain have been particularly affected by the significant austerity policies introduced by the Conservative-Liberal Democrat coalition government in power from 2010 to 2015 and continued since then by the Conservative Government, against the backdrop of the fallout from the global financial crisis and the British economic crisis. More specifically, young people from all socio-economic groups have been impacted by many recent governmental policies, which have resulted in a lack of affordable housing, high rates of youth employment, inadequate youth services, poor provision of mental health care for young people and sharp rises in university tuition fees. This crisis in youth policy and austerity are having a profoundly negative effect on the current generation of young people. As Seymour (2016, p. 78) says, "this generation is the one to suffer the most from the consolidation of neoliberalism" (see also Howker & Malik, 2013; Jones, 2017). Second, the rise in the use of social media and new technologies in political communication has encouraged and enabled young people to participate in traditional politics. However, these factors have also been at play in other countries that have not experienced a hike in traditional political participation among young people (see Grasso, 2016).

The Labour Party in Britain has been the main beneficiary of increased membership since 2015. Formed at the start of the twentieth century to represent the working-class in Parliament, at the end of 2016, its official membership was over half a million, making it the largest of any political party in Europe (Labour Party, 2016).[2] Likewise, its two youth wings, Labour Students (for young people in further and higher education) and Young Labour (for young people aged 14–26) have experienced considerable growth in paid up members (Pickard, 2018b). Whilst the detrimental austerity policies and youth policies of the Conservative governments, as well as the proliferation of digital technologies go some way to explain the rejuvenation of the Labour Party's membership and traditional politics, two other key factors have been influential. Namely, Jeremy Corbyn became the new leader of the Labour Party in September 2015, and immediately afterwards the organisation Momentum was founded to support his leadership. Young people have been very active in Momentum and this grassroots network has channelled their energy, enthusiasm and expertise in digital technologies, as part of its ambition for a leftist participatory democracy.

This chapter explores the roles played by Momentum in the regeneration of interest in traditional politics among many young people and the roles young supporters of Momentum have played in regenerating the Labour Party. It focuses on the important relationship between Momentum and young people. How have Momentum and young people regenerated traditional politics in Britain? In the chapter, I first outline the genesis, creation, organisation, ideology and goals of Momentum. I then examine Momentum's supporters and members, before analysing its campaigning methods and campaigns especially via social media. The chapter goes on to deal with some of the criticisms made of Momentum and concludes by addressing its prospects.

Refounding Labour to Include Grassroots Support: 'A New Kind of Politics'

Soon after Ed Miliband became leader of the Labour Party and Leader of the Opposition in September 2010, he announced he wanted to fundamentally reorganise the party in a bid to modernise it (as did Tony Blair with the rewriting of Clause IV of the party's constitution in the mid-1990s). His reasoning was based on the notion that greater involvement of Labour sympathisers would "strengthen democratic participation in the Labour Party" (Dawson, 2016, p. 16). Ed Miliband's pronouncement led to a consultation paper entitled *Refounding Labour: A Party for the New Generation* that formulated a series of recommendations, which were then outlined in *Refounding Labour to Win* (Labour Party, 2011). In particular, it introduced the concept of a 'Registered Supporters Scheme' with the reasoning that "these supporters can be mobilised to back local campaigns and add to local party efforts at election time; be invited to local events and be consulted on local and national matters by email" (Labour Party, 2011, p. 5). It also considered allowing these non-members of the Labour Party to vote in leadership elections.

The recommendations were backed massively at the Labour Party annual conference in 2011. Subsequently, the *Collins Review* made further recommendations on the reorganisation of the Labour Party (Collins, 2014). Many of the original ambitions expressed on reshaping the party were largely watered down, but two changes were voted in with a big majority, at a special Labour Party conference held in March 2014: who could vote in a leadership election and how. There was thus a key shift away from the longstanding tripartite electoral college system, consisting of (1) Members of the Parliamentary Labour Party (PLP) (Westminster

Members of Parliament—MPs and Members of the European Parliament—MEPs), (2) Trade unions and affiliated socialist societies, and (3) Labour Party members, where each group had a third of the votes (regardless of the number of people in that group). It was replaced by a One Member One Vote (OMOV) electoral system (with no multiple voting) for each of three groups (1) Labour Party members, (2) Affiliated supporters (including trade union members), and (3) Non-member 'registered supporters' having paid the nominal sum of £3. This moved decisional power away from the National Executive Committee (NEC) of the Labour Party, Labour MPs and trade unions to ordinary members and supporters: the grassroots.

The Labour Party lost the 7 May 2015 general election and its leader Ed Miliband immediately resigned as party leader, triggering a leadership election within his party under the new rules. Four Labour MPs were nominated by fellow MPs to stand for election: three moderate or right-wing candidates Andy Burnham, Yvette Cooper and Liz Kendall, as well as the radical Jeremy Corbyn who obtained enough support with 36 nominations from Labour MPs just before the deadline, on 31 July 2015 (to go forward candidates required nominations from 15% of the 232 Labour MPs, i.e. 35 MPs). The leadership electoral campaign took place over the summer with voting from 14 August to 10 September and the winner was announced on 12 September 2015, a few days before the Labour Party annual conference.

The number of people able to vote in the Labour leadership election was tripled by the surge in individuals (re)joining the Labour Party or becoming registered supporters online, including many young people.[3] Consequently, over half a million people were eligible to take part in the ballot for the Labour leader and deputy leader; 54% were full party members, 26% were affiliated supporters (mostly trade union members) and 20% were registered supporters who had paid £3. Three quarters of the eligible electorate voted (76.23%), and the vast majority of votes were cast online: 343,995 (81.3%) "making it the UK's largest ever online ballot" (BBC, 2015). Strikingly, Jeremy Corbyn won decisively among all three groups, in a landslide victory, which he would have won even without the votes of the new registered supporters (see Table 7.1). The success of the outsider whose nomination by certain fellow MPs was only to 'broaden the debate' and 'widen the field' was not at all expected at the outset of the leadership election campaign. The new electoral system that shifted the power balance and enfranchised registered supporters explains much of

Table 7.1 Results of the Labour Party leadership election, Britain, 2015

Candidate	Total %	Total Votes	Party members %	Party members Votes	Affiliated supporters %	Affiliated supporters Votes	Registered supporters %	Registered supporters Votes
Jeremy Corbyn	59.48	251,417	49.59	121,751	57.61	41,217	83.76	88,449
Andy Burnham	19.04	80,462	22.69	55,698	26.00	18,604	05.83	6,160
Yvette Cooper	17.02	71,928	22.18	54,470	12.64	9,043	07.97	8,415
Liz Kendall	04.46	18,857	05.54	13,601	03.75	2,682	02.44	2,574
Total	100.00	422,664	100.00	245,520	100.00	71,546	100.00	105,598

Eligible voters: 554,272, turnout: 422,871 (76.29%), spoilt ballots: 207

Source: The Labour Party (2015) Results of the Labour leadership elections

his success, but also the campaign methods employed to reach out to sympathisers of Jeremy Corbyn, especially young people, which later would be used by Momentum.

#JezWeCan, #JezWeDid

As well as the fundamental changes to rules about who could vote in the Labour leadership election, the political ideology, policies and personality of Jeremy Corbyn also played an important role in his success, as did the campaigning methods used.[4] As a traditional Socialist, Jeremy Corbyn filled the political vacuum left vacant when the Labour Party shifted to the centre-ground during the late 1980s and 1990s, especially the New Labour years under Tony Blair (1997–2010) considered by many traditionalists to be lacking in values and too moderate.[5] Jeremy Corbyn's traditional Labour left ideology centred on a pro-social justice, pro-economic equality and anti-austerity, anti-war platform appealed to both older traditional left-wing partisans who had felt adrift with New Labour and a new generation of young people enthused by a new Old Labour. Jon Lansman, who led Jeremy Corbyn's Labour leadership campaign (and who would go on to found Momentum) explains:

> Young people, a whole generation, more than one generation of young people, have been presented by some old people with some ideas that they have never come across before and actually they sound quite interesting. If an idea is good, bring it back. (Lansman, 2016a)

Part of the appeal of Jeremy Corbyn as an ideologue politician is that he is considered decent, humble and authentic in the eyes of his sympathisers, but also his adversaries—be they Blairites or Conservatives—although many of the latter view him as ridiculous, deluded and dangerous too. Corbynites, supporters of Jeremy Corbyn, have been ascribed the nickname 'Corbynistas,' which is used pejoratively by both politicians and the media.[6] Indeed, Jeremy Corbyn faced considerable hostility during the Labour leadership campaign from fellow Labour MPs and opposition MPs, as well as the traditional media, which may have worked in his favour, as Seymour suggests:

> With little support from any of the traditional media, Corbyn's campaign turned to social media. [...] Through these means he built his mass

meetings without recourse to the old media that were denying him due publicity, while the other candidates' meetings struggled to attract a dozen or so stragglers despite ample coverage. (Seymour, 2016, p. 15)

Jeremy Corbyn's leadership campaign was based on three intertwined elements aimed at spreading the message and the enthusiasm. First, by organising mass mobilisations including 99 rallies (alluding to Occupy's 'We are the 99%'), where Jeremy Corbyn spoke and enthused sympathetic crowds. Second, by encouraging grassroots supporters to set up and participate in physical events. Third, by using digital technologies to inform and mobilise interest in these events and Jeremy Corbyn via the internet, emailing and social media, especially Twitter. The Twitter handle #JezWeCan was trending throughout the summer of 2015, and there were and have been many other accounts including #JC4PM, #VoteForCorbyn, #VoteCorbyn, #Vote4Corbyn. According to Seymour, "The campaign's ability to summon enthusiastic participation was matched by its online reach, and indeed the two aspects of the campaign were mutually supporting" (Seymour, 2016, p. 22).[7] Young people—but not exclusively—played a fundamental role is this digital campaigning for Jeremy Corbyn.

A database of all the new registered supporters of the Labour Party proved essential to the success of 'Jeremy Corbyn for Leader' campaign. When registering, official supporters provided not only £3 that cumulatively supplied funds to the Labour Party, they also supplied contact details to keep in touch, i.e. an email address, a telephone number and a postcode. This personal data was stored in a database created and owned by Jon Lansman who led Corbyn's leadership campaign. It meant that all the new supporters could be contacted cheaply and efficiently.

In brief, during the 2015 Labour leadership campaign, Jeremy Corbyn seemed to sympathisers as the antidote to the New Labour years associated with Tony Blair when presentation, personality, soundbites and spin trumped substance and ideology. Jeremy Corbyn caught the political imagination of many young people in terms of authentic style and substance, offering a "coherent, inspiring and, crucially, a hopeful vision" (Jones, 2015 August). Jeremy Corbyn also benefitted from an effective leadership campaign centred on digital communication that generated much enthusiasm, which translated into votes for him. As activists and supporters of Jeremy Corbyn, young people were at the heart of his successful campaign that constituted the precursor to Momentum.

Momentum: Old Is the New New

Momentum was launched as a Leftist political organisation in October 2015, following the election of Jeremy Corbyn at the head of the Labour Party the previous month. Crucially, Momentum was founded by Jon(athan) Lansman (born 1957) who had been director of operations for Jeremy Corbyn's Labour leadership campaign. It was not created by a young tech-savvy activist, but by a long-standing friend and political ally of Jeremy Corbyn. He capitalised on his access to the 'Jeremy for Labour Leader' campaign and notably the database of registered supporters who had given their contact details: a political communication goldmine.[8]

Momentum initially described itself as "a network of people and organisations that will continue the energy and enthusiasm of Jeremy's campaign" (Momentum website, 2015 October). Momentum claims to uphold traditional Labour Party values that reflect the Socialist origins of the Labour Party and distances itself from the New Labour years of Tony Blair. Momentum is independent of the Labour Party, but declares it supports the Labour Party and Jeremy Corbyn as leader of it:

> Momentum represents a politics fit for the twenty-first century, a member-led democratic social movement, embedded in the Labour Party and the labour movement, that simultaneously builds popular power and electoral prospects. It has a politics and a purpose: to transform society so that wealth and power lodges in the many, not the few. We are at a point where politics and society shifts. The moment is open. Let's take it. (Schneider, Rees & Klug, 2016 October)

At the start of 2017, Momentum declared on its website that it "works to increase participation and engagement in the party to enable it to win elections and enter Government" (Momentum, 2017).

Six months after its creation, in April 2016, Momentum claimed it had 100,000 online registered supporters, at which point it launched a membership scheme that costs £10 a year for the waged and £5 a year for the unwaged. In January 2017, Momentum claimed on its website, to have over 20,000 members and 200,000 supporters. Momentum supporters can participate in Momentum events, but they cannot stand for office or vote in elections, which only members can do. Momentum also says it has over 150 local groups (https://groups.peoplesmomentum.com), which are "committed to electing a Labour Government and building a fair society that leaves no one behind" (Momentum, 2017 January).

The thousands of supporters who initially joined Momentum by registering online for free or who are now paid up members are by no means all young. Momentum can be divided largely (but not entirely) along generational lines. First, there are the older, veteran, traditional Leftists (including many active trade unionists) who reflect the radical political views of Jeremy Corbyn (and John McDonnell his Shadow Chancellor). They had become disillusioned with the Third Way and Blairism. Second, there are the newly politicised young people, many of whom were not even born when Tony Blair became Prime Minister in 1997.[9] According to Seymour (2016, p. 193) "Jeremy Corbyn's supporters, the potential missionaries of twenty-first-century socialism, are disproportionately young and working class."

Some of these young Momentum supporters are starting out on their political socialisation and political participation. Other young Momentum supporters became politically socialised during recent global, national and local social movements or networks: movementists. Indeed, since the Conservatives came to power in Britain, in 2010, the country has experienced a revival in youth-led protests that form part of a global anti-neoliberal, anti-austerity conversation (see other chapters in this volume). In Britain, these include Occupy London (2011–2012), movements hostile to austerity measures and the increase in university tuition fees, such as UK Uncut and the National Campaign against Fees and Cuts (NCFC), as well as climate camps and anti-fracking protests (see Pickard, 2014a, 2014b, 2018a, 2018b). The radical agenda of ideological politics with the strong emphasis on traditional socialism that is at odds with more centrist politics of the past years is appealing to many young people and comes across as authentic and cool. Young people have found attractive the potential of this fledgling, grassroots political organisation to make a democratic difference through direct democracy and its ethos of encouraging the grassroots to have a say and get involved. Momentum is removed from the shackles of rigid, top-down party structures. It is a less hierarchical, new way of doing politics that functions more like a traditional, horizontal social movement network familiar to young movementists. Moreover, there is a similar sense of belonging to a positive and constructive community. In this way, Momentum asserts that it has energised large numbers of the population who are disillusioned by mainstream politics, especially young people. For Owen Jones, a sympathiser (see Jones, 2016b), "Momentum offers hope to young people who have long been demoralised by politics" (Jones, 2016a, December).

The dynamic and interactive use of social media comes naturally to many in this age group, the so-called 'digital natives' (Prensky, 2001, see also Bessant, 2014). A young woman explains why she joined the Labour Party and then Momentum after the general election defeat of 2015 on Momentum's YouTube channel, Momentum TV:

> [There is] something that young people and that members can use to actually try and make a difference instead of feeling disenfranchised, which so many people do. […]. We do a lot of our politics on the internet and Momentum was a really good members-led, grassroots campaign, involving lots of young people, where we could actually stop talking and start doing things and that really appealed to me. (Momentum TV, 2016 September)

This multi-generational mass membership combined with active and reactive young people online are part of Momentum's strength and they have been fundamental in the organisation's campaigns and campaigning methods.

Spreading the Momentum Message #MomentumGrassroots

Momentum's mass membership and registered supporter network enables the 'Momentum message' to be spread quickly and easily. For Jon Lansman, it is part of Momentum's strategy:

> I think that the mass membership of the party which has flooded in is actually the key to the electoral success that we hope for. We've got over half a million people. That is more people than in any other party in Europe. […] That is half a million people who can have conversations with lots of people—and they want to talk about politics and issues that matter to people and not just knock on doors at election time. […] We can use very large numbers of people who are very motivated to talk to people about the issues that matter to them, to have conversations about policy issues, to persuade people. That is our strategy. (Lansman, 2016b)

Young people are at the heart of Momentum's critical mass whose energy and enthusiasm have played a fundamental role in organising, participating in and informing about Momentum's physical events. They have also been active in spreading the message digitally, by building on tactics used in the 'Jeremy for Leader' campaign.

Physical and digital events are organised by individual supporters and members of Momentum, small local Momentum groups, larger regional umbrella Momentum groups and the Momentum national committee. Across Britain from Aberdeen to Penzance, Momentum has organised rallies, but also community centred activities, such as assemblies, group discussions, debates, forums, public meetings, seminars, informal gatherings, pop-up political education meetings, political literacy events ('People's PPE'), meet ups and policy consultations. Large and small, these have taken place in the streets, in community centres, town halls, chapels, church halls and pubs, etc. Numerous local, national and international subjects have been discussed, including the National Health Service (NHS), social care, 'Corbynomics' and Donald Trump. There have also been more informal Momentum social events, such as music concerts and gigs (#Dance for Corbyn, #Jam for Jez, #Keep Corbyn), film screenings (Ken Loach's *I, Daniel Blake*), pub quizzes, meals ('Curry for Corbyn,' 'Curry and a few words'), picnics and football matches, etc. The emphasis is on community events with people coming together to share in grassroots activities.

Canvassing for Jeremy Corbyn and Labour Party candidates has taken the form of traditional knocking-on-doors and leafleting. But Momentum also initiated a project called 'Calling for Corbyn' using pop-up phone banks. Volunteers come together with their own or supplied laptop computers or tablets and phones to access Momentum's 'Calling for Corbyn' web-app to ring up and canvass potential supporters. The app can also be used by supporters to canvass other voters from home (https://call.peoplesmomentum.com) and participants are encouraged to tweet or post a photo on Facebook of themselves using the phone canvassing web-app including the hashtag #MomentumGrassroots.

In short, pivotal to organising, canvassing, mobilising and informing has been the successful use of volunteer 'Big Organising' where volunteer activists are empowered and trusted with tasks usually "reserved for staffers in other political campaigns" (Klug, Rees, & Schneider, 2016, p. 40) via digital technologies. This is done through Momentum's official communication organs, such as its official Facebook page, Twitter account and YouTube Channel, as well as emailing on a regular basis, etc., but also through member- and supporter-generated material primarily on Facebook, but also on Twitter, Tumblr, YouTube, Instagram, Snapchat, etc.

The use of social media has been fundamental to Momentum's success for several reasons. (1) Social media are a means to bypass traditional media, especially the newspapers that are overwhelming right-wing in Britain and most are vociferously anti-Corbyn and anti-Momentum. (2) Social media provide a direct link between Momentum and grassroots supporters, thus bypassing or overriding formal Labour Party structures, which are generally against Jeremy Corbyn as party leader. (3) Social media gives a voice to the grassroots and allows them to generate content, which reflects the more participatory and direct democracy ambitions of Momentum. (4) Social media create a sense of community so essential to Momentum. (5) Social media is almost cost free in both financial and effort terms. (6) Social media is fast (for information and rebuttal) and has a large reach. (7) Social media is in the moment and of the moment, capturing and encapsulating the zeitgeist of Momentum and the enthusiasm it engenders.

By harnessing social media thanks to the database, Momentum has been able to be in touch fast and wide to key segments of the population. Young people who generally have free time and energy to invest in campaigning and more digital technology knowledge than older age group have been participating enthusiastically in these activities.

Campaigning for Corbyn and Labour

Momentum campaigns for Jeremy Corbyn played a fundamental role in his re-election as the Labour Party leader in September 2016, following the leadership challenge bid from within the Parliamentary Labour Party (PLP), which underlined the divisions within Labour. Momentum also campaigns to encourage people to join the Labour Party; it is involved in mobilising Labour Party members and supporters for Labour candidates in elections (local elections, council elections, Mayoral elections and by-elections):

> Momentum exists to channel the energy and enthusiasm from the Jeremy Corbyn for Labour Leader campaign, using the experiences and creativity of ordinary people to increase power and activity at a grassroots level, based on the principles of participatory democracy and solidarity. Through this process, we aim to make people more powerful in society and build Labour into the transformative governing party of the twenty-first century. (Momentum website, 'A New Kind of Politics,' January 2017)

During the 2016 Labour Party annual conference, in Liverpool, Momentum hosted 'The World Transformed' event (with music, arts, politics and culture), which it described "as part of the Labour Party conference fringe." It was condemned by opponents in the party as an alternative Labour conference event that snubbed the official Labour Party, adding to party disunity.

More generally, Momentum holds debates and discussions across the country on local, national and international issues (see above). The first specific Momentum campaign, 'Democracy SOS,' was launched in December 2015 to encourage people to register on the electoral roll in order to be able to vote in elections. This is due to changes made by the Conservative-Liberal Democrat coalition government to voter registration from household registration to Individual Electoral Registration (IER), which disenfranchised thousands of potential voters, especially young students (see Pickard, 2015, 2018b).

Following an online survey of Momentum supporters, in March 2016, the priority campaign for Momentum became 'Defending the NHS' (National Health Service). 'Momentum NHS' is "a national campaign to stand up for the NHS against further Tory cuts and privatisation." After another consultation of members, Momentum launched 'Your Referendum' to campaign in favour of remaining in the European Union prior to the 'Brexit' referendum (that took place on 23 June 2016), providing local Momentum groups with resources to facilitate campaigning across the country.

Lastly, Momentum launched its 'Your Party' campaign, in November 2016, calling for Momentum members to have a greater say in the Labour Party, to transform Labour into a party led by its members, and a party capable of winning power. Part of this initiative is the 'Grassroots Now' campaign: "Change happens from the bottom up, and we can all be agents of that change. Get involved in #GrassrootsNow today" (Momentum, 2017), which emphasises Momentum's ideology.

Thus, while Momentum campaigns for Jeremy Corbyn, the Labour Party and very traditional Labour Party policies, it has been accused of dividing the Labour Party and being the root of its demise. Further criticisms have been made of Momentum as examined in the next section.

CRITICISMS OF CORBYNISTAS: MILITANT MARK 2

Momentum has been vilified vigorously in the overwhelmingly right-wing British press, by the Left (especially moderate and centrist Labour supporters, such as the Blairite group Progress), as well as Conservatives and Liberal Democrats. Criticism has focused on two connected issues.

First, there is speculation that Momentum is an extremist movement and that it has been infiltrated by members of extremist groups. These entryists would be seeking to influence the future direction of Labour Party without being members of it. More specifically, they would aim to take Momentum (and by extension the Labour Party) further left and to introduce mandatory reselection of MPs before elections (Diamond, 2016, p. 22) as a way to deselect moderate, centrist or 'conservative' Labour MPs. Malevolent entryists would be from the TUSC (Trade Union and Socialist Coalition), the Socialist Party (formerly Militant), the Socialist Workers Party (SWP), the Alliance of Workers Liberty, and the Green Party among others. There are very distinct echoes here of the Militant Tendency (Trotskyist) faction that penetrated the Labour Party during the 1970s and 1980s (see Crick, 1984). Importantly, Militant was particularly "successful among the young" (Crick, 1984, p. 244)[10] and the current allegation is that Momentum is a 'Militant Tendency 2.'

Second, there is conjecture that members of Momentum are aggressively harassing moderate Labour MPs. Abuse would include "online bullying, often of a misogynistic, sometimes threatening nature" (Prince, 2015, p. 371). For example, Momentum activists have been accused of cyberbullying, i.e. sending "threatening" emails (from the same email addresses used by Momentum supporters) and intimidating social media messages to Labour MPs (notably to Stella Creasy) who voted in favour of airstrikes against Syria in Parliament during the autumn of 2015. Moreover, "recipients of such abuse complain that the occasional statements from Corbyn and the Momentum leadership calling on supporters to be respectful are both insufficient and often tardy" (Prince, 2015, p. 378). When Jeremy Corbyn was asked by Labour MP Chuka Umunna during a Home Affairs Committee meeting whether Momentum should be shut down, in reaction to these accusations, the Labour leader replied evasively:

> Momentum is a place where many people who have come into political activity for the first time, or returned to political activity, are activating themselves on housing issues, on transport issues, on wage issues, and many,

many other issues. Surely that degree of engagement in political activity is a good thing? (Corbyn, 2016 July 4)

Momentum launched a national initiative 'Momentum Kids,' in September 2016, "to provide childcare for those with caring responsibilities who want to be politically active." It was dubbed "Tiny Trots" (a term used by Liberal Democrats leader Tim Farron)[11] and lambasted in much of the media, being described, for example, as "the creepiest thing I've ever heard of," by Anna Rhodes, in *The Independent* (Rhodes, 2016). Tom Watson, Deputy Leader of the Labour Party also claimed that Momentum meetings were infiltrated by Trotskyists and he commented: "I'm not a member of Momentum, they look like a bit of a rabble to me" (Watson, 2015 December 4). Significantly, Watson evoked the need for Momentum to have a code of conduct about how people should behave on social media.

Momentum initially denied claims about infiltration, intimidation and bullying within its ranks and aims to deselect moderate Labour MPs. However, it took measures at the start of 2017 to address these issues, as it moved on to the next stage of its existence.

Moving Momentum Forward

Momentum's over 20,000 supporters were asked in December 2016 via email and social media to participate in an online survey about how it should be organised and run in the future. According to the organisation, a substantial majority took part in the consultation (for results see Momentum, 2016). On the basis of their views, Momentum's founder Jon Lansman dissolved the existing governing structures, including the National Coordinating Group (NCG) and established a new steering committee in January 2017, consisting of three permanent staff members—a National Organiser (Groups and Organising) Emma Rees, a National Organiser (Communication, Campaigns and Digital) Adam Klug, and a Group Development and Volunteer Coordinator Santiago Bell-Bradford. They approved a new constitution and a Code of Ethics that came into force on 10 January 2017 (Momentum, 'constitution,' 2017). At the same time, Jon Lansman resigned as director of Momentum (though he retains access to the database of contact details) and he was replaced by Christine Shawcroft. Furthermore, decision-making in Momentum will no longer based on delegate votes, but by a One Member One Vote (OMOV) system.

Moreover, Momentum underlined its will to affiliate with the Labour Party. It announced that existing members of Momentum would have to be/become members of the Labour Party before July 2017 and all new members of Momentum will have to be members of the Labour Party. Thus, to join Momentum, three criteria must be met: "I am a member of the Labour party and no other political party. I also support the aims of Momentum and agree to abide by its constitution, including the code of ethics and equal opportunities policy. I am 14 years old or over" (Momentum website, 'join,' 2017 January).

These important changes to Momentum perform multiple roles. Officially they have been carried out to democratise the organisation, although they have garnered complaints centred on the exact opposite because there was no official vote by delegates or members, only a consultation of members and supporters. The modifications were carried out no doubt in an effort to settle disputes and divisions within Momentum, and to prepare its future. They also distance Momentum from elements who have been expelled or suspended from the Labour Party. It is an attempt for Momentum to distance itself from extremist entryism and stop entryists taking decisional roles within the organisation. It is also an attempt to dampen speculation that Momentum is trying to bring about the deselection of non-Corbynite MPs before the next general election and it enables Jeremy Corbyn to disassociate himself from extremist factions. The official move of Momentum towards the Labour Party opens the prospect of its official affiliation. All these changes may well change the nature of Momentum and reduce its appeal among young people (Avril, 2018).

Political parties are diversifying the channels through which individuals can engage with them (Scarrow, 2015) and there is a blurring of "the boundaries between formal dues paying and looser modes of affiliation" (Chadwick & Stromer-Galley, 2016), as well as "multi-speed" party membership (Margetts, 2006). The Labour Party in Britain, like other traditional political parties around the world is being renewed "from the outside in," largely due to young people "as digitally enabled citizens breathe new life into an old form by partly remaking it in their own participatory image" (Chadwick & Stromer-Galley, 2016, p. 3). The transition to being affiliated with the Labour Party is uncertain (Avril, 2018). It is not clear whether such a shift from the more informal and community based Momentum towards the more staid and rigid Labour Party will appeal to young people, or whether the Labour Party will reach out to young members of Momentum.[12]

Conclusion

Momentum was created to harness the energy and enthusiasm released when Jeremy Corbyn became a candidate in the Labour Party leadership election, which he won convincingly in September 2015, a victory confirmed by his re-election in October 2016. His landslide wins were made possible due to many intertwined factors, including changes to the Labour leadership electoral system, the use of digital technologies as a means of political communication and the dynamism of his numerous young supporters as political activists.

Momentum rejuvenated the Labour Party, participating in the substantial growth in membership and supporters. Many of these are young people who are drawn to Momentum because they are drawn towards Jeremy Corbyn as an ideological leader, his traditional Socialist policies and his hopeful message. This echoes or parallels the popularity among young people of Bernie Sanders as a Democrat presidential candidate presidential campaign in 2016, in the United States. At the same time, the hitherto more informal nature of Momentum that functions outside the rigid Labour structure appeals to young people in the way horizontal, less hierarchical social movements often do. The effective use of digital technologies, as well as the community spirit that drives it have played to Momentum's strengths and made it attractive among young people. Young people have found politics energising, inspirational and cool due to both the medium and message of Momentum.

At the start of 2017, Momentum is entering a new stage of its existence. After months of internal divisions, the organisation has introduced structural and constitutional reforms that will be decisive in its future capacity to mobilise and enthuse its members and supporters of all ages. Tribalism has always existed in the Leftist politics, and Momentum has been divided and has divided the Labour Party, whilst generating interest in left-wing politics. Momentum cannot be everything to everyone on the Left. It galvanises the left of the party—especially young members and supporters—but it disgruntles more moderate and centrist members, especially the Parliamentary Labour Party (PLP), i.e. Labour MPs who consider Momentum to be a source of extremism leading to the un-electability of the party. Jeremy Corbyn also repels many in the voting public at large who have been exposed to substantial media negativity surrounding both him and Momentum. Moreover, Momentum is indelibly linked to the fortunes of Jeremy Corbyn, which raises the question of what will happen when he is no longer leader of the Labour Party.

Momentum has been the political awakening for many young people and young people have been the life-blood of Momentum. A new generation of hopeful and positive young people has been drawn to the fundamentals of traditional politics—being a member of a political party and voting in elections—at a time when a crisis of populism and anti-politics sentiment is abound. Young people and the youth vote will be crucial to the fortunes of Jeremy Corbyn and the Labour Party, as part of the regeneration of politics in Britain.[13]

Notes

1. According to the British Election Study (BES) based on surveys after general election, the turnout rate of 18–24-year-olds went up from 62.5 in 1979, to 63.9% in 1983, to 66.6% in 1987, to 67.3% in 1992, down to 40.4% in 2001 and to 38.2% in 2005, then up to 51.8% in 2010 and to 58.0% in 2015. However, turnout of young people remains lower than the average for the British population: 59.4% in 2001, 61.3% in 2005, 65.0% in 2010, 66.1% in 2015. Ipsos MORI electoral turnout statistics are estimates based on voting-intention surveys conducted in the run-up to general elections and their statistics are lower for 18–24-year-olds: 39% in 2001, 37% in 2005, 44% in 2010 and 43% in 2015 (Ipsos MORI, 2010, 2015). See Pickard (2015) and (2018b) for further discussion.
2. In May 2015, the day before the general election, the Labour Party had 201,000 members; by the end of the year it had 400,000 members, which went up to 515,000 by July 2016. At the end of December 2016, the Labour Party claimed it had a membership of 550,000.
3. According to a YouGov survey of new full members joining the Labour Party after May 2015 the average age was 51 years of which 10% were members of Momentum (Bale, 2016). Registered supporters of the Labour Party, as well as Momentum supporters and members do not pay full membership fees and so may be younger than full paid up members, and they might be using the registered supporters scheme as a cheap 'taster.'
4. Jeremy Corbyn was a backbencher MP for 32 years from 1983 to 2015. During this time, he was an especially 'rebellious' Labour MP who defied the Labour Party whip more than 400 times in the House of Commons, i.e. he voted against his own party when it was in and out of government (see Cowley, 2016).
5. Tony Blair stated in a speech at an event hosted by Progress (a pro-New Labour group) on 22 July 2015 that "I would not want to win on an *old-fashioned* Leftist platform." And during an interview afterwards, he

commented about anyone contemplating voting for Jeremy Corbyn as Labour leader because "my heart says I should really be with that politics—well *get a transplant* because that's just dumb."

6. 'Corbynistas' is used in a derogatory way by some of Corbyn's critics. It alludes to the 'Sandinistas,' members of the Sandinista National Liberation Front (*Frente Sandinista de Liberación Nacional*) in Nicaragua named after Augusto César Sandino who led the country's resistance against its occupation by the United States, during the 1930s. Jeremy Corbyn was one of 28 signatories of an early day motion in Parliament in 1990 that "congratulates the Sandinistas on their many achievements" (House of Commons, 1990).

7. According to Ben Sellers (cited in Seymour, 2016, pp. 22–23) who coordinated Jeremy Corbyn's social media team "There were three strands to the social media campaign. There were the official [social media] accounts which consisted mainly of standard fare, official statements and so on. They grew huge, naturally. But there were also a number of semi-official accounts which we ran, where we had contact with press offices and people working on the ground in the offices in London, with whom we could discuss rebuttal strategies informally. We also had a slight distance from them. […] Then there was a huge volume of people doing smaller projects that were nothing to do with us or even necessarily the Labour Party—pages like 'Kittens 4 Corbyn', and so on. We had some tangible contact with these pages, and we could discuss things with them now and again, but they actually did a lot of the rebuttal work off their own back." See also Sellers (2015).

8. Jeremy Corbyn Campaign (Supporters) Ltd. was registered at Companies House on 24 June 2015. Its name was changed to Momentum Campaign Ltd. on 23 October 2015. Its name was changed again on 8 July 2016 to Jeremy for Labour Limited (Companies House, 2017).

9. According to Klug, Rees and Schneider (2016, p. 37): "Momentum reflects the diverse coalition of people who supported Jeremy for leader. Within this group, we can pick out four main tendencies, with the caveat that these overlap and are not comprehensive: (1) Extra-parliamentary, social movement activism—particularly post-financial crisis movements along the lines of UK Uncut and Occupy. (2) More traditional left-wing protest coalitions, such as the People's Assembly; and Stop the War Coalition. (3) The existing Labour left—its remaining MPs, its organisations such as the Labour Representation Committee, and others who "kept the flame alive" in the party. (4) The left of the trade union movement, including both unions that have been affiliated to Labour all along, and those such as the Fire Brigade Union that are now reaffiliating."

10. For excellent analysis of the popularity of Militant among young people, see Crick (1984).

11. Tim Farron at the Liberal Party annual conference, Brighton, 20 September 2016: "One thing you cannot accuse Jeremy Corbyn of is short-term thinking. His lot have waited over a hundred years for this. Finally, they have taken over the Labour Party. Like all good Marxists, they have seized the means of production. They have even seized the nurseries too, opening branches of 'Momentum Kids.' Otherwise known as 'Child Labour,' or my particular favourite 'Tiny Trots.'"
12. In January 2017, there was no weblink to the Momentum website from the Labour Party, Labour Students or Young Labour websites, but weblinks to Labour Party websites from the Momentum website.
13. I would like to thank Emmanuelle Avril for her helpful comments on this chapter.

References

Avril, E. (2018). The "movementisation" of the Labour party and the future of Labour organising. In E. Avril & Y. Béliard (Eds.), *Labour united and divided from the 1830s to the present.* Manchester: Manchester University Press, Chapter 14, [forthcoming].

Bale, T. (2016). Corbyn's Labour: Survey of post-2015 Labour members and supporters. Retrieved from http://www.qmul.ac.uk/media/news/items/178403.html

Bessant, J. (2014). *Democracy bytes: New media and new politics and generational change.* Basingstoke: Palgrave Macmillan.

British Broadcasting Company (BBC). (2015, September 12). The Labour leadership results in full. Retrieved September 13, 2015, from http://www.bbc.com/news/uk-politics-34221155

British Election Study (BES). (2015). *British Election Study,* 2015. Retrieved from http://www.britishelectionstudy.com

Chadwick, A., & Stromer-Galley, J. (2016). Digital media, power, and democracy in parties and election campaigns: Party decline or party renewal? *The International Journal of Press/Politics, 21*(3), 283–293.

Collins, R. (2014). *Building a one nation labour party. The Collins review into Labour Party reform.* London: The Labour Party.

Companies House. (2017). Company history 09655767. Retrieved from https://beta.companieshouse.gov.uk/company/09655767/filing-history

Corbyn, J. (2016, July 4). Home Affairs Committee meeting. House of Commons.

Cowley, P. (2016, May 16). Jeremy Corbyn and the Labour Whip. *Revolts. Philip Cowley and Mark Stuart's research on Parliament.* Retrieved February 17, 2017, from http://revolts.co.uk/?p=932

Crick, M. (1984). *Militant.* London: Faber and Faber.

Dawson, M. (2016, October 4). Jeremy Corbyn, the PLP and historical visions of the Labour Party. *Discover Society, 37*.

Diamond, P. (2016). Assessing the performance of UK opposition leaders: Jeremy Corbyn's "straight talking, honest politics". *Politics and Governance, 4*(2), 15–24.

Farron, T. (2016, September 20). *Leader's speech*. Liberal Democrat annual conference. Brighton.

Grasso, M. T. (2016). *Generations, political participation and social change in Western Europe*. London: Routledge.

House of Commons. (1990). 'Nicaragua and the Sandinistas.' Early Day Motion 621. House of Commons. Retrieved from http://www.parliament.uk/edm/1989-90/621

Howker, E., & Malik, S. (2013). *Jilted generation. How Britain has bankrupted its youth*. 2nd edition. London: Icons Books.

Ipsos MORI. (2010). *How Britain voted since 1974*. Retrieved from https://www.ipsos-mori.com/researchpublications/researcharchive/101/How-Britain-Voted-Since-October-1974.aspx

Ipsos MORI. (2015). *How Britain voted in* 2015. Retrieved from https://www.ipsos-mori.com/researchpublications/researcharchive/3575/How-Britain-voted-in-2015

Jones, O. (2015, August 3). Jeremy Corbyn's supporters aren't mad—They're fleeing a bankrupt New Labour. *The Guardian*. Retrieved from https://www.theguardian.com/commentisfree/2015/aug/03/jeremy-corbyn-new-labour-centre-left

Jones, O. (2016a, December 7). Momentum is a beacon of hope. It must be saved from the saboteurs. *The Guardian*. Retrieved from https://www.theguardian.com/global/commentisfree/2016/dec/07/momentum-hope-saved-saboteurs-sectarian-labour

Jones, O. (2016b, December 8). My articles on Momentum. Retrieved from https://medium.com/@OwenJones84/my-articles-on-momentum-and-trotskyists-281ec6b7163c#.f2bcbk2ge

Jones, O. (2017, January 12). The Tory policy for young people in Britain is victimisation by design. *The Guardian*. Retrieved from https://www.theguardian.com/commentisfree/2017/jan/12/tory-policy-young-people-britain-wellbeing

Klug, A., Rees, E., & Schneider, J. (2016, May 31). Momentum: A new kind of politics. *Renewal: A Journal of Labour Politics*, 36–44. Retrieved from https://www.lwbooks.co.uk/sites/default/files/ren24.2_05klug_rees_schneider.pdf

Labour Party (The). (2011). *Refounding Labour to win*. London: The Labour Party. Retrieved from http://www.leftfutures.org/wp-content/uploads/2011/10/Refounding-Labour-to-win.pdf

Labour Party (The). (2015). Results of the Labour leadership elections. Retrieved from http://www.labour.org.uk/blog/entry/results-of-the-labour-leadership-and-deputy-leadership-election

Labour Party (The). (2016, July 7). Brexit bounce means Labour now has over half a million members. Retrieved from http://labourlist.org/2016/07/post-referendum-boost-means-labour-now-has-over-half-a-million-members

Lansman, J. (2016a, June 20). *At Lunch With.* BBC Radio 4. Retrieved from http://www.bbc.co.uk/programmes/p03yxqt8

Lansman, J. (2016b, October 15). *Week in Westminster.* BBC Radio 4. Retrieved from http://www.bbc.co.uk/programmes/b07z2f3q

Margetts, H. (2006). The cyber party. In R. Katz & W. Crotty (Eds.), *The handbook of party politics* (pp. 528–535). London: Sage.

Momentum. (2015–2017). Momentum official website. Retrieved from http://www.peoplesmomentum.com

Momentum. (2016). Momentum Members' Survey 2016/17. Retrieved February 27, 2017, from https://d3n8a8pro7vhmx.cloudfront.net/momentum/pages/939/attachments/original/1484068264/Momentum_members_survey_16-17.pdf?1484068264

Momentum. (2017). Constitution. Retrieved February 27, 2017, from https://d3n8a8pro7vhmx.cloudfront.net/momentum/pages/939/attachments/original/1484079394/momentum-constitution.pdf?1484079394

Momentum TV. (2016, September 19). Young People talk about Momentum. Momentum YouTube channel. Retrieved from https://www.youtube.com/watch?v=wPBn_fuvx_o&index=6&list=PLV2Z4fYa903sY2Ed0AALRLGH-ChqWUJXBe

Pickard, S. (2014a). Productive protest? The contested higher education reforms in England under the Coalition Government. In E. Avril & J. Neem (Eds.), *Democracy, participation and contestation: Civil society, governance and the future of liberal democracy* (pp. 93–106). London & New York: Routledge.

Pickard, S. (2014b). Keep them kettled! Protesting and policing and anti-social behaviour in Britain. In S. Pickard (Ed.), *Anti-social behaviour in Britain. Victorian and contemporary perspectives* (pp. 77–91). Basingstoke: Palgrave Macmillan.

Pickard, S. (2015). Trying to turn up the turnout. Youth wings and the youth vote in the 2015 general election. *Revue Française de Civilisation Britannique— French Journal of British Studies, 20*(3). Retrieved from https://rfcb.revues.org/503

Pickard, S. (2018a). The nature of environmental activism among young people in Britain in the twenty-first century. In: D. Haigron & B. Prendiville, (Eds.), *Political ecology and environmentalism in Britain* [forthcoming].

Pickard, S. (2018b). *Politics, protest and young people. Political participation and dissent in Britain in the 21st century.* London: Palgrave Macmillan [forthcoming].

Prensky, M. (2001). Digital natives, digital immigrants. *On the Horizon, 9*(5).
Prince, R. (2015). *Comrade Corbyn. A very unlikely coup.* London: Biteback Publishing.
Rhodes, A. (2016, September 19). Momentum kids—Or Corbyn's tiny Trots. *The Independent Online.* Retrieved from http://www.independent.co.uk/voices/the-momentum-kids-plan-or-corbyn-s-tiny-trots-as-some-would-have-it-is-the-creepiest-thing-ive-ever-a7316216.html
Scarrow, S. (2015). *Beyond party members: Changing approaches to partisan mobilization.* Oxford: Oxford University Press.
Schneider, J., Rees, E., & Klug, A. (2016, October 29). What is Momentum? *Red Pepper.* Retrieved from http://www.redpepper.org.uk/what-is-momentum
Sellers, B. (2015). #JezWeDid: From Red Labour to Jeremy Corbyn—A tale from social media. *The world turned upside down.* Retrieved from https://theworldturnedupsidedownne.wordpress.com/2015/09/27/jezwedid-from-red-labour-to-jeremy-corbyn-a-tale-from-social-media
Seymour, R. (2016). *Corbyn. The strange rebirth of radical politics.* London: Verso Books.
Watson, T. (2015, December 4). *Today programme.* BBC. Radio 4.

Sarah Pickard is Senior Lecturer at the Université Sorbonne Nouvelle, Paris, France. Her research in contemporary Youth Studies focuses on the interaction between youth policy and youth politics. She is publishing *Politics, Protest and Young People. Political Participation and Dissent in Britain in the 21st Century* with Palgrave Macmillan in 2018.

CHAPTER 8

Right-Wing Populism and Young 'Stormers': Conflict in Democratic Politics

Judith Bessant

INTRODUCTION

The political landscape of contemporary global politics is being redefined by the rise of right-wing populist parties and movements that are proving to have a powerful appeal to many young people. The shift rightwards is generally evident in political successes enjoyed by ultra-right populists in 2016 including Nigel Farage's role as then leader of the United Kingdom Independence Party's (UKIP) in the Brexit referendum campaign, in the election of President Rodrigo Duterte in the Philippines, and the election of Donald Trump in Presidential election in the United States. While these instances of electoral support for the right are new, the rise of right-wing populism is not. Right-wing populist political movements and parties have persistently attracted support over the last century, not least of all from young people.[1]

Although populist far-right movements waned immediately after the Second World War, they began resurfacing in the 1960s.[2] Contemporary

J. Bessant (✉)
School of Global, Urban and Social Studies, Royal Melbourne Institute of Technology (RMIT) University, Melbourne, VIC, Australia

support for right-wing populism was galvanised by the 2008 Great Recession (and austerity policies) creating a series of global socio-economic crises. Added to this was the refugee and humanitarian crisis triggered by war in Syria after 2011, and sporadic Islamist terrorist attacks in England, France and Germany and Spain (Fielitz & Laloire, 2017; Goodwin, 2010). From that time, most European states witnessed the rise of right-wing populist parties which began attracting substantial electoral support in local and national elections.[3] Since 2015, electoral support has also grown significantly for right-wing populist and ultra-nationalist political parties.[4]

While many of these contemporary parties and movements rely on mobilising anti-Muslim, immigrant sentiment and nationalist politics, their interests are broader (Meleagrou-Hitchens & Brun, 2013; Wodak, 2015). Like earlier populist movements, contemporary populists rely on narratives about threats to a homogenous 'national community' (*gemeinschaft*) or 'people' by 'Others' who can be Jews, Muslims, African-Americans, refugees, gays, or women who are represented as minorities whose interests are allegedly being promoted at the expense of 'the people's' interests by corrupt elites, i.e., professional politicians and media conglomerates (Fritzsche, 1990). The populist party positions itself as the authentic voice of 'the people' (Wodak, 2015; Wodak, Mral, & Khosravinik, 2013).

These features of ultra-right politics may help explain why populists prefer direct democracy models including the extensive use of social media to inform, mobilise support and circumvent mainstream media (Greven, 2016, p. 1). They loathe mainstream or status quo parties and rely on truculent styles of political communication and conspiratorial narratives portraying a world as dominated by powerful minorities and elites who use political correctness to deny them and 'the people' their viewpoints and the legitimacy of their position. The rhetorical styles of ultra-right populists is one that oversteps conventional modes of respectful discourse, and are contemptuous of norms that define civility and rely on emotional appeals, personal insult, trolling and invented or 'alternative facts' or 'post-truth politics.'[5] Conspiracy theories and biological or generative violent metaphors are used to reduce the diversity of the world to race, gender and eugenics style 'facts' about genetic supremacy and rehearsals of 'master race' propaganda.[6]

While most chapters in this book document various democratic and progressive political traditions, it is important to acknowledge that some young people are also drawn to right-wing populist politics. Here I ask what role do young people play in the growth of right-wing populist politics? As I show in this chapter, we have considerable evidence of significant levels of support by some young people for right-wing populist politics. Moreover, some of the same motives and rationales that move young people toward democratic and leftist politics identified in other chapters are evident among young right-wing populists. In both cases, we see the transformation of powerful emotions into action (Castells, 2012, p. 29). Many young right-wing populists like those I focus on this this chapter, who are 'members' of The *Daily Stormer*, express hope and confidence they can make changes toward what they see as a good life through their politics.

YOUNG PEOPLE AND RIGHT-WING POPULISM

Based on their extensive survey work, Mierina and Korojeva point to a recent and notable rise in support for ultra-right populism among young Europeans (2015, pp. 183–205). Many others confirm that increasing numbers of young people are attracted to far-right politics (Koronaiou, Lagos, Sakellariou, Kymionis, & Chiotaki-Poulou, 2015, pp. 231–249; Pilkington, 2014b). The establishment of the French Identitarian movement (*Génération Identitaire*), likewise affirms this finding (Virchow, 2015). *Génération Identitaire* was established in 2002 by the youth wing of *Bloc Identitaire* to oppose non-European migration into Europe and to organise anti-Islamic 'defence groups.' The Identitarian movement now has active chapters not only in France, but also in Austria, Denmark, Germany, Italy, Lithuania, Poland and Slovenia. Likewise, researchers investigating the English Defence League (EDL) found young people provide much of the leadership and the rank-and-file membership (Pilkington, 2014a, 2014b). A Demos study of the English Defence League estimated the number of active members to be 'at least' 25,000–30,000 of whom 72% were under 30 (Bartlett & Littler, 2011, p. 5).

The popularity of right-wing populism is producing electoral effects. The National Front in France and the Freedom Party (*Freiheitliche Partei Österreichs*) in Austria are examples of far-right nationalist parties getting increasing support from younger voters. Although the National Front did not win the regional elections in 2015, it did pick up 35% of votes from 18-to-34-year-olds in the first round. In state parliamentary elections in Austria's Vienna district, the Freedom Party gained 24% of the vote among under-30-year-olds in 2015. By May 2016, a poll taken by the Institut français d'opinion publique (Ifop) found that between 27%

and 31% of young French (aged 18–25) supported Marine Le Pen and the right-wing populist *Front National* (Sibum, 2016). In Germany, support by young people for the right-wing populist *(Alternative für Deutschland)* grows. According to the Berlin political research institute Infratest dimap, Alternative for Germany was the first choice of 26% of voters aged 18–24 in the regional Saxony-Anhalt elections held in March 2016, compared with 16% for Angela Merkel's Christian Democratic Union (*Christlich Demokratische Union Deutschlands*) and only 11% for The German Greens (*Bündnis 90/Die Grünen*) and Social Democratic Party (*Sozialdemokratische Partei Deutschlands*).

While researchers agree we are seeing a significant rise in ultra-right populism among young people, they disagree about the reasons for this development and the appeal of right-wing populism to younger people. Some like Grasso, Farrall, Gray, Hay & Jennings (2017) argue it is the product of long-term 'political socialisation.' People growing-up under Margaret Thatcher's and John Major's governments (1979–1997) (now 41–58 years-old) and under Tony Blair's and Gordon Brown's New Labour governments (1997–2010) (now aged 27–40) have more right-authoritarian political values about issues like income redistribution, welfare and crime (Grasso et al., 2017). Others point to the combination of the post-2008 crash, subsequent widespread youth unemployment, austerity measures and the reaction to large numbers of immigrants and fear of Islamic terrorism (Jackson & Feldman, 2011). Bartlett and Littler (2011) and Pilkington (2014a) point to high rates of unemployment estimated to affect half of the young members of the English Defence League (EDL). Others refer to the positive endorsement of themes like anti-Islamic sentiment promoted in mainstream media (Goodwin & Ford, 2014). According to Goodwin and Ford (2014), the press are more sympathetic to the Islamophobia of the English Defence League (EDL) than they were to the anti-Semitism of the National Front in the 1970s.

While much of this research presupposes structural explanations, others like Pilkington are interested in how young people themselves understand their own preferences and motivations (2014a, p. 13). According to Pilkington, we can better understand the political preferences and sentiments of young people by listening to what they say. Her interviews with young EDL activists support Castells's (2012) claim that social movements start with "the transformation of emotion into action." She points to the role of anxiety and fear of 'external' threats over which people say they feel little or no control. Such anxiety can be mitigated through expressions of anger, outrage and by a sense of togetherness experienced through their action. The experience of activism for members of the EDL, shares many of the emotional dimensions with those from quite different movements (Castells, 2012).

What follows is a case study of a far-right populist website based in the United States, The *Daily Stormer*, and its founder Andrew Anglin (born 1985). Anglin and his colleagues use the website for significant political interventions. His political style draws on the practices and ethos of sites like 4chan generally understood to be a platform for democratic-left politics organised by Anonymous (Coleman, 2014). I use The *Daily Stormer* case because it helps in understanding why some young people engage with right-wing populist ideas typically expressed in anti-immigration sentiment, white racism, xenophobic nationalism, and opposition to liberal democracy.

This is not intended to be representative of young people's involvement in right-wing populist politics, but to provide an evocative account that gives some insight into the lives of young people, what moves them to act and how they engage. While it adheres to an ethnographic imagination, it is not an ethnographic study based on intensive face-to-face interviews (like Pilkington, 2014a). It is closer to studies like Bartlett and Littler (2011), which used online resources to survey members of the English Defence League to better understand the motivations of members of the EDL, and how they interpreted their own actions.

THE *DAILY STORMER*

The *Daily Stormer* is a website based in the United States that promotes far right-wing populist communitarian racist politics. It is used to post dozens of daily news items on various local and international events. Authors declare it is a 100% non-profit organization whose aims include 'attempting to preserve Western Civilization.' It is anti-black, anti-Semitic, anti-Muslim, anti-liberal, anti-gay and misogynistic. As its founder and editor Anglin explained, he created the website because:

> The present situation is so unsettling that it's necessary to have an extreme response ... [and] I believe strongly that European people have a right to a continued existence as an independent culture and ethnic group'. (Anglin, cited in Kavanaugh, 2014)

It is also an exercise in mobilising new forms of political intervention like trolling, street protest, hacktivism and denial of service action. The Southern Poverty Law Center's (SPLC) annual *Year in Hate* report describes the *Daily Stormer* as the "top hate site in America" (Potok, 2017), a claim paralleling the *Daily Stormer*'s own boast to be "the world's most visited Alt-right website."

Anglin grew up in Worthington, Ohio, US, in a family that did not share his Nazi sympathies (Hankes, 2017).[7] It was his engagement with the internet and 4chan in particular that seems to have catalysed Anglin's political views while providing a platform for propagating ultra-right politics. As he explained: "I had always been into 4chan as I am at heart a troll":

> This is about the time [...] [a particular 4chan board] was going full Nazi, and so I got into Hitler, and realized that through this type of nationalist system, alienation could be replaced by community in a real sense, while authoritarianism would allow for technology to develop in a direction that was beneficial rather than destructive to the people. (cited in Hankes, 2017a)

He developed an interest in contemporary Nazism, creating a short-lived website called Total Fascism, on which he posted essays on fascism, race and alleged Jewish conspiracies against America.

On 4 July 2013, Anglin launched *The Daily Stormer* website. His choice of name channels the Nazi magazine *Der Stürmer*, an anti-Semitic pornographic magazine started by prominent Nazi party member, Julius Streicher, in 1923. By 2015, *The Daily Stormer* had over 300,000 registered users, and was in the top 14,000 of the most visited websites globally and in the top 4000 sites in the US (Hankes, 2017a).

Anglin believes that 'the American people,' that is, white Christian Americans are victims of an all-out attack by Jewish, Muslim, gay, feminist, liberal and black cultural antagonists, all of whom are morally perverse and subverting normal family life throughout America and Europe. All these groups are said to be supported by mainstream media and even by the Republican Party (Anglin, cited in Kavanaugh, 2014). Such views underscore his claim the mainstream media cannot be trusted to deliver such truth, while the Republican Party is too weak to stand up for white America.

Hence Anglin's strong support for Trump who he says is the 'great leader' America needs. During the 2016 American Presidential election campaign, Anglin's claimed that "Jews, Blacks and lesbians will be leaving America if Trump gets elected [...] This alone is enough reason to put your entire heart and soul into supporting this man" (2016e). Celebrations at *The Daily Stormer* began with the presidential election:

> We've won, brothers. All of our hard work this year has paid off. And make no mistake—every meme you posted, every comments section you trolled—all of that is what made this happen. Kek sent us Trump. Sent the crazy old bastard right down an elevator into our laps. Take a bow, brothers. This is a small step for memes. But it is a giant leap for our agenda to secure a homeland for our people and a future for White children. (Anglin, 2016a)

In one post-election headline, he wrote "Female Hajis Fear to Wear the Headtowel in Public After Trump Win—You Should Yell at Them" (Anglin, 2016b). He later continued: "[...] We want these people to feel unwanted. We want them to feel that everything around them is against them. And we want them to be afraid" (Anglin, cited Hankes, 2017). He added: "This was not a presidential Election [...] It was a referendum on the international Jewish agenda. And the biggest part of that agenda is multiculturalism" (ibid).

The *Daily Stormer* message is that 'white people' are being disadvantaged by the privileging of 'other groups' and by crimes committed by 'black' and 'Jewish people.' Much of the material posted is white racist and anti-Semitic. Anglin and others who post on the site are apologists for Hitler, claiming he was the most lied about man of all time. Like Streicher's '*Der Stürmer*,' the *Daily Stormer* is deeply anti-Semitic. Anglin claims, e.g., that "Jews and Moslems have long been friendly with one another. Now Jews are helping Moslems invade every white country" (Anglin, 2017d). He argues that the 'hoax' Holocaust memorial in Berlin should be replaced "with a statue of Hitler 1000 feet tall" (Anglin, cited SPLC, n.d.). He also claims 'they' are persecuting him (Anglin, 2017b). Standard white racist claims about African-Americans are also always on full display (Anglin, 2015a), and his misogyny is florid. (Anglin, 2015b).

New Media and Politics

Like many political movements and parties shaped and populated by younger people, they draw on older ideas, practices and arrangements to reproduce the old and to create the new. In *The Daily Stormer* case, older ultra-right politics is channelled through new technology and the culture of young people who play *World of Warcraft* or troll antagonists in bulletin boards. While young people draw directly on their own experience, as well as research and reading, many also rely more directly on older political actors, and in this sense politics of all persuasions typically involves some intergenerational collaboration.[8]

The Daily Stormer production team are prolific and highly competent social media producers dedicated to creating a new generation of ultra-right devotees using new communication technology. According to Don Black (born 1953) *Daily Stormer's* webmaster, the website has modernised how the ultra-right organize and communicates with a new generation of tech-savvy advocates. As he explains, the older style of membership-based organization has become redundant: "There's really not a lot out there as far as membership organizations" (Black, cited in Wines & Saul, 2015). According to Black, the internet provides a new platform that supersedes older style ultra-right member-based organisations and allows white supremacists to expand their influence:

> But there is a huge number, I think more than ever, as far as people actively working in some way to promote our cause. Because they don't have to join an organization now that we have this newfangled internet. (Black, cited in Wines & Saul, 2015)

New media has been used to extend their reach and enlarged their capacity for political communication enormously enabling contact with anyone with access to the internet and with an interest in their trappings or curiosity about ultra-right politics. In this way, digital communication media has augmented their ability to communicate with many more people across the globe and particularly with young people given their propensity to engage with digital media. In doing so, it has also enabled new forms of recruitment and new forms of participation.

Like all movements or parties using websites and related media, the people behind the *Daily Stormer* uses digital technology to extend their reach, to inform and mobilise millions of young people in ways hitherto unimaginable. Websites in conjunction with blogs, Twitter, Facebook, YouTube, etc., allows those interested in promoting ultra-right politics to go 'to air' immediately with images, videos, commentaries and their own eyewitness accounts and in doing so, invite an immediate interactive response. In short, digital media in the hands of ultra-right groups allows for direct, and importantly, uncensored communication with young people and others. It is technology that allows for the sidestepping of gatekeepers thereby enabling unmediated communication.

Digital communication technology also facilitates interactive relationships between participants themselves and between instigators and participants without having to be physically present in real time or space. It is interaction that invites participation in ways opens up discussion on any issue. It provides opportunities to access information and to develop stories from a variety of locations, which would be unlikely to make its way on to the agenda in more traditional forums. In this way, digital media allows participants to voice their views. In doing so, they get a sense that they matter and feel they can directly shape conversation about issues they consider important. Whether their voice is in fact heard and has a real effect, or whether they are simply persuaded that is the case and believe it, is another question.

Traditional media technology in the context of the corporate media model also saw a clear division between the creators of content, who tended to be employed in the mainstream industry, and the 'audience' who used or consumed media. Digital media has helped dissolve that producer and consumer distinction. This is due in part to reductions in the cost of digital technology, its ease of access and an increase in the technological literacy of many young people. This has enabled and encouraged users to generate their own content. Moreover, the open-networked nature of the technology has seen more 'non-experts' producing and disseminating content to broader and specific audiences off their own bat and without the services of industrial and technical complex operations of traditional media corporations. Digital technologies have thus enabled the proliferation of low-cost communication that can target particular groups and individual and world-wide audiences. It has enabled many young people to access low-cost production technologies and the affordances inherent in those technologies to create a wider variety of content and to disseminate it to whom they wish.

'Users' can now not only simply respond to what is said by writing commentary, they can produce content themselves drawing interviews, by recordings of their own events (e.g., rallies) or by creating remixes of news, or by generating political skits or satire in the form of images and videos. That material is then uploaded onto YouTube and/or their own website, thereby allowing them to actively participate in debates, while at the same time broadening the medium for 'discussion' and by opening new or expanding existing sites for information exchange. (e.g. https://www.youtube.com/user/DailyStormer). In these ways, supporters of the *Daily Stormer*, and any others using digital media in such ways, bypass conventional media practices and thus build new and expand existing network cultures (see Pickard in this volume). These strategies and opportunities to communicate are not unique to the *Daily Stormer*, or indeed the ultra-right, but are shared broadly by a variety of political interests (Bessant, 2014, 2016b).

Given the demographic or generational appeal of digital technology it is unsurprising that their communication with and solicitation of young people has been so effective (Bessant, 2014). The *Daily Stormer* uses new forms of recruitment that are radically different to conventional modes of drafting young new comers and political socialisation into political movements that tended to rely on actual networks, pamphleteering and organised events to canvas material and to further their causes (clubs, camps, etc.).

The recourse to victimhood and freedom-of-speech platform is a significant part of the material found on *Daily Stormer*. In response to one Twitter ban of its posts, Anglin declared: "[…] today, our revolution against Twitter begins. We shall have our revenge. […] And we shall bring the entire system to its knees." His plan borrows heavily from Anonymous:

> […] my trolls have on-hand approximately 1000 fake black person accounts, which are going live in the biggest trollstorm Twitter has ever seen. […] Today they will begin the operation to bring down #blacktwitter. And we need your help. The primary goal is revenge on Twitter for having launched this attack on free speech, and specifically on the Alt-Right. (Anglin, 2016c)

Anglin also attacks other far-right groups using trolling and hacktivism because, he claims, they are not sufficiently far-right. In November 2015, for example, he encouraged 'members' to troll his Alt-right enemies as part of 'Operation: Kikebart.' It was an attack on the right-wing news outlet Breitbart News after it opened a bureau in Jerusalem. *Daily Stormer* trolls, also referred to as the 'Stormer Troll Army,' flooded the Breitbart site with denunciations demanding it close its Israel office and accusing it of participating in Jewish conspiracies. The plan was to fill the site with neo-Nazi propaganda to the point "where they just give up on trying to ban people, and then we guide their readership toward Jew-hatred by informing them of the truths we possess" (Anglin, cited in Hankes, 2017a). It was a targeted campaign, involving young people, using what is now a well-known practice 'Distributed Denial of Service (DDoS) action,' designed to make a computer or network of computers temporarily or indefinitely unavailable. It typically involves mobilising numerous computers to target a website at specified time so the target site is inundated with traffic to the point where it floods, crashes or otherwise becomes dysfunctional. DDoS are the digital counterpart to older styles of protest like sit-ins that work to flood a site, create bottlenecks and disrupt or deny access to it. It is a popular and effective strategy used by many leftist and anarchist groups to engage in protests, by broad social movements, by government and corporates (Bessant, 2016a, pp. 921–937; see also Watts in this volume).

The *Daily Stormer* was also deploying a closely related strategy known as 'DNS Zone transfers', which saw hackers intercept client-server communication and redirected traffic away from the Breitbart News website to other sites or servers. Readers would then be provided with 'alternative news.' As Anglin explained, the plan was to guide Breitbart News readership towards sites populated with the 'truths' they possess.

Similar strategies included "Operation: Jew Wife," where Stormer sympathisers were similarly directed to flood the website of Alt-right conspiracist Alex Jones, who was considered insufficiently anti-Semitic. Another campaign targeted Julia Ioffe, an American journalist, subjecting her to a barrage of vicious electronic attacks after Donald Trump criticized her for reporting on his daughter Ivanka Trump who in 2010 converted to Judaism after marrying Jared Kushner an Orthodox Jew (and now a key adviser to Donald Trump). Such tactics were also deployed in 2016, when neo-Nazi Andrew Auernheimer, a computer hacker working with Anglin, developed a code that caused thousands of printers around the country, mostly in universities, to spontaneously print. They printed a pamphlet reading: "White man are you sick and tired of the Jews destroying your country through mass immigration and degeneracy? Join us in the struggle for global white supremacy at the *Daily Stormer*" (SPLC, n.d.). Such outrageous actions are part of a deliberate attention seeking strategy. The intention is to be as transgressive, as shocking and outrageous as possible to attract attention and to amplify information. That will encourage people to talk and share whatever was said or whatever scandalous action was taken until the shock value diminishes and it ceases to be so extreme and newsworthy.

Besides the constant internet commentary and trolling, the *Daily Stormer* organised other forms of hacktivism. Anglin promotes trolling on

Twitter encouraging followers to open Twitter accounts pretending to be black users and to spread fear and confusion among African-Americans. "Chaos is the name of the game. So basically, you just want to cause blacks to freak out and argue with each other nonstop. Here are some basic suggestions of how to accomplish that." To aid this strategy he provided 'notes' based on his 'research into black twitter' (Anglin, 2016c). They included:

- Most of them use twitter on their phones, so spelling is often autocorrected.
- [...] homophones are often used ("no" instead of "know") as well as abbreviations and texting slang recognized by phone spell-checkers ('u' instead of 'you,' 'n' instead of 'and').
- They use a lot of emoticons [...] [and] not use much punctuation.
- They mainly follow whichever hashtag is trending, and there is always a black or black-related hashtag to jump on.
- The basic concept is to start arguments (Anglin, 2016c).

He added: "As always, we also want to have a lot of fun. As I always say: it's not our revolution if we can't lol" (Anglin, 2016c). The website also promotes anti-Islamic rallies, and much of that activity is documented, filmed and distributed online.

Ultra-right sites like the *Daily Stormer* offer a kind of virtual solidarity, an opportunity to belong and it builds a sense of community. They are micro-communities that cluster around particular commentators or events or around wider 'alt-right' or *Daily Stormer* groupings or community. One reason such communities form is because participants feel strongly about matters discussed; they love, like or hate it. In this way, discussions can quickly become polarised and with that the quality of commentary and discussion typically declines into abusive tirades. This nonetheless clearly energizes discussion, increases participation and attracts further attention to the *Daily Stormer* website.

The *Daily Stormer* includes forums for commentary, information updates, a book club, general discussion, a meme machine and Facebook. Users can respond with 'likes' and 'love' and share material by re-tweeting and-or through Facebook. In these ways, those who visit or use the website can cease being simply part of an audience can become part of a group and importantly part of communication processes. This can be seen when a political action 'goes viral' when content is shared to others in their networks and spread to others through different social media outside the field of the *Daily Stormer*. It is a development that attracts attention to specific issues, to a part of the website, and to the ultra-right politics thereby increasing participation in it. There are also options to purchase *Daily Stormer* paraphernalia like T-shirts, and space for merchandise feedback-promotion. Thus, the *Daily Stormer* offers a sense of camaraderie, a sense of purpose and of being part of bigger project something replicated in many similar websites.

There are also opportunities to 'surrender to the cause.' On 23 August 2016, Anglin called supporters to 'Register Now for the IRL [In Real Life] Troll Army AKA The Stormer Book Club.' He described the club as 'groups to prepare for the coming race war,' a place to 'form cells, build bonds, develop brotherhood. You will become stronger, better men. It's a bit like Fight Club' (Anglin, 2016d). The call produced results. According to Southern Poverty Law Center, by late 2016, the *Daily Stormer* produced 31 distinct active chapters in Anglin's Troll Army. Soon after, he urged followers to 'BUY GUNS!' in case Clinton won the presidential contest. "The race war is coming …and it is coming quickly" (Anglin, cited in Hankes, 2017c).

Interpreting Young People's Ultra-Right Politics

The messages promoted by the *Daily Stormer* are disturbing and objectionable. They are worrying given the history of political violence produced by ultra-nationalist populism over the last century. As Arendt observes himself, Hitler's national socialism began as a populist movement (Arendt, 1958).

Yet as offensive as they are, it is a mistake not to take young people's participation in ultra-right politics seriously, or to dismiss figures like Anglin simply as rabble-rouser hooligans mobilising people displaying a nasty socio-pathological bent. To do this not only ignores the dangers of this kind of politics, it disregards its appeal, and represses the 'uncomfortable knowledge' that members are often moved by moral emotions like patriotism, loyalty, a sense of communal belonging and righteous anger (Flyvbjerg, 2013). That 'uncomfortable knowledge' is that what moves many young people to participate in ultra-right political action, including the same values and political emotions many mainstream liberals valorise, like injustice, loyalty, love of country or patriotism, a sense of heroism or need to protect kin and kind, all moral and political emotions found in respectable liberal communities.

The activities exhibited by 'groups' like those who read and respond to the *Daily Stormer* reveal serious commitments to politics in a context where many young people feel distrustful of and disillusioned with power elites not just in government, but with many religious, community leaders and the corporate sector to the point where they seek alternatives. It is a context, however, where viable political alternatives are thin on the ground and where ultra-right groups provide what seem (for some) viable options. They also present opportunities to vent righteous anger, a sense of abandonment concomitant with unemployment, feelings disenfranchised and little confidence in future they seem to have little real capacity to control or shape.

That said, the more significant problem posed by the rise of right-wing populism amongst young people is how to interpret and respond to it. Given the often objectionable and threatening nature of right-wing populist rhetoric and actions how should a liberal democratic polity respond? The need to address this question is indicated by the way many modern liberal political cultures generally tend to be intolerant of dissent or difference. Nonetheless, the increased popularity of the ultra-right amongst young people does raise questions about what is acceptable social action and what is not. It is an issue considered by Mouffe when she asked how should democratic politics deal with conflict?

For Mouffe, antagonism is inherent in all human societies. Drawing on Schmitt's (1997) account of the political as the relation between friends and enemies, Mouffe argues that *the political* refers to antagonism which can take many forms and that always emerges in diverse social relations. Antagonism is something that can never be eradicated (Mouffe, 2016, p. 1). *Politics,* however as distinct from the political, refers to all the practices, discourses and institutions that seek to establish civil order and to organise human coexistence.

As she argues, while the typical liberal gesture is to deny and wish *antagonism* away, what democratic politics requires is that 'others' (however defined) are not regarded "as *enemies* to be destroyed, but as *adversaries* whose ideas would be fought, even fiercely, but whose right to defend those ideas will never be put into question" (Mouffe, 2016, p. 1). As she explains:

> [...] what is important is that conflict does not take the form of an 'antagonism' (struggle between enemies), but the form of an 'agonism' (struggle between adversaries). We could say that the aim of democratic politics is to transform potential antagonism into an agonism. (Mouffe, 2016, p. 2)

Mouffe has raised an important question about how we might recognise the legitimacy and value of the type of opposition to democratic processes presented in movements like the *Daily Stormer*. Is there capacity in a democratic polity to transform antagonism (enemies) into agonism (adversaries)? Can democratic politics be used to transform the antagonistic politics of ultra-right groups into an agonistic relationship? These are questions we may begin addressing while considering the extent to which many of the motivations identified above that attract many young people to far right politics are the same and very similar to moral and political emotions found in respectable liberal communities. They include a sense of belonging, love of country, the desire to protect, righteous anger and sense of justice and so forth. They manifest in deeply objectionable ways, but they are political and moral emotions that mark a common ground and thus some opportunity transforming antagonists (enemies) into agonists (adversaries) following democratic principles of processes.

Conclusion

This chapter provided a case study of ultra-right populism that highlights the diversity of young people's politics. It also considered how digital media is used to recruit, to extend the reach of ultra-right groups. Attention was also given to the interactive nature of this technology and to how it allows for collaborative practices, as well as direct action and direct communication in ways that bypass traditional media gate-keepers. It is this technology that has enabled young people to create content themselves in a variety of forms, to disseminate it and in doing so enhance their sense of empowerment, engagement and feeling of belonging.

The chapter also considered the appeal of ultra-right populist groups and recognised that while many of their themes and arguments are abhorrent, what attracts many young people are on the same emotions, fears and values that many of "us" recognize: loyalty, love of county and kind, a sense of altruism, and self-sacrifice for a higher good. It is in this way that the centrality of political emotions and ethical impulses become apparent;

outrage, hatred, fear, or a yearning for justice are what Critchley says play a major role in motivating us to become particular kinds of political beings or to engage in specific political activity (2007).

As Mouffe intimates, urgent attention needs to be given to what actions might be taken to help transform antagonistic politics of the kind represented by those ultra-right groups into an agonistic relationship. How this might be achieved be structural and relate to issues like increased employment opportunities and access to resources that provide a basis for a decent life. It may also rely on the availability of more viable political alternatives that young people can turn to, can create and build and in so doing fill a void that is being now being filled by populists and fascistic style politics. The task of transforming antagonistic politics into agonists politics also rests on a capacity to recognise the moral and political emotions that attract young people to an ultra-right worldview, and to consider what provisions and opportunities can be created to allow young people to express and enact those political emotions in ways that are guided by a democratic ethos.

Notes

1. Contemporary right-wing populist and ultra-nationalist political groups have a long history of left-wing and right-wing populism through the twentieth century (Canovan, 1981; Mueller, 2016).
2. In Europe, this was often a reaction against renewed immigration and the evolution of pan-Europeanism signified by the establishment of the European Union in 1992. The British National Party (BNP) e.g., formed in 1960, to promote anti-immigrant policies later joined forces (1967) with the remnants of the League of Empire Loyalists to form the National Front (Tournier-Sol, 2015). While they failed to win enough electoral support, National Front rallies were regular in British political landscape throughout the 1970s. In France, Jean-Marie Le Pen created the *Front National* in the 1980s to promote economic protectionism, a tough law and order agenda, alongside fierce opposition to immigration and to prevent France from joining the European Union (Davies, 1999). In Germany, many small movements and parties appeared and disappeared without making the same mark as right-wing populism in the UK or France (Betz, 1993; Fritzsche, 1990) The Free German Workers' Party (*Deutsche Arbeiterpartei*) founded in 1979 was outlawed in 1995. The Nationalist Front (*Nationale Front des Demokratischen*) was active during the 1980s, while the German People's Union (*Deutsche Volksunion*) (founded in 1987), and the German Alternative (founded in 1989) are more durable.

3. For example, The Alternative for Germany (*Alternative für Deutschland*), the National Front *(Front National)* in France, Lega Nord (*Lega Nord per l'Indipendenza della Padania*) in Italy, Geert Wilders's Party for Freedom (*Partij voor de Vrijheid*) in the Netherlands, and the Law and Justice Party (*Prawo i Sprawiedliwość*) and the *Congress of the New Right* (*Kongres Nowej Prawicy*) in Poland.
4. The Freedom Party (*Freiheitliche Partei Österreich*) in Austria (Jörg Haider) won 26% of the vote in 2015, while the Swiss People's Party won 24% of the vote also in 2015. The same year in France, Le Pen's National Front won over 40% of the vote in regional elections and Marine Le Pen is making a serious bid for power in the April-May 2017 Presidential elections. Across the Atlantic, right-wing populism signified by the Tea Party became increasingly significant as it contested the Obama Administration by drawing on older networks of American conservatives and 'Alt-right' groups including white supremacists, anti-Semites, anti-immigrants, religious conservatives and anti-liberals (Hochschild, 2016). In 1997, in Australia, Pauline Hanson founded the One Nation party based on an anti-immigrant and anti-Muslim agenda. One Nation won four out of 76 Senate positions in 2016 and are influential in state and national elections.
5. These refer to right-wing populist beliefs promoted across the past century, e.g., the Jewish conspiracy to dominate the world, claims the Holocaust never happened, that the 9/11 attacks were fabricated by the Bush presidency, that climate change is a hoax, that former President Obama is a Muslim and not American, and that Islam, or Islamist terrorism, constitutes an existential treat to the West (Blake, 2017; Keyes, 2004).
6. In line with the anti-pluralism of its monistic conception of 'the people,' right-wing populists see parliamentary political compromise as evidence of weakness and promote radical solutions to what they describe central issues like crime epidemics by certain minority groups, or too many immigrants in their country (Greven, 2016, p. 2). Most right-wing populists also combine cultural conservatism with 'left-wing' policies hostile to neoliberal and globalisation provoked by the 2008 economic crisis. Poland's Law and Justice Party (*Prawo i Sprawiedliwość*), for example, is campaigning for a lower retirement age and state aid to Poland's coalmines. In France, the National Front wants a lower retirement age and more protectionist agricultural policies. In the Netherlands, Wilders' Party for Freedom argues that money now spent on housing refugees should be used for the cancer treatment for Dutch citizens.
7. According to Anglin, as a young person he was spoon-fed America's 'liberal brand of politics.' In high school, he read Noam Chomsky and dabbled in 'all that Communist, Jewish stuff.' He claims to have studied Islam, Buddhism and major twentieth century French philosophers, like Jean Baudrillard and Jacques Ellul. Ellul's critique of technology seems to have

resonated with Anglin. He decided, for example, that Ted Kaczynski, the anti-technology terrorist known as the Unabomber, was "right with regards to a coming apocalypse" (cited in Hankes, 2017).
8. One stand out example of such cross generational alliance within the progressive left political domain was evident in the partnership between two founding editors of the Canadian *Adbuster* magazine. It was 69-year-old Kalle Lasn and 29-year-old Micah White who have been identified as responsible for launching and orchestrating the NY Occupy Wall Street protests (Gerbaudo, 2012).

REFERENCES

Anglin, A. (2014, March 20). Cited in Kavanaugh Dixon, Shane, 'The man bringing back the Nazi movement in America.' *Vocativ*. Retrieved from http://www.vocativ.com/usa/race/man-bringing-back-nazi-movement-america

Anglin, A. (2015a, June 20). Who is actually responsible for the Charleston shooting? *The Daily Stormer*. Retrieved from http://www.dailystormer.com/who-is-actually-responsible-for-the-charleston-shooting

Anglin, A. (2015b, June 20). Pro-white feminists attack Daily Stormer and white males generally. *The Daily Stormer*. Retrieved from http://www.dailystormer.com/pro-white-feminists-attack-daily-stormer-and-white-males-generally

Anglin, A. (2016a, October 29). Donald J. Trump is now president of the United States of America. *The Daily Stormer*. Retrieved from http://www.dailystormer.com/donald-j-trump-is-now-president-of-the-united-states-of-america

Anglin, A. (2016b, December 9). How to be a nigger on Twitter. *The Daily Stormer*. Retrieved from http://www.dailystormer.com/how-to-be-a-nigger-on-twitter

Anglin, A. (2016c, August 3). Register now for the IRL troll army AKA the stormer. Book Club. The *Daily Stormer*. Retrieved from http://www.dailystormer.com/register-now-for-the-irl-troll-army-aka-the-stormer-book-club

Anglin, A. (2016d, April 26). Get Em Outta Here: Glorious leader calls for Kike Lena Dunham to leave America. *The Daily Stormer*. Retrieved from http://www.dailystormer.com/get-em-outta-here-glorious-leader-calls-for-kike-lena-dunham-to-leave-america

Anglin, A. (2016e, November 10). Female Hajis fear to wear the headtowel in public after Trump win—You should yell at them. *The Daily Stormer*. Retrieved from http://www.dailystormer.com/female-hajis-fear-to-wear-the-headtowel-in-public-after-trump-win-you-should-yell-at-them

Anglin, A. (2017a, February 9). Cited in Hankes, Keegan. 2017 'The eye of the stormer.' *Intelligence Report*. Southern poverty law center. Retrieved from https://www.splcenter.org/fighting-hate/intelligence-report/2017/eye-stormer

Anglin, A. (2017b, February 3). 'Choking last Jew gasp: Daily Stormer has mailing address and bitcoin shutdown in the same week...!' *The Daily Stormer.* Retrieved from http://www.dailystormer.com/daily-stormer-has-address-and-bitcoin-shutdown-in-the-same-week

Anglin, A. (2017c, February 9). Cited in Hankes Keegan. Propelled by The Trump campaign and a new focus on the 'Alt-right.' The Daily Stormer is now the top hate site in America. *Intelligence Report.* Retrieved from https://www.splcenter.org/fighting-hate/intelligence-report/2017/eye-stormer

Anglin, A. (2017d, February 17). Brooklyn: Jews and Moslems come together to show solidarity against the Goyim/Kaffir. *The Daily Stormer.* Retrieved from http://www.dailystormer.com/brooklyn-jews-and-moslems-come-together-to-show-solidarity-against-the-goyimkaffir/

Anglin, A. (n.d.). Cited Southern Poverty Law Center (SPLC), Andrew Anglin, SPLC. Retrieved from https://www.splcenter.org/fighting-hate/extremist-files/individual/andrew-anglin

Arendt, H. (1958). *The origins of totalitarianism* (2 Rev.). New York: Meridian.

Bartlett, J., & Littler, M. (2011). *Inside the EDL: Populist politics in a digital age. A Report for Demos.* Retrieved from https://www.demos.co.uk/files/Inside_the_edl_WEB.pdf?1331035419

Bessant, J. (2014). *Democracy bytes: New media and new politics and generational change.* Basingstoke: Palgrave Macmillan.

Bessant, J. (2016a). Democracy denied: Youth participation and criminalizing digital dissent. *Journal of Youth Studies, 19*(7), 921–937.

Bessant, J. (2016b). New politics and satire: The euro financial crisis and the one-finger salute. *Information, Communication & Society,* 1–16. doi:10.1080/1369118X.2016.1206138

Betz, H.-G. (1993). New politics of resentment: Radical right wing populist parties in Western Europe. *Comparative Politics, 25*(4), 413–427.

Black, D. (2015, July 5). Cited in Wines, Michael and Saul Stephanie. 'White supremacists extend their reach through websites.' *New York Times.*

Blake, A. (2017, January 22). Kellyanne conway says Donald Trump's team has 'alternative facts.' which pretty much says it all. *Washington Post.* Retrieved from https://www.washingtonpost.com/news/the-fix/wp/2017/01/22/kellyanne-conway-says-donald-trumps-team-has-alternate-facts-which-pretty-much-says-it-all/?utm_term=.afd306bab1bd

Canovan, M. (1981). *Populism.* London: Junction Books.

Castells, M. (2012). *Networks of outrage and hope: Social movements in the internet age.* Cambridge: Polity Press.

Coleman, G. (2014). *Hacker, hoaxer, whistleblower, spy: The many faces of anonymous.* London: Verso Books.

Critchley, S. (2007). *Infinitely demanding: Ethics of commitment, political of resistance.* New York: Verso Books.

Davies, P. (1999). *The National Front in France: Ideology, discourse and power*. Abingdon: Routledge.
Fielitz, M., & Laloire, L. (Eds.). (2017). *Trouble on the far right. Contemporary right-wing strategies and practices in Europe*. New York: Columbia University Press.
Flyvbjerg, B. (2013). How planners deal with uncomfortable knowledge: The dubious ethics of the American Planning Association. *Cities, 32*, 157–162.
Fritzsche, P. (1990). *Rehearsals for fascism: Populism and political mobilization in Weimar Germany*. New York: Oxford University Press.
Gerbaudo, P. (2012). *Tweets and the streets: Social media and contemporary activism*. London: Pluto Books.
Goodwin, M. (2010). *The new extremism in 21st century Britain*. Abingdon: Routledge.
Goodwin, M., & Ford, R. (2014). *Revolt on the right: Explaining support for the radical right in Britain*. Abingdon: Routledge.
Grasso, M. T., Farrall, S., Gray, E., Hay, C., & Jennings, W. (2017). Thatcher's children, Blair's babies, political socialisation and trickle-down value-change: An age, period and cohort analysis. *British Journal of Political Science*, 1–20.
Greven, T. (2016). *The rise of right-wing populism in Europe and the United States*. Berlin: Friedrich Ebert Stiftung.
Hankes, K. (2017, February 17). Eye of the stormer. *Southern Poverty Law Centre*. Retrieved from https://www.splcenter.org/fighting-hate/intelligence-report/2017/eye-stormer
Hochschild, A. (2016). *Strangers in their own land*. New York: WW Norton.
Jackson, P., & Feldman, M. (2011). *The EDL: Britain's 'new far right' social movement*. Northampton: The University of Northampton.
Keyes, R. (2004). *The post-truth era: Dishonesty and deception in contemporary life*. New York: St Martin's Press.
Koronaiou, A., Lagos, E., Sakellariou, A., Kymionis, S., & Chiotaki-Poulou, I. (2015). Golden dawn, austerity and young people: The rise of fascist extremism among young people in contemporary Greek society. In H. Pilkington & G. Pollock (Eds.), *Radical futures: Youth, politics and activism in contemporary Europe, The sociological review monograph series* (Vol. 63, pp. 231–249). Hoboken, NJ: Wiley.
Meleagrou-Hitchens, A., & Brun, H. (2013). *A Neo-Nationalist Network: The English Defence League and Europe's Counter-Jihad Movement*. London: International Centre for the Study of Radicalisation and Political Violence. Retrieved from http://icsr.info/wp-content/uploads/2013/03/ICSR-ECJM-Report_Online.pdf
Mierina, I., & Korojeva, I. (2015). Support for far right ideology and anti-migrant attitudes among youth in Europe: A comparative analysis. *The Sociological Review*, 63: 183–205. doi:10.1111/1467-954X.12268

Mouffe, C. (2016). Democratic politics and conflict: An agonistic approach *Political Comun*. Retrieved from https://quod.lib.umich.edu/p/pc/12322227.0009.011/--democratic-politics-and-conflict-an-agonistic-approach?rgn=main;view=fulltext

Mueller, J.-W. (2016). *What is populism?* Philadelphia and Pennsylvania: University of Pennsylvania Press.

Pilkington, H. (2014a, November 20). Are young people receptive to populist and radical right political agendas? Turning evidence into policy MYPLACE policy forum, Brussels.

Pilkington, H. (2014b). 'Loud and Proud': Youth activism in the English Defence League. University of Manchester. MYPLACE (Memory, youth, political legacy and civic engagement. Grant agreement no: FP7-266831WP7: Interpreting activism (Ethnographies)). Retrieved from http://www.fp7myplace.eu/documents/D7_1/Cluster%201%20Right%20Wing%20and%20Patriotic%20movements/MYPLACE_WP7.1REPORT_UM_English%20Defence%20League%20(UK).pdf

Potok, M. (2017, February 17). The year in hate and extremism. *Southern Poverty Law Centre*. Retrieved from https://www.splcenter.org/fighting-hate/intelligence-report/2017/year-hate-and-extremism

Schmitt, C. (1997). *The concept of the political* (G. Schwab, Trans.). Chicago: University of Chicago Press

Sibum, H. (2016, December 12). Right-wing populism and young voters "a virtual social movement." Goethe Institute. Retrieved from https://www.goethe.de/ins/au/en/kul/mag/20879914.html

Tournier-Sol, K. (2015). Reworking the Eurosceptic and conservative traditions into a populist narrative: UKIP's winning formula? *Journal of Common Market Studies, 53*(1), 147–169.

Virchow, F. (2015). *The "Identitarian movement": What kind of identity? Is it really a movement? Digital media strategies of the far right in Europe and the United States.* Lanham: Lexington Books.

Wodak, R. (2015). *The politics of fear: What right-wing populist discourses mean.* London: Sage.

Wodak, R., Mral, B., & Khosravinik, M. (Eds.). (2013). *Right wing populism in Europe: Politics and discourse.* London: Bloomsbury Academic.

Judith Bessant is Professor in the School of Global, Urban and Social Studies at the Royal Melbourne Institute of Technology (RMIT) University, Melbourne, Australia. She publishes in the areas of sociology, youth studies, politics, policy and history, and has worked as an advisor to governments and to non-government organisations.

CHAPTER 9

'How Not to Be a Terrorist': Radicalisation and Young Western Muslims' Digital Discourses

Andrew Hope and Julie Matthews

INTRODUCTION

Such is the perceived danger of terrorism that some politicians claim "Europe is in crisis" (Verhofstadt, 2017, p. 1), while elements of the media report similarly that there is a "surveillance and security crisis" (Jalalzai, 2017). Partly this can be seen as a response to terrorist attacks and plots in European countries including France, Belgium, Germany, the United Kingdom and Spain. Though not dismissing the impact of deaths from terrorist activities, it is important to note that the resultant perpetual feelings of risk and unease among the general public allow for normalisation of "illiberal practices of liberal regimes" (Bigo & Tsoukala, 2008). Thus, in the name of combating terrorism certain groups become labelled as 'suspect communities' by governments, the media and the security industry. They are then subjected to state policies and practices that promote invasive surveillance, racist interventions and media scapegoating. In contemporary Western societies, suspicion has overwhelmingly fallen upon

A. Hope (✉) • J. Matthews
University of Adelaide, Adelaide, SA, Australia

© The Author(s) 2018
S. Pickard, J. Bessant (eds.), *Young People Re-Generating Politics in Times of Crises*, Palgrave Studies in Young People and Politics,
DOI 10.1007/978-3-319-58250-4_9

young Muslims who are labelled as being 'at risk' of radicalisation and becoming violent extremist by governments, the mass media and associated elements of the security industry. Key to understanding how counter-terrorism strategies can result in the harassment of these minorities is the contemporary conceptualisation of radicalisation.

Since 2004, the notion of radicalisation has become central to the study of terrorism and counter-terrorist policy, functioning as "the master signifier of the late war on terror" (Kundnani, 2012, p. 3), and "the dominant trope for Western discussion of counterterrorism" (Monaghan & Molnar, 2016, p. 393). This partly reflects the exponential growth of a billion-dollar government-funded industry within which "professionals of the management of unease" (Monaghan, 2013, p. 5), including advisors, analysts, academics, entrepreneurs and 'community facilitators,' purport to offer insights into the 'radicalisation process.' Indeed, so developed in this approach that within academia there has emerged a sub-discipline of 'radicalisation studies' seeking to assist both state and private organisations in addressing perceived issues of terrorism and (in)security. The resultant conceptualisation of radicalisation allows governments and security industries to avoid focusing on possible 'root causes' of terrorism, such as military conflict, political unrest and economic exploitation. Rather the risk of terrorism is pathologised, as it becomes regarded as a psycho-social abnormality that can be treated through intervention programs. Individuals are blamed for becoming 'radicalised' and risk 'indicators' are constructed drawing upon anecdotal interpretations seen through the prism of various psychological, behavioural and theological models.

Despite claims of scientific objectivity, the focus in the West falls overwhelmingly upon young Muslims as a 'suspect community,' who become labelled as at-risk of radicalisation and prone to violent extremism. As a consequence, "normal teenage behaviour becomes scrutinised and suspicious" (Akbarzadeh, 2016, p. 329). Although terrorism is an important security issue, talk of crisis should not dwell solely on this threat. Rather it should also include consideration of the consequences of counter-terrorist strategies that alienate, isolate and victimise sections of society.

In exploring these negative policy impacts, this chapter addresses two main issues. First, the use of radicalisation to socially construct young Muslims as a 'suspect community' will be explored. Thus, the semantic drift of the concept of radicalisation and the 'anticipatory logic' of indicators that seemingly problematise young Muslims will be critically examined. Second, the online responses of young Muslims to anti-radicalisation policies and practices will be considered. In exploring these Muslim digital discourses, it will be argued that the vast majority of online content is mundane in nature and that humour plays an important role in online resistance to negative media stereo-types. This latter point will be elaborated through a discussion of responses to the British right-wing *Daily Telegraph* newspaper article "How to spot a terrorist living in your neighbourhood" (Judd, 2013). In conclusion, ways in which young Muslims' respond to the complex interplay of notions of radicalisation, violent extremism and terrorism will be considered, as their discursive resistance through humour is highlighted.

The Semantic Drift of Radicalisation

As Neumann (2013) notes, the meaning of radicalisation is ambiguous, with no universally accepted definition. Nevertheless, prior to the terrorist attacks of September 11th 2001, in the United States, the term was predominantly used to indicate a movement towards more radical politics, which sought to alter social structures in a revolutionary manner and change value systems in fundamental ways. Emerging from the political rumblings of the late eighteenth century, this conceptualisation of radicalism became associated with political support for a host of reforms, such as extensions of the franchise (the right to vote), the curbing of monarchical power, the provision of social welfare, freedom of the press and the civil rights movement. In some of the policy literature focusing on terrorism and radicalisation, this earlier usage of the term radicalisation is not completely absent. Thus, in a guide to radicalisation issued by the Canadian police (RCMP, 2009) 'radical figures' such as Martin Luther King and Gloria Steinem are used to illustrate the argument that radical ideas do not necessitate violence. Although the publication still draws the conclusion that political violence is the result of radical ideas (Monaghan & Molnar, 2016, p. 398). Nevertheless, such limited examples are best seen as exceptions to current policies and media discourses that overwhelmingly reject the positive potential of political radicalisation, instead associating it with violent extremism and terror. Consequently, in contemporary society, the concept of radicalisation is utilised in a largely negative, adversarial manner to signify terrorist crimes.

At the heart of this current hostility towards processes of radicalisation is the semantic drift that has seemingly disconnected it from notions of social and political reform, instead associating it with terrorism. Thus, as

Miller (2013, p. 189) notes, there is a tendency to treat words such as radicalisation, extremism, terrorism and 'fundamentalist' as if they were synonyms, when clearly they are not. For example, terrorism involves intentionally indiscriminate violence to achieve political, religious or ideological objectives. It is a criminal activity outlawed by anti-terror legislation in all western jurisdictions. Radicalisation itself is rarely defined as a crime, with its status in the criminal justice system heavily dependent on its perceived associations with acts labelled as terrorist. Even words that might appear closer in meaning, such as extremism, are misused. Thus, whereas the etymology of radical from the Latin *radix* meaning root, suggests that it is something that lies at the very foundation of civil society, extremism, derived from the Latin *extremus*, suggests a thing situated at the edge, on the periphery of a community.

Furthermore, it is not just that words with dissimilar meanings are substituted for one another; slippage means that extremism is 'understood' as violent extremism, while anti-terrorism and counter-terrorism become conflated as terms. As Miller (2013, p. 191) observes, this last distinction is particularly problematic insofar as anti-terrorism historically meant what might be done legally to address the problem of terrorism, whereas counter-terrorism suggests the adoption of terrorist methods. Confusion such as this inevitably raises concerns about the attrition of civil rights.

In addition to the use of fallacious synonyms and slippage, it is also worth noting that in policy documents there is often an indistinct use of these concepts, which "allow for the re-construction, re-interpretation and re-articulation of what constitutes radicalisation" (Coppock, 2014, p. 119). Nevertheless, common to most articulations is the idea that radicalisation is harmful to the individual and broader society through potentially undermining the values of 'mainstream society' and resulting in acts of violence. Consequently, if a young person ends up with radical ideas, then this is to be understood as a failure of educational processes, which should have socialised individuals into conformity (Sukarieh & Tannock, 2016, p. 31). Indeed, the extent to which radicalisation has become a problematic concept is starkly illustrated in the Australian Government's (2015) anti-radicalisation kit that, in an attempt to make its indicators more agnostic, used a fictional case study to link green activism and alternative music to terrorism.

Ultimately, contentious synonyms, the slippage of meanings and the re-interpretation of what constitutes radicalisation matters. This is because the resulting conceptualisations are used in anti-terrorist policies and practices. Consequently, risk indicators are generated using flawed definitions and skewed information that precipitate the injudicious labelling of young Muslims as members of a 'suspect community.' Such processes will now be considered in more detail.

Operationalising Radicalisation: Risk Indicators and the 'Usual Suspects'

The semantic drift of radicalisation is best understood with reference to the booming political economy of securitisation. Indeed, the contemporary conceptualisation of the term has been heavily promoted in the last fifteen years by the United States and European security industries, at least partly in response to governmental desire to avoid focusing on the 'root causes' of terrorism (Sukarieh & Tannock, 2016, p. 28). Western governments labelled attention to these root causes as tantamount to justifying terrorism, a discursive feint that allowed them to avoid addressing the underlying political, economic and military conflicts that might have resulted in terrorist responses. Radicalisation became deeply embedded in counter-terrorism policy, with Kundnani's (2012, p. 7) asserting that "by 2004 the term [signified] a psychological or theological process by which Muslims move towards extremist views." This highlights two key elements of policy focusing upon (de)radicalisation, its tendency to seek to 'objectively' pathologise and its focus upon Muslims. Each of these issues will be examined in turn.

Much of the academic research on radicalisation has focused upon the pathways taken by individuals into terrorism. It is assumed that if key indicators of engagement with 'violent radicalisation' can be identified then these can be used to isolate future threats. Consequently, a number of radicalisation theories have been proposed that draw upon cognitive psychology, behavioural approaches and theological processes. All of these approaches claim to have predictive powers. Yet as Coppock (2014, p. 121) notes "most research in this area is based on retrospective case studies of 'extremists,' most of which are highly personal, inevitably subjective and lack the level of scientific rigour that would render them reliable as predictors of potential future behaviour." Furthermore, not only are such approaches empirically flawed, they also lack explanatory power. Rather, vague references to cognitive radicalisation or behavioural radicalisation help to pathologise the term, recasting "social and cultural problems as psychological ones" (Furedi, 2003, p. 27). This hints that individuals are to blame for the acquisition of a 'terrorist mindset.' Significantly such "radicalisation models [...] have encouraged national security establishments to believe that they can pre-empt future terrorist attacks through intensive surveillance of the spiritual and mental lives of Muslims" (Kundnani, 2012, p. 21).

Media narratives have long constructed Muslims as 'folk devils' (Cohen, 1973) associating them with problems of domestic violence, urban unrest, immigration and social welfare (Morgan & Poynting, 2012; Saeed, 2007). Moreover, research on representations of Islam in the British media between 2000 and 2008 highlights that the dominant representations include associations with terrorism and extremism (Moore, Mason, & Lewis, 2008). Indeed, in the forty times that former Australian Prime Minister Tony Abbott talked publicly about Muslims between September 2013 and November 2014, upon each occasion they were mentioned in relation to terrorism (Lentini, 2015). Consequently, the use of risk indicators that associate 'radicalisation' with young Muslims could be seen as the latest iteration of an inherent prejudice. Yet, users of these 'predictive' models seek to avoid the label of racism or religious prejudice by differentiating the use of indicators from the maligned practice of profiling. It is claimed that risk indicators are agnostic and non-discriminatory tools. Despite such assertions, the discourses of fear and the anticipatory logics of the counter-terrorist imagination result in a fixation upon the perceived threat posed by young Muslims. Thus, the activities of security agencies continue to promote and reinforce the stereotype that problems of 'radicalisation' and terrorism are primarily located within Muslim communities, being deeply rooted in Islamic cultural and religious practices (Coppock, 2014; Hickman et al., 2011). Accordingly, "the broad array of indicators posited as drivers of radicalisation have furthered discriminatory practices targeting the Muslim community as usual suspects" (Monaghan & Molnar, 2016). Such problems are conflated as the counter-terrorist gaze extends far beyond terrorist crime, into the broader realm of perceived ideological threats to the state (Richards, 2015). Hence the British Government changed its focus from violent extremism to "views which fall short of supporting violence and are within the law, but which reject and undermine our shared values and jeopardise community cohesion" (HMG, 2009, p. 87). Policy creep occurs as the problem is redefined, not as terrorism but as extremism, not as ideological motivated violence but as cultural religious difference at odds with 'mainstream values.' Thus, de-radicalisation policy and practice create a 'suspect community.'

Rather than focusing solely on questionable behaviour, young Muslims are labelled as 'at risk' and dangerous as a consequence of racial, ethnic and religious indicators. Consequently "respectful and law-abiding people are put through a process of risk subjectification through which they become defined as dangerous by virtue of sharing some or other of the characteristics of the typical terrorist" (Mythen, Walklate, & Khan, 2013, p. 390). From this perspective, risk can be interpreted as moral technology (Castel, 1991) that acts as a rhetorical disciplinary tool (Dean, 1999). This is not to deny the existence of terrorist violence, but rather to highlight the questionable capacity to calculate and ameliorate 'danger' through technological processes such as indicators. Blame is mobilised as risk labels are used unscientifically and highly subjectively to stigmatise and mistreat young Muslims.

Having considered how the notion of radicalisation is used to imprudently label young Muslims as members of a 'suspect community,' the focus will now turn in the next section to the subsequent responses of these individuals to such processes.

Responses to Anti-radicalisation Policies and Practices

Although young Muslims are not socially, economically, politically or even religiously homogenous, contemporary notions of radicalisation and racist risk indicators result in them being collectively constructed as 'suspect communities.' As Lynch (2015, p. 173) notes "the attention to the Muslim young people potential for radicalisation and terrorism masks not only the reality of life for these youth but also serves to shroud the everyday experiences of youth in a veil of suspicion." Alongside the increase in racism directed at Muslims (Hopkins, 2007), they are also subjected to far more routine surveillance and scrutiny. Research undertaken by Mythen, Walklate & Khan (2009, p. 745) suggests that young British Muslims respond to such victimisation in three main ways, namely infuriation, disenchantment and responsibilisation. Infuriation arose from the sense of injustice and resentment at the discriminatory treatment received. Disenchantment grew from feelings of bewilderment and resignation to the impact of racist policies and practices. Beyond infuriation and disenchantment, some young Muslims engaged in responsibilisation, wherein "victimization had generated the desire to challenge ignorance and misunderstandings about Islamic faith and traditions ... [they] saw themselves as having an important social role as educators on history, culture, faith and politics" (Mythen et al., 2009, p. 746). Yet, such desire to clarify issues and educate others is only one element of responsibilisation. Grounded in Foucault's (1978) work on governmentality, responsibilisation describes strategies that attempt to shift certain liabilities away from the state through encouraging individuals to see social risks such as ill health, poverty and crime as issues of self-care, rather than purely the responsibility of the state. In this context, problems related to radicalisation and fear of violent extremism are partly divested by the state and thrust upon those who are members of the 'suspect communities.' From this perspective, it becomes the responsibility of young Muslims to monitor and adjust their own behaviour in an attempt to manage 'risk perceptions.' This can result in a 'dramaturgical safety push.' Thus, as Hopkins (2007, p. 197) notes, to reduce notions of 'riskiness' some young people play down their 'Muslimness,' at least in terms of appearance, performing 'safeness' through avoiding wearing 'religious clothing' or using objects such as backpacks. Within this category fall such practices as hushing, embodied in the public moderation of religious and political views, and checking, which include the selective use of dialect, normalising of dress and limiting certain behaviours in public (Mythen et al., 2013, p. 391).

Nonetheless, another response is also possible. Humour can be utilised to challenge stereotypes, engaging in playful, skilled performance that seeks to expose the limitations of oppressive discourses. Beyond performance, Gournelos and Greene (2011, p. xxvii) argue that humour has an important role to play in challenging terrorist related discourse in politics and the media. They maintain that it can be used to contest simplified notions of good and evil, while constructing a counter-narrative that challenges mainstream news media and official state narratives. Consequently, humour can serve as an instrument of resistance to dominant ideologies and associated norms (James, 2015). In so doing, it can attack racist truth claims and points of ambivalence, while nurturing a shared sense of identity (Weaver, 2010). Thus, humour can function not only as politically charged, nuanced action, intended to expose the limitations of mainstream interpretations, but also as a way to foster shared vocabularies of resistance and motivation. This suggests that such satirical practices are soundly collective, thoroughly cultural and inherently bound up with identity. Such issues will be further explored in the next section as the threat of radicalisation through social media and young Muslims' use of online materials to politically engage with such ideas are considered.

Young Muslims and 'Radical' Online Media

The online environment offers fertile ground for the circulation of stereotypical and racialising discourses, as well as their contestation. Like others of their generation, young Muslims are "youth of the digital age" (Collins et al., 2011). They make extensive use of the online environment to communicate with friends on social networking sites (such as Facebook). Sixty-seven per cent of the respondents in Collins et al. (2011) study of Australian Muslims between the ages of 15–25 used the internet socially, with 49% utilising it for leisure and entertainment. Only 11% used it for religious information or to access news.

The risks posed by Muslim online engagement with radical, political and religious views are a common narrative in media debates, policy discourse and academic research. Such preoccupation reflects that social media has proven to be a seductive medium through which terrorist organisations seek to disseminate information. Sophisticated, production-quality images, slick promos mimicking Hollywood action films and hip music videos are distributed through social media such as Facebook, Twitter and YouTube to target the so-called 'Millennial generation' (Blaker, 2015). Yet, studies and accounts of the relationship between online media and radicalisation are often informed by crude assumptions about the overwhelming power and influence of media discourse to mesmerise, captivate, and convince. This moral panic about the capacity of social media to radicalise young Muslims is hardly surprising given racist stereotypes and dominant discourses labelling them as part of a 'risky' minority. Nevertheless, despite the availability of online extremist posts most young people do not use the media to access 'radical' political and religious views but rather to communicate with friends (Collins et al., 2011). Consequently, social media can be a productive and creative political space for young people to undertake the work necessary to manage potentially 'risky' identities. Furthermore, while respondents in Collins et al. (2011) study identified those producing and circulating political messages online as engaging in political action, individuals who read or watched such material were not labelled as participating in political action. This is not the assumption held by those state organisations undertaking surveillance, which have an apparent propensity to conclude that observing 'radicalisation' media is inherently political and the first step on route to terrorism. Such stereotypical judgements are often given pseudo-legitimacy when they become embodied in 'objective indicators.'

The internet provides social science research with new and challenging sites of research and data. Blogs are a rich and accessible source of qualitative 'user-generated data' and are widely read but they raise methodological challenges including data sampling, data collection and analysis. Furthermore, the dynamic and colossal nature of the internet makes it difficult to undertake a detailed content analysis of the online media activities of young Muslims. Consequently, any study focusing on this topic will provide little more than a momentary glimpse into an almost limitless networked mediascape. Yet, even limited glances have value.

As is the case with many small scale qualitative research studies, the purpose of study is not to generate overarching generalisations, but to discern the subtle details and generate insights that may be otherwise be missed in larger positivist approaches. Thus, this research should be seen as exploratory in nature, offering initial insights into some of the discursive activities of young Muslim's online, rather than as an attempt to develop a framework detailing their political responses to (de)radicalisation discourses.

Websites were selected via opportunity sampling, following Boolean searches using key words and phrases. Initial searches were conducted in late 2016 using the term 'Muslim youth.' This generated a list of online groups such as MuslimYouth.net (2017), Muslim Youth Helpline (2013) and Muslim Youth Facebook (2012). A second search using the term 'Muslim youth blogs' generated UK and USA information sites. Finally, a third search utilising the blog metrics website *Blog Rank* (2013) revealed a list entitled the Top 50 blogs in Islam Category, which provided numerous sources for analysis. It should be noted that access to some of the blogs uncovered by these searches proved problematic, specifically where password protection was used and registration was required. Due to the ethical constraints of using social media data not publicly available, such sites were not included in the final study.

The searches uncovered blogs, Facebook sites and other social media posts associated with young Muslims. It is worth noting that the nature of the internet makes it problematic to ascertain identity beyond the claims made. Hence judgements regarding whether online commentators are young Muslims were of necessity taken at face value. Furthermore, judgements about what constitutes Muslim websites are also potentially problematic. For as Begum (2009) observes in her study of young peoples' internet use in Singapore, young Muslims inject variety into Muslim identities. Hence, some young people describe their personal, club or organisational sites as Islamic, while others avoided this designation. Discussion will focus on those sites that self-identify as Muslim.

Many of the blogs found were concerned with promoting religious teachings, addressing matters of health, challenging stereotypes, combatting bullying and promoting social cohesion. Some sites referenced proverbs, sermons and the work of Islamic scholars. Varisco's (2010) study of Muslim authored blogs found a similar range of topics. Some blogs were archives of materials from Muslim scholars, including video sermons, while others were resumes, commercial sites or presented art (Varisco, 2010). Though most sites listed on the Blog Rank (2013) Top 50 blogs in Islam Category were visually appealing and accessible, only www.MuslimMatters.org (2017) offered blogs designed to engage young Muslims. Yet the site had no posts for 2016 and featured one blog in 2015 about what young Muslims should do after the *Charlie Hebdo* massacre in Paris (January 2015). This was a post that generated only two responses.

Sites, like the official Muslim Youth League Facebook (2017) page (over 12,000 members) and Muslim Youth Union Power Facebook (2017) page (over 19,000 members), were dominated by images of older men and material that did not engage directly in political debate. Based in the Republic of Ireland, #Jihad on the site the Journal.ie (2017) explains the meaning of the term Jihad, while seeking to discourage young Muslims from joining radical militant groups. This site lacks high engagement and received less than 5,000 total views in 2015 and just over 800 *Facebook* likes. By way of comparison, Maniac Muslim (2015) a satirical site established in 2005 has 25,000 followers and over 38,000 likes as of 31 October 2016.

What is notable from the online searches is the difficulty of finding websites that might be labelled as 'radical.' Furthermore, the extent to which humour played a major role in young Muslims resistance to labels such as 'extremists' and 'violent radicals' is also noteworthy. To illustrate this latter point in more detail the focus will now shift to the Muslim Medicine website, which humorously responded to the British *Daily Telegraph* newspaper story "how to spot a terrorist living in your neighbourhood" (Judd, 2013).

'10 THINGS YOU CAN DO TO NOT BE A TERRORIST': RADICALISATION AND HUMOUR ONLINE

Muslim Medicine is a site established in 2011, which had 10,000 followers in 2014 and over 19,000 likes. Nowhere does the Muslim Medicine website state its authors or its target audience. Indeed, the website meets every question of authorship with ambiguous and spoof responses. Nevertheless, the cartoons, images, photos, the style of language suggest that the target audience is 'Muslim youth.' The site features both serious newspaper reports as well as satirical commentary on the absurdity of stories such as "How to spot a terrorist living in your neighbourhood." The original *Daily Telegraph* story starts with the author calling for individuals, and "Muslim communities in particular," to inform on neighbours they suspect of extremism, a term which is viewed unproblematically as "we already know all we need to know about radicalisation" (Judd, 2013). The article then offers 'insights' into how to identify those becoming radicalised, warning against those adopting traditional Arab dress (or abandoning it to avoid suspicion!), collecting Jihadi material or withdrawing from contact with non-Muslims.

The spoof response of the young Muslim's entitled '10 things you can do to NOT be a Terrorist' begins by poking fun at the image posted as part of the *Daily Telegraph* story, "of a random white guy using binoculars to spy on what I can only assume must be Muslims up to no good" (Muslim Medicine, 2013). The author then responds to the ten 'identifiers' covered in the original article before concluding that in order to avoid becoming a terrorist Muslims need to ensure that they are:

> A fat, lazy, clean shaven doctor who never bathes, brushes his teeth, or bothers to change his clothes, but is a big-time social party-animal and is a ladies' man as well (despite already being married)—he also dresses as Sailor Moon on Fridays, collects Pokémon cards for a hobby, and is an avid Rebecca Black fan. (Muslim Medicine, 2013)

As ludicrous as this image might be, the author of this spoof is merely responding to Judd's (2013) 'identifiers' by suggesting opposites and in doing so, using humour to reveal the ridiculous nature of the original suggestions. In the comments section, Fatima A notes the crude ignorance of the initial report and the inability of the authors to comprehend it as such, stating "I think you did an awesome job of destroying the telegraphs' article through your humour and satire. I can imagine the people at the telegraph reading through this post and not getting it though because they clearly thought their piece was journalistically credible." Similarly, another commentator responds to the satire, posting the comment "You guys are the bomb! You're killing me!"

It could be argued that some young Muslims are more likely to be attracted to informative blogs able to develop sharp, engaging and humorous modes of information delivery, than those sites produced with explicit intention of presenting point by point rebuttals to the radicalisation discourse. This illustrates that young people are not uncritical consumers of mainstream media, but active political agents able to develop content and engage in deliberative practice in various forums. One way in which they address the semantic drift of the notion of radicalisation and the misapplication of flawed risk indicators is through humour. After all, "joking is one way of resolving the semantic side-effects" (Weaver, 2010, p. 35). Satire can be used to challenge misguided ideas of truth, as tropes are utilised to manipulate meaning, expose racist practices and challenge dominant ideology (Back, 1996). Young Muslims' use of political satire is particularly important insofar as a lack of humour is seen in the West to denote social exclusion. For as Kuipers (2011, p. 76) maintains "[h]umour encompasses many traits central to modern personhood: being a free, reflexive, self-controlled, socially flexible individual. Therefore, accusing people of not having a sense of humour indicates not only their social exclusion, but their unsuitability for modernity." In this context, not only is humorous engagement with radicalisation and its operationalisation a form of resistance and an assertion of collective identity for young Muslims, but it also starkly challenges the misguided perception that this group is not integrated into mainstream society.

Conclusion

Following appropriation by Western governments and the security sector, the notion of radicalisation has been used to create disciplinary regimes that seek to reconstruct maligned Muslim subjectivities in a coercive and punitive manner. Prejudices are given form through the 'anticipatory logic' of indicators and related practices. Given this interplay of (de)radicalisation practices and risk discourses, the manner in which young Muslims choose to engage in political and religious discussion online is inevitably complex and multi-faceted. Yet where they have engaged in dialogue about 'radicalisation' their responses have moved beyond infuriation, disenchantment or responsibilisation to engage with racist stereotypes through the creative use of humour. As Orwell (1968, p. 284) observed "A thing is funny when it upsets the established order. Every joke is a tiny revolution". Thus, young Muslims simultaneously confirm their sense of belonging and revolt against prejudicial practices through the use of satire. Future research needs to start to map how such humorous resistance fits into the broader political discourse of young Muslims online.

In conclusion, some young Muslims use humour online to combat the ill-considered de-radicalisation and counter-terrorist strategies that threaten to alienate large sections of society. Not only does such practice politically empower those involved, but also, as Kuipers (2011) notes, such discussions serve to challenge the racist stereotype that Muslims are humourless.

References

Akbarzadeh, S. (2016). The Muslim question in Australia: Islamophobia and Muslim alienation. *Journal of Muslim Minority Affairs, 36*(3), 323–333.

Australian Government. (2015). *Preventing violent extremism and radicalisation in Australia*. Canberra: Attorney-General's Department, Commonwealth of Australia.

Back, L. (1996). *New ethnicities and urban culture. Racisms and multiculture in young lives*. London: University College London Press.

Begum, R. (2009). Singapore youths and internet-mediated Muslim identities: Negotiating with traditional authority. In M. Nawab & F. Ali (Eds.), *Igniting thought, unleashing youth: Perspectives on Muslim youth and activism in Singapore* (pp. 23–54). Singapore: Select Publishing.

Bigo, D., & Tsoukala, A. (Eds.). (2008). *Terror, insecurity and liberty: Illiberal practices of liberal regimes after 9/11*. London: Routledge.

Blaker, L. (2015). The Islamic State's use of online social media. *Military Cyber Affairs, 1*.1, *Article 4*. Retrieved December 2, 2016, from http://scholarcommons.usf.edu/mca/vol1/iss1/4

Castel, R. (1991). From dangerousness to risk. In G. Burchell, C. Gordon, & P. Miller (Eds.), *The Foucault effect: Studies in governmentality* (pp. 281–298). London: Harvester/Wheatsheaf.

Cohen, S. (1973). *Folk devils and moral panics: The creation of the mods and rockers*. London: Paladin.

Collins, J., Jakubowicz, A., Chafic, W., Al-momani, K., Hussain, J., Ghosh, D., Cole, D., & Pennycook, A. (2011). *Voices shaping the perspectives of young Muslim Australians*. Cosmopolitan civil societies research centre university of technology, Sydney. Retrieved December 2, 2016, from https://www.dss.gov.au/our-responsibilities/settlement-and-multicultural-affairs/publications/voices-shaping-the-perspectives-of-young-muslim-australians

Coppock, V. (2014). Can you spot a terrorist in your classroom? Problematising the recruitment of schools to the "war on terror" in the United Kingdom. *Global Studies of Childhood, 4*(2), 115–125.

Dean, M. (1999). Risk, calculable and incalculable. In D. Lupton (Ed.), *Risk and sociocultural theory: New directions and perspectives* (pp. 131–159). Cambridge: Cambridge University Press.

Foucault, M. (1978). Governmentality. In J. Faubion (Ed.), *Power: Essential works of Foucault 1954–1984* (pp. 201–222). London: Penguin.

Furedi, F. (2003). *Therapy culture: Cultivating vulnerability in an uncertain age.* London: Routledge.

Gournelos, T., & Greene, V. (2011). Introduction. In T. Gournelos & V. Greene (Eds.), *A decade of dark humor: How comedy, irony and satire shaped post 9/11 America* (pp. xi–xxxv). Jackson, Mississippi: University of Mississippi Press.

Hickman, M., Thomas, L., Silvestri, S., & Nickels, H. (2011). *Suspect communities? Counter-terrorism policy, the press and the impact on Irish and Muslim communities in Britain.* London: London Metropolitan University. Retrieved December 2, 2016, from https://www.city.ac.uk/__data/assets/pdf_file/0005/96287/suspect-communities-report-july2011.pdf

HM Government. (2009). *The United Kingdom's strategy for countering international terrorism.* London: Home Office.

Hopkins, P. (2007). Young Muslim men's experiences of local landscapes after 11th September 2001. In C. Atkinson, P. Hopkins, & M.-p. Kwan (Eds.), *Geographies of Muslim identities: Diaspora, gender and belonging* (pp. 189–200). Aldershot: Ashgate.

Jalalzai, M. K. (2017). Surveillance and security crisis in Europe. *Daily Times.* Retrieved January 11, 2017, from http://dailytimes.com.pk/opinion/10-Jan-17/surveillance-and-security-crisis-in-europe.

James, A. B. (2015). Humour as resistance: Disaster humour in post-9/11 United States. *The European Journal of Humour Research, 2*(3), 28–41.

Journal.ie. (2017). *#Jihad.* Retrieved February 6, 2017, from http://www.thejournal.ie/jihad/news

Judd, A. (2013). How to spot a terrorist living in your neighbourhood. *The Daily Telegraph.* Retrieved December 2, 2016, from http://www.telegraph.co.uk/news/uknews/terrorism-in-the-uk/10084172/How-to-spot-a-terrorist-living-in-your-neighbourhood.html

Kuipers, G. (2011). The politics of humour in the public sphere: Cartoons, power and modernity in the first transnational humour scandal. *European Journal of Cultural Studies, 14*(1), 63–80.

Kundnani, A. (2012). Radicalisation: The journey of a concept. *Race & Class, 54*(2), 3–25.

Lentini, P. (2015). Demonizing ISIL and defending Muslims: Australian Muslim citizenship and Tony Abbott's "death cult" rhetoric. *Islam and Christian–Muslim Relations, 26*(2), 237–252.

Lynch, O. (2015). Suspicion, exclusion and othering since 9/11: The victimisation of Muslim youth. In J. Argomaniz & O. Lynch (Eds.), *International perspectives on terrorist victimisation* (pp. 173–200). London: Palgrave Macmillan.

Maniac Muslim. (2015). *Maniac Muslim*. Retrieved February 6, 2017, from http://maniacmuslim.com

Miller, J. (2013). Resilience, violent extremism and religious education. *British Journal of Religious Education, 35*(2), 188–200.

Monaghan, J. (2013). Terror carceralism: Surveillance, security governance and de/civilization.' *Punishment & Society, 15*(1), 3–22.

Monaghan, J., & Molnar, A. (2016). Radicalisation theories, policing practices, and the future of terrorism? *Critical Studies on Terrorism, 9*(3), 393–413.

Moore, K., Mason, P., & Lewis, J. (2008). *Images of Islam in the UK: The representation of British Muslims in the national print news media 2000–2008*. Cardiff School of Journalism, Media and Cultural Studies. Retrieved December 2, 2016, from http://orca.cf.ac.uk/53005/1/08channel4-dispatches.pdf

Morgan, G., & Poynting, S. (2012). Introduction: The transnational folk devil. In G. Morgan & S. Poynting (Eds.), *Global Islamophobia: Muslims and moral panic in the west* (pp. 1–14). London: Ashgate.

Muslim Matters. (2017). *MuslimMatters.org*. Retrieved February 6, 2017, from www.MuslimMatters.org

Muslim Medicine. (2013). 10 things you can do to not be a terrorist. *Muslim Medicine*. Retrieved December 2, 2016, from http://muslimmedicine.net/?p=919

Muslim Youth Facebook. (2012). *Muslim youth official*. Retrieved February 6, 2017, from https://www.facebook.com/pg/muslimyouthofficial/about/?ref=page_internal

Muslim Youth Helpline. (2013). *MYH Home*. Retrieved February 6, 2017, from http://www.myh.org.uk

Muslim Youth League Facebook. (2017). *Muslim Youth League*. Retrieved February 6, 2017, from https://www.facebook.com/pg/iumyl/about/?ref=page_internal

Muslim Youth Union Power Facebook. (2017). *Muslim Youth Union Power*. Retrieved February 6, 2017, from https://www.facebook.com/Muslims-youth-union-power-1372335739460567

MuslimYouth.net. (2017). *Homepage*. Retrieved February 6, 2017, from http://www.muslimyouth.net/home

Mythen, G., Walklate, S., & Khan, F. (2009). "I'm a Muslim, but I'm not a terrorist": Victimization, risky identities and the performance of safety. *British Journal of Criminology, 49*(6), 736–754.

Mythen, G., Walklate, S., & Khan, F. (2013). Why should we have to prove we're alright? Counter-terrorism, risk and partial securities. *Sociology, 47*(2), 383–398.

Neumann, P. (2013). The trouble with radicalization. *International Affairs, 89*(4), 873–893.
Orwell, G. (1968). Funny, but not vulgar. In S. Angus & I. Angus (Eds.), *The collected essays, journalism and letters of George Orwell* (pp. 284–290). London: Secker & Warburg.
Blog Rank. (2013). *Blog rank home.* Retrieved February 6, 2017, from http://www.blogmetrics.org
RCMP (Royal Canadian Mounted Police). (2009). *Radicalization: A guide for the perplexed.* Ottawa: RCMP.
Richards, A. (2015). From terrorism to radicalization to extremism. *International Affairs, 91*(2), 371–380.
Saeed, A. (2007). Media, racism and Islamophobia: The representation of Islam and Muslims in the media. *Sociology Compass, 1*(2), 443–462.
Sukarieh, M., & Tannock, S. (2016). The deradicalisation of education: Terror, youth and the assault on learning. *Race & Class, 57*(4), 22–38.
Varisco, D. (2010). Muslims and the media in the blogosphere. *Contemporary Islam, 4*(1), 157–177.
Verhofstadt, G. (2017). *Manifesto: For the renewal of European democracy.* Retrieved January 11, 2017, from http://alde.eu/uploaded/manifesto_for_the_renewal_of_european_democracy.pdf
Weaver, S. (2010). The other laughs back: Humour and resistance in anti-racist comedy. *Sociology, 44*(1), 31–48.

Andrew Hope is Associate Professor in the School of Social Sciences at the University of Adelaide, Australia. Drawing upon a sociologically informed approach his research focuses upon the relationships between young people, the internet, risk and surveillance. His recent writings have focused upon the discursive construction of radicalisation in the public sphere.

Julie Matthews is Associate Professor and Associate Head Research in the School of Education at the University of Adelaide, Australia. She is a sociologist of education with research expertise in refugee education, reconciliation, sustainability and international education. Her current projects focus on refugee education policy and anti-radicalisation education.

CHAPTER 10

Young People's Political Participation in Europe in Times of Crisis

Maria Grasso

INTRODUCTION

In the 1990s, authors started discussing the idea of an 'anti-political' zeitgeist marked by growing apathy and widespread cynicism about politics. Stoker (2011) identified the features of an 'anti-political' culture in Britain: alienation from the mainstream political parties, a growing disdain for formal politics and an increasing disengagement from all modes of conventional political participation. This chapter examines young people and the regeneration of politics through new forms of political participation across Europe in times of crisis. To speak to these theoretical debates from a comparative perspective, this chapter analyses survey data from across Europe collected in 2015, in the context of a collaborative European project, which aimed to analyse how citizens experienced and responded to the economic crisis that started in 2007–2008. The data comes from France, Germany, Greece, Italy, Poland, Spain, Sweden, Switzerland and the United Kingdom (UK) (see Grasso & Giugni, 2016a). The chapter outlines some of the key theoretical debates in the study of youth politics and political participation, before analysing differences between young

M. Grasso (✉)
Department of Politics, University of Sheffield, Sheffield, UK

© The Author(s) 2018
S. Pickard, J. Bessant (eds.), *Young People Re-Generating Politics in Times of Crises*, Palgrave Studies in Young People and Politics,
DOI 10.1007/978-3-319-58250-4_10

and older people in their modes of political participation. In so doing, the chapter sheds light on the spheres where young people are most likely to be regenerating politics.

Young People in the Current Context

To analyse political action, I examine a variety of repertoires. For some authors, young people today are apolitical and their civic disengagement threatens the legitimacy of democratic political systems (Grasso, 2011a), whereas others have argued that young people are not disinterested, but rather simply interested in a different type of politics to their elders (Marsh, O'Toole, & Jones, 2007). Moreover, it should be noted that political action takes on a new meaning in the current context marked by the legacy of the 2008 global financial crisis (Giugni & Grasso, 2015a), by the adoption of neoliberal policy frames (Temple et al., 2016), by high unemployment and unprecedented levels of debt, and by major changes brought about by technology.

While the last century has brought forth great strides in the development and the rise in living standards, it has also witnessed deepening economic crises, leading to austerity policies, which have particularly impacted on the most vulnerable sections of society, i.e. young people, old people and those in poverty, or in receipt of government benefits (Giugni & Grasso, 2015a). In particular, young people have been understood as one of the most affected groups by the recent economic crisis that emerged out of the 2008 global financial crisis (Grasso & Giugni, 2016b). Given that the crisis has occurred while young people are in their "impressionable years" and currently entering the labour market it is likely to have a disproportionate effect on their lives relative to other age groups (Grasso, 2016a). In *Understanding Youth in the Global Economic Crisis*, France (2016), examines policies directed at youth in Australia, Canada, New Zealand and the UK. He notes how youth is currently viewed as an inherently problematic life-stage and how increasingly governmental agendas have acted to anticipate young people's responsibility for their own welfare to hasten the transition to adulthood, i.e. productivity and responsibility. Trends identified include: lengthening of educational pathways and an increasingly individualised understanding of 'human capital'; a strengthening of the imperative to work, while work is becoming more precarious; an increasing tendency for young people to have to invest in their long term financial welfare, resulting in parents being responsible for children longer and generating inter-generational inequalities. Moreover, in the current context, international mobility has become a key component of young people's mode of developing their human capital in precarious employment contexts—with this opportunity in turn patterned by inequalities. Given these developments, the current period can be understood as fundamentally recasting youth citizenship. This situation is further problematised since the current context is characterised by growing economic uncertainty and insecurities (finding employment, affordable housing, pensions and welfare), economic precariousness and social exclusion. The austerity policies enacted by many countries across Europe have recently sparked a series of protests bringing to the fore questions of inequality and the redistribution of resources and a number of scholars have begun re-examining these questions in light of recent events (Giugni & Grasso, 2016; Grasso & Giugni, 2013).

Repertoires of Political Action

Political participation is made up of all those political activities that citizen can become involved in as they to attempt to influence political decision-making (Pattie, Seyd, & Whiteley, 2004). Political participation is typically understood as essential for democratic government, since it allows citizens to promote their individual and collective interests. Political participation can be understood as made up for more mainstream, conventional types of actions, such as voting or being members of political parties—or more confrontational or unconventional modes of actions, such as protesting on a march or occupying a square (Grasso, 2011a, 2016b). Participation is understood as a fundamental feature of democracy for effective representation. Despite the key importance of political participation, several scholars have argued that young citizens in particular are increasingly withdrawing from politics, particularly through formal means (e.g. voting and party membership) (Grasso, 2016a). While scholars have argued that we have witnessed 'the normalisation of protest' (Van Aelst & Walgrave, 2001) and the proliferation of 'new social movements,' including more recent incarnations such as Occupy London (Giugni & Grasso, 2015b), we also know there still exist large inequalities in participation based on socio-demographics and political attitudes (Grasso & Giugni, 2016a; Inan & Grasso, 2017).

In this section, I analyse differences in the repertoires of political action between age groups. While recent events, such as major protests against austerity might suggest a rise of youth activism, examination of the data across repertoires of activism will allow for testing this assumption. Most discussions of political participation posit a key distinction between 'conventional,' e.g. voting and joining political parties, and 'unconventional' participation, e.g. protesting and participating in social movements. While this distinction is rather basic, it is a useful starting point for any analysis of participation, since the key argument tends to be that young people are less active than older people in conventional means and more active in the non-institutional modes. While voting is still the most common form of political participation, the argument is that it is becoming increasingly less important to citizens today than at any time since the franchise was extended to women in 1918 (Franklin, 2004; Hay, 2007; Mair, 2006). Studies have shown that the majority of young citizens have little or no contact with political bodies or organisations and that most forms of political participation are on the decline if we take into account generational differences (Grasso, 2016a). Declining party membership is also taken to show the extent to which citizens—and young ones in particular—have grown increasingly disenchanted with formal politics (Dalton & Wattenberg, 2000; Van Biezen, Mair, & Poguntke, 2012). Additionally, in recent times, online activism has come to be conceived as an increasingly important dimension of participation (Pickard, 2018).

The results presented in Table 10.1 show that people aged under 35 tend to be less likely than the older age groups to engage in conventional activities, such as voting in both national and European elections or contacting a politician. However, they are more likely to be party members and there are no significant differences between age groups for volunteering for a party, attending meetings, donating money or wearing campaign symbols. Under 35 s were, in general, more likely to be involved in unconventional activities, though there were no age group differences for the more mainstream means: signing a petition and boycotting products. Under 35 s were generally more likely than the older age group to engage in online activism. As such, overall, this suggests that while young people are less likely to engage in some conventional activities, they are more likely to be involved in extra-institutional modes of political engagement and online activism.

Table 10.1 also shows that only voting is consistently practiced by a majority. The next most frequent activity, searching for political information online, barely featured. Even signing a petition (whether online or

Table 10.1 Age group differences in political activism (last 12 months)

Type of political activism	18–34	35+	Sig.
Conventional			
Voted at last national election	67	84	***
Voted at last European election	57	68	***
Party member	14	12	**
Volunteered for a party	5	5	ns
Contacted or visited a politician or government official (online or offline)	10	14	***
Donated money to a political organisation/party or action group (online or offline)	8	9	ns
Displayed/worn a political or campaign logo/badge/sticker (online or offline)	9	8	ns
Attended a meeting of a political organisation/party or action group	9	10	ns
Unconventional			
Signed a petition/public letter/campaign appeal (online or offline)	33	33	ns
Boycotted products for political/ethical/environment reasons (online or offline)	26	25	ns
Deliberately bought products for political/ethical/env't reasons (online or offline)	24	21	**
Attended a demonstration, march or rally	12	10	**
Joined a strike	7	5	***
Joined an occupation, sit-in, or blockade	4	2	***
Damaged things like breaking windows, removing roads signs, etc.	2	1	***
Used personal violence like fighting with the police	2	1	***
Online activism			
Searched for information about politics online	52	46	***
Visited the website of a political party or a politician	34	30	***
Discussed or shared opinion on politics on a social network site e.g. Facebook	28	25	***
Joined or started a political group on Facebook/followed a politician or party	16	11	***

Data: LIVEWHAT project survey 2015 (see Grasso & Giugni, 2016a)
Cells are %; Significance $*p < 0.05$; $**p < 0.01$; $***p < 0.001$ from two-tailed tests; ns means not significant at $p < 0.05$

offline) an unconventional activity that can be done simply and without cost, and visiting political websites, the next two most popular activities, were only carried out by about a third of respondents. Despite the emergence of a number of online petitioning platforms, such as 38 Degrees and Change.org, it is compelling that on average, only one third of citizens say they have ever signed a petition. Contacting a Member of Parliament

(MP) even in the age of e-mail is practiced by only around 1 in 10 of citizens. Despite the numerous free trade and 'green living' campaigns, fewer than 1 in 5 of citizens said that they practiced some form of ethical consumerism. From Table 10.1, it is clear that the more demanding the activity in terms of effort, time and other resources, the lower the proportion practicing it. The more challenging activities, such as joining an occupation, damaging property or fighting with the police are reported by only a tiny fraction of the population (though under-reporting due to social desirability might also be at play here).

Young people's disengagement from formal politics has been an increasing worry particularly in some countries. This is since their non-participation threatens the legitimacy of the political system. Some have argued that young people are active in non-mainstream types of politics, but others argue they are simply apathetic (Marsh et al., 2007). Low voter turnout is generally used to evidence these claims. In the UK, for example, this has led to the development of groups such as Bite the Ballot (Pickard, 2015) and campaigns to raise awareness of National Voter Registration Day (#NVRD) for over 16 s. Bodies like the British Youth Council are also active in trying to raise youth political participation particularly through Youth Parliaments (Pickard, 2018). As such, while voting is still the most common mode of participation, small groups of young people also participate in alternative modes of engagement, such as occupations, sit-ins, protests and boycotts. These unconventional modes tend to be associated with social movements and other forms of identity or lifestyle politics (Saunders et al., 2012). Moreover, the rising prominence of social media has contributed to 'clicktivism.' The rise of digital technology has had wide-ranging repercussions for the way young people express themselves and participate politically. While the results presented above examined age group differences in participation for the entire sample available from the nine European democracies analysed, we might wonder whether these countries exhibit interesting differences among themselves in terms of the age group differences in participation. I turn to this question in the next section.

Cross-national Differences in Patterns of Youth Participation

Table 10.2 presents the results by country. As we can see, there is a considerable degree of congruence between countries. Across countries, young people's lower propensity to turnout to vote is confirmed. Young people

Table 10.2 Age group differences in political activism, by country (last 12 months)

Type of political activism	France			Germany			Greece			Italy		
	18–34	35+	Sig.	18–34	35+	Sig.	18–34	35+	Sig.	18–34	35+	Sig.
Conventional												
Voted (nat)	47	81	***	70	82	***	80	91	***	79	87	***
Voted (EU)	46	76	***	61	70	***	77	88	***	76	81	**
Party member	12	9	*	9	9	ns	12	16	*	21	15	**
Volunteered for a party	5	3	ns	5	6	ns	3	4	ns	8	4	**
Contacted politician	6	8	*	8	11	*	10	14	**	12	11	ns
Donated money	4	5	ns	8	9	ns	6	5	ns	6	7	ns
Displayed badge	3	4	ns	10	8	ns	7	8	ns	10	8	ns
Attended a meeting	4	6	ns	7	8	ns	13	13	ns	16	13	*
Unconventional												
Signed a petition	16	19	ns	38	29	***	25	38	****	36	34	ns
Boycotted products	19	17	ns	32	28	ns	30	39	***	21	20	ns
Bought products	14	11	ns	32	29	ns	18	25	***	21	15	***
Demonstration	13	14	ns	10	7	*	22	24	ns	13	11	ns
Joined a strike	6	5	ns	5	3	*	13	14	ns	12	12	ns
Joined occupation	3	1	*	2	2	ns	7	4	*	6	4	*
Damaged things	2	1	**	2	1	**	2	1	**	3	2	ns
Used violence	2	1	*	1	1	ns	2	1	**	4	2	**
Online activism												
Searched pol info online	27	30	ns	50	50	ns	69	71	ns	50	41	***
Visited political website	15	19	*	30	28	ns	36	38	ns	30	25	**
Discussed/shared politics	19	15	ns	19	17	ns	40	45	**	35	29	*
Joined/started pol group	6	6	ns	10	6	***	20	18	ns	17	12	***

(continued)

Table 10.2 (continued)

	Poland			Spain			Sweden			Switzerland			UK		
	18–34	35+	Sig.	18–34	35+	Sig.	18–34	35+	Sig.	18–34	35+	Sig.	18–34	35+	Sig.
	58	82	***	72	84	***	88	95	***	27	56	***	88	93	**
	60	72	***	71	78	***	65	73	***	na	na	na	55	74	***
	9	6	*	13	11	ns	19	15	ns	13	11	ns	19	13	***
	3	2	ns	8	7	ns	4	5	ns	4	3	ns	8	5	*
	12	15	*	12	14	ns	9	16	***	9	12	ns	18	26	**
	11	11	ns	6	7	ns	10	10	ns	10	11	ns	14	15	ns
	9	5	**	9	10	ns	12	12	ns	9	6	*	13	12	ns
	8	9	ns	12	13	ns	7	9	ns	6	8	ns	10	8	ns
	29	22	***	38	39	ns	30	30	ns	35	32	ns	52	51	ns
	14	12	ns	23	23	ns	35	33	ns	27	27	ns	33	28	ns
	17	12	**	16	15	ns	34	31	ns	32	27	*	30	25	ns
	8	5	*	17	18	ns	8	7	ns	8	5	*	6	4	*
	2	2	ns	15	6	***	13	4	*	4	1	***	3	2	***
	3	2	*	5	2	**	1	1	ns	3	1	**	1	1	ns
	3	1	**	2	1	**	1	0	ns	2	1	**	0	0	ns
	3	1	**	2	1	**	0	0	ns	2	1	**	0	0	ns
	51	44	***	49	47	ns	56	46	ns	46	42	ns	63	50	***
	36	31	*	40	30	***	44	34	***	27	28	ns	46	37	**
	27	24	ns	31	25	**	24	25	ns	22	17	*	36	27	***
	19	11	***	20	13	***	13	12	***	14	7	***	19	12	***

Data: LIVEWHAT project survey 2015 (see Grasso & Giugni, 2016a)
Cells are %; Significance * $p < 0.05$; ** $p < 0.01$; *** $p < 0.001$ from two-tailed tests; ns means not significant at $p < 0.05$

are also less likely to contact politicians on the whole. The differences in the other modes of conventional political action are less marked, also since these tend to be practiced by smaller proportions of citizens. There is an interesting exception in Italy, where young people are more likely to be involved with political parties than older citizens, perhaps owing to the emergence of the *Movimento Cinque Stelle* (Five Star movement—the new populist party in Italy) in this period, which garnered much support from younger citizens. As for the differences in unconventional participation, we find little evidence of major age group differences. On the whole, there are small or no differences in the more mainstream activities, such as petitioning and consumer politics. There are more marked age differences in the more confrontational modes of unconventional activism, though here the absolute proportions practicing these activities also tend to be lower. These findings thus confirm the insights from theories of biographical availability, the idea that younger citizens tend to have more spare time to engage in this sort of high risk activism (Saunders et al., 2012). Also, confirming insights from the literature, particularly in in Italy, Poland, Spain, and the UK, young people tend to be more active in online activism. All in all, results suggest that other than voting, young people tend to slightly more active in more confrontational political actions, though it should be borne in mind that these tend to be practiced by smaller proportions of citizens.

Age Groups and Generations

While the previous sections have examined age group differences in participation, we need to be wary not to extrapolate all too readily from these patterns any 'generational' differences. This is because we need to leave intact the possibility that young people may become more politically active as they grow up. Mannheim (1928) spoke of the impressionability of young people: the idea that the events of an epoch leave the greatest imprint on those undergoing socialisation. Despite the expansion of education and rising technological developments, turnout and other modes of participation, such as party membership, have been shown to be declining across Europe. This suggests underlying changes in the political choices that new generations are faced with (Grasso, 2016a). While in the past communities would have been clearly divided along political lines and Left and Right had real resonance in the daily lives of people, today social democratic parties are in crisis and the axes of political allegiances are

Table 10.3 Levels of political activism by generations (%)

Formative period	1930–1944	1945–1964	1965–1978	1979–1996	1997–2010
Years of birth	1910–1924	1925–1944	1945–1958	1959–1976	1977–1990
Contacting					
Contacted your MP	14	20	21	14	6
Contacted a government department	3	5	6	4	2
Contacted radio, TV or newspaper	3	6	8	5	2
Contacted an influential person	3	6	7	4	3
Group activism					
Raised an issue with group you belong to	4	6	7	4	2
Formed a group of likeminded people	1	2	3	1	1
Protest activism					
Gone on a demonstration	3	7	15	12	9
Signed a petition	27	39	48	46	39

Data: British Social Attitudes 1983–2012 (see Jennings et al., 2015)
Cells are %

shifting to encompass other attitudinal dimensions such as values of openness and tolerance versus cultural protectionism.

Table 10.3 shows levels of participation by generation (only for the UK with the necessary long-term longitudinal data available from the British Social Attitudes surveys collated from 1983 to 2012, see Jennings, Gray, Hay, & Farrall, 2015 and Grasso, Farrall, Gray, Hay, & Jennings, 2017 for details on the dataset). The data is pooled from all the different surveys so we can actually compare generations in their patterns of participation using data from when they were in different life stages. In this way, we can avoid the pitfall of assuming that age group differences examined only in one cross-section of time—e.g. a survey year—are real generational differences. To deal with this issue, pooling data from the 1983–2012 surveys allows us to examine members of different generations in different life stages. Table 10.3 shows that the youngest generation, 'Blair's Babies,' are less likely than older generations to be involved in political activities including protest. This evidence presented in Table 10.3 and supported by other studies of political participation across generations (Grasso, 2014, 2016a) challenges the idea that the youngest generations are just as active as the older ones, just acting through unconventional avenues (Dalton, 2009; Marsh et al., 2007; Sloam, 2007). This evidence suggests that it is not quite a simple story of younger generations being more likely than older ones to engage in unconventional activism such as sign petitions, join boycotts, or demonstrations (Inglehart & Welzel, 2005).

Earlier it was shown how younger people seem slightly more likely to engage in the more confrontational modes of participation, but these activities tend to attract very small proportions. Others have argued that young people's political involvement is increasingly mediated through new technologies and social media linked to the idea of 'clicktivism' (Castells, 2000; Pickard, 2018). For some, the rise of lifestyle politics twinned with the popularity of social networking sites such as Facebook and Twitter has encouraged young people to construct their own sense of community through the internet often based around identity politics and campaigning around issues surrounding the politics of recognition (Castells, 2000). In this respect, one of the key processes impacting on the changing nature of participation is individualisation and for young citizens in particular this means that political action tends to be conducted on the basis of personal interests and single-issues rather than as expression of group solidarity, such as a shared class interest or identity (Furlong, 2009; Marsh et al., 2007). Scholars have suggested that young people prefer single issue campaigns that deal with practical issues in concrete and personal ways (Marsh et al., 2007).

Related to these trends is also the emergence of the New Politics and the rise of post-material values. Post-materialism is understood as a shift in values emerging from the 1970s linked to the transition from industrial to post-industrial societies and increasing affluence of the post-war period as charted in Inglehart and Welzel (2005). Inglehart and Welzel (2005) show that between 1970 and 1999 each new birth cohort is more post-materialist than the previous one and this produces an inter-generational a shift toward post-materialist values as younger cohorts replace older ones in society. This shift has also been linked to the rise of organisations championing what are seen as post-material concerns including nature protection (Giugni & Grasso, 2015b). The rise in support for the Greens, the environmental and anti-war movements are often linked to the growth of post-materialist values. Yet, while the narrative on post-materialism emphasises the importance of 'new' values for drawing young people to unconventional political action, the economic crisis of 2008 might be linked to the rise of material concerns (Giugni & Grasso, 2016; Grasso & Giugni, 2013, 2016a, 2016b). The crisis can be seen to have acted as a catalyst spurring the young to political action against political elites. Young people in Europe can be understood to have many grievances: precarious employment; diminishing prospects of home ownership; soaring rents in cities; all suggest young people may come to be worse off than their parents for the first time since the Second World War (Sloam, 2007). The crisis has seen a growth in protest movements against austerity and spending cuts to social services including movements such as Occupy. Yet, these movements tend to attract only relatively small proportions of participants. Moreover, these types of participation are often ignored by mainstream political parties since young people are the least likely to turnout to vote. While young people active in social movements have contested austerity, there remains no widely identified alternative.

Class-Based Inequalities in Political Participation

The importance of generational differences, however, should not lead us to overlook other inequalities in political participation. Arguably these, too, are on the rise. In this context, a crucial variable is social class, which can be measured through type of occupation of the chief wage earner in the household (Dunn et al., 2014). As Table 10.4 shows, there is a clear and consistent difference in participation levels between individuals with manual and non-manual occupations. Individuals in non-manual occupations are more active in all but the very demanding, confrontational unconventional activities attracting very small numbers. This evidence supports claims that while unconventional participation does not attenuate age based inequalities in participation (as we have seen demonstrations only attract very small numbers), it also does not rectify socioeconomic inequalities. Participation is demanding of resources and as such more likely to be practiced by highly educated, wealthy citizens. This suggests a feedback effect, in which only the already well-off and highly educated are the only ones who have the time and resources to defend their interests. Thus, based on this data, social movements do not look likely to improve existent problems of voice and equality in political action (Verba, Schlozman, & Brady, 1995).

Table 10.4 Class differences in political activism (last 12 months)

Conventional	Manual %	Non manual %	Sig.
Voted at last national election	75	80	***
Voted at last European election	61	66	***
Party member	10	13	***
Volunteered for a party	3	5	***
Contacted or visited a politician or government official (online or offline)	11	14	***
Donated money to a political organisation/party or action group (online or offline)	6	9	***
Displayed/worn a political or campaign logo/badge/sticker (online or offline)	7	9	**
Attended a meeting of a political organisation/party or action group	8	10	***
Unconventional			
Signed a petition/public letter/campaign appeal (online or offline)	30	34	***
Boycotted products for political/ethical/environment reasons (online or offline)	21	27	***
Deliberately bought products for political/ethical/env't reasons (online or offline)	16	23	***
Attended a demonstration, march or rally	10	11	**
Joined a strike	5	6	**
Joined an occupation, sit-in, or blockade	2	2	ns
Damaged things like breaking windows, removing roads signs, etc.	1	1	ns
Used personal violence like fighting with the police	1	1	ns
Online activism			
Searched for information about politics online	42	50	***
Visited the website of a political party or a politician	27	32	***
Discussed or shared opinion on politics on a social network site e.g. Facebook	24	26	*
Joined or started a political group on Facebook/followed a politician or party	12	12	ns

Data: LIVEWHAT project survey 2015 (see Grasso & Giugni, 2016a)
Cells are %; Significance *$p < 0.05$; **$p < 0.01$; ***$p < 0.001$ from two-tailed tests; ns means not significant at $p < 0.05$

Other than class and age, gender and education have also traditionally been identified as important socio-economic predictors of political participation (Almond & Verba, 1963). As politics has historically been the domain of 'public man,' the 'private woman' has traditionally been excluded from politics (Verba, Nie, & Kim, 1978). However, the growing liberalisation of gender roles has been argued should diminish the gender gap and more so amongst the young (Inglehart & Welzel, 2005). Since Almond and Verba (1963), education level also has been linked to a citizen's level of political knowledge, interest and sophistication and the better educated have been found to be more likely to have the time, money, access to political information, knowledge and ability to become politically active (Dalton, 2008; Grasso, 2013).

Moreover, party attachment has been found to influence participation (Dalton, 2008). This could lead to growing inequalities in participation between those that support parties and those instead that feel like they have been left behind. Also, membership in voluntary organisations offers the opportunity to develop skills prompting more overtly political participation (Verba et al., 1995). Individuals with greater resources will have more time and money to be involved in organisations in turn leading to growing inequalities in participation between members and non-members. Additionally, ideological identification, satisfaction with the way democracy works and other political values may help explain variations in levels of political involvement. Dissatisfaction with the way democracy works in one's country could influence participation but some argue that satisfaction increases support for the political process whereas others suggest that it might stimulate efforts for change (Dalton, 2008). Finally, the literature also discusses the role of ideology and political values; if participation influences the law-making processes, whether activists are drawn equally from different political camps has implications for democracy.

Conclusions: The Future of Youth Participation in Europe

As we have seen, a number of authors have spoken of a crisis of citizenship (Stoker, 2006) and of our hate for politics (Hay, 2007). This crisis has been linked to declining civic life and associational participation (Putnam, 2000), low trust in institutions (Norris, 2011; Pharr & Putnam, 2000), an increasingly individualist culture and the rise of post-material values

(Inglehart & Welzel, 2005), the depoliticisation of the public sphere and the rise of technocratic managerialism (Hay, 2007; Mair, 2006), as well as growing cynicism (Grasso, 2011b; Stoker, 2006). Mair (2006) in particular emphasised how the transformation of political parties and in particular their withdrawal from civil society and decreased mediation and representation of group-based interests in favour of a form of centralised managerialism (Whiteley & Seyd, 2002) has been a major shift breaking down the trust that existed between constituents and their representatives.

This chapter has presented evidence on young people's political participation in a range of conventional, unconventional and online political activities showing differences with older people. It also examined differences cross-nationally from a comparative perspective and considered the issues of generation and class. It was shown that there are interesting cross-national differences though on the whole patterns for youth participation are relatively similar across Europe. The younger generations coming of age since the more radical 1960–1970s were shown to be less participatory than this generation. Class was also shown to have an effect with individuals in manual occupations being generally less politically active so that important inequalities remain in political action based on resources in society. These are important issues for political equality that will need to be addressed if societies want to be truly democratic. Moreover, the results from this chapter confirm the argument that younger generations tend to be detached from conventional politics. Against this picture, some have argued that while young people vote and participate in conventional politics less than older people, they may be more active in unconventional forms of participation. Yet, evidence shows these activities only attract small numbers. The results presented show that young people are active in online 'clicktivism,' which attracts more participants, so youth regeneration of politics is likely to come either from social change enacted by social movement activists or by increased mobilisation through social media and other forms of technological advances for the practice of political engagement.

References

Almond, G., & Verba, S. (1963). *The civic culture: Political attitudes and democracy in five nations*. London: Sage Publications.

Castells, M. (2000). *The rise of the network society*. Oxford: Blackwell.

Dalton, R. (2008). *Citizen politics: Public opinion and political parties in advanced industrial democracies*. Washington, DC: CQ Press.

Dalton, R. (2009). *The good citizen: How a younger generation is reshaping American politics*. Washington, DC: CQ Press.

Dalton, R., & Wattenberg, M. (2000). *Parties without partisans: Political change in advanced industrial democracies*. Oxford: Oxford University Press.

Dunn, A., Grasso, M. T., & Saunders, C. (2014). Unemployment and attitudes to work: Asking the "right"' question. *Work, Employment, and Society, 28*(6), 904–925.

France, A. (2016). *Understanding youth in the global economic crisis*. Bristol: Policy Press.

Franklin, M. (2004). *Voter turnout and the dynamics of electoral competition in established democracies since 1945*. Cambridge: Cambridge University Press.

Furlong, A. (Ed.). (2009). *Handbook of youth and young adulthood*. London: Routledge.

Giugni, M., & Grasso, M. T. (Eds.). (2015a). *Austerity and protest: Popular contention in times of economic crisis*. London: Routledge.

Giugni, M., & Grasso, M. T. (2015b). Environmental movements in advanced industrial democracies: Heterogeneity, transformation, and institutionalization. *Annual Review of Environment and Resources, 40*, 337–361.

Giugni, M., & Grasso, M. T. (2016). How civil society actors responded to the economic crisis: The interaction of material deprivation and perceptions of political opportunity structures. *Politics & Policy, 44*(3), 447–472.

Grasso, M. T. (2011a). *Political participation in Western Europe*. D. Phil., University of Oxford.

Grasso, M. T. (2011b). *[With the assistance of Jonathan Rose and the Committee's Research Advisory Board] Surveys of public attitudes towards conduct in public life*. London: Committee on Standards in Public Life.

Grasso, M. T. (2013). The differential impact of education on young people's political activism: Comparing Italy and the United Kingdom. *Comparative Sociology, 12*(1), 1–30.

Grasso, M. T. (2014). Age-period-cohort analysis in a comparative context: Political generations and political participation repertoires. *Electoral Studies, 33*, 63–76.

Grasso, M. T. (2016a). *Generations, political participation and social change in Western Europe*. London: Routledge.

Grasso, M. T. (2016b). Political participation. In R. Heffernan, P. Cowley, & C. Hay (Eds.), *Developments in British politics 10*. London: Palgrave Macmillan.

Grasso, M. T., Farrall, S., Gray, E., Hay, C., & Jennings, W. (2017). Thatcher's children, Blair's babies, political socialisation and trickle-down value-change: An age, period and cohort analysis. *British Journal of Political Science*. https://doi.org/10.1017/S0007123416000375

Grasso, M. T., & Giugni, M. (2013). *Anti-austerity movements: Old wine in new vessels?* Paper presented at the XXVII Meeting of the Italian Political Science Association (SISP), University of Florence, Florence, September 12–14.

Grasso, M. T., & Giugni, M. (2016a). Protest participation and economic crisis: The conditioning role of political opportunities. *European Journal of Political Research, 55*(4), 663–680.

Grasso, M. T., & Giugni, M. (2016b). Do issues matter? Anti-austerity protests' composition, values, and action repertoires compared. *Research in Social Movements, Conflicts and Change, 39*, 31–58.

Hay, C. (2007). *Why we hate politics*. Cambridge: Polity Press.

Inan, M., & Grasso, M. T. (2017). A participatory generation? The generational and social class bases of political activism in Turkey. *Turkish Studies, 18*(1), 10–31.

Inglehart, R., & Welzel, C. (2005). *Modernization, cultural change and democracy: The human development sequence*. Cambridge: Cambridge University Press.

Jennings, W., Gray, E., Hay, C., & Farrall, S. (2015). Collating longitudinal data on crime, victimization and social attitudes in England and Wales: A new resource for exploring long-term trends in crime. *British Journal of Criminology, 55*(5), 1005–1015.

Mair, P. (2006). Ruling the void? The hollowing of western democracy. *New Left Review, 42*, 25–51.

Mannheim, K. (1928). *The problem of generations essays on the sociology of knowledge*. London: Routledge.

Marsh, D., O'Toole, T., & Jones, S. (2007). *Young people and politics in the UK. Apathy or alienation?* Basingstoke: Palgrave Macmillan.

Norris, P. (2011). *Democratic deficit: Critical citizens revisited*. Cambridge: Cambridge University Press.

Pattie, C., Seyd, P., & Whiteley, P. (2004). *Citizenship in Britain: Values, participation and democracy*. Cambridge: Cambridge University Press.

Pharr, S., & Putnam, R. (Eds.). (2000). *Disaffected democracies: What's troubling the trilateral countries?* Princeton, NJ: Princeton University Press.

Pickard, S. (2015). Trying to turn up the turnout. Youth wings and the youth vote in the 2015 general election. *Revue Française de Civilisation Britannique—French Journal of British Studies, 20*(3). Retrieved from https://rfcb.revues.org/503

Pickard, S. (2018). *Politics, protest and young people. Political participation and dissent in Britain in the 21st century*. London: Palgrave Macmillan [forthcoming].

Putnam, R. (2000). *Bowling alone: The collapse and revival of American community*. New York: Simon & Schuster.

Saunders, C., Grasso, M. T., Olcese, C., Rainsford, E., & Rootes, C. (2012). Explaining differential protest participation: Novices, returners, repeaters and stalwarts. *Mobilization, 17*(3), 263–280.

Sloam, J. (2007). Rebooting democracy: Youth participation in politics in the UK. *Parliamentary Affairs, 60*(4), 548–567.

Stoker, G. (2006). *Why politics matters: Making democracy work*. Basingstoke: Palgrave Macmillan.
Stoker, G. (2011). Anti-politics in Britain. In R. Heffernan, P. Cowley, & C. Hay (Eds.), *Developments in British politics*. Basingstoke: Palgrave Macmillan.
Temple, L., Grasso, M. T., Buraczynska, B., Karampampas, S., & English, P. (2016). Neoliberal narrative in times of economic crisis: A political claims analysis of the UK Press, 2007–2014. *Politics & Policy, 44*(3), 553–576.
Van Aelst, P., & Walgrave, S. (2001). Who is that (Wo)Man in the street? From the normalisation of protest to the normalisation of the protester. *European Journal of Political Research, 39*(4), 461–486.
Van Biezen, I., Mair, P., & Poguntke, T. (2012). Going, going, ... gone? The decline of party membership in contemporary Europe. *European Journal of Political Research, 51*(1), 24–56.
Verba, S., Nie, N., & Kim, J.-O. (1978). *Participation and political equality*. Cambridge: Cambridge University Press.
Verba, S., Schlozman, K. L., & Brady, H. (1995). *Voice and equality: Civic voluntarism in American politics*. Cambridge, MA: Harvard University Press.
Whiteley, P., & Seyd, P. (2002). *High-intensity participation: The dynamics of party activism in Britain*. Ann Harbor: University of Michigan Press.

Maria Grasso is Senior Lecturer in Politics and Quantitative Methods, Department of Politics, University of Sheffield. She is Deputy European Editor of *Mobilization*, the author of *Generations, Political Participation and Social Change in Western Europe* (2016) and co-editor of *Austerity and Protest: Popular Contention in Times of Economic Crisis* (2015).

PART III

Young People, Collective Identity and Community Building

CHAPTER 11

The Gezi Resistance of Turkey as Young People's Counter-Conduct

Nilay Çabuk Kaya and Haktan Ural

Introduction

In 2013, an initially small protest against the construction of a shopping mall in central Istanbul, Turkey, turned into a countrywide uprising that became known as the Gezi Resistance. It brought together unusually diverse groups of people including feminists, Alevis, LGBTQ (lesbian, gay, bisexual, transgender and queer) communities, football club fans, environmentalists and Sunni Islamist groups such as Anti-Capitalist Muslims, among others.[1] The resistance movement was unprecedented in the country's political history; the display of popular discontent against the ruling party had never reached such a level and, indeed, Turkey witnessed the emergence of a distinct type of political dissent. According to Navaro-Yashin (2013), diverse groups of people came onto the streets for the purpose of "crying out all their issues with the AKP [JDP][2] government" in a carnivalesque way. The resistance was an expression of what is described as "spoiling memorization" (ibid.), a Turkish idiom meaning to remake the taken-for-granted.

N. Çabuk Kaya • H. Ural (✉)
Department of Sociology, Ankara University, Ankara, Turkey

The development of such widespread resistance, bringing together so many different social groups in terms of gender, class, sexuality, ethnicity and religion, attracted immense scholarly attention. The growing body of literature provides two interrelated accounts of the rise of the resistance. Firstly, the socio-economic and socio-political background that engendered this political mobilisation is widely debated and it is argued that the Gezi Resistance can best be interpreted as the rise of discontent against JDP's political hegemony (Gürcan & Peker, 2014; Öncü, 2014; Tuğal, 2013; Yörük, 2014). Secondly, the 'who' question predominates in major debates on the Gezi movement. The social composition of protesters has been widely debated. In these debates, particular attention has been paid to the class of protesters (see Keyder, 2013; Tuğal, 2013; Yörük & Yüksel, 2015); however, many other dimensions that characterise protesters remain under-examined.[3]

The role played by young people is one such dimension that deserves particular attention. Our focus in this chapter is to examine the Gezi Resistance as an example of young people's practices of protest. We demonstrate that young people have played a pivotal role in these protest waves and, by that means, they construct an alternative political subjectivity, which concurrently transforms their depictions as individualist, consumerist and cynical subjects.

The study is framed by "the analytics of protest" (Death, 2010), which is inspired by Foucault's (2007) concepts of conduct and counter-conduct, developed in his lectures at the Collège de France, in Paris, in 1978. In Foucault's (2007, p. 96) view, government is the conduct of people's actions, mobilities, thinking and feeling through cultivating a milieu of possible actions. Furthermore, diverse practices of government themselves entail certain modes of counter-conduct, struggling "not to be governed thusly, like that, by these people, at this price" (Foucault, 2007, p. 75).

Death (2010, pp. 240–242) reworks Foucault's conceptual tools of conduct and counter-conduct to create a heuristic for analysing protest. He suggests that protests are a form of counter-conduct, which works as a political rationality and relies on a particular regime of knowledge. This leads to the performative character of protests; protesters construct a particular political rationality, while performing their acts of defiance. These acts are also concatenated to the performative construction of resistant subjectivities. Thus, we discern that viewing the Gezi Resistance through the lens of counter-conduct helps us to go beyond static approaches that see resistant identities through protesters' pre-existing social positions. Instead, this approach provides a deeper insight into what is constructed and performed by young protesters.

We then argue that the Gezi Resistance is young people's counter-conduct directed against the ruling party's political reason that imposes its own image of ideal society and political order upon the country. The resistance movement counteracts the promotion of consumerist lifestyles, conservative and family-based social policies, and the silencing of the media by the JDP. The spaces associated with the movement comprise a creative and innovative site, where an alterity in the name of "Gezi Spirit" is invented and performed. The performance of political subjectivity known as "the Gezi Spirit" thus strives to put openness, inclusiveness, autonomy and freedom into practice.

In what follows, we first demonstrate the role played by young people in the Gezi Resistance and show the forms of knowledge they constitute that run counter to the neoliberal, conservative and authoritarian rule of JDP. Following this, we reveal that these young protesters create and perform a certain mode of alterity, in the name of the 'Gezi Spirit,' in order to act against the JDP's rule and construct a novel way of being and doing.

Gezi Resistance as Young People's Dissent

Young people have played a pivotal role in the Gezi Resistance movement. Research investigating the social composition of the protesters who occupied Gezi Park in early June 2013 reported that 52.8% of the occupiers were 25-years-old or younger. Of this group, 64.4% were students, 28.4% were employed and the remaining 7.2% were unemployed (Konda, 2014). Although the social composition of the group of protesters was heterogeneous, it can be discerned that Gezi Resistance was predominantly a youthful political mobilisation, mostly led by student activists.

Young protesters acquired a pioneering and iconic stance in the Gezi Resistance and a couple of young people became the figureheads of the movement, due to the striking images of them that were widely circulated through local and international media. The most prominent example was 'the woman in red dress.' On the very first day of events, a graduate student activist was photographed in Gezi Park; she was standing in front of armed police forces and turning her head to avoid the pepper spray that was blasted directly into her face by them. Shortly after the circulation of this image in national and international media, the activist became known as the woman in the red dress and the image was reproduced in graffiti and on banners. Another example was the 'activist reading a book.' During another encounter with police forces in Gezi Park, a young protester was photographed reading a book out loud to police officers. Following the publication of this photograph in the mainstream media, the protester's image gained an iconic stance by means of its hasty circulation through social media.

Both images (of non-violent resistance) have been powerful tools in constituting the visual repertoires of the movement. They have been graphic accounts of the movement's character. They revealed the decisive peacefulness and creativity that characterised the resistance movement. Furthermore, they illustrated how young people of the movement were determined, courageous, confident and ready to play a pioneering role in the Gezi Resistance.

It is widely debated that young people in Turkey are dramatically disinterested in traditional/conventional politics, as they do not trust political institutions (see Demir, 2012). Besides, as Neyzi (2001) states, youth subjectivities are constructed through the consumption-based and individualist cultures of the post-1980 period.[4] These ideas lead to the representations of youth in Turkey as apathetic and cynical about politics. However, the Gezi outburst of resistance was a turning point for young people in Turkey. The rise of this political mobilisation subverted the image of apathetic and cynical youth (Alemdaroğlu, 2013). It has been a transformative moment for young people, allowing them to re-imagine themselves as active citizens of Turkey who are seeking to re-establish a democratic society (Bee & Kaya, 2016). The Gezi Resistance indicates a determined desire of young people to actively construct more engaged and participatory political subjectivities.

Young protesters construct their political subjectivities by employing certain regimes of knowledge. As Death (2010, p. 241) suggests, protests are based on certain styles of thinking and feeling, and on rationalities which are directed against dominant political rationalities. In the case of the Gezi Resistance, as the movement has grown markedly in size and diverse groups have participated, it is not possible to identify the movement's political rationality through a single pattern of thinking. We instead examine three forms of regimes of knowledge that come to constitute the forms of thinking in the Gezi Resistance.

Defending Mobile Urban Subject

The first dimension of political opposition was a consideration of the mobilities in urban public spaces, which was central especially at the initial stage. The Gezi Resistance started as an occupation of Gezi Park, in May 2013, by a few dozen protesters acting against the construction of a shopping mall on the site. Protesters aimed at preventing the park's demolition for business interests. In that regard, as Kuymulu (2013) states, the claiming of an open, inclusive and non-commercial use of space was central to the resistance movement.

Since the beginning of the century, Istanbul's urban government regimes steadily aimed to transform the urban economy into one based on service economies (Aksoy, 2012). To that end, the long-desired goal of attracting flows of financial and commercial capital to Istanbul has become more manifest in recent years. With the advent of new legislative frameworks requiring local governments to promote, initiate and regulate neoliberal urban government, municipal actors—who are also ruled by the JDP—have presented a fervent desire to undertake entrepreneurialist projects (Türkün, 2011). Authorities have embarked upon numerous initiatives, ranging from 'mega-projects' to urban renewal or regeneration projects in squatter settlements and inner cities.

The demolition of Gezi Park to construct a shopping mall was a directive of the municipal government that is committed to such a neoliberal worldview. The project was driven by a desire for profit; the objective was to remake urban space into a site for consumerism. However, the demolition of the park mattered greatly to the activists. The park was located at the very centre of Beyoglu, the social and cultural hub of Istanbul. More importantly, it was one of the few public spaces in the inner city. From this perspective, the park was occupied as a fight against the priority of profitability and private interests over open and non-commercial uses of space.

In a similar way to the Occupy movements across the world (see Bulley, 2016, p. 244), members of the Gezi Resistance claimed an alternative use of public space. In this alterity, young protesters employed a particular knowledge that embraces the free mobility and circulation of urban subjects across urban spaces. Indeed, there lies a denial of consumerism in this embrace of the mobile urban subject. The resistance movement counteracted the construction of the shopping mall because in this project the freely mobile urban subject was to be replaced by the freely mobile consumer subject.

Concerns over Conservative Regimes of Government

Insofar as the resistance movement has grown and deepened since its inception, protesters have become more variegated, coming to include those concerned with the JDP's conservative regime of government. Young people's voices against restrictions on alcohol consumption, pro-natalist discourses and practices, as well as against proposals to ban abortion, among other issues, clearly reflected popular discontent with the JDP's imposition of conservative values and norms.

Consolidating massive support by combining populist and conservative political discourses and practices in recent years (Öncü, 2014; Yörük, 2014), the JDP has constituted a political rationality that imposes a conservative image of society onto the Turkish population. Such a conservative political rationality puts forward the ideal of moral and family values. As Kaya (2015, p. 60) suggests, within this political rationality lies a call for the "strong family" as the best model of living.[5] In this way of thinking, women's bodies and practices were regarded as the markers of societal order. Consequently, a series of policy changes—or attempts to make changes—directly targeting women's bodily practices came to the fore (Acar & Altunok, 2013). These most prominently included policies promoting/favouring the three-child family, discourses against pre-marital and queer sexualities, restrictions on caesarean deliveries and the submission of a bill to parliament on the prohibition of abortion, among many others.

Certain regulations concerning alcohol consumption are also linked to the will to establish moral order. The JDP has made serious changes in this area, such as prohibition of the late-night purchase of alcoholic beverages from shops, restrictions on alcoholic drinks appearing in public (including in advertisements), and substantial increases in tax levies on alcohol consumption (Evered & Evered, 2016).

The Gezi Resistance was a struggle against such conservative policies. Young people showed their concerns about such governmental interventions regarding their own bodies and practices. They made claims for a different conduct from the government, or more accurately, for their lives not to be directed or controlled to such an extent. Public utterances in slogans, graffiti and tweets all reflected demands for increased autonomy, creativity and pleasure. The utterances were wildly diverse in content, yet they commonly defied the government's imposition of a strict moral order. They were nothing short of an outcry over a drift towards a "socially impoverished" and "monotonous" life, in Tuğal's (2013, pp. 167–169) words.

Struggling Against Silenced Media

Another factor that stirred discontent was the JDP's authoritarian rule as manifested in its silencing of mainstream-traditional media. Many media companies remained quiet about the dissent, especially in the initial stages of the Gezi Resistance. The biased and inaccurate coverage or silence of the media when it came to reporting on the protests and on the disproportionate use of police violence triggered concerns over freedom of expression being repressed by the state authority. The protesters discerned that these omissions and limitations revealed the extent to which the flow of information through the media was controlled by the political elites.

The prominent media companies in Turkey have been amalgamated into the hands of a few business elites in recent decades. This process has gone hand in hand with the reinforcement of political parallelism and with decreasing journalistic autonomy (Kaya & Çakmur, 2010). Akser and Baybars-Hawks (2012) identify the key mechanisms used by the JDP to repress media criticisms. They note that the media critique is blocked in numerous ways that include the imposition of economic pressures on media investors, and discouragement of journalists or other content producers/providers to report openly (through to prosecution and the regulation of the internet, the surveillance of particular individuals, and accreditation regimes). In addition, almost half of the media companies in Turkey are owned by investors who have close relationships with the ruling party (Kurban & Sözeri, 2012).

The JDP's sovereignty over media companies became apparent during the resistance movement. In the initial stage of the protests, with reference to a news channel's choice to air a documentary about penguins rather than covering the dissent on the streets, young protesters called the silenced media the "Penguin Media." The broadcast was a decisive moment for reinforcing rising concerns that the JDP has increasingly been exercising sovereign power to silence the domestic media. Thus, many people who were informed about the demonstrations through social media joined the protests in order to show their discontent with the silenced media (Buğra, 2013; Tunç, 2013).

All things considered, the JDP's policies regarding urban space, family life and flows of information are designed to promote particular subjectivities that chime with consumerism, morality, pro-family policies and silence. However, young people of the Gezi Resistance invoked an alternative to this. The protesters contested government policies directed towards the privatisation of public space, hyper-consumerism, family-based morality, and the silencing of critique.

THE PERFORMANCE OF "GEZI SPIRIT"

In Death's (2010, p. 245) account, the analytics of protests draws attention to acts of defiance. Accordingly, resistance subjectivities are performatively constructed through diverse acts of defiance. Considering the resistance movement in this way, we examine the ways that the famous "Gezi Spirit" was constructed and performed across virtual and physical places of the Gezi Resistance. It incorporated a diversity of practices, involving all sorts of protests, such as online activism, barricades, street marches, graffiti, public forums, video streaming, and more. Many of these practices served the purpose of communicating and spreading young people's words across virtual or physical places (see Juris, 2012). In the same way, the use of social media had an especially strategic role in movements struggling against authoritarian rule, such as the Arab Spring (Khondker, 2011). Demirhan (2014) argues that these dynamics were enormously influential in the use of social media during the Gezi movement.

Furthermore, Malmvig (2014, 2016) suggests paying close attention to the creative and subtle practices that avoided overtly political expression. Following this, we discern that the motionless stance of a performance artist that spontaneously turned into a collective performance of passive resistance is a good example of creative and subtle practices.[6] Likewise, the humour and carnivalesque style of young people were also important dimensions of the protests (Dağtaş, 2013). As Arda (2015, p. 90) states, this humorous and carnivalesque tone reflects the preponderance of youthful subjectivities and its capacity to introduce a new political language into public life through extended use of social media. For instance, young people's strategic action to subvert the image of themselves as 'spoilers' (*capulcu*), an ostensibly critical epithet given to them by Turkish Prime Minister Recep Tayyip Erdogan during the events, sets a good example. This derogatory term and its derivations (such as *chapuller, chapulling* and so forth) have been re-appropriated as an honourable and reputable label in texts and images circulated in social media.

It is not possible to fully portray and examine every individual defiant practice here. Instead, we probe the way that a particular mode of resistant subjectivity is created and performed. As Malmvig (2016, pp. 264–265) contends, the concept of counter-conduct points out the will to be governed differently as it seeks to cultivate an ethos of novelty. It implies one's individual and collective involvement in inventive, critical and bold practices to create a new conduct of life. In that sense, according to Davidson (2011, p. 29), the ethical dimension of counter-conduct resides in this disposition. Counter-conduct is conceived as an attitude of aspiring a new way of being and acting.

In order to invent this new conduct of life, a whole new way of being and acting is not deemed to be an individual activity. Davidson (2011, p. 34) suggests that friendships are auspicious for cultivating these new ways, as follows:

> The kinds of counter-conduct made possible by these friendships [that involve affective relations] both changed the force relations between individuals and modified one's relation to oneself. One conducts oneself in another way with friends, fabricating new ethical and political possibilities. (Davidson, 2011, p. 34)

We suggest that the Gezi Resistance was a practice of counter-conduct to invent a new way of being and acting; it was committed to creating (Karakayalı & Yaka, 2014, p. 128). Furthermore, it facilitated a social space where experiences of encounters and mutual recognition were translated into a novel way of being and acting by means of new or reinforced friendships. The "Gezi Spirit" derived from the development of affective ties through which young protesters were individually and collectively bound to another. Yet it is not only shaped by openness and inclusiveness, but also by othering discourses constantly negotiated by the protesters themselves.

New or Reinforced Friendships

The spontaneity of the resistance movement gave rise to a self-organising political defiance across online and offline spaces. The interactions between young people, during which they exchanged and circulated information and ideas, allowed for network formation and the development of an alternative mode of sociality based on emotional ties. The idea of a "Gezi Spirit" bears the marks of these emotional registers that emerged from encountering differences and the blurring of boundaries. Such processes effectively triggered the establishment of friendly ties among diverse individuals and collectives.

A stunning example of creating or reinforcing friendships concerns the remarkable presence and visibility of LGBTQ communities within the movement. Zengin (2013) aptly attributes the heightened visibility of LGBTQ communities to the fact that "queers painted seized bulldozers pink, waved the rainbow flag on top of barricades, pitched the 'LGBT Blok' tent at the center of the park, and organised frequent drag-queen dances and small-group parades with slogans and songs." As Pearce (2014) observes, a remarkable crowd of young LGBTQ activists were seen in the front lines, especially in Istanbul's Beyoglu.

Such commitment from LGBTQ young people helped them build solidarity with other protesters. This could best be seen in the substantial increase in numbers of demonstrators taking part in Istanbul's Pride Parade in the same month. The Pride Parade dates back to 2003, when it attracted 30 marchers. In the course of time, attendance has increased, but the parade in 2013 was unprecedented in terms of size. The number of demonstrators was estimated at 10,000 and, indeed, it was announced as the largest Pride Parade taking place in a Muslim-majority society.

Pearce (2014) observes that LGBTQ young people's active involvement in diverse acts of defiance paved the way for encounters between LGBTQ individuals and other protesters. These encounters were suitable for creating greater sympathy and solidarity. Substantially increased interest in the Pride Parade clearly revealed how these affective ties led to increased solidarity. The embrace of openness and inclusiveness in the movement's regimes of knowledge, as illustrated above, has been translated into reality by virtue of that strengthened solidarity. Larger attendance at the Pride Parade is linked to the movement's rationality that favours the will not to be governed too much.

Another example is an Islamist group's participation in the resistance movement. A couple of weeks after the Gezi protests, the Anti-Capitalist Muslims group organised "Communal Meals" (*Yeryüzü Sofralar*) events in which people sat on the ground for *iftar* (fast-breaking) during Ramadan. These events, as part of the Islamic ritual of breaking fast, were a meeting spot for resistance groups. Thousands gathered at a single (one-kilometre-long) table in Istanbul streets. Damar (2016) notes that LGBTQ communities, leftists, feminists, and football fans were among the participants of these "Communal Meals."

In this way, the "Communal Meals" opened up a space for encounters between religious and secular communities of Turkey. According to Damar (2016), these activities enabled the formation of an alliance between religious and secular political groups, creating the potential to transgress existing boundaries and participate in a collective struggle (see also Karakayalı & Yaka, 2014). These activities also bear the marks of "publicness" with freely mobile urban subjects favoured over consumerism and entrepreneurialism. Defiance through "Communal Meals" creatively put the "Gezi Spirit" into practice. Shared dinner tables welcoming a diversity of people have been the marker of "Gezi Spirit," advocating for openness and inclusiveness instead of consumerism, exclusion and profit-seeking.

In all these examples, it is crucial to emphasise that we do not intend merely to point out mutual recognition of different identities and establishment of solidarities between diverse groups when speaking of the "Gezi Spirit." We argue that a new political subjectivity has been constructed and performed in conformity with young protesters' regimes of knowledge, namely defending the mobile urban subject over the consumer subject, individual autonomy against family-based social order, and freedom of expression against silenced media. The performance of this political subjectivity, namely the "Gezi Spirit", refers to this novel way of being and acting. That mode of being and acting is directly linked to a political rationality of resistance that favours publicness, autonomy and freedom, as has been illustrated above. In that sense, it is directed against the JDP's government as its forms of thinking and feeling starkly contrast with its neoliberal, conservative and authoritarian rationality.

Negotiating Friendships

We consider counter-conduct to be a force that is vested in what it counteracts. Thus, it may have a polyvalent character that vibrantly takes on the meanings of resistance and compliance at the same time (Bulley, 2016, p. 243). In that regard, we avoid providing an enthusiastic account of the "Gezi Spirit" that portrays only its open and inclusive facets. Rather, we claim that the "Gezi Spirit" contemporaneously accommodates othering discourses that have been questioned, negotiated and transformed during the protests.

Homophobic, transphobic and sexist discourses that were to some extent fostered by the humorous and carnivalesque style of young protesters set the precedent. Although the "Gezi Spirit" gave rise to inclusiveness and openness embracing queer communities, these tenets were not always easily maintained. Moments that undermined this inclusiveness and openness (such as the slogans and graffiti including derogatory terms about sex workers or LGBTQ individuals) could be challenged and transformed by various means. As Zengin (2013) observes:

> By painting over offensive graffiti, altering some swearword letters with the female symbol, and organizing an alternative "Swearword Workshop" (Küfür Atölyesi) to dispute the humiliation of women, gays, and sex workers, queers, together with feminists, challenged the misogynist, homophobic, and transphobic language of the resistance.

All these factors reveal that while the Gezi Resistance was comprised of plural existences, the "Gezi Spirit" illustrated above was also highly vulnerable and ambivalent; it could be easily disrupted and undermined, although its discourses were constantly negotiated during the protests. In regard to the Occupy movements, Bulley (2016, p. 254) discerns that emotional ties could be fleeting and momentary; similarly, the performance of the "Gezi Spirit" could in fact be transitory.

Conclusion

Gezi Resistance can be considered as young people's counter-conduct directed against the JDP's political project to establish neoliberal, conservative and authoritarian forms of government. We argue that the young people of resistance have created a regime of knowledge revolving around openness, inclusiveness, individual autonomy and creativity, intended to reverse the consumerist, profit-oriented, pro-family and repressive rule of the JDP. The "Gezi Spirit" acts upon this regime of knowledge; and its performance, which is marked by a carnivalesque style, translates that political rationality into reality. By this means, given that young people in Turkey are represented through the terms of individualism, consumerism and cynicism (Neyzi, 2001, p. 423), the protesters subvert this imposed image of youth and come to construct an alternative political subjectivity.

However, we state that the "Gezi Spirit," while being mostly characterised by openness and inclusiveness was also vulnerable and could easily be disrupted. Its ambivalent relationship with queer communities is a clear revelation of this aspect. On the one hand, the "Gezi Spirit" helped to establish or reinforce political alliances between queer communities and other components of the resistance moment; on the other hand, the humorous and carnivalesque style of "Gezi Spirit" chime with homophobia, transphobia and sexism, and have called its openness and inclusiveness into question.

The creative energy of the movement was boosted by Turkish young people displaying discontent with the JDP's conduct. They struggle to be governed differently, or not to be governed that much. Yet, in point of fact, the JDP maintains its electoral support and rule. The resistance seemingly could not entail an immediate transformation in electoral politics. The question of whether the practice of the "Gezi Spirit" will constitute a different way of being and acting may be resolved in the course of time, as Özel (2014) states. At this stage, we can say that such an experience convincingly reveals how young people of Turkey are determined to construct a brand new world. However, we insist on the importance of understanding the limits of what it promises to construct.

Notes

1. The protests started on 27 May 2013 as an occupation of Gezi Park to oppose its demolition. Yet, on 29 May 2013, after brutal police violence directed against the occupiers, the protests dramatically increased in both size and scale. On 30 May, the police attacked once again. This was a turning point. The protests turned into a countrywide uprising, recruiting hundreds of thousands of people. From then on, the Gezi Resistance was transformed into a movement which was about more than Gezi Park alone.
2. JDP [AKP] stands for Justice and Development Party (*Adalet ve Kalkınma Partisi*). The party has continuously won legislative elections and ruled the government since 2002. Its political tradition is rooted in political Islam. The party was derived from the Islamist Virtue Party after its closure. During its rule in the 2000s, the JDP has been aligned with pro-Western, pro-market and conservative politics. The party's political rationality is built on neoliberal ideas blended with conservatism, particularly in social and moral issues.
3. Yörük's (2014) study would count as an exception. He rightly shows that diverse social groups such as women, LGBTQ communities and Alevis (a religious minority group) had remarkable visibility and a pioneering role in the movement.
4. The emphasis on the post-1980 period in identifying the emergence of youth subjectivities relies on the fact that 1980s became a very important watershed in the social, economic, political and cultural history of Turkey. In this period, Turkey was incorporated into the flow of global capital and its economy was increasingly transformed into a free market economy. In this way, youth cultures and identities have been constructed through consumption-based practices (see Neyzi, 2001).

5. The government's family-based discourses can best be observed in the employment and social care regimes. Buğra (2012) demonstrates that the advent of flexible employment and the replacement of institutional care with cash transfer systems in the JDP period resulted in an intensified role for informal networks. That is to say, establishing such welfare provisions reinforces the normative principle that sees women as the principal care providers. Indeed, such pro-family social policy framework works in harmony with neoliberal rationality advocating financial austerity, budget cuts, privatization and market rule.
6. On 17 June 2013, a young man started to stand, unmoving, in Taksim Square. Shortly after, others joined in and his solo performance turned into a collective one. This action, known as *Duran Adam* [Standing Man], was a very effective form of passive resistance, attracting local and international media coverage. It became a symbolic marker of the protesters' peaceful attitude (see Baydar, 2015).

References

Acar, F., & Altunok, G. (2013). The "politics of intimate" at the intersection of neo-liberalism and neo-conservatism in contemporary Turkey. *Women's Studies International Forum, 41*, 14–23.

Akser, M., & Baybars-Hawks, B. (2012). Media and democracy in Turkey: Toward a model of neoliberal media autocracy. *Middle East Journal of Culture and Communication, 5*(3), 302–321.

Aksoy, A. (2012). Riding the storm: "New Istanbul". *City, 16*(1–2), 93–111.

Alemdaroğlu, A. (2013). From cynicism to protest: Reflections on youth and politics in Turkey. *Jadaliyya*, 18 July. Retrieved January 2, 2017, from http://www.jadaliyya.com/pages/index/13048/from-cynicism-to-protest_reflections-on-youth-and-

Arda, B. (2015). The construction of a new sociality through social media: The case of the Gezi uprising in Turkey. *Conjunctions, 2*(1), 75–99.

Baydar, G. (2015). Embodied spaces of resistance. *Women's Studies International Forum, 50*, 11–19.

Bee, C., & Kaya, A. (2016). Youth and active citizenship in Turkey: Engagement, participation and emancipation. *Southeast European and Black Sea Studies*, 1–15.

Buğra, A. (2013). *Turkey: What lies behind the nationwide protests?* 6 August. Retrieved October 28, 2016, from https://www.opendemocracy.net/5050/ayse-bugra/turkey-what-lies-behind-nationwide-protests

Buğra, A. (2012). The changing welfare regime of Turkey: Neoliberalism, cultural conservatism and social solidarity redefined. In S. Dedeoğlu & A. Y. Elveren (Eds.), *Gender and society in Turkey: The impact of neo-liberal policies, political Islam and EU accession* (pp. 15–31). London: IB Tauris.

Bulley, D. (2016). Occupy differently: Space, community and urban counter-conduct. *Global Society, 30*(2), 238–257.
Dağtaş, S. (2013). The politics of humor and humor as politics during Turkey's Gezi park protests. *Cultural Anthropology Website,* 31 October. Retrieved October 17, 2016, from https://culanth.org/fieldsights/397-the-politics-of-humor-and-humor-as-politics-during-turkey-s-gezi-park-protests
Damar, E. (2016). Radicalisation of politics and production of new alternatives: Rethinking the secular/Islamic divide after the Gezi Park protests in Turkey. *Journal of Contemporary European Studies. Routledge, 24*(2), 207–222.
Davidson, A. I. (2011). In praise of counter-conduct. *History of the Human Sciences, 24*(4), 25–41.
Death, C. (2010). Counter-conducts: A Foucauldian analytics of protest. *Social Movement Studies, 9*(3), 235–251.
Demir, I. (2012). The development and current state of youth research in Turkey: An overview. *Young, 20*(1), 89–114.
Demirhan, K. (2014). Social media effects on the Gezi Park movement in Turkey: Politics under hashtags. In B. Patrut & M. Patrut (Eds.), *Social media in politics: Case studies on the political power of social media* (pp. 281–314). Cham: Springer International Publishing.
Evered, E. Ö., & Evered, K. T. (2016). From Rakı to Ayran: Regulating the place and practice of drinking in Turkey? *Space and Polity, 20*(1), 39–58.
Foucault, M. (2007). *Security, territory, population: Lectures at the Collège de France, 1977–78.* (G. Burchell, Trans.). Basingstoke: Palgrave Macmillan.
Gürcan, E. C., & Peker, E. (2014). Turkey's Gezi Park demonstrations of 2013: A Marxian analysis of the political moment. *Socialism and Democracy, 28*(1), 70–89.
Juris, J. S. (2012). Reflections on #occupy everywhere: Social media, public space, and emerging logics of aggregation. *American Ethnologist, 39*(2), 259–279.
Karakayalı, S., & Yaka, Ö. (2014). The spirit of Gezi: The recomposition of political subjectivities in Turkey. *New Formations: A Journal of Culture/Theory/Politics, 83,* 117–138.
Kaya, A. (2015). Islamisation of Turkey under the AKP rule: Empowering family, faith and charity. *South European Society and Politics, 20*(1), 47–69.
Kaya, R., & Çakmur, B. (2010). Politics and the mass media in Turkey. *Turkish Studies, 11*(4), 521–537.
Keyder, Ç. (2013). *Yeni Orta Sınıf.* Bilim Akademisi website, no date. Retrieved October 19, 2016, from http://bilimakademisi.org/yeni-orta-sinif-caglar-keyder
Khondker, H. H. (2011). Role of the new media in the Arab spring. *Globalizations, 8*(5), 675–679.
Konda. (2014). *Gezi raporu: Toplumun 'Gezi Parkı Olayları' algısı—Gezi Parkındakiler kimlerdi?* Istanbul: KONDA.

Kurban, D., & Sözeri, C. (2012). *Caught in the wheels of power: The political, legal and economic constraints on independent media and freedom of the press in Turkey*. Istanbul: TESEV.
Kuymulu, B. (2013). Reclaiming the right to the city: Reflections on the urban uprisings in Turkey. *City, 17*(3), 274–278.
Malmvig, H. (2014). Free us from power: Governmentality, counter-conduct and simulation in European democracy and reform promotion in the Arab world. *International Political Sociology, 8*(3), 293–310.
Malmvig, H. (2016). Eyes wide shut: Power and creative visual counter-conducts in the battle for Syria, 2011–2014. *Global Society, 30*(2), 258–278.
Navaro-Yashin, Y. (2013). Editorial-breaking memory, spoiling memorization: The Taksim Protests in Istanbul, Cultural Anthropology website. 31 October. Retrieved September 16, 2016, from https://culanth.org/fieldsights/411-editorial-breaking-memory-spoiling-memorization-the-taksim-protests-in-istanbul
Neyzi, L. (2001). Object or subject? The future paradox of "youth" in Turkey. *International Journal of Middle East Studies, 33*(3), 411–432.
Öncü, A. (2014). Turkish capitalist modernity and the Gezi revolt. *Journal of Historical Sociology, 27*(2), 151–176.
Özel, S. (2014). A moment of elation: The Gezi protests/resistance and the fading of the AKP project. In U. Özkırımlı (Ed.), *The making of a protest movement in Turkey* (pp. 7–24). Basingstoke: Palgrave Macmillan.
Pearce, S. C. (2014). Pride in Istanbul. *Societies Without borders, 9*(1), 111–128.
Tuğal, C. (2013). "Resistance everywhere": The Gezi revolt in global perspective. *New Perspectives on Turkey, 49*, 157–172.
Tunç, A. (2013). Freedom of expression debates in Turkey: Acute problems and new hopes. *International Journal of Media & Cultural Politics, 9*(2), 153–163.
Türkün, A. (2011). Urban regeneration and hegemonic power relationships urban regeneration and hegemonic power relationships. *International Planning Studies, 16*(1), 61–72.
Yörük, E. (2014). The long summer of Turkey: The Gezi uprising and its historical roots. *South Atlantic Quarterly, 113*(2), 419–426.
Yörük, E., & Yüksel, M. (2015). Gezi eylemlerinin toplumsal dinamikleri. *Toplum ve Bilim, 133*, 132–165.
Zengin, A. (2013). *What is queer about Gezi?*, Cultural Anthropology website, 31 October. Retrieved September 19, 2016, from https://culanth.org/fieldsights/407-what-is-queer-about-gezi

Nilay Çabuk Kaya is Professor of Sociology at Ankara University, Turkey. She holds a PhD from Durham University, UK. She is mainly interested in sociology of gender, youth, education and rural sociology. She is also the member of the executive committee of European Sociological Association (ESA).

Haktan Ural is a Research Assistant in Department of Sociology at Ankara University, Turkey. He holds a PhD in Sociology from Middle East Technical University, Turkey. He is mainly interested in gay subjectivities, youth, emotions and affect. His recent publications have appeared in the journals *Emotion, Space and Society* and *Journal of Middle East Women's Studies*.

CHAPTER 12

Off the Radar Democracy: Young People's Alternative Acts of Citizenship in Australia

Lucas Walsh and Rosalyn Black

INTRODUCTION

At the time of writing of this chapter, Australia was in an election year. In the lead up to the federal election in July 2016, the media noted that around half of Australia's 18-year-olds were not on the electoral roll. This was seen to be particularly significant in light of Australia's compulsory system of voting (Australian Broadcasting Commission, 2016). While there are many reasons why so many young people were not registered to vote (Collin & Walsh, 2016), this type of media coverage reflects an ongoing concern about young people's participation in Australian democracy. This concern has particular resonance in the wake of the Global Financial Crisis (GFC) and the austerity measures, which have followed it across various countries.

Compared to many other countries, Australia's young population was shielded from the worst effects of the Global Financial Crisis: while youth

L. Walsh (✉)
Department of Education, Monash University, Melbourne, VIC, Australia

R. Black
Department of Education, Deakin University, Geelong, VIC, Australia

© The Author(s) 2018
S. Pickard, J. Bessant (eds.), *Young People Re-Generating Politics in Times of Crises*, Palgrave Studies in Young People and Politics,
DOI 10.1007/978-3-319-58250-4_12

unemployment remains an issue here, the impact of the Global Financial Crisis has been lower by comparison with the catastrophic effects on young people in parts of Europe and the United Kingdom. This is not to suggest that young people in Australia are not feeling the effects of austerity policy, however. Many austerity measures have been proposed in recent years in relation to young people. These include Work for the Dole; Youth Jobs PaTH (Prepare, Trial, Hire), an youth internship program that pays young interns at a rate lower than the poverty line; the defunding of various youth support networks and agencies, and the deregulation of higher education.

These measures mimic those of recent United Kingdom Conservative governments (since 2010), both in their form and justification in terms of austerity (Walsh, 2016b, 2017a, 2017b). Measures such as Youth Jobs PaTH also serve to shift the responsibility of an insecure labour market onto young people as part of a wider policy movement away from a commitment to full employment and towards low-paid, piecemeal or voluntary work. While some of these measures have failed to win legislative support, and some are still in a nascent state, they have contributed to a wider cultural and policy climate in Australia, which evokes the language of austerity: scarcity, market competition and entitlement.

The Global Financial Crisis also affected young people in tangible ways. In the years immediately following the Global Financial Crisis, the proportion of Australian young people not learning or earning full-time increased by the highest level since the recession of the early 1990s (from 13.4 per cent to 16 per cent). Unemployment for those aged 15–19 and not in full-time education increased by over six per cent, one of the largest annual increases for this age group in two decades. In 2009, one quarter of young people aged 20–24 were not engaged in full-time work or full-time education (Robinson & Lamb, 2009): one journalist estimated that all but 400 of the 30,600 jobs shed between January and July 2009 had been lost by "teenagers" (Martin, 2009). Insecure, part-time work also increased, much of it undertaken on an involuntary basis (Walsh, 2016a).

Conditions for young people have improved since that time, but Australia, like other nations, is still characterised by a persistently negative discourse of youth politics in crisis, which portrays young people as civically and politically alienated or apathetic (see Walsh & Black, 2011). On the one hand, this discourse positions young people as democratically precarious because they are seen to be retreating from conventional democratic institutions and processes (Williamson, 2014). On the other, when they engage in what may be seen as alternative acts of citizenship, such as protest or social unrest, it portrays them as democratically deviant and dangerous. In so doing, it contributes to the demonisation and, in fact, to the criminalisation of increasingly large groups of young people as well as the acts or sites of citizenship which they choose to use or create (Bessant, 2016; Bessant, Farthing, & Watts, 2016; Pickard, 2014b). It positions them as a threat to the social and political order even while it cements their tenuous or marginalised relationship to that order (Bradford & Cullen, 2014; Cooper, 2012). As Pickard notes, in the age of austerity, "youth remains a problem" (2014a, p. 58).

The studies mentioned above are part of a still emerging body of scholarship which argues that most young people are not in fact democratically disengaged, but are engaging as citizens in ways that are 'off the radar' of conventional institutions and processes (also see Mansouri & Kirpitchenko, 2016; Percy-Smith, 2016; Peterson & Bentley, 2016). In Australia, the widespread youth protests and unrest in recent years have been less dramatic than in Europe or the Middle East. Many young people are, nevertheless, choosing alternative ways of expressing or enacting their citizenship. Some of these include conventional modes and sites such as the frequently informal and everyday spaces of youth volunteering. There are also newer modes and sites, such as the socially dynamic spaces of social enterprise, in which young people work interstitially between the government, business and not-for-profit sectors while drawing on tools and resources from each or all of them (Walsh & Black, 2011; Walsh & Owen, 2015).

This shift in young people's citizenship is indicative of something wider: an established but apparently escalating shift away from representative bodies (e.g. mainstream political parties) and institutions of the twentieth century towards more cause- or issue-based politics and a greater engagement with the 'small p' politics of the local (Kallio, Mills, & Skelton, 2016; Staeheli, Attoh, & Mitchell, 2013; Wood, 2016). Yet despite the scope of this shift, there has been insufficient analysis of the ways in which young people in countries such as Australia are seeking to influence change in an era of austerity. Young people's changing acts of citizenship are only poorly recognised through the conventional lenses or blunt measures of political participation, which still tend to emphasise traditional political institutions, channels and affiliations.

This chapter seeks to address this lack of analysis by exploring the growth of youth volunteering and social enterprise as alternate spaces for youth citizenship in the austerity era. It is divided into three parts. The first part of our discussion critically examines the patterns of young people's volunteering in Australia, drawing on an evidence review conducted by the authors for the Australian Research Alliance for Children and Youth (Walsh & Black, 2015). We consider the paucity of data that is available to describe young people's volunteering and the problems with how that volunteering is defined. Drawing on direct field research conducted by the authors with young social entrepreneurs,[1] the second part of our discussion considers young people's engagement in social enterprise, the dispute regarding what constitutes a social enterprise and the lack of data about the scope and scale of young people's involvement in this area. Finally, we build on our discussion to consider the implications of these interstitial or 'off the radar' acts of citizenship for conventional notions and practices of citizenship and the political, and for ways of moving beyond the trope of youth politics in crisis.

WHY YOUNG PEOPLE VOLUNTEER IN THE AGE OF AUSTERITY

According to conventional definitions of volunteering, around one in three young Australians volunteer, but the proportion of young people who volunteer *regularly* is much lower than this. Those most likely to volunteer are young women, those in education or paid work, those who have completed the final year of schooling, those who live outside of major cities, those who speak English at home, and those who give money to charity (Muir et al., 2009).

The question remains as to why such young people give their time. Young people's perceptions of what constitutes volunteering, and their motivations for volunteering, are as diverse as most other aspects of the volunteering landscape. The limited government data available suggest that young people volunteer to help others or the community, to gain personal satisfaction, to do something worthwhile, and for personal or family reasons (Muir et al., 2009). These motivations are worth unpacking in further detail.

Moffatt's typology of motivations for volunteering outlines three potential sets of motivations or 'asks' which young people seek from their volunteering. Firstly, there are the "You's," which comprise community based asks; "i.e. those who want to use this particular role to contribute to their community, 'make a difference,' or for social interaction." Secondly there are the "Me's," consisting of "solely personally based asks—i.e. those who want to use this particular role for personal reasons, such as to develop their skills, to enhance their career prospects, or to pursue a personal interest." Thirdly, there are the "Us's—Mixed asks—i.e. those who want to use this particular role partly for community reasons and partly for their own personal reasons" (Moffatt, 2011b, p. 68).

The first and most altruistic set of these motivations appears to be a powerful driver of volunteering for many young people in Australia. Many appear to see volunteering as an expression of good or active citizenship (Australian Youth Forum, 2012) and an opportunity to make a difference (Ferrier, Roos, & Long, 2004; Moffatt, 2011a). This is echoed by a national United Kingdom study, which found that the chief reason given by 16–24-year-olds for volunteering was to help people (Hill, Russell, & Brewis, 2009).

Other appeals of volunteering include the social benefits of being with friends, strengthening relationships and working collaboratively with others (Moffatt, 2011a). In particular, young people look for volunteering opportunities that link them to other young people (Ferrier et al., 2004; Volunteering ACT, 2013). There is also evidence that volunteering delivers the social benefits and outcomes that it promises: in a number of studies, young volunteers describe experiences of acknowledgement, appreciation and a sense of being socially engaged (Ferrier et al., 2004; McBride, Johnson, Olate, & O'Hara, 2011).

The second, more personal set of motivations proposed by Moffat is also a factor in many young people's choice to volunteer in Australia. The opportunity to learn or exercise new skills, especially skills that may be useful in progressing or obtaining work and career opportunities, is a key motivation for many young volunteers (Australian Youth Forum, 2012). It is also one that has particular resonance in the era of austerity, when many young people offer their unpaid work as volunteers and interns in the hope that it will position them more competitively in insecure and highly contested labour markets. This is where the rhetoric of citizenship may be misleading increasingly large numbers of young people. The "cult of experience" (Holdsworth, 2015, p. 1) has the potential to exacerbate existing inequalities between young people as voluntary internships and work placements displace or replace paid employment and, as Holdsworth observes, "create new cleavages of distinction and advantage" (2015, p. 6). More systemically, as Mills notes, these "new geographies of voluntarism" (2015, p. 532) provide a rationale for further cuts to public services and supports, including those services and supports needed by young people trying to cope with the vicissitudes of austerity, as well as the proposal of new policy measures (e.g. Work for the Dole) as mentioned above.

The third set of motivations in Moffat's typology involves a mixture of reasons that can shift over time. Some studies note that while altruism—the desire to contribute to the community and make a difference—may be what leads young people to volunteer in the first instance, they continue volunteering because they regard it as a way of accessing the more personal benefits mentioned above (Cornelis, Van Hiel, & De Cremer, 2013; Harris, 2013). Others suggest that young people may initially volunteer for shorter-term reasons of personal or professional gain, but that this frequently converts to a lifelong commitment to voluntary work (Nicol, 2012). What this commitment looks like in a precarious and increasing competitive labour market remains to be seen, as young people navigate and try to balance competing demands of insecure work, study and training.

Measuring Young People's Volunteering

It is difficult to ascertain the true nature of young people's volunteering in Australia because the data on youth volunteering is generalised from very limited information and its accuracy is often questionable. One reason for this lies in how volunteering is defined.

The Australian Bureau of Statistics (ABS) defines volunteering as "the provision of unpaid help willingly undertaken in the form of time, service or skills, to an organisation or group" (ABS, 2007). This definition excludes what it calls "direct volunteering"; that is, direct help that is not mediated through a formal organisation (ABS, 2012, p. 2). It also excludes what is commonly called 'informal' volunteering: volunteering that occurs outside not-for-profit organisations and without a position description (Volunteering Australia, 2006).

These exclusions foster an ambiguity about young people's volunteering, in relation to whether youth volunteering is in fact voluntary. While it is a key principle of volunteering that it is a freely chosen activity that takes place without compulsion, there are numerous contexts in which young people's choice to volunteer is not entirely free. As we have already discussed, the need to compete within the fluid labour markets of the austerity era is one of these contexts. Another relates to schooling, where volunteering in the form of service learning may be part of the compulsory curriculum or where students are given academic credit for it. Such contexts conflate the voluntary nature of young people's acts of citizenship with other, more instrumental goals. A blurring of purposes is also likely to occur in mutual obligation programs (Bessant, 2000) and where schemes are implemented that allow young people to reduce their university-fee debt through community volunteering, a proposal that has been circulating for some years in Australia (Left Right Think-Tank, 2011).

Young people's own understandings of volunteering are subject to a similar blurriness. One Australian House of Representatives Standing Committee Report into volunteering found that some young people failed to recognise their own activities as such (House of Representatives, 2008). Other studies have found that some young people dislike and do not identify with the term 'volunteer' (Geale, Creyton, Tindoy, & Radovic, 2010). Harris suggests that a crucial element in Australian school students' understanding of volunteering is intent: "if the intent was to do something for the greater good, rather than because one was compelled to through policy or for money, then it was viewed as volunteering" (Harris, 2013, p. 4). Our earlier observations raise the question of whether such distinctions remain valid in an era when the lines between paid and unpaid work, and between personal and public goods, are being increasingly blurred.

Much of the literature discussed earlier suggests an orientation of young people towards a 'politics of choice' (see Vromen & Collin, 2010). It documents the desire of many young people to make an active contribution and to have their voices and actions taken seriously by institutions of power. The evidence is, however, that this desire is largely being treated tokenistically at best, or—at worse—dismissed. The literature on youth volunteering suggests that negative discourses about young people's civic disengagement are devaluing the scope of their contribution. Civic and political institutions need to take a more positive view of young people's citizenship and social participation if they are to draw on their enthusiasm and energy, but the contributions of young people through volunteering remain largely off the radar because they are not recognised by the predominant (adult) gaze(s) of those institutions. This is despite evidence that volunteering matters to young people in Australia. In Mission Australia's 2015 survey of young Australians aged 15–19, volunteering was reported as one of the three top activities in which young people were involved (Cave, Fildes, Luckett, & Wearring, 2015). This follows the pattern of previous surveys (e.g. Buckley et al., 2012).

This evidence tends to slip through the gaps in the formal ABS data collection, which only reports on the volunteering activities of people between the ages of 18–24. Defining what constitutes young people's volunteering and who defines this are both important here. For example, informal volunteering by young people is less likely to be recorded because it is not necessarily seen as volunteering, especially within culturally and linguistically diverse communities where young people's contribution is viewed as a community or family obligation. As Kerr and her colleagues note, this contribution often occurs outside the commonly acknowledged definitions and purposes of volunteering (2001). This means that it may also be insufficiently recognised, supported or valued (House of Representatives, 2008).

Some young volunteers are also involved in 'hidden' voluntary activities that are not included in public measures or assessments of volunteering. A 2007–2008 survey of young people in the United Kingdom, for example, found that 16–24 year olds are more likely to volunteer informally than any other age group (41 per cent compared to an average of 35 per cent) but also less likely than any other age group to volunteer formally (Hill et al., 2009). In Australia, this informal volunteering is not monitored or measured by the ABS. There is also a paucity of empirical information about non-traditional volunteering roles such as online social action, e-volunteering, time-banks, and young people's engagement in volunteer tourism during their gap year.

This lack of data and consistency means that many policy proposals with regards to youth volunteering are made without real knowledge or substantial research into young volunteers' values, activities and attitudes (Bassett, Troy, Scarce, & McLaren, 2011). Traditional definitions of volunteering also provide few insights into the organisational contexts or locations in which young people volunteer. While these are often not-for-profit organisations, the growth in non-traditional volunteering roles, which we note earlier presents an increasing challenge to the notion that youth volunteering is necessarily mediated by a formal organisation at all. This leads us to the issue of how young people's increasing engagement in youth-led social enterprises is recognised and understood.

The Emergence of the Social Enterprise

In recent years, young people have become part of a new wave of voluntary activity that seeks entrepreneurial responses to contemporary social and political challenges. Through what are often called social enterprises, young people operate at the intersection of the government, business and not-for-profit sectors (Black, Walsh, & Taylor, 2011).

Social enterprises are exclusively voluntary, yet they are not measured according to the conventional ABS definition of volunteering. The emergence of youth-driven social enterprises is widely feted—young social entrepreneurs are almost breathlessly valorised within the not-for-profit sector (Walsh, Black, & Berman, 2013)—yet there is virtually no official recognition of this activity by standard measurements of citizenship participation and no systematic data exists on the scope and scale of youth social enterprise in Australia. This means that it represents one of the 'hidden' voluntary activities we discuss above.

This is not helped by blurry definitions of the field. Like volunteering more broadly, the notion of what constitutes a social enterprise is itself debated. Broadly defined, a social enterprise targets perceived unmet areas of need or gaps in service delivery, pursuing a social or political purpose while engaging in commercial activities such as the sale of products and/or services (Battilana, Sengul, Pache, & Model, 2015). According to Crawford-Spencer and Cantatore (2016, p. 48), a social enterprise is characterised by:

> (a) a social purpose that prevails over the aim of delivering profit to shareholders; (b) an organizational culture, structure, management, processes, and resources that are less centralized than those of strictly commercial enterprises; (c) imperatives to collaboratively prevail over market competition; and (d) greater complexity in the involvement and interests of stakeholders/customers.

These themes certainly emerged from our conversations with 18 young social entrepreneurs, in which many expressed frustration with the slowness of government responses to issues of key concern to young people such as education, the environment, health and human rights. These young people have chosen to engage in social enterprises out of a need for more dynamic, responsive and efficient forms of change-making (Walsh & Owen, 2015). They draw from business, government, and not-for-profit sector resources and approaches, working between the spaces typically occupied by these sectors.

At the same time, they are keenly aware of how they and other young people seeking to drive social change are negatively portrayed by some of those sectors and by the traditional discourses of politics and power. Despite their commitment, these young people suffer from the effects of the stereotypes that are still used to characterise young people as a collective. As one young social entrepreneur observed, "as a society we problematise young people, so young people are a problem to solve."

This problematisation of youth was seen by some young entrepreneurs as a systemic issue. As another observed, "society doesn't put young people in the top job and we see that in the government, we see that with big organisations ... taking responsibility off young people." This same young person spoke with some bitterness about the cultural and institutional blindness that infantilises contemporary young people:

> [...] you go way back to the 1400's and Joan of Arc led an entire country to victory at the age of sixteen. We now treat our sixteen year olds like they can't wipe their own arse and they need to be, like, managed or they need to be sorted out.

As with volunteering, the value and recognition of youth-led social enterprise is arguably delimited by adult discourses. In a previous study of young social entrepreneurs, we found a related and potential significant divergence in how some young people characterised their participation. One example was Jack, who was involved in a social enterprise seeking to address homophobia in a regional Australian setting. Though passionate about social justice, Jack did not consider his enterprise to be 'political,' despite the fact that its success depended on a shift in social norms, attitudes and power relations in determining who could be included and excluded based on sexual orientation (Walsh & Black, 2011).

There is one final but important question to arise in relation to social enterprises. This is whether they reflect the neoliberal responsibilisation of young people to address the complex social problems of our time rather than conventional institutions, such as the state. Given the pervasiveness of neoliberalism, young entrepreneurs may themselves be the subjects of neoliberal discourses valorising the "entrepreneurial self" as a means of governance (Kelly, 2006, p. 18). But to reduce their entrepreneurialism to some kind of by-product of neoliberalism underplays their reflexive understandings, struggles and capacities to influence their worlds (for more about this, see France & Threadgold, 2015). It could be argued that social enterprises function interstitially between sectors because young people and the conventional avenues of influence have been relegated to the margins. Young people might be attempting to adopt this model in the absence of other means of influence.

Conclusion

Andersson has argued that "young people, when given the opportunity, have the capacity to create their own political spaces and places as political actors" (2015, p. 14). Our main contention here is that a lack of recognition and misrecognition of these key aspects of young people's citizenship limits our capacity to understand how they are seeking to shape their worlds in the austerity era.

The forms of youth volunteering and social enterprise described in this chapter appear to be largely invisible to researchers and commentators, suggesting a need for more nuanced ways of mapping and measuring the scope and impact of young people's citizenship activities (Walsh & Black, 2015). This has important implications not only for youth studies scholars but also for organisations and political institutions seeking to engage young people as citizens. At the very least, better recognition, measurement and acknowledgement of the ways in which young people are choosing to enact their citizenship could create more meaningful and more positive opportunities for other young people. At the time of writing, a more inclusive definition of volunteering was developed by Volunteering Australia (2016), according to which "volunteering is time willingly given for the common good and without financial gain." This definition is promising because it takes into account activities such as activism, more nuanced forms of volunteerism and, potentially, some forms of social enterprise.

It could also help to focus policy attention on the key question of who is included and who is excluded in the 'off the radar' acts of citizenship considered in this chapter. Educated young people, young people from higher socioeconomic groups and young people who are already confident, already civically engaged and who already possess the skills required to volunteer are also the most likely to choose to volunteer (Hardy, Pratt, Pancer, Olsen, & Lawford, 2010). Such young people demonstrate higher membership of cultural associations, participation in politics and other organisations than those who do not volunteer (Hill et al., 2009). They are also more likely to report positive beliefs about the importance of volunteering (Jahromi, Crocetti, & Buchanan, 2012) and to sustain their civic and citizenship participation (Walsh & Black, 2015). A similar pattern emerges within the social enterprise area.

This has the potential to set up new patterns of inequality amongst young people, as well as to reinforce and exacerbate existing inequalities.

The austerity era is cementing the neoliberal expectation that young people foster their own life opportunities as well as the discourse that holds them responsible for any failure to secure those opportunities (Walsh, 2017b; Walsh & Black, 2011). Without a clearer analysis and understanding of young people's preferred acts of citizenship, the dominant and institutional constructions of what constitutes citizenship will continue to foster limited understandings of youth politics in crisis that either devalue the ways that young people are participating and seeking to shape their worlds, or overlook them entirely. It will also perpetuate cruel patterns of exclusion for rapidly growing numbers of young people.

Note

1. In 2013, the authors conducted a focus group with young people who were seeking to make social or political change. The focus group involved 18 participants from the 'Foundation for Young Australians' Young Social Pioneers', a program designed to develop social enterprises. Our discussions explored the extent to which those young people believe they have the power to influence society; the ways in which they seek to influence; the barriers to that; and what they believed would enable them to have greater influence.

References

Andersson, E. (2015). Situational political socialization: A normative approach to young people's adoption and acquisition of political preferences and skills. *Journal of Youth Studies, 18*(8), 967–983.

Australian Broadcasting Commission (ABC). (2016). Concerns one in two 18-year-olds not enrolled to vote: Australian electoral commission. *World Today*, 9 May. http://www.abc.net.au/worldtoday/content/2016/s4458565.htm

Australian Bureau of Statistics (ABS). (2007). *Voluntary work*. Canberra: Australian Government. http://www.abs.gov.au/AUSSTATS/abs@.nsf/DetailsPage/4441.02010?OpenDocument

Australian Bureau of Statistics (ABS). (2012). *A comparison of volunteering rates from the 2006 Census of Population and Housing and the 2006 General Social Survey*. Canberra: Australian Government. http://www.abs.gov.au/AUSSTATS/abs@.nsf/DetailsPage/4441.0.55.002Junper.

Australian Youth Forum (AYF). (2012). *Submission to Australian curriculum and reporting authority on proposed Australian curriculum*. Department of Education Employment and Workplace Relations, Office for Youth. Retrieved

March 21, 2013, from http://www.youth.gov.au/sites/Youth/ayf/weHearYou/Documents/AYF_Sub_ACARA_Civics.pdf

Bassett, K., Troy, D., Scarce, L., & McLaren, A. (2011). *Youth volunteering*. Fortitude Valley: Left Right Think-Tank.

Battilana, J., Sengul, M., Pache, A.-C., & Model, J. (2015). Harnessing productive tensions in hybrid organizations: The case of work integration social enterprises. *Academy of Management Journal, 58*(6), 1658–1858.

Bessant, J. (2000). Civil conscription or reciprocal obligation: The ethics of "work-for-the-dole". *Australian Journal of Social Issues, 35*(1), 15–33.

Bessant, J. (2016). Democracy denied, youth participation and criminalizing digital dissent. *Journal of Youth Studies, 19*(7), 921–937.

Bessant, J., Farthing, R., & Watts, R. (2016). Co-designing a civics curriculum: Young people, democratic deficit and political renewal in the EU. *Journal of Curriculum Studies, 48*(2), 271–289.

Black, R., Walsh, L., & Taylor, F. (2011). Young people on the margins: What works in youth participation. *Youth Studies Australia, 30*(1), 42–48.

Bradford, S., & Cullen, F. (2014). Youth policy in austerity Europe. *International Journal of Adolescence and Youth, 19*(1), 1–4.

Buckley, H., Dalton, B., Fildes, J., Ivancic, L., Matkovic, L., Perrens, B., et al. (2012). *Youth survey 2012*. Sydney: Mission Australia.

Cave, L., Fildes, J., Luckett, G., & Wearring, A. (2015). *Mission Australia Youth Survey Report 2015*. Sydney: Mission Australia.

Collin, P., & Walsh, L. (2016). Many young people aren't enrolled to vote—But are we asking them the wrong question? *The Conversation*. 16 May. Retrieved July 29, 2016, from http://theconversation.com/many-young-people-arent-enrolled-to-vote-but-are-we-asking-them-the-wrong-question-59248

Cooper, C. (2012). Understanding the English "riots" of 2011: "Mindless criminality" or youth "Mekin Histri" in austerity Britain? *Youth and Policy, 109*(6), 6–26.

Cornelis, I., Van Hiel, A., & De Cremer, D. (2013). Volunteer work in youth organizations: Predicting distinct aspects of volunteering behavior from self- and other-oriented motives. *Journal of Applied Social Psychology, 43*(2), 456–466.

Crawford-Spencer, E., & Cantatore, F. (2016). Models of franchising for social enterprise. *Journal of Marketing Channels, 23*(1–2), 47–59.

Ferrier, F., Roos, I., & Long, M. (2004). *Passions, people and appreciation: Making volunteering work for young people*. Canberra: National Youth Affairs Research Scheme.

France, A., & Threadgold, S. (2015). Youth and political economy: Towards a Bourdieusian approach. *Journal of Youth Studies, 19*(5), 612–628.

Geale, J., Creyton, M., Tindoy, M., & Radovic, A. (2010). *Youth leading youth: A look at organisations led by young people*. Queensland: Volunteering Queensland.

Hardy, S. A., Pratt, M. W., Pancer, S. M., Olsen, J. A., & Lawford, H. L. (2010). Community and religious involvement as contexts of identity change across late adolescence and emerging adulthood. *International Journal of Behavioural Development, 35*(2), 125–135.

Harris, C. (2013). *Promoting youth engagement and wellbeing through student volunteer programs in schools.* Canberra: Volunteering ACT.

Hill, M., Russell, J., & Brewis, G. (2009). *Young people, volunteering and youth projects: A rapid review of recent evidence.* London: Institute of Volunteering Research.

Holdsworth, C. (2015). The cult of experience: Standing out from the crowd in an era of austerity. *Area.* doi:10.1111/area.12201.

House of Representatives Standing Committee on Family, Community, Housing and Youth. (2008). *The value of volunteering.* Canberra: Parliament of the Commonwealth of Australia.

Jahromi, P., Crocetti, E., & Buchanan, C. M. (2012). A cross-cultural examination of adolescent civic engagement: Comparing Italian and American community-oriented and political involvement. *Journal of Prevention and Intervention in the Community, 40*(1), 22–36.

Kallio, K. P., Mills, S., & Skelton, T. (Eds.). (2016). *Politics, citizenship and rights.* Singapore: Springer.

Kelly, P. (2006). The entrepreneurial self and 'youth at-risk': Exploring the horizons of identity in the twenty-first century. *Journal of Youth Studies, 9*(1), 17–32.

Kerr, L., Savelsberg, H., Sparrow, S., & Tedmanson, D. (2001). *Experiences and perceptions of volunteering in indigenous and non-English speaking background communities.* Adelaide: Social Policy Research Group, University of South Australia.

Left Right Think-Tank. (2011). *Youth volunteering: Increasing engagement and participation.* Queensland: Left Right Think-Tank.

Mansouri, F., & Kirpitchenko, L. (2016). Practices of active citizenship among migrant youth: Beyond conventionalities. *Social Identities, 22*(3), 1–17.

Martin, P. (2009). Women make jobs gains while men lose out. *The Age,* 10 July. Retrieved May 25, 2015, from http://www.theage.com.au/national/women-make-jobs-gains-while-men-lose-out-20090709-dep7.html

McBride, A. M., Johnson, E., Olate, R., & O'Hara, K. (2011). Youth volunteer service as positive youth development in Latin America and the Caribbean. *Children and Youth Services Review, 33*(1), 34–41.

Mills, S. (2015). Geographies of youth work, volunteering and employment: The Jewish lads' brigade and club in post-war Manchester. *Transactions of the Institute of British Geographers, 40*(4), 523–535.

Moffatt, L. (2011a). *Engaging young people in volunteering: What works in Tasmania? Executive summary.* Hobart: Volunteering Tasmania.

Moffatt, L. (2011b). *Engaging young people in volunteering: What works in Tasmania? Full report*. Hobart: Volunteering Tasmania.

Muir, K., Mullan, K., Powell, A., Flaxman, S., Thompson, D., & Griffiths, M. (2009). *State of Australia's young people*. Canberra: Australian Government, Office for Youth.

Nicol, S. (2012). Volunteering and young people. *Youth Studies Australia, 31*(3), 3–5.

Percy-Smith, B. (2016). Negotiating active citizenship: Young people's participation in everyday spaces. In K. P. Kallio, S. Mills, & T. Skelton (Eds.), *Politics, citizenship and rights* (pp. 1–18). Singapore: Springer.

Peterson, A., & Bentley, B. (2016). A case for cautious optimism? Active citizenship and the Australian civics and citizenship curriculum. *Asia Pacific Journal of Education*. doi:10.1080/02188791.2016.1142424.

Pickard, S. (2014a). French youth policy in an age of austerity: Plus ça change? *International Journal of Adolescence and Youth, 19*(1), 48–61.

Pickard, S. (2014b). "The trouble with young people these days": "Deviant" youth, the popular press and politics in contemporary Britain. *French Journal of British Studies, 19*(1), 91–121.

Robinson, L., & Lamb, S. (2009). *How young people are faring 2009*. Melbourne: The Foundation for Young Australians.

Staeheli, L. A., Attoh, K., & Mitchell, D. (2013). Contested engagements: Youth and the politics of citizenship. *Space and Polity, 17*(1), 88–105.

Volunteering ACT. (2013). *About us*. Retrieved July 15, 2016, from http://www.volunteeringact.org.au/about/about-us

Volunteering Australia. (2006). *Involved and valued? Findings from a national survey of Australian volunteers from diverse cultural and linguistic backgrounds*. Canberra: Volunteering Australia.

Volunteering Australia. (2016). *Definition of volunteering*. Canberra: Volunteering Australia.

Vromen, A., & Collin, P. (2010). Everyday youth participation? Contrasting views from Australian policymakers and young people. *Young, 18*(1), 97–112.

Walsh, L. L. (2016a). Will the internships program help young people get jobs? *The Herald Sun*. 10 May. Retrieved July 29, 2016, from http://www.heraldsun.com.au/business/work/will-the-internships-program-help-young-people-get-jobs/news-story/d0763044b0f14501c6fcf868037d174d

Walsh, L. L. (2016b). *Educating generation next: Young people, teachers and schooling in transition*. London: Palgrave Macmillan.

Walsh, L. L. (2017a). Treading water? The roles and possibilities of adversity capital in preparing young people for precarity. In P. Kelly & J. Pike (Eds.), *Neoliberalism and austerity: The moral economies of young people's health and wellbeing*. London: Palgrave Macmillan.

Walsh, L. L. (2017b). Beyond hope and outrage: Conceptualizing and harnessing adversity capital in young people. In P. Kelly, P. Campbell, L. Harrison, & C. Hickey (Eds.), *Young people and the politics of outrage and hope*. Leiden and Boston: Brill Publishers.

Walsh, L. L., & Black, R. (2011). *In their own hands: Can young people change Australia?* Melbourne: ACER Press.

Walsh, L. L., & Black, R. (2015). Youth volunteering in Australia: An evidence review. In *Report prepared for the Australian Research Alliance for Children and Youth*. Canberra: Australian Research Alliance for Children and Youth.

Walsh, L. L., Black, R., & Berman, N. (2013). Walking the talk: Youth research in hard times. In K. te Riele & R. Brooks (Eds.), *Negotiating ethical challenges in youth research* (pp. 43–54). London: Routledge.

Walsh, L. L., & Owen, J. (2015). Young people, change making and democracy. In P. Crisp (Ed.), *So you want to be a leader: Influential people reveal how to succeed in public life* (pp. 216–227). Melbourne: Hybrid Publishers.

Williamson, H. (2014). Radicalisation to retreat: Responses of the young to austerity Europe. *International Journal of Adolescence and Youth, 19*(1), 5–18.

Wood, B. E. (2016). A genealogy of the "everyday" within young people's citizenship studies. In K. P. Kallio, S. Mills, & T. Skelton (Eds.), *Politics, citizenship and rights* (pp. 1–14). Singapore: Springer.

Lucas Walsh is Associate Professor and is Associate Dean (Academic Staff) in the Faculty of Education at Monash University, Australia. He was previously Director of Research and Evaluation at the Foundation for Young Australians. His recent book, *Educating Generation Next: Young People, Teachers and Schooling in Transition* was published with Palgrave Macmillan.

Rosalyn Black is Senior Lecturer in Education at Deakin University, Australia. Her coming co-authored books include *Rethinking Youth Citizenship after the Age of Entitlement* (with Lucas Walsh, to be published by Bloomsbury) and *Risk, Resilience, Inclusion and Citizenship: Young People's Perspectives on Digital Life* (Palgrave Macmillan).

CHAPTER 13

(Re)Politicising Young People: From Scotland's Indyref to Hong Kong's Umbrella Movement

Susan Batchelor, Alistair Fraser, Leona Li Ngai Ling, and Lisa Whittaker

INTRODUCTION

In the aftermath of the 2008 global financial crisis, young people across the world have experienced increased precariousness of work, housing, stability and confidence in the future. In some contexts, this has led to alienation and apathy; in others, it has led to increased politicisation and

S. Batchelor (✉)
School of Social and Political Sciences, University of Glasgow, Glasgow, Scotland

A. Fraser
School of Social and Political Sciences, University of Glasgow, Glasgow, Scotland

L.L.N. Ling
Department of Sociology and Centre for Criminology, University of Hong Kong, Pok Fu Lam, Hong Kong

L. Whittaker
Tenovus Cancer Care, Cardiff, UK

© The Author(s) 2018
S. Pickard, J. Bessant (eds.), *Young People Re-Generating Politics in Times of Crises*, Palgrave Studies in Young People and Politics,
DOI 10.1007/978-3-319-58250-4_13

protest. In particular, a backlash against globalisation and disillusionment with political elites has contributed to the rise of nationalist movements, commonly associated with right-wing populism and opposition to immigration. Yet nationalism can take many forms, as evidenced by the recent campaigns for self-determination in both Scotland and Hong Kong.

In Scotland, the 2014 referendum on independence (locally referred to as IndyRef) from the United Kingdom (UK) saw young people mobilised as never before: campaigning on behalf of non-partisan political groups, participating in rallies and debates, engaging in online discussions, and turning out to vote in high numbers (Electoral Commission, 2014; McLaverty et al., 2015). While the outcome of the referendum was a vote against independence, young people—especially those living in marginalised communities—were amongst those most likely to vote for independence, motivated by concerns about social inequality and a desire to have their voices and their interests reflected in public life (Breeze, Gorringe, Jamieson, & Rosie, 2015). Rather than focusing on the perceived negative consequences of immigration, frustration in Scotland was targeted at a UK Westminster government led by right-wing politics and an agenda of austerity.

This emphasis on self-determination from a larger territorial government was also the driving force behind the youth-led pro-democracy movement in Hong Kong. The 2014 'Umbrella Movement' lasted three months and at its peak brought over 100,000 people to the streets to campaign to elect the Chief Executive without interference from Beijing (see Watts in this volume). In doing so, it 'reaffirmed the civic character of the people to resist political and economic integration with China by attempting to reassert the values of universal suffrage and self-determination' (Kwan, 2016, p. 965). Protesters occupied three major road junctions, transforming them from spaghetti-style intersections choked with traffic to spaces of quiet defiance. At the largest of these protest sites, in Admiralty, the civic nature of the occupiers drew global attention: a social ecology built around interdependence and recycling, makeshift study groups and free exchange of goods and services.

Drawing on a wider study of youth leisure in Scotland and Hong Kong, this chapter compares the participation of young people in these two independence movements, highlighting the similarities and differences that emerge. In doing so, it challenges static representations of both nationalism and youth politics, and points to the ways in which the narratives underpinning the activities of young people in each setting reflected their distinctive political heritages. The chapter is set out in four sections. The first engages with sociological debates about the nature and form of contemporary youth politics, in particular those focused on questions of apathy, disengagement and disorder. The second introduces the research project, the two case study locations and the focus group sample characteristics. The subsequent sections draw out analytical insights from the study, examining themes of self-determination and social justice. The conclusion offers some brief observations relating to the implications of these findings for youth politics in Scotland and Hong Kong.

The Character of Contemporary Youth Politics

Young people's political engagement, or perceived lack thereof, has been a major focus for academic research in recent years (Brooks & Hodkinson, 2008; Henn & Foard, 2012; Marsh, O'Toole, & Jones, 2007). Studies have repeatedly shown that many young people are dissatisfied with and alienated from traditional institutional political participation. Compared to older generations, young people have lower levels of electoral turn out (Phelps, 2005; Wattenberg, 2003), lower levels of party membership (Sloam, 2007; Van Biezen, Mair, & Poguntke, 2012), and lower levels of knowledge about and interest in formal political processes (Henn, Weinstein, & Forrest, 2005; Kimberlee, 2002). These patterns have led some commentators to conclude that young people in the twenty-first century are apolitical:

> Today's young people say they are not interested in politics and do not regard political activity as worthwhile. They know little about the institutions of government at various levels, and feel little loyalty to the communities of which they are a part. (Pirie & Worcester, 2000, p. 35)

This rather bleak picture of contemporary youth politics is often linked to the breakdown of traditional identities and practices (Beck, 1999; Giddens, 1991), alongside the depoliticising effects of consumerism and mass media. As Furlong and Cartmel note:

> In the context of late modernity, young people may increasingly find it difficult to make connections between their own life circumstances and those of others occupying similar positions or sharing core experiences.

As a consequence, identification with a broader collectivity in the shape of a social class or a community of interests, and hence the political orientations and values associated with class positions, is seen as having weakened. (Furlong & Cartmel, 2012, p. 14)

Yet, whilst many may lack interest and involvement in electoral politics, a number of studies demonstrate that young people participate in other, more unorthodox forms of political activity (Henn & Foard, 2014). A key finding to emerge is that young people may have a particular propensity towards issue-based or 'cause-oriented' politics, which focus on specific concerns and 'non-traditional' methods of political activity, such as boycotts, petitioning, demonstrations, and direct action (Loader, 2007; Marsh et al., 2007), as well as local forms of social action, for example membership of informal community networks or volunteering (Brooks, 2007; Eden & Roker, 2002; Roker, Player, & Coleman, 1999; Vromen, 2003). Some social theorists characterise these activities as evidence of a shift towards individualised 'life politics' (Giddens, 1991), concerned with post-materialist values like autonomy, belonging, and self-actualisation. (Inglehart, 1997)

In recent years, however, narratives of fragmentation and post-material politics have been tempered by evidence of the continuing salience of materialist, economic concerns amongst young people. As a number of contemporary studies have indicated, there is continuity as well as change in young people's political engagements, with place-based structural inequalities and political traditions continuing to play an important role in shaping attitudes and practices. Furlong and Cartmel (2012), for example, found that young people's political views varied from, and were similar to, those of older generations. In particular, there was shared concern across the generations about the state of the economy, as well as a shared distrust of conventional politics and political institutions. In their analysis of survey data from Australia, the UK and the United States (US), Vromen, Xenos and Loader (2015) also found that the economy was ranked as a key issue of political importance for young people, together with other materialist concerns relating to work and education. Focus group data from the same three countries demonstrated that young people's understanding of these issues was often framed by neoliberal ideas of choice and responsibility, but these were tempered by differing lived experiences rooted in particular places. This merging of materialist and post-materialist concerns is also highlighted by Rheingans and Hollands's (2013) in their case study of the 2010 UK university student occupation movement (following the rise in tuition fees). Participants in their research located their actions in relation to an established tradition of student activism, but also made connections with other collective actions and entities (e.g. the trade union movement) and wider concerns (the banking crisis and public sector cuts).

Most recently, these economic concerns have merged with a new collectivist politics of nationalism and the 'rise of the right' across Europe (see Bessant in this volume). In England, young people in insecure labour market positions have increasingly been involved in new forms of street politics, including organised demonstrations against immigration and more spontaneous forms of violent disorder (McDowell, Rootham, & Hardgrove, 2014; Treadwell, Briggs, Winlow, & Hall, 2013). The rise of a new English nationalism, evidenced by the growth of support for the United Kingdom Independence Party (UKIP) and groups like the English Defence League (EDL), has been attributed to the failure of established political parties to adequately defend working-class interests (Winlow, Hall, & Treadwell, 2016). It is important to note, however, that there is a degree of cultural and social heterogeneity to young people's political responses to economic crisis. As will be discussed, independence movements in Scotland and Hong Kong were characterised by strains of a more 'civic' nationalism, which combined materialist and post-materialist concerns, and focused less on narrow, inward-looking identity politics and more on self-determination and opportunities to address broader issues of inequality.

(Re)Imagining Youth in Glasgow and Hong Kong

The research reported on here was originally designed as part of a wider, comparative study of youth leisure in Glasgow and Hong Kong.[1] We set out to explore the values, attitudes and habits of young people in two geographically disparate cities, in order to interrogate contemporary debates relating to youth, globalisation and social change (Batchelor, Whittaker, Fraser, & Ling, 2017; Fraser, Batchelor, Ling, & Whittaker, 2017). The Scottish fieldsite, Dennistoun, is a residential neighbourhood located in the East End of the city. Typical of many post-industrial areas in the UK, Glasgow's East End is known largely for its high rates of poverty and unemployment, poor health and low mortality, and is often stigmatised as a breeding ground for welfare dependency and violent gang culture (Fraser, 2015a; Gray & Mooney, 2011; Mooney, McCall, & Paton, 2015). Much of the district falls within the 15% 'most deprived' data zones in Scotland (Scottish Government, 2012), though there is also a growing population of middle-class students and artists, attracted to the relatively affordable housing market and proximity to Glasgow city centre. Yat Tung, the Hong Kong fieldsite, is a large public housing estate located on Lantau Island, exhibiting similar demographics to Dennistoun: predominantly lower-income, with a mixture of social housing and owner-occupied leases, coupled with high youth populations and perceived 'problem' youth (Hong Kong Sheng Kung Hui Tung Chung Integrated Services, 2010). Unlike Dennistoun, however, it is relatively isolated from the rest of the city, built to service a new airport.

We used a qualitative case study approach, involving concurrent data collection in these two locations, including ethnographic observations (six months in each site, from October 2013 to March 2014), interviews with local community representatives (n = 8 in Glasgow and n = 7 in Hong Kong), focus groups with young people (n = 9 and n = 6 respectively) and interviews with young people (n = 22 and n = 20). The empirical material presented in this chapter is principally drawn from Phases 1 and 2 of the study, alongside a small proportion from Phase 3. Phases 1 and 2 comprised structured observations and 15 focus groups with 68 young people across the two research sites, accessed via local youth organisations, schools and colleges, as well as via employers and employment agencies, criminal justice agencies and social work, while Phase 3 consisted of 42 interviews with young people across both fieldsites. The characteristics of the focus group samples are indicated in Tables 13.1 and 13.2.

Although the study was initially designed to compare young people's leisure in these two sites, this focus was superseded by the emergent politics of the independence referendum and Umbrella Movement. These two major instances of political mobilisation happened at almost exactly the same time across our two field sites and were raised as a significant issue by research participants, particularly in the Glasgow setting. In this sense, the study was very much in the right place at the right time, and as events unfolded, we decided to explore the opinions and experiences of the young people involved.

Table 13.1 Focus group sample, Glasgow (N = 42)

	Age				Total
	15 and under	16–19	20–25	26 and over	
Female	4	9	1	–	14
Male	2	18	7	1	28
Total	6	27	8	1	42

Table 13.2 Focus group sample, Hong Kong (N = 26)

	Age				Total
	15 and under	16–19	20–25	26 and over	
Female	2	3	3	–	8
Male	3	9	2	–	14 (4 data missing)
Total	5	12	5	–	26

In the sections that follow, young people's views and experiences are brought into dialogue with the debates mentioned above regarding young people and politics. In Glasgow, research participants expressed an overwhelming support for Scottish independence from the UK, with an emphasis on self-determination and social justice. It was particularly notable that young people were reluctant to identify themselves explicitly as 'nationalist,' but the language of class—specifically working-class politics—featured heavily in their accounts. By contrast, while Hong Kong participants were also animated by a desire for self-determination, political freedom and universal suffrage formed the foreground of their narratives. These differences suggest the need to explore the role of place, history and political heritage in understanding contemporary configurations of youthful politics (Pilkington & Pollock, 2016).

(Re)Politicising Youth? Indyref and the Umbrella Movement

On 18 September 2014, the population of Scotland were presented with a single question: 'Should Scotland be an independent country?' With the vote extended to 16- and 17-year-olds, it was the first time that under-18s in the UK had the franchise on a major matter of state (see Pickard, 2018). In the weeks leading up to the referendum, debate was energised by the involvement of a new cohort of voters who participated in a range of online and offline forms of engagement, and who were widely reported in the media as likely to tip the balance towards independence. Student activism played an important role on both sides of the campaign, with organised debates taking place in schools, colleges and universities up and down the country, alongside spontaneous grassroots gatherings in major city centres. On the day, an estimated 75% of 16–17 year olds turned out to vote, compared to 54% of those aged 18–24 (and 85% of eligible voters overall) (Electoral Commission, 2014). The outcome was a vote against independence, with 55% returning No and 45% returning Yes. Following the result, however, the pro-independence Scottish National Party (SNP) experienced a huge surge in membership (from approximately 26,000 to over 120,000—around 2% of the Scottish population) and went on to make historic gains in the 2015 UK General Election, winning 56 out of 59 Scottish seats.[2] Though there was some variability in polling data, several exit surveys found that young adults and those living in socio-economically disadvantaged areas were most likely to vote Yes to independence (Curtice, 2014).

Just two weeks after the Scottish referendum, on 28 September 2014, the youth-led Umbrella Movement brought the world's media spotlight to Hong Kong. While organised protest and occupations are not entirely new to the city (Chiu & Lui, 2000; Lam, 2004), the scale and intensity of the Umbrella Movement was unprecedented. Several major roads in three different neighbourhoods were blocked, with people from diverse backgrounds camping out overnight, some for several weeks, after finding out about the action via social media (Cheng and Chan, 2017). Forms of involvement varied—from occupiers to online translators, contributors to logistical coordinators—but young people were unified under a common concern to promote the democratic autonomy of Hong Kong (Ortmann, 2015). The movement lasted until 15 December 2014, at which point protesters were forcibly removed by police. Although unsuccessful in obtaining universal suffrage, the protest had 'reverberating effects on society which fundamentally changed Hong Kong's political atmosphere […] result[ing] in the rapid rise of localism and the new political awakening among a generation of youth to defend their home' (Kwan, 2016, p. 949).

During our fieldwork, participants in both sites were swept up in the excitement and fervour of political conversation. In Glasgow, participants valued the fact that the referendum allowed their voices to be heard and highlighted the role of social media in creating shared spaces for engagement and interaction. The following excerpt is drawn from a group of young people discussing the referendum in the weeks leading up to the vote. Echoing the later survey polls, the group discuss both their engagement in debate and their feelings in relation to the age-based patterning of voting preferences:

> *LW*: Has there been a lot going on in school about the referendum?
> *Alex*: Everyone is talking, arguing, fighting.
> *Nicola*: Our Modern Studies teacher is taking two periods out tomorrow to talk about it because everyone was just going on about it.
> *LW*: Is there quite a mixed view in the school?
> *Nicola*: No, mainly Yes [voters].
> *Mairi*: We went to a referendum debate last week at the Hydro [entertainment venue] and our teacher was finding it really hard to find No voters.
> *Alex*: A lot of the No voters are, like, old people.

These comments reflect a general sentiment in favour of independence among the young people we engaged. However, our participants were often careful to distinguish this support for independence from support for the SNP, focusing instead on the possibility of democratic and social reform. As one young woman commented, "independence isn't a vote for the SNP, it's a vote for independence" (Young woman, Glasgow focus group 1). This pre-referendum disavowal of the SNP was often linked to young people's desire to distance themselves from the negative connotations of nationalism, portrayed as "exclusionary" and "inward-looking." Against a backdrop of a decline in support for the Labour Party in Scotland,[3] independence was regarded as vehicle for a more progressive politics:

> I'm not saying that being a Nationalist is right, I'm not saying that their policies are right, but they're a step in the right direction. See as soon as you've got Independence, you'll vote for Joe Bloggs … It's not about being British or being Scottish, it's nothing to do with that. It's the power. It's the Westminster Government that's the problem and needs to be sorted. (Young man, Glasgow focus group 8)

Amongst our Glasgow participants there was a general of lack of enthusiasm for conventional political parties and, more specifically, a lack of trust in Westminster politicians sitting in the House of Commons in London. This was articulated in their frustrations about the handling by the Westminster government of the 2008 banking crisis and the parliamentary expenses scandal (see Pickard, 2013). It was also evident in their criticisms of Scottish Labour's lack of political autonomy from Westminster and the party's decision to campaign alongside the Conservatives as part of the Better Together (i.e. vote No) campaign. Voting for independence, for many of our Glasgow-based research participants, was thus motivated less by nationalist sentiment and more by a desire for influence, which they felt could best be achieved at a national level (see also Breeze et al., 2015).

In Hong Kong, participants became similarly more engaged in political discussions during the Umbrella Movement, though levels and forms of involvement varied. Some participants had visited the main Admiralty site, which was principally associated with student-led activism and deliberate efforts to create a self-sustaining protest camp. Others visited the Mong Kok site, which was more associated with grassroots politics and diversity. Mirroring the separatist politics of the Scottish independence referendum, young people who visited the camps were animated by a desire for political self-determination and protection of basic freedoms from the perceived threat of mainland China. As one participant noted, young people felt that they had no choice but to take to the streets in a way that marked out a different form of political engagement from their parents' generation (DeGolyer, 2010):

> *LL*: You've been to Admiralty. Why did you go there?
> *Ng*: There're times you'll be moved, and you'll want to go. For example, the scenes you saw on TV. At that moment, you'll have that impulsion to go.
> *LL*: Can you talk about your opinion on the movement as a whole? So far, it's been two months.
> *Ng*: I personally think that the biggest starter of the whole thing is the government. Sometimes, they may want to hold things off for a while. They hope that it'll lead to citizens fighting against citizens. The real root of the problem is the government. But the older generation—Like, my mother—I often talk about this with my mum—she'll scold the people when it's shown on TV. Actually, it's not the students who are to blame, who're causing the troubles. They're forced to do so.
> *LL*: The situation now, what do you think about this?

> *Ng*: I feel helpless. Because the protest is a tied match. There won't be a side who can win. The police and citizens are like on the opposite sides, students are beaten by the police, the reputation of the police goes bad as they beat the citizens. No-one in the society can win. Everyone loses. Students have lost their time to prepare themselves, to strengthen themselves. The atmosphere in the society is tense. The government does not care about you. They're ok with this. Everyone loses in this thing.

While the movement energised many students, and drew them into action (Fraser, 2015b), the housing estate where our research participants lived was quite distant from the protest sites, and so some of the young people we spoke to said that they felt like the protest was going on elsewhere. For these young people, there was not optimism but pessimism about the potential for political enfranchisement:

> *Ying*: We just do not have any influence on anything.
> *LL*: Why don't you think you can have influence on anything?
> *Ah Yat*: We just have 7 million people … Is it possible we can choose our own governor?
> *LL*: So you are quite pessimistic about Hong Kong politics and future?
> *Ah Yat*: Yes.

In both Glasgow and Hong Kong, therefore, young people were animated by a political sentiment of self-determination, expressed as a desire for independence. Though articulated differently, there were striking parallels in the political context and animus for both movements, involving a desire for fuller control of a smaller geographical territory from a larger, more powerful, neighbour. Indeed, this similarity drew the attention of Scotland's First Minister, Nicola Sturgeon, who on a visit to Hong Kong pointed to Scotland's independence referendum as a potential lesson in 'political engagement' (Fraser, 2015c). In both cases, too, there was intense disappointment in the aftermath of events. As the following excerpt from Glasgow demonstrates, young people felt let down by "the older generation," and frustrated that the opportunity to enact change had been missed:

> *Mary*: I stayed up all night.
> *Carol*: I stayed up all night too, I didn't mean to—I just wasn't tired!

LW: What do you think about the result?
Keir: It was rigged.
Robert: It wasn't rigged, it was just people bottled it and there was too many old people involved in it.
Nicola: I don't see why they even got the vote.
Keir: I would agree with that.

A further similarity between the two movements was the shift from non-partisan campaign groups to political parties as vehicles of engagement. In Hong Kong, Joshua Wong, the prominent student activist and public face of the Umbrella Movement, sought to stand for election after co-founding Demosisto, a new political party advocating the 'democratic self-determination' of Hong Kong (Phillips, 2016). Other post-Umbrella Movement political parties include Hong Kong Indigenous, Youngspiration and the Hong Kong Nationalist Party. These latter groups are more localist and radical in orientation, advocating 'national self-determination' via 'whatever effective means' available (Lam, 2016). Research into young people's post-referendum political activity in Scotland points to a similar upsurge in youth membership of political parties (McLaverty et al., 2015), especially the SNP, the Scottish Green Party (SGP) and RISE (a new left-wing, pro-independence political alliance). These developments not only challenge dominant representations of young people's lack of interest in party politics, but also complicate the picture of their predilection for narrow, inward-looking identity politics over material and/or class-based concerns. Growth in SNP support, for example, can be explained in part by their resistance to Westminster rule, but also their success in positioning themselves (rhetorically) as more left wing than Labour. SNP policies that were popular with participants included their scrapping of medical prescription charges and student tuition fees in Scotland, and their long-standing commitment to nuclear disarmament.

Youth Politics, Austerity and Place

One of the main points of difference between young people's orientations towards Scotland's independence referendum and Hong Kong's Umbrella Movement relates to the issue of austerity. While in Glasgow young people articulated a clear vision of material concerns over jobs, housing and security, in Hong Kong these issues featured less prominently. In our Glasgow data, traditional notions of collective services and state responsibility were recurrent themes and, as indicated above, young people reported that their support for independence was primarily motivated by a sense of democratic deficit and a desire to have more control over issues such as education and employment:

> I'd love nothing more than a working-class man to work his way up and say, 'Right well I'm here for the working-class people and the majority.' 'Cause as soon as you start working for the majority of your country, the country is behind you, and not divided. And although we are united in terms of the United Kingdom, we're a divided nation—I don't care what anybody says ... And that leads back to unemployment and the state of the country. That's the reason we're having an Independence referendum, it's because the country is absolutely broken ... so many young people wanted change. They'd been let down badly. Every time I see adverts for jobs, its jobs the average Joe can't go for. You come out of college or university and there's no support there. It's a disgrace. (Young man, Glasgow focus group 8)

These findings are in some ways unsurprising, if one considers that Glasgow has the highest rate of youth unemployment in Scotland, and one of the highest figures in the UK (Hudson, Liddell, & Nicol, 2012). For the young people who were unemployed at the time of interview, the search for work dominated discussions:

> *Tony*: A lot of colleges tell you, 'If you do voluntary work like that'll usually lead you into a job.' But I've done over 100 hours of voluntary work and none of its led me into a job. Like it's basically rubbish.
> *Rylan*: It's a zero hours contract. Honestly, a zero hours contract!
> *Dylan*: They're cutting far too many jobs. They're cutting too many corners. They're like, 'We'll pay off 50 people and just overload them with work.'
> *Tony*: I went for an interview yesterday and there was another guy there wi' us, and I was talking away to him in the job centre. He'd been there for a year and they're saying, 'Why can't you get work?' and he was saying, 'Well, I'm on the wrong side of 50.' He was just coming up for retirement too and the job centre's making him feel bad because-....
> *Rylan*: Television and the media and stuff all tar all the young people in the country with 'They're just layabouts that don't want to

work.' Every single person sitting round this table wants to better their life. Every single person. Everybody's got skills, everybody wants to better their life.
Tony: There's no jobs.

As intimated in this excerpt, young people were able to make connections between their own life circumstances and those occupying similar positions—but this generally did not translate into support for the party traditionally associated with the Scottish urban working class (i.e. Labour).

By contrast, while work and employment came to the fore in conversation with young people in Hong Kong, these were not connected with discussions relating to the Umbrella Movement. Unlike the broader, global 'Occupy' movement—which had its own imprint in Hong Kong—the direct action of the Umbrella Movement was focused on political democracy and self-determination as an end in itself. The quest for political independence from mainland China, in fact, coloured the view of participants towards the Scottish independence referendum. In the following excerpt, a group of students draw connections between the separatist politics in Scotland and Hong Kong, seen clearly through a lens of territorial rather than economic concerns:

LL: Oh, by the way, people in Scotland are going to have a referendum on the independence issue….
Ying: What?
LL: They have the vote to determine the future of Scotland and whether they will be separated from the UK….
Ah Yat: That's good!
Ying: But there will be wars? Or they should turn to China? Hahaha!

In this context, it is important to note the different economic and political situations in Hong Kong and Glasgow. While the Glasgow economy has experienced long-term cycles of unemployment and underemployment, brought to crisis point in the context by recent austerity measures, Hong Kong is often considered to be the 'jewel in the crown' of the rising economic strength of China. Even so and as in Glasgow, a great many young people in Hong Kong have been left behind by this economic transformation—relative inequality, as measured by the Gini-coefficient, is among the highest in the world. However, there is one clear difference between the politics of Hong Kong and Glasgow. As a result of a colonial political administration, a system of 'utilitarian familialism,' and *laissez-faire* economic policy, Hong Kong has traditionally been defined by a non-adversarial political ethos (Lam, 2004). With a number of notable exceptions (Chiu & Lui, 2000), society at large, and young people in particular, have been denied full suffrage, and the opportunity to fully participate in political life. Though the Umbrella Movement represents clear evidence of a generational shift in youthful politicisation, this is nonetheless a very different political heritage to that of Glasgow, with its tradition of radical politics and resistance to elitism and oppression.[4]

Conclusion

This chapter contributes to ongoing debates about young people and politics in a global context, by drawing on emerging data from a comparative study of young people in Glasgow and Hong Kong. Against the masternarratives of political apathy and disengagement, both the Scottish independence referendum and the Umbrella protest represented significant instances of youth activism and political mobilisation. Further parallels included support for democratic self-determination from a larger territorial government regarded as resistant to change, involving the formation and sustaining of new spaces for dialogue and discussion including: organised debates in schools and universities, spontaneous gatherings in city centres, and creative engagements with digital social media. Beyond the lifespan of the two movements, young people in each setting shifted their activities from issue-based campaigns to membership of non-traditional political parties (which often had young people as figureheads).

That said, there were also some significant differences between the two sites, specifically regarding the ways in which young people constructed these moves toward independence. In Glasgow, participants' desire for self-determination was informed by a keen sense of social (in)justice and the promise of a more progressive politics in an independent Scotland. Against a backdrop of labour market restructuring and state funding cuts, the politics of austerity, unemployment and working-class identity remained significant for young people in Glasgow. In Hong Kong, a city with a generational reputation for political disengagement, discussion was focused more squarely on changing the discourse and terms of engagement for political conversation. The political priorities of our Hong Kong participants revolved around voting rights, participatory democracy, and fundamental political freedoms. While both sets of participants were actively engaged in debate, and some in action, by the magnetism of both movements, their concerns were thus patterned by the political context and cultural history of their respective environments. These arguments suggest the need to examine the role of place, history and political heritage when considering young people's engagement—or lack thereof—in mainstream politics.

Notes

1. Funded jointly by the Economic and Social Research Council and Research Grants Council of Hong Kong, ESRC Project Code: ES/K010409/1. A detailed description of the research is available on the (Re)Imagining Youth website: https://reimaginingyouth.wordpress.com
2. The Scottish National Party (SNP) is a left of centre, social democratic and progressive party. It explicitly promotes civic nationalism, claiming that membership in the Scottish nation is to be defined not by ethnic origin but by voluntary attachment to Scotland and participation in its civic life.
3. In previous UK elections, Scotland has overwhelming voted for Labour, a centre-left political party that grew out of the Trade Union and socialist movements of the nineteenth century. Despite this, the centre-right Conservative and Unionist Party has frequently been elected as Westminster government, based on the English vote.
4. The repeated invocation of 'Red Clydeside' during the campaign for Scottish independence indicates the cultural significance of this heritage for working-class people across the city, and indeed the nation more broadly (Griffin, 2015).

References

Batchelor, S., Whittaker, L., Fraser, A., & Ling, L. (2017). Leisure lives on the margins: (Re)imagining youth in Glasgow's East end. In S. Blackman & R. Rogers (Eds.), *Youth marginality in Britain. Contemporary studies of austerity*. Bristol: Policy Press and Oxford University Press.

Beck, U. (1999). *World risk society*. Cambridge: Polity Press.

Breeze, M., Gorringe, H., Jamieson, L., & Rosie, M. (2015). Everybody's Scottish at the end of the day: Nationalism and social justice amongst young yes voters. *Scottish Affairs, 24*(4), 419–431.

Brooks, R. (2007). Young people's extra-curricular activities: Critical social engagement—Or something for the CV? *Journal of Social Policy, 36*(3), 417–434.

Brooks, R., & Hodkinson, P. (2008). Young people, new technologies and political engagement: Introduction. *Journal of Youth Studies, 11*(5), 473–479.

Cheng, E., & Chan, W. (2017). Explaining spontaneous occupation: Antecedents, contingencies and spaces in the Umbrella Movement. *Social Movement Studies, 16*(2), 222–239.

Chiu, S., & Lui, T.-L. (2000). *The dynamics of social movement in Hong Kong.* Hong Kong: Hong Kong University Press.

Curtice, J. (2014). So who voted yes and who voted no? *What Scotland Thinks.* Retrieved February 3, 2017, from http://blog.whatscotlandthinks.org/2014/09/voted-yes-voted

DeGolyer, M. (2010). *Protest and post-80s youth: Sources of social instability in Hong Kong.* Hong Kong Transition Project. Retrieved February 3, 2017, from http://www.hktp.org/list/protest_and_post_80s_youths.pdf

Eden, K., & Roker, D. (2002). *"Doing something." Young people as social actors.* Leicester: National Youth Agency.

Electoral Commission. (2014). *Scottish independence referendum research: Post-polling day opinion research report.* London: Electoral Commission.

Fraser, A. (2015a). Umbrella sociology. *International Institute for Asian Studies Newsletter,* 70: 10–11. Retrieved February 27, 2017, from http://iias.asia/the-newsletter/article/umbrella-sociology

Fraser, A. (2015b). *Urban legends. Gang identity in the post-industrial city.* Oxford: Oxford University Press.

Fraser, A., Batchelor, S., Ling, L., & Whittaker, L. (2017). City as lens. (Re)imagining youth in Glasgow and Hong Kong. *Young—Nordic Journal of Youth Research, 25*(3), 1–17.

Fraser, N. (2015c). Scottish referendum could be lesson in political engagement for Hong Kong, Says first Minister Nicola Sturgeon. *South China Morning Post,* 30 July.

Furlong, A., & Cartmel, F. (2012). Social change and political engagement among young people. Generation and the 2009/10 British Election Survey. *Parliamentary Affairs, 65*(1), 13–26.

Giddens, A. (1991). *Modernity and self-identity. Self and society in the late modern age.* Cambridge: Polity.

Gray, N., & Mooney, G. (2011). Glasgow's new urban Frontier. "Civilizing" the population of "Glasgow East". *City, 15*(1), 4–24.

Griffin, P. (2015). *The spatial politics of red clydeside: Historical labour geographies and radical connections.* PhD Thesis, University of Glasgow.

Henn, M., & Foard, N. (2012). Young people, political participation and trust in Britain. *Parliamentary Affairs, 65*(16), 47–67.

Henn, M., & Foard, N. (2014). Social differentiation in young people's political participation. The impact of social and educational factors on youth political engagement in Britain. *Journal of Youth Studies, 17*(3), 360–380.

Henn, M., Weinstein, M., & Forrest, S. (2005). Uninterested youth? Young people's attitudes towards party politics in Britain. *Political Studies, 53*(3), 556–578.

Hong Kong Sheng Kung Hui Tung Chung Integrated Services. (2010). *Evaluation research on HKSKH Tung Chung integrated services, model building and service development 2010.* Hong Kong: HKSKH Tung Chung Integrated Service.

Hudson, N., Liddell, G., & Nicol, S. (2012). *Youth unemployment. Key facts*. Edinburgh: Scottish Parliament.

Inglehart, R. (1997). *Modernization and postmodernization. Cultural, economic, and political change in 43 societies*. Princeton, NJ: Princeton University Press.

Kimberlee, R. (2002). Why don't young people vote at general elections? *Journal of Youth Studies, 5*(1), 85–97.

Kwan, J. (2016). The rise of civic nationalism: Shifting identities in Hong Kong and Taiwan. *Contemporary Chinese Political Economy, 2*(2), 941–973.

Lam, J. (2016). They're young, vocal and very, very determined … but how do Hong Kong's newest political parties differ? *South China Morning Post*, 11 April.

Lam, W.-M. (2004). *Understanding the political culture of Hong Kong. The paradox of activism and depoliticization*. London: Routledge.

Loader, B. (Ed.). (2007). *Young citizens in the digital age. Political engagement, young people and new media*. London: Routledge.

Marsh, D., O'Toole, T., & Jones, S. (2007). *Young people and politics in the UK. apathy or alienation?* Basingstoke: Palgrave Macmillan.

McDowell, L., Rootham, E., & Hardgrove, A. (2014). Precarious work, protest masculinity and communal regulation: South Asian young men in Luton, UK. *Work, Employment and Society, 28*(6), 847–864.

McLaverty, P., Baxter, G., MacLeod, I., Tate, E., Goker, A., & Heron, M. (2015). *New radicals: Digital political engagement in post-referendum Scotland. Final report*. Working papers of the communities & culture network+ 6.

Mooney, G., McCall, V., & Paton, K. (2015). Poverty, territorial stigmatisation and social insecurities as social harms. *Scottish Justice Matters, 3*(3), 27–28.

Ortmann, S. (2015). The Umbrella Movement and Hong Kong's protracted democratization process. *Asian Affairs, 46*(1), 32–50.

Phelps, E. (2005). Young voters at the 2005 British general election. *The Political Quarterly, 76*(4), 482–487.

Phillips, T. (2016). Hong Kong's Umbrella Movement spawns new political party. *The Guardian*, 10 April.

Pickard, S. (2013). Sleaze, freebies and MPs: The British parliamentary expenses and allowances scandal. In D. Fée & J.-C. Sergeant (Eds.), *Ethique, Politique et Corruption au Royaume-Uni* (pp. 117–141). Aix-en-Provence: Presses Universitaires de Provence.

Pickard, S. (2018). *Politics, protest and young people. Political participation and dissent in Britain in the 21st century*. London: Palgrave Macmillan. [forthcoming].

Pilkington, H., & Pollock, G. (2016). "Politics are bollocks": Youth, politics and activism in contemporary Europe. *The Sociological Review, 63*(2), 1–35.

Pirie, M., & Worcester, R. (2000). *The big turn-off: Attitudes of young people to government, citizenship and community*. London: Adam Smith Institute.

Rheingans, R., & Hollands, R. (2013). "There is no alternative?" Challenging dominant understandings of youth politics in late modernity through a case study of the 2010 UK student occupation movement. *Journal of Youth Studies, 16*(4), 546–564.

Roker, D., Player, K., & Coleman, J. (1999). Young people's voluntary and campaigning activities as sources of political education. *Oxford Review of Education, 25*(1), 185–198.

Scottish Government. (2012). *Scottish index of multiple deprivation 2012.* Edinburgh: Scottish Government.

Sloam, J. (2007). Rebooting democracy: Youth participation in politics in the UK. *Parliamentary Affairs, 60*(4), 548–567.

Treadwell, J., Briggs, D., Winlow, S., & Hall, S. (2013). Shopocalypse now: Consumer culture and the English riots of 2011. *British Journal Criminology, 53*(1), 1–17.

Van Biezen, I., Mair, P., & Poguntke, T. (2012). Going, going, … gone? The decline of party membership in contemporary Europe. *European Journal of Political Research, 51*(1), 24–56.

Vromen, A. (2003). People try to put us down … participatory citizenship of "Generation X". *Australian Journal of Political Science, 38*(1), 79–99.

Vromen, A., Xenos, M., & Loader, B. (2015). Young people, social media and connective action. From organisational maintenance to everyday political talk. *Journal of Youth Studies, 18*(1), 80–100.

Wattenberg, M. (2003). Electoral turnout. The new generation gap. *British Elections and Parties Review, 13*(1), 159–173.

Winlow, S., Hall, S., & Treadwell, J. (2016). *The rise of the right: English nationalism and the transformation of working class politics.* Bristol: Policy Press.

Susan Batchelor is Senior Lecturer in Criminology in the School of Social and Political Sciences at the University of Glasgow, Scotland, based in the Sociology subject area. Her research interests revolve around intersecting issues of youth, gender, culture and crime.

Alistair Fraser is Lecturer in Criminology and Sociology in the School of Social and Political Sciences at the University of Glasgow, Scotland. Prior to this he spent four years at the University of Hong Kong in the Department of Sociology. His research focuses on young people and globalisation, with a particular focus on youth 'gangs.'

Leona Li Ngai Ling is Senior Research Assistant and Honorary Lecturer at the Department of Sociology and Centre for Criminology, University of Hong Kong.

Lisa Whittaker was previously Research Assistant at the University of Glasgow, Scotland. She now works as Research Engagement Officer for Tenovus Cancer Care, Cardiff, Wales.

CHAPTER 14

New Forms of Solidarity and Young People: An Ethnography of Youth Participation in Italy

Nicola De Luigi, Alessandro Martelli, and Ilaria Pitti

INTRODUCTION

The global financial crisis, which began in 2008, is having an impact on a range of socio-political actions of Italian young people. Amongst other things, this is evident in the changes emerging in the nature of their civic and political engagement.

This chapter proposes an analysis of three solidarity projects that started between 2010 and 2015 by leftist youth groups in the city of Bologna, Italy, looking at the re-actualisation of mutualistic practices of help as a means of political action. These practices are particularly relevant because they shed light on the influences of the crisis on civic and political engagement. We consider two elements frequently underlined by the literature

---

N. De Luigi (✉) • A. Martelli
Department of Sociology and Business Law, University of Bologna, Bologna, Italy

I. Pitti
Centre for Studies on Civic Engagement, Örebro University, Örebro, Sweden

© The Author(s) 2018
S. Pickard, J. Bessant (eds.), *Young People Re-Generating Politics in Times of Crises*, Palgrave Studies in Young People and Politics, DOI 10.1007/978-3-319-58250-4_14

on youth participation and on social movements: the recent increase of young people's involvement in unconventional forms of engagement (Sloam, 2013), and the return of certain forms of participation, inspired by mutualistic experiences of the past, as a possible answer to the effects of the crisis (della Porta, 2015).

We start by depicting the living conditions of young Italian people during the years of the global financial crisis, discussing their main influences on young Italians' current relationship with politics. After presenting the background, context and methodology of the study, this chapter provides an in-depth analysis of the three socio-political youth projects, aimed at pointing out how the repertoires and goals of youth involvement are shaped in reaction to the crisis. The last section is dedicated to discussing the results and their broader implications for the study of youth engagement.

Youth, the Crisis and (New) Mutualistic Experiences

Even before the global financial crisis, Italy[1] could be depicted as 'no country for young people' (Barbieri, 2011).[2] Since the beginning of the twenty-first century, many studies have pointed to significant and persistent social and economic disadvantage in young people's life experiences, in Italy. These studies also highlight the increase in subjective insecurity evident in young people's attitudes and feelings about their future. One crucial topic at the turn of the twenty-first century in Italy was the issue of labour market deregulation and its effect on young Italians. Italy, like many other European countries, embraced the neoliberal orthodoxy, which holds that labour laws are the main reason for the persistence of unemployment and promoted the deregulation of its labour market from the mid-1990s onwards (Barbieri & Scherer, 2009). Esping-Andersen and Regini (2000) argue that the Italian reaction to globalised competition involving 'partial' and 'targeted' labour market deregulation and increasingly non-standard forms of employment for labour market entrants, while leaving the regulation of existing employment relations largely unchanged, had a major impact on young job-seekers. Although deregulation did contribute to reducing the youth unemployment rate,[3] primarily by lessening the search time for first jobs, it also increased the likelihood of only finding temporary positions for new entrants. Given the characteristics of the Italian welfare system, this affected the capacity of young people to access social welfare entitlements (Berton, Richiardi, & Sacchi, 2012). It has proved difficult to realign the social protection system with changed labour market conditions, therefore access to social entitlements is essentially granted only to workers having steady employment. Moreover, labour market deregulation has raised young people's sense of job insecurity and reinforced their dependence on their families. Thus, families who are able and willing to provide support have come to play an increasing role in young people's chances of success. In this new context, families are expected to provide financial and housing support, not only for as long as their children experience difficulties in entering the labour market, but also until they find some form of employment stability, which is even more unlikely.

Scholars have pointed out that young people's job insecurity translates into growing uncertainties over their life course (Mills, Blossfeld, & Klijzing, 2005) and reduced agency in planning their lives (Standing, 2011). For instance, young people's employment difficulties have contributed to the postponement of leaving the parental home, affecting long-term decisions such as setting up home independently or starting a family.

Undoubtedly, the worsening of economic conditions triggered by the 2008 global financial crisis has exacerbated unresolved long-term problems affecting young Italians. Many analysts warn of the risk of a 'lost generation,' indicating not only the sharp rise in rates of youth unemployment and young people not in education, employment or training (NEET), but also a change in subjective perceptions concerning the lack of opportunities and hopes for a positive and meaningful future (Argentin, 2015; De Luigi, Rizza, & Santangelo, 2012).

For a long time, social science research pointed out that Italian society is characterised by a low level of intergenerational mobility. However, more recent analyses have highlighted that new generations will likely experience a decline in opportunities in comparison to those of their parents (Schizzerotto, Trivellato, & Sartor, 2011). In many public discourses, young people are presented as the first generation since the Second World War who will struggle to achieve the same standard of living as their parents (Sgritta, 2014). The adoption of austerity policies, in the name of controlling the rise of sovereign-debt and only partly caused by the crisis, has negatively affected the already weak capacities of the Italian welfare state to alleviate social risks related to employment, thus increasing young people's structural dependency on their families' socio-economic status. How did the pressing feeling of an impending breakdown in the socio-economic system affect young people's relationship with politics, which was already marked by mistrust and a distancing from conventional forms of engagement?

Many young people—not only in Italy—tend to display a low level of interest in the formal political process and democratic institutions, as suggested by declining voter turnout and a marked reduction in membership numbers of political parties (Quaranta, 2016; Sloam, 2013). Consequently, they are frequently described as "disaffected" and "disillusioned" in many public discourses (Farthing, 2010). However, young people's current relationship with politics appears much more complex than the one suggested by these labels (Harris, Wyn, & Younes, 2010; Pickard, 2018). The individualised and ambivalent behaviour many young people (and adults) adopt towards social and political engagement was defined, before the global financial crisis, as "conditional participation" (Martuccelli, 2015). With this concept, Martuccelli highlights a peculiar, apparently contradictory orientation towards politics in which activism and disaffection exist simultaneously. Ekman and Amnå (2014) propose the concept of "stand-by citizens," indicating the existence of a significant number of young people who adopt a passive role, but are waiting for a chance to be heard and included in decisional processes at a collective level.

The global financial crisis exerts different effects on the various forms of youth political engagement (Quaranta, 2013; Vassallo & Ding, 2016). Recent research reveals that in many European countries, and particularly in Italy, young people's disaffection and aversion towards formal politics are deeper today than they were before the outbreak of the crisis (Alteri & Raffini, 2014; Sloam, 2013). This growth in disaffection is generally explained as a reasonable reaction not only to political elites who claim there is no viable alternative to austerity measures, but also to institutions that seem able to offer only a few and often ineffective answers to the challenges and social risks young people are experiencing. Likewise, declining support for mainstream political parties by young people who do vote— mainly expressed through their increasing support for political organisations promoting populist messages or extreme positions (e.g. in relation to contemporary migration processes)—can be considered as additional evidence of this aversion to formal, professional politics (Roberts, 2015).

However, young people's alienation from political institutions and their evident detachment from conventional national elections have not merely turned into a passive attitude. On the contrary, scholars have shown that young people's forms of civic and political engagement have become progressively multifaceted, with a marked increase in less-conventional practices. Specifically, in recent decades, research has focused on the rising participation of young people in volunteering and non-profit initiatives active in aid and caring, service provisions, leisure-time activities, advocacy, and global issues (Biorcio & Vitale, 2016; Cuzzocrea & Collins, 2015). Despite being frequently framed in a discourse of non-partisan benevolence, which impedes the possibility of understanding its connections with the sphere of political struggle (Henriksen & Svedberg, 2010), young people's volunteering testifies that the younger generation is far from being indifferent or apathetic when faced with many social problems.

The global financial crisis and the consequent austerity policies adopted by European countries—beside increasing frustration and resignation—have also triggered social discontent, anti-(formal) political feelings and stimulating young people's engagement in anti-austerity movements. Furthermore, particularly at a local level, pessimism and difficulties have fuelled innovative revisions of the political language used, its style, spaces and goals, as well as various attempts at building new forms of solidarity-based exchanges and networks of collective action (della Porta, 2015). Even if these attempts tend to be less visible than protest action, they are contributing to enlarging the forms of political engagement among young people in times of economic hardship, also responding to their material and immaterial needs with concrete, self-managed activities. These include such things as urban gardening, new consumer-producer networks and cooperatives, local saving groups, free legal advice and medical services. Other features involve urban squatting, housing occupation, as well as self-management of abandoned public and private buildings, factories, cinemas, theatres and other spaces of cultural and artistic production (Alteri & Raffini, 2014; D'Alisa, Forno, & Maurano, 2015).

To further understand these various experiences of youth, civic and political participation, the concept of 'mutualism'—intended as an updated version of a type of collective action embedded in the nineteenth century cooperative and workers' movements (Ferraris, 2011)—may be useful. In a similar way to what voluntary associations have always done, mutualistic forms of participation aim to respond to increasing demand for material and immaterial needs (e.g. food, housing and health) and for free-market spaces where it is possible to meet other people and take part in cultural events. However, what distinguishes mutualistic experiences of engagement from volunteering is the political potential. Indeed, the concept of mutualism contains the aim of expressing a political vision and challenging the current socio-economic system, which is increasingly perceived as unfair. In other words, these forms of participation try to build what they claim to be right through the participants' own contributions and resources.

Specifically, there are four important potentialities that can be found in the mutualistic experiences, which the contemporary networks of solidarity among and for young people are developing:

1. The re-introduction of the self-management model, activating people's capacity to be agents of their own destiny;
2. The building of a real alternative for the same participants, namely an experience which is recognisable as a genuine opportunity for emancipation;
3. The centrality of the beneficiaries and of their professional and social skills and experience in handling life problems and needs, as opposed to the model of external assistance;
4. The affirmation of an interpretation of solidarity that is different from paternalistic, charitable or altruistic visions. This interpretation does not intend to simply compensate for the retrenchment of the welfare state caused by austerity policies, but aims at making lost rights eligible again and at promoting new ones (Ferraris, 2011; de Leonardis, 2011).

Background, Focus, and Methodology

The materials considered in this analysis have been mainly collected within the European research project 'Partispace—Spaces and Styles of Participation.'[4] Sponsored by the European Commission, Partispace seeks to understand the different ways in which young people in European countries[5] participate in decisions concerning them and, in general, the life of their communities. In so doing, the project explores young people's political and civic engagement in eight cities, adopting a qualitative methodological perspective aimed at giving voice to young people's views and practices of politics and social engagement. Specifically, the present contribution is based on the data collected in the city of Bologna, Italy, between April and December 2016.

Located in the North-East of Italy, Bologna is a university city with 400,000 inhabitants that presents a particularly rich case study when it comes to analysing young people's engagement in non-institutional politics. Bologna's population has always shown pronounced higher levels of political and civic interest compared to the Italian average, and a marked loyalty to the left-wing political tradition. Furthermore, the vivacity of the local youth movements has contributed at strengthening Bologna's reputation as a highly politicised city (Cento Bull & Giorgio, 2006). During the 1960s and the 1970s, grassroots movements of students—in combination with feminist, workerist, and gay rights groups—transformed the city into a hotbed of non-institutional politics and counter-culture. In the following decades, young people's political activism meant Bologna remains the beating heart of autonomous and antagonistic politics in Italy, enabling it to occupy a primary role in the national political scenario for what concerns the development and consolidation of leftist movements (Hejek, 2012). Within this context, a central role has been played by the numerous experiences of self-management of social spaces (*centri sociali*) started by left-wing political groups since the 1980s—with the "Isola nel Kantiere" experience—and especially in the 1990s (Mudu, 2012). Over the years, the *centri sociali* have become places of political reflection, but also meeting spots where recreational and cultural activities are proposed (Montagna, 2006).

The *centri sociali* have consistently promoted awareness campaigns concerning different types of social problems affecting disadvantaged or stigmatised social groups. However, the years of financial and economic crisis have changed the ways of young people's engagement in some of these political spaces. In particular, an array of solidarity-based projects aimed at providing a direct and practical answer to increased needs (e.g. food, housing, health services) of specific underserved segments of the population (e.g. migrants and homeless) have emerged.

In this chapter, we consider three of these civic and political initiatives of young people's engagement, started by different leftist groups within Bologna's main self-managed social centres. Within each of these projects, we conducted six months of participant observations for a total of about 150 hours, as well as carrying out 10 in-depth interviews where the young activists were asked to describe how these projects emerged and how they have developed (also in relation to the services offered by public institutions), and their personal paths within these initiatives.

In the following section, we analyse and describe these practices of young people's engagement by focusing our attention on their intentions and on the ways their goals are pursued.

Unheeded Needs: Youth Politics and Solidarity in Front of the Crisis

The three initiatives considered in this chapter consist of solidarity-based projects carried out by youth leftist groups. These experiences reside outside the perimeter of institutional political participation and express a pragmatic vision of political action aimed at creating what they claim to be right with the participants' own forces.

The first project is a help-desk for migrants who receive free professional legal support, as well as orientation concerning access to public health and housing services. The project was started in 2010 by six law students interested in making their expertise available to those in need. The second case involves a larger group of about 50 young people who, within the premises of an occupied former barracks located in the centre of Bologna, opened a shelter hosting 20 homeless persons (largely migrants and asylum seekers). The project started in 2015 and, since then, has witnessed an increasing participation of young people who keep the shelter open around-the-clock. Some spaces in the barracks serve as housing for many of the young activists, and who also organise activities for self-training on issues related to the reception of the homeless, migrants, and refugees. Lastly, in 2013, within the premises of a third autonomous space, a group of about 15 young people started a 'popular canteen' aimed at selling good quality, organic food at affordable prices to the whole population, and good quality food for free to people in need. In so doing, the project also intends to foster political reflection on access to food and practices of self-production. The canteen is open three times a week and is based on the 'self-managed price' model, by which everyone may decide to pay as much as he or she wants and can for the food.

Older activists are also involved in the *centri sociali* that hosts these projects, though the three initiatives mentioned have been started and are managed by groups of young people aged between 18 and 30. The vast majority of young activists are university students or recent graduates, confirming the significant role the student population has in the city's political scene. Both male and female activists are engaged in these groups, but the project implying a more assiduous and demanding activity of care—the homeless shelter—is mainly run by young women.

The projects do not receive funds from external bodies. While the popular canteen raises funds through the payments received for the meals, the help-desk often organises fundraising dinners, and the homeless shelter group both promotes food drives and has created a second-hand shop for additional self-funding.

The young people involved in these projects were energised by problems generated by the recession and by the desire to critique claims that the crisis is a fleeting difficulty. The projects began in the aftermath of the global financial crisis with the objective of mitigating the increased problems experienced by homeless people, migrants, and people in need, and of going beyond the 'emergency' by proposing alternative, practical, and enduring answers to long-standing social issues:

> Our economy sucks, and it has done since we were born. Migrants are considered an emergency since the 1990s. Rather than something new, "crisis" is the name we have given to problems that were already here, problems that have just worsened because we haven't really tried to solve them. (Informal conversation with Gaia, activists at help-desk for migrants—Fieldnotes, June 2016)[6]

Moving from a strong scepticism concerning the possibility of finding the right answers to these problems in private actors' services, the projects also criticise the solutions offered by public institutions. The solidarity experiences started by these young people seek to avert what the activists describe as the 'logic of the service,' namely the distinction between providers and users, which is the basis of public services' mode of functioning:

> The popular canteen seeks to overcome the logic of the service […], the canteen seeks to share a "tool box" to hold out against the crisis, to promote a proliferation of the practices and knowledge on the self-production of food. (Popular canteen, Leaflet)

From the activists' perspective, the distinction between 'the one who gives' and 'the one who receives' necessarily creates a hierarchy between the two and confines the latter in a position of marginality and dependence. According to the activists, instead of helping people find a solution to their own problems together with other people sharing similar difficulties, public services generate a vicious circle of passivity and solitude where each person becomes an isolated user:

> The classic welfare state's major limitation is that it does not think about the autonomy of the person who wants to help. The person is always passive, he/she is someone who must have a service he/she needs, whereas what we try to spread is the idea that doing things collectively can solve everybody's problems. (Tiziano, activists at homeless shelter)

The three projects considered in this chapter attempt to cancel or minimise the differences between the positions and roles of the activists and those being helped by promoting the active engagement of the latter in the same solidarity activities:

> The general framework of welfare related to food is mere assistance, it is a service, there is no real relationship between those who use charitable canteens and those who open them up. What we try to do with the popular canteen is to make people conscious, waking them up a little in relation to some issues and also involve them in the organisation of lunches. (Simone, activist at popular canteen)

However, the possibilities of reaching this objective are different from project to project, depending on the targeted social issues. When it is not possible to cancel or minimise the difference,[7] attention is given to providing help in 'a more humane way,' that is, treating those being helped as people, rather than merely clients or users:

> Each room has just two beds. We did not add other beds because we want to make the shelter a human and fair place. We believe that this is the way a person should be able to live, not in overcrowded dorms. (Martina, activists at homeless shelter)

This particular way of providing help to people is guided by the idea of fostering a process of self-activation, whereby assistance is replaced by individual and collective empowerment, and individuals' personal, social and professional skills in dealing with life problems are valued and cherished. In fact, the main political intention that all these projects have in common is to open spaces where is the potential for people to have the power to shape their own way of living and the world around them. The relevance that the issues of self-determination and self-empowerment acquire in these youth projects highlights how central these categories are in the involved young people's representation of a 'fair way of living.'

The need to provide those who approach these initiatives with the ability to adopt actives roles in their lives echoes young people's need to regain control and power on their own lives. Looking at the objectives that members of these projects seek to achieve, the analysis of the research materials reveals that two different goals—both connected to the crisis—guide their practices. The first goal refers to the willingness to help vulnerable groups, while the second has to do with the need for autonomy and independence of the same youth population.

On a primary level, the analysed projects are, in fact, all tailored to target the needs of groups living in particularly difficult conditions—the homeless, migrants, and people experiencing financial hardship. These projects are motivated through the intent to address the damage caused by the crisis, as well as the local services' and public structures' increasing difficulties concerning the management of social vulnerabilities:

> We claim everyone's right to be free to choose where to move and settle, regardless of origin and without discrimination. We reject that immigration is treated as a public order problem, or restricted by the economic needs of a country in crisis. (Help-desk for migrants, Leaflet)

Both in young people's accounts of these practices of engagement and in the groups' public statements and documentation, the need to intervene in order to face the consequences the crisis is having on vulnerable populations represents a central argumentation for getting politically involved and for behaving in a particular political way:

> We are ready. One month ago, we announced our idea to open a homeless shelter free from approaches based on the logics of emergency and assistance [...] and now we are ready to start. On Sunday, we will cut the ribbon and we are inviting [to this event] the part of Bologna's population that, faced with crisis, doesn't surrender to racism, war among the needy, and terror. (Homeless shelter, Facebook event)

The global financial crisis influences young activist's participation by encouraging them toward actions that are aimed at mitigating the direct and indirect damages caused by the economic downturn to particular vulnerable groups. At the same time, the analysed socio-political experiences also appear to emerge in connection with the young people' own difficulties and personal needs. Young people's reconstructions of their civic and political participation points to a link between the experience of personal problems and the use of political activism as a means to solve these difficulties.

> Antonio explains that he has always been interested in studying and working in the field of migration law, but finding a law firm where receiving field training on this is practically impossible and thus he decided to join the help-desk

as a side activity. He tells that, since the beginning of the crisis, many law firms have stopped hiring young trainees because they cost too much and also, if you get hired, you don't get training since they just use you for 'doing photocopies.' [...] According to Antonio, "if nobody helps us become who we want to be, we must find our own way and here we are finding our own way together". (Fieldnotes, August 2016—Help desk for migrants)

The aforementioned problems refer to a series of 'generational needs' pertaining to the lives of young people during the years of the crisis. In their accounts, these individual fears and difficulties are presented relative to collective ones and, later, to the need to find new solutions through their political activism:

Before gaining experience in the popular canteen, Michele worked in several restaurants as a sous-chef, but his contracts were no longer than 3–6 months and he often did not know where to find money to eat [...]; the popular canteen and the idea of the self-managed price, he says, comes also from this personal experience of uncertainty, shared with other young people in the group who have the same problems. This experience has stimulated the creation of something that allows them and others to have the certainty that "there is a place where I can go and have lunch, paying what I can, which necessarily changes whether or not I have a job". (Fieldnotes, June 2016—Popular canteen)

While offering help to migrants, starving or homeless people, these projects also provided answers for young people helping them to address some of the difficulties, fears, and doubts they experienced living and growing up in the context of the global financial crisis. These difficulties include accessing food, housing, work, training and social spaces. Considered as a whole, they all mirror young people's needs and willingness to take back space, visibility and power, both as individuals and as a generational group:

Our generation has been stopped; it has to deal with limits, limits, and limits [...]; it is clear that we have been stopped, that we cannot reach any goal [...] We started the occupation saying that we are the 'no future generation' that takes back its future. (Cristian, activist at homeless shelter)

In so doing, young activists' participation not only addresses other people' needs and difficulties, but it also becomes a means of self-help within the context of a long-lasting economic and occupational crisis affecting their living conditions and limiting their possibilities for self-determination. In all these practices of social and political activism, young people have taken on a primary role in finding the solution to a personal and collective problem, becoming 'agents of change' for themselves and for others, trying to shape a world where nobody feels excluded from the opportunity to have a say and to be recognised (Honneth, 1995):

> The project includes many people who are coordinated through collective meetings where everyone can express their ideas, while the others listen and comment. The great thing is that all these people do not think the same way. They don't all have similar ideas, ideals, lifestyles, studies, interests, etc. It is a mix, a group of very different people that, with this system, works well. (Michele, activists at popular canteen)

Sharing a critical perspective on the current socio-economic order, these experiences seek to expand the domain of political and democratic decision-making, moving from private territory to public, from individual needs to collective action. In so doing, practices that can be considered typical of voluntary activities (i.e. providing food to homeless people) are embedded in codes that transform them into a means of political action.

> This is not just a homeless shelter; it is the place where people have found dignity again, begun or started again on a path towards autonomy, reacquired confidence in themselves. [...] What we have done this year goes beyond what is commonly called "volunteering". Here we do solidarity, social activism, mutualism to meet needs that are neglected by the institutions, needs that are addressed through emergency policies. (Homeless shelter's public communication—December, 2016)

By promoting this reconfiguration of solidarity in a way that fosters the dynamics of individual and collective self-empowerment and self-help, young activists also revise their way of being politically active, placing at the centre of their engagement a new understanding of the role of non-institutional activism in society. A conflictual relationship with the institutions remains, but in line with the idea of finding collective solutions to collective problems, they assume more open positions in relation to the surrounding community:

> [Politics means] feeling good together [...] I think it is crucial, especially in times of misery and individualism to feel good together in the very moment

of the political discussion and action [...]; in the last year and a half we have changed our way of doing politics in order to gain recognition from more people, to be recognised more, to be attractive to the people [...] we have created moments when people can feel good. (Cristian, activist at homeless shelter)

The significance and implications of these findings in relation to the analytical framework previously proposed will be discussed in our conclusion.

Conclusion

In this chapter, we described some changing relationships between young Italian people's political engagement facing the global financial crisis of 2008 and its aftermath. In particular, we focused on three solidarity initiatives promoted by political youth groups in Bologna, highlighting the emerging connections between these forms of engagement, their objectives and practices, and the difficulties—in terms of access to material and immaterial resources—the young activists are experiencing in the current period of recession and austerity.

The account has shown that young people's political activism is fostered by a mix of collective goals in support of disadvantaged groups as well as meeting a number of needs of young people involved in these projects. New connections for collective action are experienced within these projects, turning them into 'laboratories of civic and political resistance' in the face of specific dynamics of socio-economic and social transformation.

These findings align with those of other researchers who have interpreted contemporary youth practices of social engagement in terms of "collaborative individualization," highlighting "how some young people, faced with significant economic uncertainties, concurrently sow the seeds of more equitable and resilient socio-economic systems and do so specifically through collaboration among peers" (Cuzzocrea & Collins, 2015, p. 136).

These initiatives, constitute young people's active attempts to collectively reclaim their own power as social actors in response to generational inequalities that are limiting their access to the rights and services long associated with citizenship (Percy-Smith, 2015; Rossi, 2009). When the willingness and the possibility of participation combine, engagement takes the form of active citizenship (Martelli, 2013), understood as that condition where the distance between 'being a citizen'—that is, enjoying the rights of citizenship necessary for social and political participation—, and 'acting as a citizen'—that is, actively fulfilling those rights—(Lister, 2008) tends to disappear. In this dialectical and unstable relationship between the two elements of citizenship, participation becomes a means of social change, which demands or proposes a revision of the traditional patterns of social solidarity and citizenship. This takes place when the existing set of shared values and rules comprising the *status quo* about things like the division of labour or the distribution of economic resources appears no longer to be adequate or legitimate.

In this perspective, the projects described here question the conventional idea that the crisis is just a transitory difficulty and create new and sustainable answers to some long-lasting difficulties Italians have had in accessing social entitlements. These initiatives suggest a pragmatic vision of participation, by adopting a logic of action aimed at autonomously generating solutions to these problems.

Self-determination, self-empowerment, and self-management are thus placed at the centre of initiatives where the relevance of beneficiaries' skills, know-how and capabilities is emphasised in order to de-construct both the neoliberal narrative and the ineffective forms of solidarity typical of the more traditional paternalistic and bureaucratic approaches to policymaking. The actions aim to open up "spaces—physical, virtual, social, political—to fuller participation from a wider citizenry, and, through the diversity which necessarily accompanies such a move, build communities, cities, nations—and individuals—with greater resilience" (Cuzzocrea & Collins, 2015, p. 149).

The projects we explored aligned with the model generated by the traditional grassroots mutualistic experiences, inasmuch as they express young people's capacity to be agents of their own destiny, promote a new approach to solidarity, and foster the consolidation of mutual help practices where individuals' capacities and competences are both valued and cultivated. Due to their only recent launch, these projects are still largely undergoing a process of consolidation, in terms of both the human and economic resources they can mobilise, and of their impact on the social problems they want to tackle. Nevertheless, they also demonstrate an interesting potential in terms of building actual opportunities for emancipation both for the individuals being helped and also young people in general, offering them a possibility to have a say in their own lives and in the world around them.

This chapter has shed light on some of the significant traits of young people's current forms of political participation. Further analyses of these and similar initiatives should focus also on the relationships with the institutions and the neighbourhood, as well as look at young people's relation with the adult generation (Martelli & Pitti, 2014; Percy-Smith, 2015). Young people, in fact, always act (or are resigned to act) with respect to a specific space and to the other generations around them.

Notes

1. Despite being the third largest national economy in the Eurozone, Italy suffers from several structural economic problems (such as low levels of GDP growth, high public debt, and economic stagnation), which have been exacerbated by the global financial crisis and the austerity policies requested by the European Union. Concerning the political sphere, since the end of the last centre-right government in 2011, following the worsening of the economic national condition and the rapid escalation of the sovereign debt crisis, a series of unelected and rather unstable technical and coalition governments have administered the country. Populist parties increased their electoral support among the Italian population that, despite remaining highly engaged in non-profit organisations and civic associations, appears less and less involved in trade unions and professional associations (For a more complete analysis, refer to Mammone, Giap Parini, & Veltri, 2015).
2. The American movie *No Country for Old Men* was released in 2007. It is a bitter, cruel thriller directed by Joel and Ethan Coen, based on Cormac McCarthy's homonymous 2005 novel.
3. In Italy, labour market deregulation began in the second half of the 1990s. In 1995, the unemployment rate among young people (15–29 years old) was 25.2%. During the following decade, it decreased more than 10 percentage points, reaching 14.5% in 2007, on the eve of the global financial crisis.
4. This project receives funding from the European Commission's Horizon 2020 research and innovation programme under grant agreement No 649416.
5. The countries involved in the study are: Bulgaria, France, Germany, Italy, Sweden, Switzerland, Turkey, and the United Kingdom.
6. All names have been changed.
7. We refer, in particular, to the case of the help-desk for migrants where the distance between the role of young activists and the role of the people in need of legal help is impossible to remove when it comes to defend the migrant's rights in a legal action, but also to the case of the homeless shelter

where the young activists need sometimes to assume a coordinating role in relation to the hosted homeless.

REFERENCES

Alteri, L., & Raffini, L. (Eds.). (2014). *La nuova politica. Mobilitazioni, movimenti e conflitti in Italia*. Napoli: EdiSes.

Argentin, G. (2015). New generation at the crossroad: Decline or change? Young people in Italy and their transformation since the nineties. In A. Mammone, G. E. Parini, & G. Veltri (Eds.), *Handbook of contemporary Italy* (pp. 77–88). London: Routledge.

Barbieri, P. (2011). Italy: No country for young men (and women): The Italian way of coping with increasing demands for labour market flexibility and rising welfare problems. In H.-P. Blossfeld, S. Buchholz, D. Hofäcker, & K. Kathrin (Eds.), *Globalized labour markets and social inequality in Europe* (pp. 108–145). Basingstoke: Palgrave Macmillan.

Barbieri, P., & Scherer, S. (2009). Labour market flexibilization and its consequences in Italy. *European Sociological Review, 25*(6), 677–692.

Berton, F., Richiardi, M., & Sacchi, S. (2012). *The political economy of work security and flexibility: Italy in comparative perspective*. Bristol: Policy Press.

Biorcio, R., & Vitale, T. (2016). *Italia Civile. Associazionismo, Partecipazione e Politica*. Roma: Donzelli Editore.

Cento Bull, A., & Giorgio, A. (Eds.). (2006). *Speaking out and silencing: Culture, society and politics in Italy in the 1970s*. London: Routledge.

Cuzzocrea, V., & Collins, R. (2015). Collaborative individualization? Peer-to-peer action in youth transitions. *Young, 23*(2), 136–153.

D'Alisa, G., Forno, F., & Maurano, S. (2015). Grassroots (economic) activism in times of crisis: Mapping the redundancy of collective actions. *Partecipazione e conflitto, 8*(2), 328–342.

De Luigi, N., Rizza, R., & Santangelo, N. (2012). La disoccupazione giovanile in tempo di crisi: nuovi squilibri e vecchie segmentazioni. In G. Cordella & S. Masi (Eds.), *Condizione giovanile e nuovi rischi sociali. Quali politiche?* (pp. 59–82). Carocci: Roma.

della Porta, D. (2015). *Social movements in time of austerity. Bringing capitalism back into protest analysis*. Cambridge: Polity Press.

Ekman, J., & Amnå, E. (2014). Political participation and civic engagement: Toward a new typology. *Human Affairs, 22*(3), 283–300.

Esping-Andersen, G., & Regini, M. (Eds.). (2000). *Why deregulate labour markets?* Oxford: Oxford University Press.

Farthing, R. (2010). The politics of youthful antipolitics: Representing the issue of youth participation in politics. *Journal of Youth Studies, 13*(2), 181–195.

Ferraris, P. (2011). *Ieri e domani. Storia critica del movimento operaio e socialista ed emancipazione dal presente*. Roma: Edizioni dell'Asino.

Harris, A., Wyn, J., & Younes, S. (2010). Beyond apathetic or activist youth: "Ordinary" young people and contemporary forms of participation. *Young: Nordic Journal of Youth Research, 18*(1), 9–32.

Hejek, A. (2012). Francesco è vivo, e lotta insieme a noi! Rebuilding local identities in the aftermath of the 1977 student protests in Bologna. *Modern Italy, 17*, 289–304.

Henriksen, L. S., & Svedberg, L. (2010). Volunteering and social activism: Moving beyond the traditional divide. *Journal of Civil Society, 6*(2), 95–98.

Honneth, A. (1995). *Struggle for recognition*. Cambridge, MA: MIT Press.

de Leonardis, O. (2011). E se parlassimo un pò di politica? In A. Arjun (Ed.), *Le aspirazioni nutrono la democrazia*. Milano: Et al. Edizioni.

Lister, R. (2008). Unpacking children's citizenship. In A. Invernizzi & J. Williams (Eds.), *Children and citizenship* (pp. 9–19). London: Sage.

Mammone, A., Parini, G. E., & Veltri, G. (2015). *Handbook of contemporary Italy*. London: Routledge.

Martelli, A. (2013). The debate on young people and participatory citizenship. Questions and research prospects. *International Review of Sociology, 23*(2), 421–437.

Martelli, A., & Pitti, I. (2014). Searching for adulthood: Young people, citizenship and participation. *SocietàMutamentoPolitica, 5*(10), 173–192.

Martuccelli, D. (2015). La partecipazione con riserva: al di qua del tema della critica. *Quaderni di Teoria Sociale, 1*(1), 11–34.

Mills, M., Blossfeld, H.-P., & Klijzing, E. (2005). Becoming an adult in uncertain times. In H.-P. Blossfeld, E. Klijzing, M. Mills, & K. Kurz (Eds.), *Globalization, uncertainty and youth in society* (pp. 423–441). London: Routledge.

Montagna, N. (2006). The commodification of urban space and the occupied social centres in Italy. *City, 10*(3), 295–304.

Mudu, P. (2012). I Centri Sociali italiani: verso tre decadi di occupazioni e di spazi autogestiti. *Partecipazione e Conflitto, 9*(1), 69–92.

Percy-Smith, B. (2015). Negotiating active citizenship: Young people's participation in everyday spaces. In K. P. Kallio, S. Mills, & T. Skelton (Eds.), *Politics, citizenship and rights* (pp. 401–422). London: Springer.

Pickard, S. (2018). *Politics, protest and young people. Political participation and dissent in Britain in the 21st century*. London: Palgrave Macmillan. [forthcoming]

Quaranta, M. (2013). Measuring political protest in Western Europe: Assessing cross-national equivalence. *European Political Science Review, 5*(3), 457–482.

Quaranta, M. (2016). An apathetic generation? Cohorts' patterns of political participation in Italy. *Social Indicators Research, 125*(3), 793–812.

Roberts, K. (2015). Populism, political mobilisation, and crisis of political representation. In C. de la Torre (Ed.), *Promises and perils of populism: Global perspectives* (pp. 140–159). Lexington: Kentucky University Press.

Rossi, F. (2009). Youth political participation: Is this the end of generational cleavage? *International Sociology, 24*(4), 467–497.
Schizzerotto, A., Trivellato, U., & Sartor, N. (Eds.). (2011). *Generazioni disuguali. Le condizioni di vita dei giovani di ieri e di oggi: un confronto*. Bologna: Il Mulino.
Sgritta, G. (2014). Degenerazione. Il patto violato. *Sociologia del Lavoro, 136*(1), 279–294.
Sloam, J. (2013). Voice and equality: Young people's politics in the European Union. *West European Politics, 36*(4), 836–858.
Standing, G. (2011). *The precariat: The new dangerous class*. London and New York: Bloomsbury Academic.
Vassallo, F., & Ding, P. (2016). Explaining protest in the aftermath of the great recession in Europe: The relevance of different economic indicators. *Partecipazione e Conflitto, 9*(1), 101–126.

Nicola De Luigi is Associate Professor of Sociology at the University of Bologna, Italy. He has carried out extensive research at national and European levels and published in the field of youth studies. He is currently involved in the European research project PARTISPACE—Spaces and Styles of Youth Participation.

Alessandro Martelli is Assistant Professor at the University of Bologna, Italy, where he teaches Social Policies and is member of the 'Sociology and social research' PhD Programme. His research concerns two main fields: youth condition, active citizenship and social change; transformations of social needs and organization of welfare policies.

Ilaria Pitti is Marie Skłodowska-Curie Fellow at the Centre for Studies on Civic Engagement at Örebro University and holds a visiting position at the University of Bologna, Italy. Her main research interests focus on youth civic and political engagement (with an emphasis on unconventional forms of participation) and intergenerational relationships between young people and adults.

CHAPTER 15

Youth Heteropolitics in Crisis-Ridden Greece

Alexandros Kioupkiolis and Yannis Pechtelidis

INTRODUCTION

Since the global financial crisis hit Greece in 2009, the country has seen the emergence of an authoritarian political regime characterised by harsh austerity, massive precarity, collective disempowerment and atomisation, which has affected the majority of the population and particularly young people. However, collective resistances have also arisen. Young people in particular have looked for other political practices regarding their direct participation in public life and social self-reconstruction. They engage in community building on a footing of equality and self-governance, and they seek to open knowledge, education and politics to all social actors. This embodies a widespread search for another politics. We call this heteropolitics (hetero means other in Greek), featuring various strategies of collective problem-solving in response to exclusion, youth unemployment and underemployment, state violence, the crisis of politics and democracy.

A. Kioupkiolis (✉)
School of Political Science, Aristotle University, Thessaloniki, Greece

Y. Pechtelidis
Department of Early Childhood Education, University of Thessaly, Volos, Greece

© The Author(s) 2018
S. Pickard, J. Bessant (eds.), *Young People Re-Generating Politics in Times of Crises*, Palgrave Studies in Young People and Politics,
DOI 10.1007/978-3-319-58250-4_15

In this chapter, we shed light on certain aspects of 'alternative' political engagements pursued by young people in times of crisis. We draw on several case studies, to indicate the presence of various modes of youth politics that escape the radar of more conventional frames of political analysis. We start by offering some background information on the ongoing crisis in Greece, focusing on young people, their precarisation and retreat from formal politics. This helps to situate our discussion of youth heteropolitics within the wider debate about young people's politics in times of crisis, in order to challenge dominant ideas about young people's political ability and to bring out less visible forms of political participation by young people today. In our subsequent analysis of the case studies, we make the following claims: many young people are politically engaged and they belong thus to a politicised generational unit. Although they are active in different social and political spaces, they share a common set of affects, attitudes and embodied practices, or a common (hetero)political generational habitus towards the crisis. Furthermore, although this politicised youth express deep disappointment and concern over the increasing depoliticisation of a majority of young people, they still believe in the importance of politics and collective life. They desire to engage directly in the construction of social reality, in autonomous life in collective groups, in collaborative creativity and new collective initiatives.

Methodological Framework

In 2016, we undertook several case studies that revealed particular kinds of political activism among young people in crisis-ridden Greece. We carried out ethnographic interviews (Legard, Keegan, & Ward, 2003; Spradley, 1979), tracing out young people's experiences, ideas and emotions about their involvement in hetero-political settings, located outside the political mainstream. The interviews were semi-structured and lasted 60–90 minutes each. We chose this approach to encourage the interviewees to freely express their thoughts, feelings, and emotions.

More specifically, we conducted interviews with 11 young people (22–30 years old) and we identified certain general attitudes and questions regarding politics and political participation. For this chapter, we selected six male and five female interviewees. Their names have not been changed. They were all young university students living in Volos, a middle-sized town in central Greece, and Thessaloniki, the second largest Greek city. They were all actively involved in collective groups, alternative social, political and educational groups and non-governmental organisations. They are all Greek, white, middle or working class, and come from urban areas. One participant comes from the Muslim minority in Thrace (Northern-East Greece).

All interviewees were involved in substantive forms of participatory democracy, autonomy and solidarity, 'here' and 'now.' On the whole, by engaging with their discourse, we set out to we explore processes of subjectification. We did not read their statements as representations of underlying identities, but as a frame and a way of establishing their political identities. The analysis of the interviews is organised around the following three themes:

1. The crisis. How did interviewees experience and responded to it?
2. Hetero-political actions and creative resistances. Which new modes of interaction, social relation and organisation have arisen in young people's heteropolitics? How do they look on conventional politics—the political system—and their own activity?
3. Subjectivity. Which forms of individual thought, action and feeling have emerged under critical conditions? Which figures of individual and collective subjects have been active, and which new modes of resistant subjectivity have come into being?

THE CRITICAL CONTEXT

Young people's political activity in present-day Greece should be situated in the specific contemporary context of crisis. First, democratic politics has been gravely undermined, giving rise to a deep-cutting and widespread disaffection with the political system in Greece. Moreover, the economic crisis since 2009 has brought about extensive impoverishment, insecurity, precarity and indebtedness, which are particularly acute among young people.[1] Precarity and exclusion are predominantly experienced through a certain individualism, which often engenders individual and collective impotence, if not paralysis and resigned submission.

In the 1990s and at the dawn of the twenty-first century, a post-democratic consensus was consolidated in Greece, reflecting similar shifts in liberal democracies in France, Germany, the United Kingdom and across the world. These involved the diffusion of a consumerist, apolitical individualism among citizens that went hand-in-hand with the attachment of ruling parties to the neoliberal doctrine as the sole reasonable option for a developed and prospering economy. The treatment of political issues as technical questions, the increasing authority of experts in governance, the eclipse of real alternative choices within the political system are trademarks of an impoverished form of post-democracy dominated by elites (Crouch, 2004; Kioupkiolis, 2006; Mouffe, 2005).

However, oligarchic post-democracy took a further, authoritarian turn from 2010 onwards. Under the 'state of emergency' engendered by the debt crisis and the threat of a total economic collapse, the ruling parties enforced recession policies and harsh austerity measures in line with the monetarist and neoliberal policies of European Union (EU) elites and the International Monetary Fund (IMF) that dictated the terms of the Greek bailout. Since 2010, the conduct of government in Greece has enacted thus Agamben's idea of the state of exception (Agamben, 2005).[2] Harsh, unpopular laws and measures dictated by Greece's foreign lenders were imposed apparently by 'the necessities' of the situation itself, while excessive police brutality was mobilised in crucial moments of popular unrest and protest (in 2011 against the Indignados Movement etc.), to discipline and repress large swathes of the population who did not assent to the brutal ruin of their socio-economic condition (Kioupkiolis, 2014, pp. 143–158). This political mutation bore heavily on individual and collective subjectivity. Under the state of exception, individuals tend to become "*homines sacri*," people fully exposed to the arbitrary discretion of power and extreme misfortunes (Agamben, 1998, p. 171). Likewise, since 2010, Greek citizens have lost numerous social rights (social benefits, welfare and labour rights) and their political liberties have been effectively trumped as majoritarian collective choices were systematically disregarded by their governments (Mouriki, Balourdos, Papaliou, Spyropoulou, & Fayadaki, 2012).[3]

Under these circumstances, the "fabrication of the indebted man" (Lazzarato, 2011) was a catalyst for the production of self-disciplined, disconnected and subdued individuals. The indebted subject is filled with permanent fear due to his/her constant job insecurity, the high risk of insolvency and the menace of an imminent and cataclysmic state 'bankruptcy.' The individual self in debt strives, moreover, to cope with poverty and the lack of social benefits, to manage his/her accumulating debts and to assure his/her employability in the face of job insecurity (Lazzarato, 2011, pp. 28, 41–43, 74, 97). This condition intensifies the tendencies of neoliberalism to produce atomised 'responsible individuals' who take charge of their lives without relying on collective security nets, collaboration and social guarantees (Rose, 1999).

Recasting the Political

Our case studies explore how diverse groups of young people responded critically and creatively to these conditions of material and political disempowerment, the alienation from mainstream politics, the hollowing out of democracy, and atomisation. The turn towards new modes of collective self-organisation, the attempt to construct new social bonds and to forge socially empowered forms of subjectivity should be understood in relation to the foregoing critical context.

However, before embarking on our account of alternative youth politics in such circumstances, it is necessary to engage with the concept of the political itself. As Bessant (2014) notes, a significant predicament when looking into youth politics today is the conventional understanding of the relationship between young people and the political. McCaffrie and Marsh (2013, p. 116) claim: "a pervasive problem with the mainstream participation literature [is that] a *restrictive conception of politics forces a restrictive understanding of participation*" (our emphasis). A narrow understanding of politics and participation locates them only in the formal political system: the government, parties, elections and voters. But when, as in the case of contemporary Greece, the political system is perceived as hostile or irrelevant, young people's political activity is likely to take place at a distance from it. Hence, if the political is seen through standard, systemic lenses, much of what can count as young people's political engagement will be either missed altogether or dismissed as irrelevant. And focusing our study of political engagement on conventional forms of activity and organisation (voting, party membership, etc.) would tend to confirm the thesis of young people's apathy or apoliticism. Consequently, the debate over youth politics cannot advance without reconsidering our conception(s) of 'the political' (see Pickard, 2018).

Traditionally, politics has been identified with the art of government, which in modern times is primarily the government of a nation-state. Hence, politics has been centred on the machinery of national government and the apparatus of the state: the cabinet, the parliament, political parties, public administration, etc. (Heywood, 2013, pp. 3–5; Schmitt, 2007, pp. 19–25). This conception of politics has been increasingly contested in the twentieth century, starting with Schmitt's seminal *The Concept of the Political* (2007).

Schmitt argues that the equation politics = state "becomes erroneous and deceptive at exactly the moment when state and society penetrate each other" (Schmitt, 2007, p. 2). For him, "The specific political distinction to which political actions and motives can be reduced is that between friend and enemy [...] which denotes the utmost degree of intensity of a union or separation" (Schmitt, 2007, p. 26).

Reasoning from a widely different—liberal and democratic—perspective, Lefort (1986, pp. 280–281) likewise displaced the political from the state and government and has identified it with the "generative principles" of society, its particular mode of instituting and defining society. Mouffe (2005, p. 9), among others, has likewise construed the political as "the very way in which society is instituted." Furthermore, she introduced a distinction between the political in the foregoing sense and "politics" implying the "manifold practices of conventional politics" (Mouffe, 2005, p. 8).

Other strands of contemporary political theory (Connolly, 1995; Day, 2005; Rancière, 2010), sociology (Beck, 1992; Giddens, 1991) and anthropology (Papataxiarchis, 2014; Scott, 1990) have pushed the 'decentering' of the political further away from its concentration on the state. First, they have removed the emphasis on "institution." Second, they have located the political in every act and process that struggles over established social forms and structures, seeking to contest them, to transform or to uphold them. Third, they have blurred the distinction between ordinary and extraordinary politics, conventional and unconventional, visible and invisible.

Taking our cues from such diverse and heterodox conceptions of the political, in this chapter, we broach the political engagement of young people in Greece in the times of crisis by construing 'the political' as social activity which deliberately intervenes in actual social relations, structures and embedded subjectivities—i.e. conventional modes of thought, understanding, evaluation, motivation, feeling, action and interaction—by resisting, challenging, transfiguring or striving to preserve them.

We introduce the term 'heteropolitics' to highlight (1) that such political activity is not primarily focussed on the formal political system; (2) it is not confined to revolutionary events or hegemonic acts of institution. 'The political' as deliberate collective action on social structures and subjectivities can be also part of ordinary, face-to-face interactions and attempts at coping with everyday problems; (3) 'the political' can occur on any (micro- or macro-) level in social life, in more *or less* institutionalised and visible social spaces across any social field. Hence, it can take place in informal and often obscure movements, exchanges, performances and differences of everyday life (Papataxiarchis, 2014, pp. 18–31). Finally,

(4) we place power relations, struggles and difference at the heart of the 'political,' but this involves strife and action in concert, plurality and confluence, antagonism and consensus-seeking, disruptions of normality and the crafting of 'alternative normalities.'

ANALYSIS: YOUNG PEOPLE AND POLITICAL PARTICIPATION

Participants in our research were all politically engaged. They identified their university studies as key to their politicisation. They belong to a politicised generational unit (Edmunds & Turner, 2005; Mannheim, 2001). As we see, although they were active in different social spaces, they evinced a common set of affects, attitudes and embodied practices or, otherwise put, a common habitus (Bourdieu, 1977) towards politics and the crisis.

Young Subjects in Crisis

Kostas is 25 years old, studying social anthropology and attending an MA programme (visual cultural studies) in Norway. Kostas has been a member of various heteropolitical groups in Volos, where creative resistances and new modes of interaction and organisation are being crafted, such as the '*Aftonomi Fititiki Syllogikotita tou Panepistimipiou Thessalias*' [Students' Autonomous Collectivity of University of Thessaly] (Pechtelidis, 2016), the '*Anarmonikes Ekfili*' [Unharmonic Perverts], the Students' Film Club, etc. He stresses that inequality and isolation have increased during the crisis. He adds that young people under 30 years live in dire conditions, they cannot find employment and they feel hopeless.

Kostas's account of the position of young people in crisis conveys to some extent the complexities of youth involvement with or alienation from politics:

> *Kostas*: On the one hand, some people were involved even with political parties in order to shape things together, while, on the other hand, some young people felt an aversion towards what they were perceiving in the crisis, and they did not hit back by participating politically against the crisis but by taking leave, as they saw that all this was due to political situations. [...] In the crisis, the aversion towards the parties intensified, but some new groups were formed, such as the groups in which I participate.

Stelios, Sophia and Selatin are unemployed teachers. They each teach Greek language courses to immigrants as volunteers in the *Odysseas* Solidarity School in Thessaloniki. They also participate as volunteers in the NGO *Diepafi* [Intercourse], which engages with issues of multiculturalism and multilingualism. Moreover, they work in the non-governmental organisation (NGO) *Arsis*, where they organise informal educational programmes for immigrant, refugee, homeless and marginalised children. Finally, they are radio producers on a national internet radio station where they host a radio show discussing social and educational issues. They voice a deep pessimism over political affairs, and the political system in particular:

> *Stelios*: We are concerned about politics and we don't know what to do.
> *Selatin*: Some politicians who do not represent the interests of the people should resign.
> *Sophia*: It is not a question of politicians, but of the coalescence of the working class, of the people.
> *Selatin*: Yes, but how can we organise collectively?
> *Stelios*: I am pessimistic, I have lost my hope.
> *Selatin*: Most of those who enter the political arena are corrupt.

Katerina and Iason were involved in institutional politics as members of SYRIZA's youth wing, while they are now employed as journalists and radio producers in the radio station *Sto Kokkino*, which is connected with the SYRIZA (Συνασπισμός Ριζοσπαστικής Αριστεράς) party.[4] Katerina is also a former, founding member of alterthess.gr, a journalism website based in Thessaloniki, and Iason is a current member of alterthess.gr. They stressed the emergence of a new wave of depoliticisation among young people over the last years of the crisis, in the aftermath of SYRIZA's electoral victory and the formation of the "first leftist government" in Greece in January 2015:

> *Katerina*: I think that the process [of politicisation] which started in 2008 came to an abrupt end in 2015, and our own generation has started now to distance itself from politics, saying that apparently it does not work, it does not make sense; and we are under conditions of crisis, so let's try to get a degree in case we can find a job in some months. So, there was what everybody was saying—hope—and this abruptly ceased, and it has not been explained how and why this happened ... there is a

gap … given the expectations generated by the referendum and the result of the referendum … I think that for the first time since December 2008 there has been such a big mobilisation of our age group, either for or against, either for No or for Yes [to the question of the referendum], friends broke up, boyfriends and girlfriends broke up [laughter], although the vast majority of youth mobilised around the No vote.[5]

Iason: And the retreat [from politics] into privacy seems more marked particularly among young people who defended the 'No' vote at that time, because everyone who did that had to engage in fights with their social milieu […] and the next day was a huge blow. Hence the automatic retreat and resignation, and, since we are talking about the younger generation, there has been a second wave of migration. While the former was about postgraduate and PhD students, who hoped to return home [in Greece] to work, now there is a deliberate choice to leave and stay abroad […].

The words of Katerina and Iason prompt us to consider the following three events which marked an intense period of political mobilisation of a great part of the young generation:

1. The youth revolt in December 2008, triggered by the murder of 15-year-old Alexis Grigoropoulos by the police;
2. The encampments in central squares in several cities across the country in 2011;
3. The massive youth participation in the July 2015 referendum in support of the 'No' vote, and the immediate reversal of its result by the government, which perpetuated austerity policies and increased the alienation of young people from the political system and official political representation.

The decision of the government took a heavy political toll, causing frustration and political disappointment among young voters who took part in the referendum. A generational split arose, which brought about political disorganisation and a sense of meaninglessness. From 2015 onwards, many young people distanced themselves again from social movements, mass youth political organisations, parties etc. and shifted towards an exclusive "life politics" with concerns about "lifestyle," "choice" and "self-actualization" (Furlong & Cartmel, 2007). They retreated into the apolitical tendencies of the neoliberal self which we outlined above. The following quotes are telling:

> *Katerina*: I think that what is occurring now is a retreat, and because some people were accustomed to collective life, they may turn up at some kind of solidarity initiative in favour of refugees, some kind of small-scale participation of this kind.
>
> *Iason*: And in political groupings that have been created since September 2015, participation is very different, because it has no outreach to a massive community, not even in the universities [...].
>
> *Katerina*: Whereas there were massive youth organisations, I think it was the first time that SYRIZA's youth organisation had attracted so many people...

In these quotes, Katerina and Iason express their disappointment over the steady decrease of young people's participation in large-scale politics (e.g. party politics and social movements) after the referendum, and the retreat into individualism. They manifest thus their embarrassment over the current political impasse.

Divergent Attitudes Towards Party Politics and the Formal Political System

Katerina and Iason are deeply concerned about the young people's recent sense of alienation from the political system. However, they had, and to some extent they still maintain, some ties with institutional politics and parties. Moreover, they had, in the period 2008–2015, a very positive attitude towards the prospect of collaboration between leftist parties and social movements until "hope proved to be false" (in 2015):

> *Katerina*: I believed strongly in the narrative of a combination of street action and parliamentary force which could change things, that is, that we would clash on the streets and social movements ... and this would propel an actor who was then small (SYRIZA). People who had no relation with the

movements would turn to the party, which could press for certain things and reach out to a broader audience and achieve certain concrete victories.

Iason: I had more or less the same view as Katerina who claimed that the movement puts forward political projects, which a political actor (party) can introduce in the central political system. There was a time when this issue was a lot in play, there were intense mobilisations, and particularly the squares [the social mobilisation in 2011 organising assemblies in public squares] set an agenda for the central political system and there was a connection. It was not merely a movement, there was a connection between the two [the mobilisations and a party], which helped us psychologically to entertain the view that a powerful movement can produce also political change.

We identify however, considerable discrepancies within this group, which bear mainly on their attitude towards conventional politics and the parties, and the prospect of a synergy between the two. Sophia, Stelios and Selatin occupy an intermediate position and display a mixed attitude. They recognise the "dogmatism of the parties" and the impossibility of directly participating in them, however they do not dismiss them completely:

Selatin: We are interested [in party politics], but not in embracing ideas stemming from political parties.
Sophia: What Selatin means to say is that we don't like dogmatism. […].
Selatin: If you cannot judge for yourself, how is this any different from religion? With political parties, the problem is that ideology does not translate into action […] Parties in Greece have a hierarchical organisational structure, with a leadership on top, and all others are soldiers. That's why we don't take part […] I don't think that there can be a party which will change things.
Sophia: From the existing ones … […] Without a party, perhaps it is not possible to attain anything.
Stelios: It is not our aim to establish a party […]
Sophia: How else can you bring people together? […]
Selatin: On the one hand, I agree with Stelios, on the other hand, I agree with Sophia. How can everyone rally under a single umbrella without a party?

Among the young people in our study, are those who rejected political parties:

> *Kostas*: The combination [of parties and movements] is not a solution, because when you hold certain things against the parties, regarding e.g. their mode of organisation, representation, and when you believe and you say that they should be broken up into smaller parts of collective groups and self-management, this cannot work in combination because you are against the criteria of party activity. It is not only the question of representation; it is also the question of undesirable [for parties] plurivocity and fluidity in time. A party is slower in the circulation of ideas, whereas for us fluidity is something normal, there is no burden that ties you down from the top, and something can change in a short time.

Kostas stresses, on the one hand, how many young people distanced themselves from conventional politics, and, on the other, how a politicised young generational unit is interested in collective life:

> *Kostas*: Youth participation has been on the wane since 2011, and many young people no longer participate politically. Those who are politically concerned join collectives rather than parties. What was self- evident before the crisis—that I will vote in the elections and will take part in the assemblies of political parties [their youth organisations] even in the general meetings of departments—is minimised through the participation in the assemblies of other collectives. Collectives alleviate inequality […].

Kostas is a member of the groups *Aftonomi* and *Anarmonikes*, which are close to the libertarian movement. *Anarmonikes* is concerned with gender issues, sexuality, but also with broader political issues, such as equality and autonomy, etc. It functions without an elected board of directors and other hierarchies. The group holds a weekly assembly. At the beginning, only few people took part, whereas now there is a regular participation of 15–20 individuals. In a similar vein, a core group of around 15 students are fully engaged in the *Aftonomi Fititiki Syllogikotita* [Students Autonomous Collectivity], and approximately another 20–30 students are partly involved in the everyday life of this cultural space. Their customary rite was a gathering on university premises almost every Wednesday evening, where they organised 'alternative lessons.' Those meetings were focussed on the search for an effective form of participatory democracy, autonomy and solidarity (Pechtelidis, 2016):

> *Kostas*: We encourage horizontality and critique even towards the movement itself, whether anarchist or leftist [...] There are affinities with other spaces and collectives, but no adhesion to them. They (the members of the group) will voice criticisms [...] They will uphold their autonomy. [...] Difference is recognised, but also our community against sexism, fascism, capitalism etc. and the fact that we are building another world.

Heteropolitics in Action and the Remaking of Subjectivities

Transformations of subjectivity and the crafting of a heteropolitical habitus have been traced in the narratives of all the subjects in our study, despite the fact they are involved in social sites with different political logics, modes of action and forms of organisation:

> *Kostas*: A form of self-education takes place by way of participating in the assemblies of the collective *Anarmonikes Ekfili* and, more generally, in its actions. [...] In all these spaces, another subjectivity is being created; they are spaces of encounter, opinion-formation and vindication. Hence, participating in these groups without any repression of action from the top engenders pluralism in knowledge and information and speech. There is a freedom of speech, which gives rise to diversity and difference [...] emphasis is placed on both autonomy and collectivity.

Kostas dwells on the importance of this space for the cultivation of a heteropolitical habitus:

> Upon starting university, I felt a drive and a power to participate, and upon graduating, I wanted to convey this outside the university. You have the feeling that you want to talk, and you do it with others. Hence, you carry

it outside the university [...] Many people keep acting in the same way, they establish structures for various issues. A habitus is thereby engendered. Those of us who have lived this experience, we do not discard it despite all the problems, despite all the criticisms we make, after having lost the security of the university.

Sophia, Stelios and Selatin expressed the same sentiment:

> *Sophia*: In Odysseas, we offer lessons (in the Greek language) to immigrants aged 18–65 years. Beyond the lessons, what is also important is the broader ambiance, we hold weekly assemblies to make decisions, I have never experienced this in such a way.
> *Stelios*: We decide collectively, everybody takes part, voting is open, the setup is very democratic, it bears no relation to what we know. [...] There are no hierarchies, nor differences between the old and the new [members]. It functions horizontally; everybody can express himself or herself freely.

Sophia, Selatin and Stelios state that they do not identify with any political party, and their strongest involvement with institutional politics is that they vote in national elections. However, they see what they are doing as political. As Stelios puts it succinctly: "the aim of all three of us is to change society, to improve it." It is not politics that repels them, it is the form it takes on through political parties:

> *Stelios*: What we are doing is something of our own, we have made it, we are making it, we are reshaping it over time. This is our ideology; we think that it is completely unrelated to existing political groups and parties.

What Stelios asserted is crucial: "with our actions we can affect some others and become many [a growing popular mobilisation], collective groups...."

In light of this, we can glimpse how a heteropolitical habitus can emerge from relatively different political trajectories and modes of political organisation:

Iason: My political engagement began with the 2008 events [...] I was 14, and for five years and more the events in 2008 were decisive, which introduced us as a generation in a process, at least those young people who have a critical outlook and stance in any way [...] it was a violent event on a social level, which affected all of us socially and psychologically as students throughout the country, it was a much-debated issue, there were people from school who took part for the first time in a demonstration, an assembly, it was thus something novel. [...] Although my family is left-leaning, until then, we had never had any such social ferment.

Katerina: In high school in 2006–2007, with the school occupations, I had my first significant contact with things political. [...] I remember when we first started the occupations and then formulated the demands; I remember how impressed I was by the first students' assembly in the courtyard of the school, how embarrassed I was and how I could not speak, how to speak. [...] That was the first contact [...] then I was in the Faculty of Philosophy, and I think that my entire engagement with politics was determined by the days of December [2008] and the event made me develop a much more active political life and, what is more, not in the classic party-political fashion, because those events demonstrated spontaneity, spontaneous politics and the problems of the parties [...] and those days gave rise, as it were, to the first thoughts about the creation of *AlterThess*. [...] This group operated through the assembly [...].

We did not operate in terms of majority/minority, that is, we did not vote, we would discuss things until we reached an agreement [...] *AlterThess* used to have what we see now on Twitter, that is, you would have the immediate posting of a photo from the demonstration in Thessaloniki, it would provide live updates, it used to go to events where nobody else would go, it provided live coverage of the anti-racist festival when nobody else would go [...] The first talks started then. [...] For our generation, those days were key. [...] I have been shaped by all this, I was there for many years, from when I was 20½ until when I was 26. [...] This taught me to improvise and to look for solutions that are not self-evident, it taught me to voice my opinion, it is very important and you don't find it necessarily, it taught to me to conduct enquiries with clean hands and a clear conscience. I felt independent and it gave me employment, it made me a professional, and today I have a job from which I make a living.

Iason: This experience changed me because I could compare the alternative journalism of *AlterThess*, which deconstructed the dominant one, with my experience as a student in the IEK [professional school] where we had professors who own and manage right-wing/far right-wing media.

The heteropolitical habitus, configured by participating in these collective groups, evinces also a generational dimension:

Kostas: There is also the fact that we are young, students, and we understand that we are introduced into a new logic. Older people have tried to join these groups but they failed, they tried to impose specific ideas our ways of action. Many times they have felt embarrassed, that they do not belong here, they are a different generation, e.g. the way the assembly was run was not comprehensible to them. Young people in Greece see what happens now and do not know what used to happen in the past, they think ahead and they act with what they have now in their hands.

Also, this generational dimension is evident in Katerina's interview:

Katerina: When we were younger, we were all under 30, and what impressed me was the disappointment of older journalists, they used to tell us 'don't do it.' We described in essence the creation of a blog, initially, and later on a website that would cover what others seek to hide [...] they told us, then, don't dare it, it won't work, it will have no future in financial terms, such ventures cannot hold up. In the end, we did it. I passed from an active collective life to this space, in essence it was a group of young people who tried to utter a political discourse but addressing mainly things they themselves did, and their friends and acquaintances, either because they were not covered or they were covered in a distorted way.

This heteropolitical generational habitus has some features that we found in all the young people in our study, such as the desire to participate directly in the construction of social reality, in the autonomy of collective groups, in collective creativity and in new collective initiatives. What transpires is that the young people of the study are very much aware of the political and social situation, they reflect upon it and react accordingly. Our study shows that a part, at least, of Greek youth is not withdrawn from politics and action, but resists in various ways. Young people demand more participation in society. They belong to a politicised generational unit and they develop a common heteropolitical habitus through their participation in various alternative social and cultural sites. They are informed thus by a quite common political and social dynamic, despite their differences. However, 'the political' should not be perceived through conventional, systemic political lenses, because much of what can count as young people's political engagement will be either missed altogether or dismissed as irrelevant.

Youth identity and politics tend to be naturalised and preordained, as they are usually grasped through adult grids of understanding and conventional, standard preconceptions about 'youth' and its politics. Young people tend to be either rebuked as apolitical, and thus as a serious threat to contemporary liberal democracy (Bauerlein, 2009), or hailed as radical, revolutionary, and progressive. Such polar thinking of youth politics reveals underlying differences in how 'the political' is conceptualised (Bessant, 2014). Young people's political activity in present-day Greece should be understood and evaluated in the precise context, in which social bonds and collective identities are being dismantled, while insecurity, precarity and indebtedness are experienced through a certain individualism which often engenders both individual and collective impotence, if not paralysis and resigned submission. The subjects of the study have shifted away from formal politics towards collective action on social structures and subjectivities. They have located the political in ordinary, face-to-face interactions and in attempts to deal with everyday problems. Therefore, they have blurred the distinction between conventional and unconventional politics. Such low politics and micro-political actions may have an impact only on certain social practices and relations, or they may coalesce with others to prepare and engender large-scale antagonisms and systemic macro-changes.

Conclusion

Our explorations of youth heteropolitics in crisis delved into the everyday underground of political activities, which are ongoing—rather than limited to spectacular moments of insurrection—, diffuse and heterogeneous.

What transpired from our research is that young people today are very much aware of the political and social situation, and they reflect upon it and respond accordingly. Many young Greeks do not just retreat from action, but resist in various ways and demand more political participation in society. They seek to become socially useful and they search for effective means of action. Despite the deterioration of the current situation, young people try to maintain an optimistic attitude in a world without anchors, as independent social beings. They work out strategies to access educational and professional opportunities in a spirit of cooperation. They experiment, and they constantly improvise. Furthermore, they are not narcissistic, selfish, politically disengaged and apathetic and unskilled, etc. We claim that they belong to a politicised generational unit, which develops a common heteropolitical habitus through its participation in various alternative social and cultural sites, displaying thus a common political and social dynamic despite several differences within it.

It is crucial to investigate how young people themselves approach politics and which activities they themselves understand as political (Bessant, 2014; Pleyers & Karbach, 2014). Hence, it is important to deploy an enlarged conception of the political, looking into heteropolitical activities of young people.

Notes

1. Official unemployment rates rose to 24% in 2016, up from 7.76% in 2008 (OECD, 2016). Youth unemployment reached 49.8% in 2015 (OECD, 2015). Material deprivation rose to 22.2% of the population in 2015, compared to 11% in 2009. The rate peaks among the young (ages 0–17): 25.7%. Those risking poverty amount to 35% of the entire population (Hellenic Statistical Authority, 2016). Child poverty rose to 40.5%, increasing by 17.5% between 2008 and 2012 (UNICEF, 2014, p. 8).
2. The onset of the Greek financial crisis was handled by the PASOK (social democratic) government of Giorgos Papandreou (PM), who lost the 2013 elections to Antonis Samaras, the leader of New Democracy (centre-right) party. Samaras remained in office until January 2015, supported by other parties in parliament (including PASOK in the first year). Then, led by Alexis Tsipras, the leftist coalition party SYRIZA won the general elections in January 2015, and again in September 2015, following a dramatic defeat of its anti-austerity agenda in the new negotiations held with the EU leaders during the summer of 2015.
3. The July 2015 referendum, whose anti-austerity result was ignored by the EU and the new Greek government alike, was only the last dramatic episode in a long chain of political events. See below.

4. The title means 'Coalition of the Radical Left,' as it consisted originally of one large and several small leftist groups.
5. The referendum was called by the new, leftist SYRIZA government in June 2015, when negotiations with the 'Troika' (the European Commission, the European Central Bank and IMF) reached an impasse. Since January 2015, when it was first elected, the government had been trying to negotiate a way out of the austerity policies imposed by the EU and IMF in return for new loans to the nearly bankrupt Greek state. By June 2015, the Troika offered the draft of a new loan agreement, which would perpetuate austerity policies, demanding further cuts in welfare state expenses etc. The government decided to resort to a popular referendum on the agreement, asking citizens to reject (by voting "No") the proposed EU offer or to approve it (by voting "Yes"). The referendum would be the first after 1974 when democracy was restored in Greece and a referendum took place to decide the type of the constitution (constitutional monarchy or republic). The referendum, held on 5 July 2015, caused unprecedented political divisions and tensions in Greek society, as it was considered to put into risk the very membership of Greece in the EU. The result was a resounding "No" to the proposed agreement: 61.3%. However, few days later the government, led by PM Aléxis Tsipras, gave in to the demands of the Troika and concluded a new agreement, which enforced further austerity measures. This 'capitulation' caused a deep crisis in the ruling party of SYRIZA, splits, and an exodus from the party and the government, particularly of young people mobilised in the youth organisation of SYRIZA.

References

Agamben, G. (1998). *Homo sacer. Sovereign power and bare life* (D. Heller-Roazen, Trans.). Stanford: Stanford University Press.

Agamben, G. (2005). *State of exception* (K. Attell, Trans.). Chicago and London: The University of Chicago Press.

Bauerlein, M. (2009). *The dumbest generation: How the digital age stupefies young Americans and jeopardizes our future*. Harmondsworth: Penguin.

Beck, U. (1992). *Risk society: Towards a new modernity* (M. Ritter, Trans.). London: Sage.

Bessant, J. (2014). *Democracy bytes: New media, new politics and generational change*. London: Palgrave Macmillan.

Bourdieu, P. (1977). *Outline of a theory and practice* (R. Nice, Trans.). Cambridge: Cambridge University Press.

Connolly, W. C. (1995). *The ethos of pluralization*. Minneapolis: The University of Minnesota Press.

Crouch, C. (2004). *Post-democracy*. Cambridge: Polity.

Day, R. (2005). *Gramsci is dead: Anarchist currents in the newest social movements*. London: Pluto Press.
Edmunds, J., & Turner, B. (2005). Global generations: Social change in the twentieth century. *The British Journal of Sociology, 56*(4), 559–577.
Furlong, A., & Cartmel, F. (2007). *Young people and social change: New perspectives*. Maidenhead: Open University Press.
Giddens, A. (1991). *Modernity and self identity. Self and society in the late modern age*. Polity: Oxford.
Hellenic Statistical Authority. (2016). Press release: Material deprivation and living conditions. 2015 Survey on income and living conditions. Retrieved February 15, 2017, from http://www.statistics.gr/documents/20181/677a27d3-1743-4200-a2ab-cc619a625061
Heywood, A. (2013). *Politics* (4th ed.). Basingstoke: Palgrave Macmillan.
Kioupkiolis, A. (2006). Introduction. In C. Crouch (Ed.), *Metadimokratia* (pp. 5–47). Athens: Ekkremes.
Kioupkiolis, A. (2014). Towards a regime of post-political biopower? Dispatches from Greece, 2010–2012. *Theory, Culture & Society, 31*(1), 143–158.
Lazzarato, M. (2011). *La Fabrique de l'homme endetté. Essai sur la condition néolibérale*. Paris: Editions Amsterdam.
Lefort, C. (1986). *Essais sur le politique, XIXe-XXe siècles*. Paris: Seuil.
Legard, R., Keegan, J., & Ward, K. (2003). In-depth interviews. In J. Ritchie & J. Lewis (Eds.), *Qualitative research practice. A guide for social science students and researchers* (pp. 138–169). London: Sage.
Mannheim, K. (2001). The problem of generations. In P. Kecskemeti (Ed.), *Essays on the sociology of knowledge: Collected works* (Vol. 5, pp. 276–322). New York: Routledge.
McCaffrie, B., & Marsh, D. (2013). Beyond mainstream approaches to political participation: A response to Aaron Martin. *Australian Journal of Political Science, 48*(1), 112–117.
Mouffe, C. (2005). *On the political. Thinking in action*. London and New York: Routledge.
Mouriki, A., Balourdos, D., Papaliou, O., Spyropoulou, N., & Fayadaki, E. (2012). *The social portrait of Greece—2012. Aspects of the crisis*. Athens: EKKE Editions.
Organisation for Economic Co-operation and Development (OECD). (2015). Labour market statistics: Youth unemployment rate. Retrieved February 15, 2017, from https://data.oecd.org/unemp/youth-unemployment-rate.htm
Organisation for Economic Co-operation and Development (OECD). (2016). Short term labour market statistics: Harmonized unemployment rates. Retrieved February 15, 2017, from http://stats.oecd.org/index.aspx?queryid=36324
Papataxiarchis, E. (2014). Introduction. In E. Papataxiarchis (Ed.), *Politikes tis Kathimerinotitas* [Politics of everyday life; written in Greek] (pp. 17–77). Athens: Alexandria Publishers.

Pechtelidis, Y. (2016). Youth heterotopias in precarious times. The students autonomous collectivity. *Young, 24*(1), 1–16.
Pickard, S. (2018). *Politics, protest and young people. Political participation and dissent in Britain in the 21st century.* London: Palgrave Macmillan. [forthcoming]
Pleyers, G., & Karbach, N. (2014). *Young people political participation in Europe: What do we mean by participation?* Brussels: European Union/Council of Europe Youth Partnership.
Rancière, J. (2010). *Dissensus: On politics and aesthetics,* (S. Corcoran, Trans.). London: Continuum.
Rose, N. (1999). *Powers of freedom reframing political thought.* Cambridge: Cambridge University Press.
Schmitt, C. (2007). *The concept of the political* (G. Schwab, Trans.). Chicago and London: University of Chicago Press.
Scott, C. J. (1990). *Domination and the arts of resistance hidden transcripts.* London and New Haven: Yale University Press.
Spradley, P. J. (1979). *The ethnographic interview.* New York: Holt, Rinehart and Winston.
UNICEF Office of Research. (2014). Children of the recession: The impact of the economic crisis on child well-being in rich countries. In *Innocenti Report Card 12.* Florence: UNICEF Office of Research.

Alexandros Kioupkiolis is Assistant Professor of Contemporary Political Theory in the School of Political Science, Aristotle University, Greece. His research interests are focused on contemporary theories of power and radical democracy, the 'commons,' and utopian thought. He has published several monographs and papers on these topics.

Yannis Pechtelidis is Assistant Professor of Sociology of Education in the Department of Early Childhood Education, at the University of Thessaly, Greece. His research interests lie in sociology of education, sociology of childhood and youth, discourse theory, and ethnography.

PART IV

Young People and Protest as Politics

CHAPTER 16

Youth-Led Struggles Against Racialized Crime Control in the United States

Tim Goddard and Randolph R. Myers

INTRODUCTION

Beginning in 2013, widespread protests against criminal justice policy and practice in the United States erupted across many cities, revealing a crisis in the relationship between law enforcement and urban communities of color. From Ferguson to Baltimore, from Los Angeles to New York, from Baton Rouge to Cleveland, people living in heavily-policed neighborhoods took to the streets demanding changes to a criminal justice system that has, for the last 40 years, penetrated ever-deeper into the communities, families and lives of poor people, particularly marginalized people of color (Clear, 2007). While specific acts of police violence were the immediate catalyst for these protests, decades of deepening social and economic inequalities provided the broader backdrop for this protest against criminal justice practice (Young, 2007). The American criminal justice system

T. Goddard (✉)
Department of Criminal Justice, Florida International University, Miami, FL, USA

R.R. Myers
Department of Sociology and Criminal Justice, Old Dominion University, Norfolk, VA, USA

© The Author(s) 2018
S. Pickard, J. Bessant (eds.), *Young People Re-Generating Politics in Times of Crises*, Palgrave Studies in Young People and Politics, DOI 10.1007/978-3-319-58250-4_16

has displaced a functioning social welfare system. It has been used to contain communities locked out of the labor market and increasingly cut-off from basic social goods like education and state-based family supports (Currie, 2013a). The collateral consequences of this approach are increasingly clear, both to the academic criminologists who chart the effects of mass incarceration and to the people living in marginalized communities in the US where the police officer and the parole agent have become the face of the State (Wacquant, 2009).

Mainstream news outlets often represented these protests as being 'sudden' in nature. However, the chants, signs and political demands of young people on the streets in Baltimore, Ferguson, Minneapolis and elsewhere resonated with the philosophies and demands of social justice organizations that had been working in earnest for years to bring these issues to light, often organizing young people for criminal justice reform in the process. While they have largely escaped the attention of criminologists (and the social sciences generally), a number of youth-led grassroots organizations have mobilized against the carceral state and innumerable non-custodial forms of punishment such as fines, proactive police stops, registries of suspected gang members, and civil injunctions. For some time now, young people in these organizations have politically engaged with, among other issues, the criminalization of school discipline, racialized policing practices and the devastating effects that mass incarceration has had on poor communities of color. Such social justice organizations exemplify a re-generation of youth-led political action, thus providing a counterpoint to claims that young people are increasingly apolitical and civically disengaged.

This chapter draws on interviews conducted during site visits at 12 social justice organizations working in major cities across the US. These organizations all saw crime as the product of social injustice; and many of them mobilized young people to make changes to an unjust social order, while often envisioning participation in protest as a catalyst for personal change in young people. Drawing on interviews with staff members at these organizations, this chapter details the contestations of three key injustices that affect the lives of marginalized young people in the US: the criminalization of school discipline, racialized policing practices, and mass incarceration.

All of the organizations had a social justice focus and were young people-led, young people-run, or shaped by the concern of young people. However, there were differences in the practices of the 12 organizations.

One type works primarily, but not exclusively, on social movements against 'law and order' policies and practices, often while trying to "harness the energies and anger that many young people feel toward the US criminal legal system" (Goddard, Myers, & Robison, 2015, p. 81). For example, these activist-oriented organizations routinely campaign against the presence of police in schools, the absence of due process protections for people placed on gang registries, and the construction of new jails and prisons. While some of these organizations partner with the State or philanthropies to fund some service-oriented work, advocacy and activism is at the core of what they do.

Another variety of social justice organization is more service focused, delivering youth crime prevention, intervention, and reintegration programs to young offenders, or those 'at-risk' of crime. Organizations of this type are often also involved in advocacy work, but their main efforts are to partner with state or philanthropic bodies to deliver services. Their programs are often focused on raising the social consciousness of young people, or as criminologist Currie writes (2013b, p. 6), helping young people to understand "that their troubles and frustrations have causes outside themselves—that they are rooted in the systemic injustices and deprivations that are inflicted on them by the society around them." Importantly, the programs are usually designed and revised in tandem with the young people (or at least are subject to their input) and thus they integrate the knowledge of young people into justice reform and progressive crime policy (Cunneen & Rowe, 2014). As these service-oriented groups often accept state money through public–private partnerships, they provide an interesting example of how one aspect of the neoliberal project (privatization) can provide the space to counter other aspects of the neoliberal project, a point we return to in the discussion.

As we describe the work of youth-led grassroots organizations, we also outline the basic contours of three interrelated injustices that organizations routinely contested, providing basic statistics in each of the areas. Finally, in the discussion, drawing again on interviews with staff members who work to mobilize young people for criminal justice reform in the US, we discuss how consumerist youth culture works against organizing young people for social justice and how youth organizers navigate this new reality.

We believe these organizations are important; however, we do not wish to romanticize them; nor do we want to overstate their importance, either in recent protests of mass incarceration, or in the potential struggles that still lay ahead. At the same time, we believe that paying attention to them provides an important counterpoint to what many critical scholars have characterized as a 'post-political' era. We also believe that they are important because the ideas and demands of youth-led grassroots organizations challenge the technocratic solutions put forward by our discipline, criminology, which tends to limit its policy suggestions to small changes constrained by the assumptions and limits of evaluation work.

To help understand the struggles experienced by the social justice organizations, we must understand how crime control in the US affects the activists and advocates we interviewed and the young people and communities they work with. As we detail the work of youth-focused organizations fighting against punitive policies in schools, policing and incarceration practices, we also outline the broad contours of the carceral state in these three areas.

CRIMINALIZATION OF SCHOOL DISCIPLINE

Referred to as the 'school-to-prison pipeline,' school discipline and safety practices in the US increasingly emulate criminal justice logics (Simon, 2007). Many schools since the 1990s have installed metal detectors and surveillance cameras, outlawed lockers, instituted drug sweeps, and employed school resource officers or on-site police officers (Hirschfield, 2008; Sykes, Piquero, Gioviano, & Pittman, 2015). Schools look more and more like detention centers and daily contact with security measures has become routine for young people (Hirschfield, 2008; see also Mejia Mesinas, in this volume). Moreover, zero-tolerance policies have led to increases in mandatory suspensions and expulsions: between 1974 and 2000, school suspensions increased by over 80 percent (Wald & Losen, 2003).

Racial disparities are prevalent in this school-to-prison pipeline. Mirroring observed patterns in the criminal justice system, minority youth, especially Black youth, are over-represented in school punishment and disciplinary statistics, particularly suspensions (Cregor & Hewitt, 2011; Fabelo et al., 2011). According to the US Department of Education Office for Civil Rights (2014), young people of color are suspended and expelled at a much higher rate than Whites. Specifically, African American males are three times more likely, and African American females are six times more likely, to receive an out-of-school suspension than white youth of the same gender (Goff, 2016). The emergence of zero-tolerance policies and a more punitive orientation to students sets up young people of color to fail academically; it also means that they experience disproportional criminal justice contact, which will disadvantage them in myriad social institutions in the future. In this way: "the school-to-prison pipeline may solidify systems of inequality by insuring the creation of a caste through the alteration of life chances" (Sykes et al., 2015, p. 9).

Since they were mainly young people of color from poor neighborhoods, the young people involved in the organizations we visited were disproportionately affected by the criminalization of school discipline. With their activism, they mobilized in a number of ways to chip away at these policies. The organizations we visited were typically led by a collaborative group of young people, who had been with the organization for some time, working alongside adults from the local area who sought solutions that were rooted in a tradition of social justice, community empowerment, and emancipation (and who often had gone through the organization themselves). Thus, when we speak about the actions of an organization, we are primarily referring to actions of young people, usually between the ages of 14 and 24. Moreover, even though all of the organizations had an adult director and staff (albeit often in their mid to late twenties), those staff members were almost always from the same or similar neighborhoods as the young people they now worked with. This meant that, oftentimes, they too had experience with the justice system. Or as a young adult who now directed an organization that he founded put it:

> The original young people who started the organization, we were either all gang members or affiliated with gangs. So, it's always interesting to tell that story 'cause, I mean, for us, we all understand like the reason we did that, or most young people do that, is to have like a sense of community because awkwardly enough, in our community, there's no sense of community.

This shared background helped attract young people disconnected from, and distrustful of, mainstream institutions. In addition to their grassroots origins, many of the organizations had a democratic component that gave young people control over what the programs and activities entailed. A respondent at an organization in the San Francisco Bay Area outlines the philosophy behind the youth-driven nature of her organization:

> We believe that if decisions are going to be made about services for, or activities for, or laws in place for young people, that young people need to be there to have their voice heard about it.

The school-to-prison pipeline was a significant concern for members of the organizations we visited. Moreover, many of them sought to transform the school system, or rejected mainstream school systems altogether. At many organizations, youth-led campaigns demanded physical improvements to school buildings and changes to how funding was allocated. One organization we visited went directly to state congress to demand budget changes to improve basic school infrastructure. Young people also campaigned to change the disciplinary codes in local school districts, and fought against having school resource officers (i.e. sworn law enforcement officers who are responsible for providing security and crime prevention services) permanently stationed in schools. In their place, like many organizations working across the country, they wanted to replace school police and probation officers with intervention specialists and peace workers (see Justice for Families, 2013).

The strategies employed by these social justice organizations were often highly creative. For instance, one organization attempted to educate teachers about the social ecology of their school's neighborhood by having young people involved in the organization give local teachers neighborhood tours. Many teachers lived out in the suburbs, far away from the urban schools where they taught. During the tours, young people from the social justice organization showed teachers the environment that their students were exposed on a daily basis, including "what [low] employment rates look like, and what [impoverished] households look like, and what are the services available for the students and their families they're working with." Such tours, said the organization's director, helped teachers understand why the young people in their classes might sometimes appear troubled, hostile, or "checked out" during class.

Some youth-led organizations secured state funding to open their own schools (Goddard & Myers, 2011). These were not necessarily well-funded schools with modern up-to-date classrooms. Rather, these schools were opened in spaces like a derelict storefront, an abandoned business, or an old elementary school building. One respondent described the physical state of the building where his organization opened a social justice-focused high school:

> We started realizing that the building had no internet, there was no gym for—well, there was a gym, but it wasn't fit for high school students 'cause it's really small, 'cause it's for elementary school students. There was no

science lab. High school students, they have to take, they have to be in a science lab. So [the young people in our organization] started organizing around those issues. So, laptops, internet, getting a science lab, getting books for a library, getting, college support.

Another similar organization in Los Angeles, California, established a school that operated under the charter school system in the US (Goddard & Myers, 2011). But unlike mainstream charter schools designed for remedial education, where students are taught a traditional trade like plumbing or cosmetology, students learn the vocation of activism. For example, one course, entitled 'Troublemakers,' reconsidered historical figures denounced as 'agitators' or 'criminals.' The course was a part of a larger curriculum called 'Street University,' "which introduces students to US and international movement history, as well as past critical education efforts, through readings, music, films, guest, speakers and discussion" (Goddard & Myers, 2011, p. 661).

The organizations we studied took action in response to issues and injustices that participants struggled with in their daily lives. The organizations sought to prevent "school push out" (i.e. expulsion), not mainly by changing young people, but by reforming or eliminating punitive school policies and practices. Although these small battles and the establishment of small social justice oriented schools do not make national headlines, they are crucially important. Small-scale protest victories chip away at youth criminalization without the need for large amounts of funding and without attracting political backlash. And the relatively small schools that some organizations founded usually go somewhat undetected in the neoliberal enterprise (because of its reverence for privatization).

Young People Mobilizing Against Police Misconduct

Youth-led organizations also mobilized action against police misconduct. For some time now, young people in the US (particularly young people of color) have been differentially monitored, stopped, arrested, punished, and harmed by the police (Alexander, 2010). Studies show that police disproportionately stop people of color while driving (Warren, Tomaskovic-Devey, Smith, Zingraff, & Mason, 2006). For instance, a recent study by the Bureau of Justice Statistics found that "black drivers were three times as likely to be searched during a stop as white drivers and twice as likely as Hispanic drivers" (Sentencing Project, 2013, p. 5). On sidewalks and streets, police stop, question, and frisk Black males at higher rates than Whites (Tonry, 2011). In these stops, however, the police are no more successful at finding weapons or drugs than in their stops of Whites (Center for Constitutional Rights [CCR], 2009). In New York City, for example, 80% of the people stopped were black and Hispanic young men, and 85% were frisked, but the New York Police Department (NYPD) rarely found illegal drugs or weapons. Only 10% of the time was there an arrest or summons to court. Although rare, when the NYPD did stop, question, and frisk a white person, only 8% were frisked and yet Whites were 70% more likely to be in possession of a weapon (CCR, 2009). Police disproportionately arrest people of color as well. Black young people, for example, are 2.3 times more likely to be arrested for all delinquent offenses than white young people (Sentencing Project, 2013) and black young people have the highest probability of being charged with a crime, regardless of self-reported offending (Stevens & Morash, 2015). Black young people are also over 2.5 times more likely to be arrested for violating curfew laws than white young people (Sentencing Project, 2013).

The social justice organizations help young people recognize why conflict with the police is so common in their neighborhood, and why it has been this way for a long time. As one director of an organization explained:

> It's kind of interesting 'cause we talk about the Black Panther party, we talk about the Young Lords. So, you know, you talk about what was there that made—what are the main issues that they had? It was police brutality, and all police brutality in that community.

We heard this theme repeatedly. A director at another organization in a different city put it this way: "There's been an adversarial relationship throughout the history of law enforcement in the African American community and other communities of color, in this country. Nothin's been done to shift that." And as a staff member at a third organization in another city explained, the history of police violence in neighborhoods often intersects with traditions of youth activism and organizing:

> I think part of what we try to be really intentional about is to talk about the history around [police violence]. And, the history of police violence in this [neighborhood]. And we talk about Fred Hampton, Fred Hampton being murdered by the Chicago police, which is actually a story a lot of

them know, even if they don't know (laughter) any other social movement history. Fred Hampton, he was like 22 when he was killed. He became the chairman of the Black Panthers when he was like 19. So, it's also a story of like youth activism. So, we talk about the history of it to help give them some context for what sometimes can feel so individual or like they're the only person struggling—that's not quite right, 'cause they know that they're not the only person struggling. They know that it's their community. But I think that his story actually gives them a sense of power around that a little bit, to know that their communities have been pushing back against police violence for a long time.

Adults in the organizations also taught younger members about the historical roots of poverty, low wage work, racial isolation, and how oppressed people of the past resisted against these forces. One organization connected their curriculum to Midnight Schools (i.e. illicit gatherings in the middle of the night during the nineteenth century) that, as one respondent put it, "slaves did in the woods to teach themselves how to read." These lessons aim to help young people situate their lives and those of their families within a broader political and economic system, and to decide on their own what actions to take.

Energized by a social consciousness grounded in past popular struggles, young people in the organizations we visited mobilized to take on several police-related issues. For example, these youth-led organizations work to end intrusive and discriminatory stop-and-frisk tactics by police in low-income communities of color and limit arrests for drug possession and low-level misconduct. Members of the organizations also participated in the recent protests against the police killings of (often unarmed) people of color. While they are now making the national news, protests, die-ins (a form of protest in which participants simulate being dead, i.e. murdered by the police), and marches against police violence have been going on for at least a decade, and many of the youth-led organizations we visited were involved in those smaller-scale protests.

Although recent groups such as Black Lives Matter have articulated steps needed to reform police violence, the organizations we studied worked to end several less overt policy practices. Their advocacy and protest efforts included advocating prohibiting the questioning of young people by police prior to parent or guardian notification and consultation. They also worked to eliminate the ticketing of youth for riding a bicycle on a sidewalk and worked to end 'police special orders' that give police broad powers to fight suspected terrorists, but end up criminalizing innocuous behaviors such as taking pictures near public buildings. One Los Angeles-based organization mobilized in a number of ways to push a bill through the California Legislature that would curb the practice of racial and identity profiling and increase transparency and accountability of law enforcement agencies making arrests and seizing property. Using telephone calls to government officials, visits with legislators and the Governor's Office, media interviews and storytelling, rallies, marches, signature gathering, and (along with other groups such as Black Lives Matter) shutting down the State Governor's office for a time, the bill was successfully written into California law in 2015. These smaller scale protests shine light on the sorts of everyday criminalizations that young people of color have to negotiate. One such everyday punishment was described by a staff member at an organization in California:

> For eight years, Los Angeles Unified School District issued truancy tickets. So, basically, the way it worked in practice is, literally, police officers would be waiting at the bus stop for the kids who are late to school. Not the kids who are not in school (laughter), but the kids who are arriving late to school, and ticket 'em on the way in, and the tickets were 250 dollar tickets. That's obscene (laughter).

Actions taken by youth-led organizations included not only marches and sit-ins, but a host of direct actions, such as filling a court with supporters of those identified as 'suspects' and charged with crimes. Young people would also give passionate testimonies at public hearings, petition and Tweet local and state legislators and Governors, and even hold press conferences with the media. Another tactic was to attempt to organize dialogue sessions between police officers and young people for the purpose of improving police–community relations. In some of the organizations, young people also learned about their constitutional rights when stopped by the police and what they were obligated by law to do and not do. In sum, the youth-led groups organized dozens of campaigns in protest over the problems described above. We believe that, as with the mobilization against the criminalization of school discipline in impoverished communities, the somewhat piecemeal victories that are achieved should not be overlooked. Moreover, these struggles also help bring young people mobilizing for change together, introducing them to the world of politics and collective action.

Incarceration: Direct and Collateral Consequences

The US incarcerates at a higher rate than any other major country, using prisons and jails at a rate that dwarfs Western European countries (Currie, 2013a). As with policing, significant race and class disparities exist in determining who is incarcerated in the US (Alexander, 2010). It is not only the size of the prison system that sets the US apart from other penal systems: prisons in the US are also notoriously harsh, stingy on providing rehabilitative and transitional services to prisoners, and many partner with corporations seeking nearly-free prison labor (Gottschalk, 2015).

The carceral system in the US inflicts numerous collateral consequences on the communities where mass incarceration hits hardest and deepest (Mauer & Chesney-Lind, 2002). Having a felony conviction record, for instance, significantly lowers an individual's odds of finding a secure, well-paid job (Pager, 2007). In isolation, this is bad enough. But when numerous people living in the same (isolated) areas experience this disproportionate contact with the criminal justice system, the social capital of each and every community member decreases, as their personal and professional ties are often with folks whose life chances have been dimmed by mass incarceration (Clear, 2007). The concentrated nature of incarceration in the US—the fact that the prison extracts and returns people to only a few neighborhoods—means that these places are filled with a high proportion of people experiencing some degree of civil death (Mauer & Chesney-Lind, 2002). What emerges is a multi-generational pattern of employment inequality, income inequality, and educational inequality, maintained in no insignificant way by the classed and racialized use of the prison (Wakefield & Uggen, 2010).

Youth-led organizations around the country have worked to highlight the problem of mass incarceration, and the protests of incarceration policies that we heard about in our study were varied and numerous. In one of the organizations, young members marched on to the site of a newly proposed women's prison. Another organization successfully passed a 'Bill of Rights' for young mothers in a juvenile justice system. Another group marched on a state capital to protest the use of public funds to build prisons at a time of austerity. In the organizations we visited, the young people involved in agitating for criminal justice reform often had intimate knowledge about incarceration, its exploitative conditions, and the direct and collateral consequences of a stint in jail or prison. One respondent reflected on how her personal experience with mass incarceration motivated her initial involvement in youth-led protest of the state prison system a few years back:

> And, this movement was definitely not just a movement of, you know, what we sometimes [call] *high achieving young people*. It was like young people who were like, "You're not gonna continue to incarcerate our people." Like really learning about what the prison industrial complex has done to us. I mean, we were doing trainings on like the 13th amendment inside of detention, organizing walkouts around like [prison labor] ... And, we'd sit there and be like, "Those are our parents who are making 30 cents an hour." These are our parents that they're exploiting inside prison. Like this is like new age slavery. And, so I think that, we used to always say, "You don't need to agitate us. We're already agitated!" (laughter). So let's skip that part and get right to the tools [needed to organize].

While the criminalization of poor communities is not a new problem—its now massive scale means that young people have grown up in a society where mass incarceration has always been a reality. And indeed, it is a regular and growing presence in many of their lives, and that of their family members, friends, and neighbors.

YOUTH-LED ORGANIZING IN NEOLIBERAL TIMES

The organizations we studied provide an example of young people engaging in civic and political actions to generate social change. Our research into the work of youth-led grassroots organizations' campaigns against the criminalization of school discipline, racialized policing, and mass incarceration revealed that young people are exercising their political autonomy. To claim otherwise, would be a misstep. In the area of grassroots mobilizing against the large-scale carceral system in the US, there exists a sizable and highly motivated group of young people exercising their political autonomy.

However, a good deal of work in a number of disciplines has demonstrated how social, economic and cultural shifts coinciding with neoliberalism have worked to depoliticize the subjectivities of young people. This too should not be overlooked, even if some of the conclusions in this research work may go too far. Although the youth-led actions that we described challenge the claim that we are now in a post-political age (Treadwell, Briggs, Winlow, & Hall, 2013), we do need to recognize how broader neoliberal cultural shifts, and especially the ascent of consumer culture, affects the practice of organizing young people for justice system reform. We recognize, as did our respondents, how consumer culture mitigates against organizing young people's social justice campaigns. Understanding the spread of consumer culture is important not only for theorizing criminal behavior (Anderson, 1999; Bourgois, 2003; Hall, Winlow, & Ancrum, 2008), but also for thinking through prospects for progressive social change in a post-industrial US.

In their ethnographic research into the lives of young people involved in the English Riots of 2011, Treadwell et al. (2013) make a persuasive case that the protest and discontent expressed on the riotous streets of England was driven by a consumerist logic. Those young people, they argue, came of age in communities where collective decision-making and political consciousness spurred by unionized labor—and the relatively stable communities that it created—was in serious decline (see also Hall et al., 2008). With no clear political framework to guide their understanding of the personal and material problems they faced—and surrounded by a hyper-competitive consumerist logic—especially in their less-rehearsed moments, it appeared that all that was left was to "go shopping":

> [...] in the post-political present, it seems almost impossible for a potential collective of marginalized subjects to construct a universal political narrative that makes causal and contextual sense of their own shared suffering and offers a feasible solution to it. No unifying and readily communicable political symbolism is at hand to provide a means of grasping the reality of common stresses and dissatisfactions, or the enduring sense of precariousness and lack that frames the marginalized subject's sense of being-in-the-world. Instead, subjects are forced to stew over the bleak reality of their material conditions and their durable but objectless sense of exploitation, irrelevance and anxiety in isolation. Unable to divest themselves of torment and nagging doubt, perpetually marginalized youth populations have become moody and vaguely 'pissed off' without ever fully understanding why. (Treadwell et al., 2013, p. 3)

We see these organizations—and the broader 'model' they represent—as an important, albeit partial, antidote to this sort of depoliticized lashing out. With the option of waged work having largely disappeared in many of the communities we visited, along with the decimation of labor unions and the casualization of work in service industries, community organizing may be one of the only spaces left to begin constructing more 'complete' political narratives. Moreover, members in many of the organizations were keenly aware of the new challenges that consumer culture presented. Some staff members described elements of their program that tried to show young people how neoliberal capitalism and the consumer culture that flows from it shaped their biographies, subjectivities and communities. For example, a respondent at one organization explained how their summer workshops tried to give young people an understanding of consumer cultures, but in ways that respected how symbolically powerful and instrumentally important conspicuous consumption was to the young people in this post-industrial US city:

> We talk about consumerism a lot here. And, I would say most of the young people we work with are very caught up in like what shoes they have, and what hair they have, and what … and absolutely—it's like a huge thing in their lives […].

The same respondent continues:

> They're also like young folks tryin' to like survive, and to have a certain pair of Jordan's will give them status in their school, and allows them to navigate their reality in a way. And, that's their experience. So, they, ultimately, they know how to survive, and they will survive with us or without us, right? So, we're just there to be able to give tools and allow them to question themselves, question other people, question us, right? We don't work to create shame, but we do work to develop an analysis.

Conclusion

By working to raise the social consciousness of young people living in marginalized and criminalized communities, social justice organizations like those we visited are working to create the psychic and social space needed regenerate youth-led politics. This alone, may not be enough to avert the crisis of democracy that some scholars claim is unfolding. Nevertheless, we believe there is a condition of opportunity, in part due to the peculiarities of neoliberal governance. Given the preference in the US for 'community' and the private sector over government support, community-based organizations of all political stripes are relied upon to carry out much of the social programs and day-to-day responsibilities of governing. Many of the organizations that we visited funded their work with young people using state monies, framing their activities as crime prevention, youth development or intervention services with 'at-risk' young people. The agendas of community based organizations and what they provide to young people in the way of guidance and support suggests that when the state outsources community-based organizations with the task of carrying out crime control and crime prevention activities, the solutions those agencies offer can counter aspects of neoliberalism.

In this way, our research demonstrates how one aspect of neoliberalism (privatization) can work as a catalyst for organizing against certain negative features of neoliberal policy that disrupt the daily lives of young people most acutely. In short, the organizations communities create may provoke political opposition directed against troubling aspects of neoliberalism, like the criminalization of young people and the metastasizing consumer culture. The fact that such protests are possible suggests that communities can exploit the relative autonomy encouraged by neoliberal governance—in this case, by using the gray area of privatization to mobilize young people for social and political change in these uncertain and increasingly unequal times.

References

Alexander, M. (2010). *The new Jim Crow. Mass incarceration in the age of colorblindness.* New York: The New Press.

Anderson, E. (1999). *Code of the street. Decency, violence and the moral life of the inner city.* New York: Norton.

Bourgois, P. (2003). *In search of respect. Selling crack in El Barrio* (2nd ed.). Cambridge: Cambridge University Press.

Center for Constitutional Rights. (2009). *Racial disparity in NYPD stops-and-frisks.* Retrieved November 29, 2016, from http://ccrjustice.org/files/Report-CCR-NYPD-Stop-and-Frisk.pdf

Clear, T. (2007). *Imprisoning communities. How mass incarceration makes disadvantaged neighborhoods worse. Studies in crime and public policy.* New York: Oxford University Press.

Cregor, M., & Hewitt, D. (2011). Dismantling the school-to-prison pipeline. A survey from the field. *Poverty & Race, 20*(1), 5–7. Retrieved October 8, 2016, from http://www.naacpldf.org/files/case_issue/PRRAC%20journal%20Jan_Feb%202011-%20Dismantling_the_School-to-Prison_Pipeline.pdf

Cunneen, C., & Rowe, S. (2014). Changing narratives. Colonised peoples, criminology and social work. *International Journal for Crime, Justice and Social Democracy, 3*(1), 49–67. Retrieved November 1, 2016, from https://www.crimejusticejournal.com/article/view/138

Currie, E. (2013a). *Crime and punishment in America* (Rev. and Updated ed.). New York: Picador.
Currie, E. (2013b). Consciousness, solidarity and hope as prevention and rehabilitation. *International Journal for Crime, Justice and Social Democracy, 2*(2), 3–11. Retrieved April 8, 2016, from https://www.crimejusticejournal.com/article/view/114
Fabelo, T., Thompson, M. D., Plotkin, M., Carmichael, D., Marchbanks, M. P., III, & Booth, E. A. (2011, July 19). Breaking schools' rules. A statewide study of how school discipline relates to students' success and juvenile justice involvement. *Council of State Governments Justice Center*. Retrieved August 15, 2015, from https://csgjusticecenter.org/youth/breaking-schools-rules-report/
Goddard, T., & Myers, R. R. (2011). Democracy and demonstration in the gray area of neo-liberalism. A case study of free Los Angeles high school. *British Journal of Criminology, 51*(4), 652–670.
Goddard, T., Myers, R. R., & Robison, K. J. (2015). Potential partnerships. Progressive criminology, grassroots organizations and social justice. *International Journal for Crime, Justice and Social Democracy, 4*(4), 76–90. Retrieved November 30, 2016, from https://www.crimejusticejournal.com/article/view/231
Goff, M. (2016). African American girls and the school-to-prison pipeline. Who are our sisters' keepers? *Urban Institute*. Retrieved May 24, 2016, from http://www.urban.org/urban-wire/african-american-girls-and-school-prison-pipeline-who-are-our-sisters-keepers
Gottschalk, M. (2015). *Caught. The prison state and the lockdown of American politics*. Princeton: Princeton University Press.
Hall, S., Winlow, S., & Ancrum, C. (2008). *Criminal identities and consumer culture. Crime, exclusion and the new culture of narcissism*. New York: Routledge.
Hirschfield, P. J. (2008). Preparing for prison? The criminalization of school discipline in the USA. *Theoretical Criminology, 12*(1), 79–101.
Justice for Families. (2013). *Families unlocking futures: Solutions to the crisis in juvenile justice*. Retrieved December 1, 2016, from www.justice4families.org/media/Families_Unlocking_FuturesFULLNOEMBARGO.pdf
Mauer, M., & Chesney-Lind, M. (Eds.). (2002). *Invisible punishment. The collateral consequences of mass imprisonment*. New York: New York University Press.
Pager, D. (2007). *Marked. Race, crime, and finding work in an era of mass incarceration*. Chicago: University of Chicago Press.
Sentencing Project. (2013). *Shadow report to the United Nations on racial disparities in the United States criminal justice system*. Retrieved September 15, 2016, from http://www.sentencingproject.org/publications/shadow-report-to-the-united-nations-human-rights-committee-regarding-racial-disparities-in-the-united-states-criminal-justice-system/
Simon, J. (2007). *Governing through crime. How the war on crime transformed American democracy and created a culture of fear*. New York: Oxford University Press.

Stevens, T., & Morash, M. (2015). Racial/ethnic disparities in boys' probability of arrest and court actions in 1980 and 2000. The disproportionate impact of "getting tough" on crime. *Youth Violence and Juvenile Justice, 13*(1), 77–95.

Sykes, B. L., Piquero, A. R., Gioviano, J. P., & Pittman, J. P. (2015). The school-to-prison pipeline in America, 1972–2012. In M. Tonry (Ed.), *The Oxford handbook of criminology and criminal justice* (pp. 1–27). New York: Oxford University Press.

Tonry, M. (2011). Less imprisonment is no doubt a good thing. More policing is not. *Criminology & Public Policy, 10*(1), 137–152.

Treadwell, J., Briggs, D., Winlow, S., & Hall, S. (2013). Shopocalypse now. Consumer culture and the English Riots of 2011. *British Journal of Criminology, 53*(1), 1–17.

US Department of Education Office for Civil Rights. (2014). *Civil Rights Data Collection. Data snapshot: School discipline*. Retrieved October 28, 2016, from http://ocrdata.ed.gov/Downloads/CRDC-School-Discipline-Snapshot.pdf

Wacquant, L. (2009). *Punishing the poor. The neoliberal government of social insecurity*. Durham: Duke University Press.

Wakefield, S., & Uggen, C. (2010). Incarceration and stratification. *Annual Review of Sociology, 36*(1), 387–406.

Wald, J., & Losen, D. L. (2003). Defining and redirecting a school-to-prison pipeline. In J. Wald & D. J. Losen (Eds.), *New directions for youth development: No. 99. Deconstructing the school-to-prison pipeline* (pp. 9–15). San Francisco: Jossey-Bass.

Warren, P., Tomaskovic-Devey, D., Smith, W., Zingraff, M., & Mason, M. (2006). Driving while black. Bias processes and racial disparity in police stops. *Criminology, 44*(3), 709–738.

Young, J. (2007). *The vertigo of late modernity*. London: Sage.

Tim Goddard is Assistant Professor in the Department of Criminal Justice at Florida International University, USA. He holds a PhD in Criminology, Law & Society from the University of California, Irvine. His current research focuses on community-led crime policy reform and on issues of race and class in predicting social danger.

Randolph R. Myers is Assistant Professor in the Department of Sociology and Criminal Justice at Old Dominion University, USA. He received his doctorate in Criminology, Law & Society from the University of California, Irvine. His work examines the relationship between inequality and violence, community-derived alternatives to the criminal legal system, and the lived realities of juvenile justice.

CHAPTER 17

Youth Work, Agonistic Democracy and Transgressive Enjoyment in England

Graham Bright, Carole Pugh, and Matthew Clarke

INTRODUCTION

Debates regarding the supposed crises in young people's democratic and political participation have, as other authors in this book argue, been ubiquitous in recent years. Indeed, democracy, it would seem, is in crisis (della Porta, 2013), with widespread and growing scepticism regarding the political accountability of states, coupled with a deep distrust of democratic processes on the part of many of its citizens—developments that have been exacerbated by neoliberalism's hegemony and the resultant rise of the popular right in many global contexts.

While, in the United Kingdom (UK), concerns have been voiced about overall political participation, young people are said to be particularly

G. Bright (✉)
Childhood and Youth Studies and Youth and Community Work, York St John University, York, UK

C. Pugh
Youth and Community Work, York St John University, York, UK

M. Clarke
School of Education, York St John University, York, UK

© The Author(s) 2018
S. Pickard, J. Bessant (eds.), *Young People Re-Generating Politics in Times of Crises*, Palgrave Studies in Young People and Politics, DOI 10.1007/978-3-319-58250-4_17

disillusioned (Briggs, 2017) about traditional, conventional and electoral forms of political participation (see Pickard, 2018). At the last national general election in 2015, only 76% of 18–19 year olds were registered to vote, and of those, only 43% did so (Electoral Commission, 2015; Ipsos Mori, 2015). Young people's participation in the referendum on whether the UK should remain or leave the European Union (EU) in June 2016 contradicts this trend with an estimated turnout of 64% for 18–24 year olds (Bruter and Harrison, 2016), compared to 72.2% for all groups (Electoral Commission, 2016). However, 71% of those young people who did participate in the referendum voted to remain in the European Union (Electoral Commission, 2016), highlighting the effect of demographic change in undermining the "un-written rule" of democracy—that those whose lives will be affected longest have the greatest power at elections (Berry, 2014, p. 14).

Concerns about young people's presumed political apathy have led to research and government policy interventions (Youth Citizenship Commission, 2009), resulting in the introduction of 'Citizenship Studies' in the National Curriculum, the establishment of the UK Youth Parliament in 1999, and the creation of the National Citizenship Service (NCS) in 2010. This emphasis on participatory citizenship is also reflected in policy discourses, examples of which include Positive for Youth (HM Government, 2011) and You're Welcome (Department of Health [DoH], 2011), which rhetoricise the importance of young people's voices.

However, these responses recycle increasingly narrow definitions of democracy (Pykett, 2007), which are more about compliance, than questioning the validity or desirability of the existing, or indeed any other, system. By individualising and responsibilising young people, policy makers ignore the realities of increasing disenfranchisement and marginalisation arising from the daunting array of discriminatory policies, including electoral reform that presents barriers for youth voter registration, age-based discrimination in housing rights and minimum wage entitlements, and, substantial increases in university tuition fees. Another is the large-scale closure of state-funded youth provision, which is the focus of this chapter. Taken together, these developments demonstrate a fundamental disregard for young people on the part of the government and corrode the substance of their democratic citizenship (Briggs, 2017; Jones, 2017).

Much youth service[1] provision is founded upon principles of democratic participation, association and collectivity (Batsleer, 2008; Jeffs & Smith,

1999; Ord, 2016), and while tensions exist between agendas of emancipation and control, a commitment to dissensual critical pedagogical praxis, grounded in contestation, critique and critical action (see Freire, 1972), remains discernible (Taylor, 2008). Its current ambiguous status represents a neoliberal paradox: youth work[2] is required for its capacity to engage young people in 'project global capitalism,' yet it is hated for the threat it poses of catalysing fraternity, solidarity, association and democratic collectivity amongst young people and their communities, thereby daring them to begin to think, act and resist differently. The research on which this chapter is based evidences youth work's ongoing capacity to ignite young people's critical imaginaries. In doing so, it moves beyond assumptive discourses of youth political apathy and disillusionment, to contend youth work's ability to capture and harness young people's frustration in engendering critical animation.

The chapter draws on the narrative accounts of five young adults[3] involved in national campaigns to save local youth services in England as part of wider anti-austerity movements, which responded to substantial and wide-ranging cuts introduced by the David Cameron-led Conservative-Liberal Democrat coalition government in the aftermath of the global economic crisis of 2007–2008. The chapter questions whether young people's supposed political disengagement arises from apathy, or represents a more considered rejection of neoliberal procedural democracy. We argue, that our participants' accounts reflect the characteristics of agonistic democracy, insofar as they embody a desire for the recognition of pluralistic voices; they value the disruptive and dissensual capacity of contestation, and implicitly acknowledge a tragic view of life, grounded in human finitude and fallibility, and, a recognition that choices and decisions always come at some cost. Agonistic democracy, we contend, has the capacity to serve as a source of transgressive enjoyment, and hence, to solicit democratic engagement, in a way that more banal, procedural versions of democracy, with their limited focus on regular "free and fair" elections, do not. We assert that youth services provide arenas where these democratic praxes are valued, and where the development of democratic capital can be facilitated. The chapter traces our participants' transgressive struggles with procedural democratic structures, in attempting to save local youth services, and concludes by arguing that the young adults in this study are passionately and politically engaged in promoting democratic accountability and renewal.

From Procedural to Agonistic Democracy: Resisting Neoliberalism

Popular and governmental discourses surrounding young people's political apathy presuppose a narrow reading of democracy, which privileges participation at the ballot box, parliamentary procedures and the rule of law, over, or even at the expense of, other forms of expression (Pickard, 2018; Sloam, 2017). This reading also ignores how democracy has become sutured with capitalism as 'democratic capitalism' (Dean, 2009), fuelling constructs regarding 'good' young neoliberal subjects, who diligently and compliantly perform their civic duty, without challenging, subverting or disrupting the advancement of capitalist logic (Kennelly, 2016).

Neoliberalism is, of course, a complex and contested term; but for the purposes of this chapter, we understand it as "*the disenchantment of politics by economics*" (Davies, 2014, p. 4, emphasis in original). Neoliberalism privileges the demands of capital over the welfare of people. Its rhetoric places individual 'freedom' over anything that espouses collective democratic solidarity, and its production utilises the prospect of precarity to engender fear. It marginalises the weakest, and uses them to example the consequences of non-compliance.

Certainly, it can be argued that neoliberalism has come to use an entire generation of young people as disposable fodder by disproportionately targeting austerity measures against them, all in the name of 'good' fiscal order (Cairns, de Almeida Alves, Alexandre, & Correia, 2016). Whilst in the UK, this meant an overall reduction in public spending of 2.6% between 2009–2010 and 2014–2015, this disproportionally fell on 'non-protected services,' with Youth Service funding reduced on average by a third up to 2014, and significant cuts continuing beyond that (Barton & Edgington, 2014; Nuffield Foundation, 2015). In a little over six years (2010–2017), some £387m has been cut from Youth Service budgets. Nationally, this resulted in the loss of some 600 youth centres, and more than 3500 youth work jobs (Jones, 2016; Unison, 2016). The pursuit of neoliberal policy agendas has not only reduced the quantity of youth work, it has sought to induce fundamental changes in its character. The imposition of performative market rationality, increasingly prescriptive state agendas at the expense of broader educative principles, and the prioritisation of product over process has resulted in the 'hollowing-out' of practice (Jeffs, 2015, p. 85).

Neoliberalism moulds subjects in its own image (Scharff, 2016) and, in this sense, represents not just a fiscal, but an intellectual, form of discipline, which stultifies individual and collective imaginaries with its insistence that there is no alternative to the stratifying and competitive logics of the market (De Lissovoy, 2015). Neoliberalism thereby trains subjects into what Fisher (2009) describes as "capitalist realism": a world in which capitalism is the only reality with no conceivable alternatives—where "it appears as a neutral economic system that simply exists in the absence of any political intervention" (McGowan, 2016, p. 87). Democracy, in this capital realist view, is tamed and reduced to voting and the rule of law.

Yet, at its core, democracy has always been excessive—replete with radical and unsettling forces that challenge notions of balance and orderliness. For this reason, democracy was viewed by philosophers like Plato with deep suspicion, as something threatening to the rule of the wise elders. In psychoanalytic terms, this excess is associated with enjoyment, or jouissance—an intense form of pleasure/pain analogous with venturing beyond limits or constraints (McGowan, 2013). The current appeal of populist right wing parties can be understood in these terms, insofar as such a politics enables its adherents to derive enjoyment from the transgression of the limitations imposed by democracy, such as those established by 'political correctness.' The leaders of such parties achieve success by seeming to embody this jouissance. Meanwhile, capitalism's rise and its suturing with democracy has tamed the latter's excessive nature and limited its capacity to serve as a source of transgressive enjoyment. While capitalism purports to fulfil our desire through the endless accumulation of supposedly satisfying objects, support for democracy is left reliant on people's more limited capacity for identifying with the good (McGowan, 2013, 2016). However, the political disenchantment wrought by neoliberalism has rendered democracy increasingly vulnerable, and not to be taken for granted, thus repositioning it as a source of potential jouissance.

We believe the challenge for the youth work profession—and for young people—is to articulate alternative possibilities, which might serve as sources of transgressive enjoyment. In confronting this challenge, we highlight the scope offered by agonistic democratic models (Wenman, 2013), which privilege constituent power (the demos) over constituted power (structures of governance), and foreground the need to recognise and value a plurality of voices, the positive value of contestation and dissensus, and the tragic nature of human existence. As such, agonistic democracy offers a counter-discourse to "the utterly discredited system of disciplinary neoliberalism" (Wenman, 2013, p. 297). Tellingly, it also resonates powerfully with the data generated with participants in this study.

Young People, Pluralism and Political Engagement

For our participants, the effects of neoliberal austerity are not remote and abstract, but personal and keenly felt. These young people were deeply affected by proposed spending cuts to public services and, through democratic contestation, came to reject the depersonalisation of public services, in which the faces, names and voices of young people are replaced with budget lines and performance targets. In contesting the closures, they sought to highlight a plurality of voices and experiences, otherwise hidden by budgets and reductionist statistics. For the young participants, their deep personal involvement and political investment in youth services influenced their decision to become involved in campaigning to resist the closure of provision (Harris, 2017). As Pip explained:

> [...] for me [the youth drop-in centre] has such a special place in my heart and if they had closed [it] I would feel like a part of me would have almost gone with it. Do you know what I mean? [...] To have that taken away it was like I was being robbed too. Even though I don't work with them anymore and I don't go there for support or anything it felt like they were taking away a piece of my identity. Yes I think that's it, I think it felt like a piece of my identity would have gone alongside [The youth drop-in] too.

Jade concurred:

> And after all the cuts and things it was just the worst—it felt like someone had died. Because I had been seeing this person once or twice a week for years and then no more. I can't see them anymore. That was it. [...] And instead of just being like I should do this because the cuts are bad or this is bad, it was very personal in the end. There would be times when I'd be crying about it and things like that and it got to the place where I wasn't able to talk about the cuts.

Youth services had supported young people in finding and connecting their voices, as well as in developing critical awareness regarding the processes by which some voices are amplified while others are silenced:

> At the time [young people] maybe don't even know they need that to be able to be that voice I suppose ... if you're a young person dealing with

housing, with exploitation, with family breakdown or mental health problems then they cloud your ability to have a voice. It would be very hard to be on the radio or practically organised enough to be in the right place at the right time if you're living in chaos (Lara).

In narrating their motivation for campaigning, participants explained how they embraced a pluralism, 'where everyone's voice is represented,' that resonates with an agonistic view of democracy. In recounting their reasons for 'standing up,' they articulated a complex range of emotions (rage, hope, fear, concern, optimism and passion), which suggest that for them, the democratic ideals associated with youth work were successful in offering a source for transgressive jouissance.

Democracy, Contestation and Capital

The Youth Citizenship Commission's (2009) findings that politicians and policy makers do not take young people's concerns seriously are reflected in the experiences of our participants, all of whom became involved in protests against cuts to services that they, their peers and their communities valued, but which were seen as unnecessary by local decision makers. This reflects a disconnection between the issues deemed important by young people and the priorities of politicians, as pointed out by Pip:

> The council in the local authority had made a decision because it was in their best interest and were going to see that through no matter what, or so they thought. And when we came up and said "no you're causing damage here, you're not causing positive things."

Even where young people previously engaged with organisations explicitly constructed by various levels and agencies of government to support young people's voices and participation, their experiences were of structures that were unresponsive to their ideas. As Christopher explained:

> As a member of the Youth Parliament, we'd talked about a lot of issues and did campaigns, but I think in that whole year term, I don't think there was anything tangible that we could say we'd done as the Youth Parliament.

Yet even as young people find that democratic structures do not reflect, or respond to their concerns, they continue to discover and generate alternative forms of engagement and contestation, including 'micro-politics'

(Pattie, Seyd, & Whiteley, 2004) and 'cause-orientated repertoires' (Norris, 2003). Rather than viewing young people as apathetic, we argue that dominant definitions of political participation, found for example in citizenship curricula, are premised on the fallible separation of public and private and fail to take account of the conception of politics as lived experience (Pykett, 2007). Youth services, responding to the challenge noted above of making democracy a living praxis, provide arenas for developing and enacting democratic contestation, and are instrumental in developing young people's voices as reflexive agents (Couldry, 2010), as illustrated by Pip's comments:

> For years I've tried to get people to understand where I'm coming from, I tried to get people to relate to what I was feeling and I feel like I was never really able to do it and you've [youth worker] just done it. It was so incredible. It was so empowering, it felt like you'd been silent for so long and all of a sudden to have a voice to be able to explain it. I will never forget it.

The process of young people collecting, telling, and representing their own and others' narratives was critical in contesting dominant neoliberal discourses, and central to the struggle to defend services. Established political structures had not taken these narratives into account; consequently, young people, youth workers and community members created informal networks, through, for instance, community meetings, media events and social media activity, to contest the status quo thereby becoming "self-actualising citizens" (Bennett, 2003, p. 6).

Despite recent undermining, the educative value of democratic association has been a defining feature of youth work since its inception (Smith, 2001). Kenny, Taylor, Onyx, and Mayo (2015) argue that citizenship grows through concrete educative practices, promoting reciprocally networked civic virtue in the form of social capital (Putnam, 2000). For participants in this research, however, associative approaches not only had pedagogic value, but were vital in identifying and drawing on wider support networks in contesting the closure of debates regarding the future of services.

For our respondents, participation in youth work programmes provided networked spaces, which linked individuals and agencies (including children's centres, community centres, police, universities, local newspapers, radio stations, as well as local political figures), enabling them to "come to voice" (Batsleer, 2008, p. 5) and enact contestation. Without engagement with services, participants would not have been able to build social capital and develop capacity to speak effectively in defending provision. However, threats to services ignited democratic activism and served as a source of transgressive enjoyment in contesting dominant neoliberal narratives of efficiency and austerity.

Fighting for Hope: Democratic Justice, Symbolic Resistance and Tragic Acceptance

Most campaigns began with a petition, a requirement in triggering access to local government meetings. At these meetings, participants delivered speeches and were subject to interrogation by elected officials. Participants' struggle for democratic legitimacy was characterised by a fight for dignity and hope—that alternative futures are possible, that young people matter, and should have a say in decisions that affect them. Participants narrate a struggle for recognition and justice that represents, and, in places subtly usurps the symbolic violence (Bourdieu, 1977) mobilised by the elite against them. Pip describes the disdain she felt from an elected official who rudely asked: "why are 'these people' here?", whilst continuing to focus on his phone, as she and others brought their highly personal deputations, based on their experiences of the value of services. This violence is not always overt, but is epitomised by our respondents' experiences of power. They vividly describe being the subject of stereotypical views—incapable of having, or expressing an opinion about proposed cuts to their services. As Claire explained:

> Just because you're a young person and you wear a hoodie, it doesn't mean you don't have a valid opinion and I think it allowed a lot of people's opinions to be heard when they wouldn't normally be heard.

Christopher similarly argued that:

> More than anything, a lot of the councillors were just simply surprised that young people were so engaged with politics, and things that were going on.

Some participants spoke about the warmth and surprise with which some elected officials received their deputations, and others of a disdainful ambivalence. But, whilst 'democracy's' warmth is perhaps to be cautiously embraced, surprise suggests an imbalance of power. Specifically, surprise speaks to the disorientation of democratic representatives at young people's entry into a field that does not 'belong' to them, and of the structural disconnect between young people and elected representatives (Gordon, 2010). As Collin (2015, p. 110) argues "political cultures that [keep] young people at arm's length [present] a significant barrier to engagement"—an idea further reflected in Christopher's account:

> We went from our safe environment to their meetings, to where they were, and did things how they did them to try and save our services, our youth centre. [...] We did that like 'cos we did it out of necessity 'cos it was the only way we could be heard. I don't think it was the best way to convey the young people's passion and feelings about it 'cos I don't think we articulated as much as we would like to say because we were out of our depth, out of our environment. You know it's like being in someone else's house. You can't always express yourself like you would if you were in your house and they came to visit you. And I think the prospect of going to council meetings and offices was a very daunting prospect.

Young people are required, by formal participatory structures, to cross democracy's threshold, to learn its language, to know their place.

Seal and Harris (2016, p. 44) contend that whilst many accounts of state-fuelled symbolic violence against young people and communities "are partial, contradictory and reinscribe prevailing hegemonies, there is also potential for resistance and subversion." Participants' sabotage of this violence can be seen in the data. Young people recognise the damage done to them by narratives of 'risky youth.' However, in defending services, young people drew on these discourses. By utilising popular fears that reductions in services will result in 'anti-social behaviour,' young people re-inscribe these narratives, using weapons that are fashioned against them in self-defence. This usurpation turns symbolic violence towards symbolic resistance.

Youth work can express symbolic resistance—it facilitates freely chosen associations with which to resist structural inequalities (Seal & Harris, 2016). Participants are therefore engaged in symbolic resistance to save significant associative spaces for themselves and others. Their counter-embrace of the hegemonic is a joyous and hard-won trickery; yet, it is costly, and may still return to wound them, and future generations (Bassil-Morozow, 2015). This trickery sits alongside the passionate and personally affective stories of the campaigns—of compellingly powerful narratives that speak sacrificially, in forgoing privacy and anonymity, of the transformative influence of youth services on young people's lives and communities. The victories these participants have won may be small-scale, and temporary, but they are significant for local communities nonetheless. As Seal and Harris (2016, p. 127) note, "small acts of resistance, even the symbolic ones should be celebrated." Thus, resistance's effectiveness is "that it produces a new reality, a new condition from which to resist" (Tuck & Yang, 2014, p. 13).

All participants, because they are so invested, both personally, and on behalf of their communities, describe a considerable weight of responsibility and guilt, and of fear and denial, beyond the known:

> At points it did feel like "Are we actually going to make a difference? Is anything actually going to change? Is this going to have an effect? Are we just a little stone in a lake? What change are we going to make by being here?" …. People didn't really talk about it, we tried to avoid it, what would happen if the youth centre wasn't here, what would be do instead? Those were questions we all had, but nobody really wanted to explore (Christopher).

These emotions are heightened by the alienating conditions of official democratic structures, and speak of an emotional labour (Hochschild, 1983), for which there is a cost, and no guaranteed return. As Kennelly (2016, p. 65) argues, young activists are "motivated by feelings of individual responsibility to the state and community (which turn quickly to feelings of guilt if one's perceived responsibility is not fulfilled), and ultimately curtails his or her behavior so as to not challenge the state beyond particular limits."

Each of our participants spoke forcefully about the expenditure and exchange of emotional labour, of their fight for hope, passionately recounting changing waves of emotion at different points of their respective campaigns. They recounted how encouragement from local communities, schools, businesses, media and professionals, together with a deep sense of personal and social injustice, spurred them on in their fight. They described how they created and drew upon wells of solidarity, fraternity and shared values to sustain them and how varying engagements with procedural democracy's representatives deflated, encouraged, enraged and impassioned them in their struggle. Defending youth work and the democratic values it embodies, including commitments to pluralism and contestation, against the encroaching hegemony of neoliberalisation thus offers a source of transgressive jouissance/enjoyment—of vital energies, heightened and dissipated and heightened again. This defence is inflected within a tragic acceptance that there are no guarantees, which only makes the struggle all the more vital. As Fine, Tuck, and Yang (2014, p. 50) posit: "Resistance is never pure, never simply oppositional or rejecting; it is often enacted with an affective bouillabaisse of anger, disappointment, sense of injustice, desire, yearning and ambivalence."

Conclusion: Passion, Politics and Protest as Transgression

Our participants may all vote in elections and for a range of motivations (duty, hope, despair, anger, guilt, conscience). However, they express mixed views regarding the "external efficacy" (de Moor, 2016) of official, procedural versions of democracy. They are nonetheless passionately political people who care deeply, and who are willing to act in response to a range of issues that are personally and socially significant (Harris, 2017; Harris, Wyn, & Younes, 2010; Sloam, 2017). As Lara explained:

> Yes, definitely and I suppose those things I feel passionate about I'll lend my support by signing a petition or social media, like the NHS, junior doctors, academies, privatisation. The things that I care about.

This entails a need to be actively involved in political struggle:

> [...] government is a bit messed up and we have to do a lot to get our voices heard. Whether that is protesting or riots, I think that should be done. You have to be an activist, you can write your name down on a piece of paper and that will be a number, but you need to be really involved to make a difference. Signing and things do things, but I think just being aware and being more articulate with it and knowing where to go to get your voice heard (Jade).

This is a far cry from the picture of 'youth apathy' that dominates many media discussions. As Collin (2015, pp. 155–156) notes:

> [...] ordinary young people are identifying and acting on issues that matter, and in everyday ways they are shaping the kind of society they want to live in. [...] The remoteness with which they mainly view political

institutions is in stark contrast with their often passionate commitments to particular issues and personally defined acts incorporated into their everyday lives.

Despite the implicit embodiment of agonistic politics suggested in our discussion, 'democracy,' in its dominant liberal, procedural version, has given these young people perhaps just enough for appeasement, but has failed to truly win their hearts. They have learned critical (dis-)engagement. This research has focussed on 'winning' campaigns, at least to the extent that they achieved a measure of short-term success. However, there are many more young people with stories of loss to tell. If the winners remain cynical about 'democracy,' questions must be raised regarding where this leaves those affected by the loss of their youth services.

Youth work represents a collaboration of critical voices. It offers relational and potentially democratic spaces in which dialogical learning based on young people's experiences of the world can be framed, critiqued and enacted. Yet by drawing on state resources, working to its diffuse agendas and engaging democratic structures to contest governmental decisions, youth workers and young people continue to find themselves challenging, and sometimes uncomfortably involved in the legitimation of pernicious capitalist machinery. Nonetheless, the threat to, and removal of, youth work spaces further erodes young people's opportunities to engage in democratic practices (Harris et al., 2010).

Globalisation, and the concomitant neoliberal atomisation of life, have arguably led to more fluid social ties, and resulted in more transitory, utilitarian associations (Bauman, 2009; Harris, 2017; Putnam, 2000). These changes may well coincide with generational shifts (Woodman & Bennett, 2015), in which the rising generation experience the painfully austere realities of collective civil precarity—the result of neoliberally-induced next-generation asset stripping. Consequently, they are moving beyond unattainable materialistic values, towards a new plurality that again (tentatively) embraces collective, post-materialist civic concerns (Inglehart, 1990; cited in Harris, 2017). The young adults in our study necessarily struggle within compromised democratic structures, which mean that in spite of victories in their campaigns, they still view contemporary 'democracy' as dislocated and damaged. As Harris (2017, p. 296) puts it: "[A] lack of interest in and engagement with formal politics and political institutions is not the same as a lack of interest in political issues or an ability to act politically."

Our participants have shown themselves to be passionately political in ways that makes sense given the situated fluidity of their lives. In particular, their accounts suggest they have embraced measures of pluralism, contestation and tragedy that resonate with an idea of agonistic democracy, while highlighting the shortcomings of the dominant contemporary procedural models of politics. In this sense, they can be viewed as one of Bang's (2005) 'everyday makers,' those who "participate in short-term, concrete ways that fit in with their lifestyles; they value self-led participation; and, want to engage and disengage at will" (Collin, 2015, p. 99). Yet the democratic practices explored in this chapter, are both passionate and enduring—a result and a reflection of participants' deeply felt transgressive enjoyment. In considering their experiences, our participants, as young adults, express an on-going awareness of the continuing threat to the services they fought to save, and of a willingness, if needed, to fight again. This enduring passion speaks volumes about the significance of youth services, and the campaigns to save them, in fostering our participants' personal and civic identities. The personal it would seem for these young people *is* political, and the political, personal.

Notes

1. In England, the term youth services primarily refers to state sponsored provision of services for young people aged 13–19.
2. Youth work in England is a contested term, however, for the purposes of this chapter, we define it as informal education with young people.
3. Participants in this study, as *young adults* (aged 22–27), retrospectively narrated accounts of their involvement in campaigns to save youth services, which they themselves accessed as *young people* (aged 13–25).

References

Bang, H. (2005). Among everyday makers and expert citizens. In J. Newman (Ed.), *Remaking governance* (pp. 159–178). Bristol: Policy Press.

Barton, T., & Edgington, T. (2014, March 25). Youth service spending down by one-third. *BBC News Online*. Retrieved November 28, 2016, from http://www.bbc.co.uk/news/uk-26714184

Bassil-Morozow, H. (2015). *The trickster and the system: Identity and agency in contemporary society*. London: Sage.

Batsleer, J. (2008). *Informal learning in youth work*. London: Sage.

Bauman, Z. (2009). Identity in a globalizing world. In A. Elliott & P. du Gay (Eds.), *Identity in question* (pp. 1–12). London: Sage.

Bennett, W. L. (2003). *Civic learning in changing democracies: Challenges for citizenship and civic education* (Working Paper #4). Retrieved December 1, 2016, from https://depts.washington.edu/ccce/assets/documents/bennet_civic_learning_in_changing_democracies.pdf

Berry, C. (2014). Vote early and often: Reinforcing the unwritten rule of representative democracy. In A. Mycock & J. Tonge (Eds.), *Beyond the youth citizenship commission: Young people and politics* (pp. 14–17). London: Political Studies Association (PSA).

Bourdieu, P. (1977). *Outline of a theory of practice* (R. Nice, Trans.). Cambridge: Cambridge University Press.

Briggs, J. (2017). *Young people and political participation: Teen players.* London: Palgrave Macmillan.

Bruter, M., & Harrison, S. (2016). Did young people bother to vote in the EU referendum? *ECREP.* Retrieved December 8, 2016, from http://www.ecrep.org/wp-content/uploads/2015/03/Did-young-people-bother-to-vote-in-the-EU-referendum.docx

Cairns, D., de Almeida Alves, N., Alexandre, A., & Correia, A. (2016). *Youth unemployment and job precariousness: Youth unemployment in the austerity era.* London: Palgrave Macmillan.

Collin, P. (2015). *Young citizens and political participation in a digital society.* London: Palgrave Macmillan.

Couldry, N. (2010). *Why voice matters: Culture and politics after neoliberalism.* London: Sage.

Davies, W. (2014). *The limits of neoliberalism: Authority, sovereignty and the logic of competition.* London: Sage.

De Lissovoy, N. (2015). *Education and emancipation in the neoliberal era: Being, teaching, and power.* New York: Palgrave Macmillan.

de Moor, J. (2016). External efficacy and political participation revisited: The role of perceived output structures for state- and non-state-orientated action forms. *Parliamentary Affairs, 69*(3), 642–662.

Dean, J. (2009). *Democracy and other neoliberal fantasies.* Durham, NC: Duke University Press.

della Porta, D. (2013). *Can democracy be saved?* Cambridge: Polity.

Department of Health. (2011). *Quality criteria for young people friendly health services.* London: The Stationery Office (TSO).

Electoral Commission. (2015). *Nearly 7 in 10 people don't know the deadline to register to vote in the general election—National campaign launched by the Electoral Commission to spread the word.* Retrieved October 16, 2016, from http://www.electoralcommission.org.uk/i-am-a/journalist/electoral-commission-media-centre/news-releases-campaigns/nearly-7-in-10-people-dont-know-the-deadline-to-register-to-vote-in-the-general-election-national-campaign-launched-by-the-electoral-commission-to-spread-the-word

Electoral Commission. (2016). *EU referendum results*. Retrieved February 1, 2017, from http://www.electoralcommission.org.uk/find-information-by-subject/elections-and-referendums/past-elections-and-referendums/eu-referendum/electorate-and-count-information

Fine, M., Tuck, E., & Yang, K. W. (2014). An intimate memoir of resistance theory. In E. Tuck & K. W. Yang (Eds.), *Youth resistance research and theories of change* (pp. 46–58). Abingdon: Routledge.

Fisher, M. (2009). *Capitalist realism: Is there no alternative?* London: Zero Books.

Freire, P. (1972). *Pedagogy of the oppressed*. Harmondsworth: Penguin.

Gordon, H. R. (2010). *We fight to win: Inequality and the politics of youth activism*. Piscataway: Rutgers University Press.

Harris, A. (2017). Young people, politics and citizenship. In A. Furlong (Ed.), *Handbook of youth and young adulthood* (2nd ed., pp. 295–300). Abingdon: Routledge.

Harris, A., Wyn, J., & Younes, S. (2010). Beyond apathetic or activist youth: "Ordinary" young people and contemporary forms of participation. *Young: Nordic Journal of Youth Research, 18*(1), 9–32.

HM Government. (2011). *Positive for youth: A new approach to cross-government policy for young people aged 13 to 19*. London: The Stationery Office (TSO).

Hochschild, A. (1983). *The managed heart: Commercialisation of human feeling*. Berkeley: University of California Press.

Inglehart, R. (1990). *Culture shift in advanced industrial society*. Princeton: Princeton University Press.

Ipsos Mori. (2015). *How Britain voted in 2015*. Retrieved July 19, 2016, from https://www.ipsos-mori.com/researchpublications/researcharchive/3575/How-Britain-voted-in-2015.aspx

Jeffs, T. (2015). Innovation and youth work. *Youth and Policy, 114*, 75–95.

Jeffs, T., & Smith, M. (1999). *Informal education: Conversation, democracy and learning* (2nd ed.). Ticknall: Education Now Publishing Cooperative.

Jones, H. (2016). Youth work in England: An uncertain future? In M. Heathfield & D. Fusco (Eds.), *Youth and inequality in education: Global actions in youth work* (pp. 117–135). Abingdon: Routledge.

Jones, O. (2017). The Tory policy for young people in Britain is victimisation by design. *The Guardian*. Retrieved February 1, 2017, from https://www.theguardian.com/commentisfree/2017/jan/12/tory-policy-young-people-britain-wellbeing

Kennelly, J. (2016). *Citizen youth: Culture, activism and agency in a neoliberal era*. London: Palgrave Macmillan.

Kenny, S., Taylor, M., Onyx, J., & Mayo, M. (2015). *Challenging the third sector: Global prospects for active citizenship*. Bristol: Policy Press.

McGowan, T. (2013). *Enjoying what we don't have: The political project of psychoanalysis*. Lincoln, NE: University of Nebraska Press.

McGowan, T. (2016). *Capitalism and desire: The psychic cost of free markets.* New York: Columbia University Press.

Norris, P. (2003). *Young people and political activism: From the politics of loyalty to the politics of choice?* Report for the Council of Europe Symposium, Mimeo, Harvard University, 27–28 November.

Nuffield Foundation. (2015). *Social policy in a cold climate—Summary research report 4.* Retrieved October 25, 2016, from http://www.nuffieldfoundation.org/sites/default/files/files/RR04_SUMMARY.pdf

Ord, J. (2016). *Youth work process, product and practice: Creating an authentic curriculum in work with young people* (2nd ed.). Abingdon: Routledge.

Pattie, C., Seyd, P., & Whiteley, P. (2004). *Citizenship, democracy and participation in contemporary Britain.* Cambridge: Cambridge University Press.

Pickard, S. (2018). *Politics, protest and young people. Political participation and dissent in Britain in the 21st century.* London: Palgrave Macmillan. [forthcoming].

Putnam, R. (2000). *Bowling alone: The collapse and revival of American community.* New York: Simon & Schuster.

Pykett, J. (2007). Making citizens governable? The Crick Report as governmental technology. *Journal of Education Policy, 22*(3), 301–319.

Scharff, C. (2016). The psychic life of neoliberalism: Mapping the contours of entrepreneurial subjectivity. *Theory, Culture & Society, 33*(6), 107–122.

Seal, M., & Harris, P. (2016). *Responding to youth violence through youth work.* Bristol: Policy Press.

Sloam, J. (2017). Youth political participation in Europe. In A. Furlong (Ed.), *Handbook of youth and young adulthood* (2nd ed., pp. 287–294). Abingdon: Routledge.

Smith, M. K. (2001). Young people, informal education and association. *The Informal Education Homepage.* Retrieved October 15, 2016, from http://infed.org/mobi/young-people-informal-education-and-association

Taylor, T. (2008). Youth work and politics. *Youth and Policy, 100,* 253–268.

Tuck, E., & Yang, K. W. (2014). Introduction to youth resistance research and theories of change. In E. Tuck & K. W. Yang (Eds.), *Youth resistance research and theories of change* (pp. 1–24). Abingdon: Routledge.

Unison. (2016). *A future at risk—Cuts in youth services.* Retrieved October 24, 2016, from https://www.unison.org.uk/content/uploads/2016/08/23996.pdf

Wenman, M. (2013). *Agonistic democracy: Constituent power in the era of globalisation.* Cambridge: Cambridge University Press.

Woodman, D., & Bennett, A. (2015). Cultures, transitions and generations: The case for a new youth studies. In D. Woodman & A. Bennett (Eds.), *Youth cultures, transitions and generations* (pp. 1–15). London: Palgrave Macmillan.

Youth Citizenship Commission. (2009). *Making the connection: Building youth citizenship in the UK.* London: The Stationery Office (TSO).

Graham Bright is Senior Lecturer in Childhood and Youth Studies and Youth and Community Work at York St John University, UK. His PhD with Durham University explores youth workers' life and practice narratives. He is editor of *Youth Work: Histories, Policy and Contexts* (Palgrave, 2015) and co-editor, with Carole Pugh, of *Youth Work: Global Futures* (Sense).

Carole Pugh is Lecturer in Youth and Community Work at York St John University, UK, which she joined after 15 years of professional youth and community work practice. Her PhD with Huddersfield University explores the role of youth work in supporting young people's political participation.

Matthew Clarke is Professor of Education at York St John University, UK. His research focuses on education policy and politics in the context of neoliberal globalisation focusing on the implications of the latter for the work of teachers. He co-authored *Teacher Education and the Political: The Power of Negative Thinking* (Routledge, 2017).

CHAPTER 18

Political Participation and Activism in the Post-15m Era: Young People's Political Identifications in Lleida, Catalonia

Eduard Ballesté Isern and José Sánchez García

Introduction

In 2016, young people belonging to different political groups in the city of Lleida,[1] Catalonia, organised a series of protest actions during the week prior to the 1 May International Workers' Day public holiday. The protest arose as a direct struggle against the local, regional and national institutional political power, and they used the slogan "The struggle gives us what the powerful take from us" ("*La lluita ens dona el que el poder ens treu*"). Various groups responded in different ways to this protest. What was first created as an open protest for unitary struggle by the organisers was perceived by many older activists as an attempt to change the nature

---

E. Ballesté Isern (✉)
Department of Geography and Sociology, University of Lleida, Lleida, Catalonia, Spain

J. Sánchez García
Department of Social and Cultural Anthropology, University of Lleida, Lleida, Catalonia, Spain

© The Author(s) 2018
S. Pickard, J. Bessant (eds.), *Young People Re-Generating Politics in Times of Crises*, Palgrave Studies in Young People and Politics, DOI 10.1007/978-3-319-58250-4_18

of political activism. At the same time, younger activists who identified as anti-capitalist activists tended to reject what they saw as more traditional political demands associated with 'old politics' that were mainly reformist and institutionalist.

The centrepiece of the protests was the demonstration held on 1 May in *Plaça del Treball* (Work Square), led by anti-capitalist groups and official trade unions. When the march began, however, the protest split in two. First, there was the group mobilised by the traditional trade unions, and second, was the group formed within the framework of the previous week's struggle (organised by the anti-capitalist activists). The profile of the participants in each group also reflected a generational difference, the anti-capitalist march was mostly composed of young people in their twenties, while the trade union members tended to be in their thirties and older. Regarding the actions undertaken, while the trade union demonstration followed the traditional route through the city's centre and ended with some speeches read by union representatives, the anti-capitalist march was marked by more direct action (including the writing of graffiti on bank premises and the throwing of eggs at temporary work agency offices). This generation gap highlighted how participants in the social movements encouraged by the Los Indignados 15M movement were joining one march or the other based on their age and preference for different kinds of political action.

The division between 'the institutional march' and the 'anti-capitalist march' highlighted certain internal differences within the movements over political strategy that emerged after the 15M protests in Spain.[2] The younger participants tended to support the more radical calls, such as 'the anti-capitalist week' and the march described above, while older participants tended to support the traditional political activism that was led by the trade unions.

In this chapter, we analyse the dynamics of the internal politics of what has been called the post-15M stage (Mansilla, 2015), which was mainly led by young activists. This will enable us to observe some of the ways the Los Indignados movement evolved, including its effects on the practices and the discourses of politicised young people. We analyse post-15M youth activism in the city of Lleida (Catalonia) using ethnographic material. Our focus is on the intergenerational tensions that emerged between the so-called White Tide (*Marea Blanca*), in defence of public health, and the Platform for People Affected by Mortgages (*Plataforma de Afectados por las Hipotecas*, or PAH), which was committed to stopping home evictions and fighting for citizens' rights to adequate housing (Colau & Alemany, 2013).

We trace these dynamics using data obtained[3] through participant/engaged observation in these political movements, semi-structured interviews guided by the ethnographic process and a discussion group in each movement, which were supplemented with a review of the information produced by the media and the movements themselves. This analysis enables us to examine the concepts of 'new' and 'old' politics, and the understanding that the young activists have of them.

The first section starts with a description of the conceptual approach of different types of young political activists in the post-15M era in Lleida, Catalonia. Next, we analyse the participation of young political activists in both movements (i.e., PAH and White Tide), from December 2014 until summer of 2016, to establish some conclusions on youth political participation and its relation with other (older) actors in these movements.[4]

Youth Political Activism Post-15M: Three Types of Political Trajectories

Young people have been identified as the protagonists and instigators in many of the movements that were born in 2011, such as the Arab Spring, 15M and Occupy Wall Street (Castells, 2012; Feixa & Nofre, 2013; Martí Puig, 2012). Together with their occupation of central urban spaces, young people revised their ways of doing politics at a time of 'structural crisis' and government-sponsored austerity measures. In this context, young people who were being labelled as not interested in traditional politics by the power elites (Feixa & Nofre, 2013; Navarrete, 2011) took over the public arena of politics. In doing so, they reaffirmed the need to do politics in a more direct, active and engaged manner. This approach departed from the more conventional representative democracy model and allowed space for what Rosanvallon (2008) called "mutations of democracy." This idea seems to apply well to what is considered as 'being political' and what young people understood as 'doing politics.' This distinction was based in part on the way that some young people began to engage in non-institutional spaces. It was a distinction already evident in movements like 15M, reflecting the desire of some young people to find new spaces of political participation.[5] There was also a new way of understanding politics, in which political parties, unions and other institutional channels were rejected by young people. Meanwhile, new kinds of political agencies and ways of participation emerged, creating new politicised spaces and networks (Kriger, 2016).

The Los Indignados movement evolved as a result of the formation of new groups, like 'the Tides' (which favoured public services) and the territorialisation of the protest through neighbourhood assemblies. This fast-moving evolutionary process affected our research. At the start of our fieldwork, it was difficult for us to know whether the young people involved in 15M were now participating in these post-15M movements. Many of them were no longer present in the new political spaces, and the demobilisation and their absence in the public space was increasingly tangible.

However, the participant observation and the first interviews that we conducted in December 2014 suggested the value of a provisional heuristic distinguishing between three types of political trajectories in the development of post-15M activism. This heuristic is based on the conceptual models developed by della Porta and Diani (2006) to describe the evolution of social movements.[6] We use three categories—namely, demobilisation, institutionalisation and re-politicisation—to describe the political trajectory of the young people that we interviewed.

First, we can observe a degree of demobilisation. Some of the activists who were highly engaged during the 15M are now (at the time of writing early 2017) decreasing their activity in the post-15M movements (like PAH and White Tide). That said, their demobilisation was not complete. Many of those who were politically active in the Los Indignados movement were still casual participants in demonstrations and actions. We can affirm that the less-mobilised young people are those who experienced the 15M as a personal political initiation, as a historical moment in which they would obtain all the changes they were demanding. The political activity of these young people, who were often highly engaged during the camps, assembly discussions and other forms of participation, was relegated to an ad hoc participation after this main period of protest.

Second, some of the older activists, generally people in their thirties and beyond, were clearly committed to the institutional route as the space to fight for their rights. It is worth noting that when this data was being collected (2014–2016), the Spanish political electoral scene was marked by an increase of new political parties, who claimed to be the heirs of the Los Indignados movement, *Podemos* being their greatest exponent (Subirats,

2015; Tugas, 2014).[7] During that period, which was marked by four elections (a local election, an autonomous community election and two general elections), the political demands for institutional change increased and many of those activists who were part of movements and parties at the same time, devoted a great deal of energy to the preparation of the different election campaigns. According to our explanatory categorisation, this is the group of 'institutionalised' activists.

Finally, the special focus of our analysis of the two movements is the 're-politicised' group, in the sense of increased politicisation. As we have argued, the 15M triggered an increase in participation and adhesion to more politically active groups, usually with political positions close to Anarchism, Communism or the Catalan left-wing independence movements. This was the case both for those who were not politically active, as well as for those who had had some previous experience. This group is central to our analysis because of their increased non-institutional political participation, as well as their involvement in these two movements and because of the consequences that participation had for these movements. It should be added, that this category does not necessarily capture the whole gamut of possibilities and so is best regarded as a provisional type.

The need to understand the militant experience of young people in this last 'group' is fundamental if we are to observe the internal evolution that movements undergo. To develop this understanding, we have drawn on the theoretical contributions of Matonti and Poupeau (2004) and their notion of 'militant capital.' This kind of capital is accumulated in the course of their experiences and knowledge in sites of struggle and militancy. Their oratory and the degree of skilled involvement in political groups are also important. Using this framework, we will see how (re)politicised young people occupy protagonist spaces in the two movements that are analysed, based on their involvement and experience, as well as the roles that the members had already played in their groups. Applying the idea of militant capital in the micro-analysis of the evolution of social movements also allows for the use of different theoretical perspectives, such as 'leadership(s),' normalisation and disciplinary arrangements (Foucault, 2012), as well as the political field and its internal struggles between what he calls 'professionals' and 'profanes' (Bourdieu, 2000). This points to the role of unequal internal relations and the implications for the participation of politicised youth with a high militant capital for the movement itself.

The Platform for People Affected by Mortgages: A New Distribution of Power?

After the creation of the PAH, there were two clearly visible political phases in Lleida, determining a new political course as a result of structural and symbolic change within the movement. When the PAH was established in Lleida after the 15M, it was organised around a spokesperson who acted as the representative figure of the movement and of those the movement helps, establishing relationships with the Spanish political institutions, the media and the banks. Edgar,[8] the person in this 'position,' played a significant role in shaping the movement's evolution because of his participation in earlier movements and his ability to speak and communicate well in public. He was seen as someone with great 'leadership' skills who took the lead given to him by the assembly itself in making decisions and in setting the movement's political trajectory. He was also seen as someone embodying a certain kind of reformist politics. He stayed as spokesperson for more than two years. During this period, the participation of (re)politicised young people was intermittent. Young people may have felt attracted to the movement but, at the same time, they distanced themselves from it. Many seemed uncomfortable with the way the movement functioned. For example, Pedro, a 27-year-old man who had been active in 15M and who is now an activist in the Communist group, summarises it as follows: "I got myself into the PAH […] four years ago and I left because 'X' was there. […] What I saw there was more than I could take, and, I don't know, I suggested things and they always […] I don't know, they called the shots."[9]

While all disagreements were settled by the spokesperson, young people only participated sporadically. They attended actions like demonstrations to stop an eviction, but did not get too deeply involved with the movement's internal functioning or the decision-making. In this process, which ran from the end of the 15M in 2011 to mid-2014, different young people belonging to various political groups joined and then left the movement for similar reasons. Through this first phase, the movement's commitment to a reformist politics and a willingness to negotiate, as well as its organisational format with a leader who acted as spokesperson, seemed to have ensured that the young (re)politicised people's participation remained sporadic and unsteady.

The second stage began when the spokesperson quit the movement. In mid-2014, the spokesperson decided to join an established left-wing green political party in the city ('*Iniciativa per Catalunya els Verds*'). During a long-drawn-out process accompanied by a lot of internal debate about the possibility of the PAH being swallowed up by this party, he decided to resign and headed the list of candidates for the '*Iniciativa per Catalunya els Verds*' party in the 2015 municipal elections. Consequently, the PAH experienced some upheaval, with different spokespersons being appointed, all trusted by the previous spokesperson and all of whom represented the same kinds of political styles and position. This situation triggered increasing unrest within the movement's assembly. Ultimately, the assembly decided to abolish the position of spokesperson, and instead let the assembly itself and the affected people become their own representatives. This process, which stressed equality of function and public representation, is similar to that adopted by the political groups associated with the Los Indignados movement.

This commitment to sharing power among the different actors within the assembly involved the internal mobilisation of all the participants, as well as their relocation within the movement. It was this process of internal change that enabled (re)politicised young people to see an opportunity to participate in the PAH again. Joining forces with different groups, young people became actively involved and took on a more active role. This was the case with Pedro, who explained: "we persuaded the libertarians to get involved […], I wish others would join too, I don't know, people from Arran [group of left wing, independent young people] […] The more of us wanting to go a step further than the [PAH] suggests the better."[10] Young people wanted not just to participate in this movement, but to also change the very movement itself. For this reason, they sought to increase political pressure, to make significant changes in the mortgage and housing system, to expand the movement's political discourse by increasing the numbers of participants, to intensify the nature of political action, and to put the right to housing before the rights of property owners.

This power struggle entailed the emergence of at least three groups within the PAH. The first were the young politicised activists who rapidly affiliated with those affected by the threat of eviction or with the most difficult cases. This fostered a significant change in the extension of their actions, leading to deep conflicts with authorities and banks. Among the changes in their actions, we find: an increase in the occupation of banks, an increase in the length of occupations, the search for collective solutions to specific cases, an increase in nightly actions (e.g., the sticking up of posters, the covering bank branches in paper, etc.) and an increase in the methods of pacifist resistance during actions. This hard-line provoked repressive measures that were directed at the PAH movement by political authorities, police forces and the media. We saw a variety of derogatory labels typically applied to groups that the hegemonic interests want to criminalise; for example, the movement was identified as 'radicals,' 'anti-establishment groups,' 'anarchists' and 'violent.' A direct consequence of these actions was the 'group' trials where PAH members found themselves in court facing 'occupation charges.' These events encouraged the debate within the PAH about whether it should return to the previous strategy (i.e., reformist and more conciliatory).

This episode allows us to introduce the second group of activists, who persisted by using a more conciliatory approach when dealing with banks and institutions and maintaining positive public opinion. This group was committed to fostering more State control over the housing rental market and finding a solution to the national mortgage crisis by implementing a Deed of Assignment in Payment (*Dación en pago*). Some people in this group started to raise questions about the violence and radicalism of actions promoted by more radical members of the movement.

A third group in the PAH movement was much more ideologically heterogeneous than these other two groups. It was made up of people who were not clearly in either of these two groups. During the ethnographic fieldwork, we met activists who floated between the two strategic orientations for a variety of reasons, including fear of repression. For example, they might have been outside the courthouse in solidarity with those being tried, but they did not take part in the occupation of a bank, which was the reason why the others were taken to court.

In this sense, Brubaker and Cooper (2000), talk about 'identifications' rather than 'identities' because this allows us to see how a person can identify with a group without becoming a part of that group while also treating groups as non-hermetic entities in constant evolution. We see in the movements that we have examined the salience of identifications serving as a mechanism of unity. At the same time, we also see in these movements a case of 'diffused' borders characterised by highly permeable barrier between groups in which actors may change groups at any given time depending on circumstances (Barth, 1969). The 'intermediate' group (i.e., the third group) seems to be a good example of both ideas because people hopped between groups, with plenty of short-term comings and goings.

At the same time, there is a tipping point, which comes as a consequence of both an increase in the number of political actions as well as the condemnation of their actions by governments and conventional institutions, and the judicial consequences. This is the point made by Turner (1986), a political anthropologist, who suggests that we often see in political processes a 'social drama,' which requires that different actors adopt a stance towards a new political reality. In this case, we see (re)politicised young people, together with those most active people in the movement, accumulating a lot of political capital within the assembly due to their high level of involvement, participation and discursive skills. This group of activists were committed to achieving political supremacy in the movement. Simultaneously, the more marginal and less skilled members of the second group found themselves more 'alone' in the assemblies. Confronted in a more or less direct way with the more confident and articulate members, they gradually abandoned the movement.

The White Tide: Leadership and Accumulation of Power

The White Tide in Lleida, like the PAH, was created by a group working on health issues in the town square that had also been once occupied by the 15M movement. After being evicted from the square, the movement took a new and autonomous course, joining health system workers and users to undo some of the austerity measures implemented by the Spanish government in the health system after 2008–2009. The profile of the participants was (and remains) different to the PAH. The age profile of White Tide is older: many of them are workers over forty years of age, many of whom have participated actively in labour unions and in traditional political parties, but there are also some young participants in their twenties and thirties. However, the organisation of White Tide replicates the structure of the Los Indignados movement. The assembly of White Tide is the decision-making authority; its format is designed to keep the organisation horizontal, participatory and egalitarian.

That said, like PAH, the participants in the White Tide have either brought in or developed different degrees of political capital in the movement. Those who get more involved, participate more or have more knowledge tend to be more active protagonists in the assemblies, positioning themselves as unacknowledged but recognisable leaders. Like 15M, the White Tide movement's political discourse and its actions are nonviolent. They are based on the principle that nothing they do should be interpreted in ways that that would weaken the support they get from citizens.

Participation by politicised young people in a movement dominated by older people, many of them with trade union backgrounds and a more reformist orientation, has also been, and still is, intermittent. While its political rationale is attractive to young people, participation seems to be difficult due to the reformist strategy and style. Most of the young people involved in White Tide have a loose attachment with this movement and tend to participate only in mass actions.

However, during the period that coincided with the expansion of youth participation in the PAH, members of a young Communist group attempted to approach the other movements in the city in a coordinated manner. The idea was always the same: to try to push them to go 'a step beyond' what they were doing. In the case of White Tide, this occurred when two young people began suddenly to attend all the assemblies and actions. At first, these young people simply listened to what the most active members (or 'leaders') had to say. Afterwards, they began to participate more actively when some of the habitual leaders happened to miss an assembly. In a more or less direct way, they promoted ideas about actions that would present a more politicised discourse and that ultimately sought to expose the capitalist basis of all the problems that the movement was addressing. Disagreements with some other members, especially older ones, started to become more visible and increased as the days went by.

The point when this process became impossible to ignore came during one of the assemblies, immediately prior to the demonstration of 1 May. The assembly debate was about which demonstration their movement should join: the one with the institutional unions or the 'anti-capitalist' one. There was a thorough debate, which was dominated by the issue that taking up an openly anti-capitalist stance might lead to a loss of popular support the citizens, who might see the movement as too radical or potentially dangerous. The two young people made their position clear during the debate, actively seeking to intensify the anti-capitalist stance. However, some other leading members positioned themselves against these lines very quickly. Most of the assembly supported these leading members and set aside the ideas that the two young people had put forward. Finally, it was agreed to support both demonstrations, but not to make their support visible during the demonstration, assuming that every person could participate on an individual basis.

This key moment allows us to see how parallel processes within these movements (i.e., the White Tide and the PAH) had a completely different outcome.

In the White Tide, the deployment of political capital by actors who had been present from the beginning of the movement led to increasing disaffection on the part of the highly politicised young people, who saw how their contributions were being side-lined, encouraging greater confrontation between the two 'groups.' The young people, who received the support of other young people in the movement, gradually left the movement and stopped attending the assemblies. Identifications between the older members, which had happened before the movement's creation, and the accumulation of power by some of them did not enable the kind of political course that the young activists wanted. In this case, once the Labour Day demonstration was over, these young activists, simply stopped attending the movement's meetings, limiting their participation to occasional actions and mass mobilisations, just as had been happening at the start of White Tide.

We can conclude that the presence and deployment of political capital among the older and more active members of the White Tide prevented the young and radical people from promoting their political goals or the transformations they were proposing. The core group of older participants at the heart of the White Tide movement, consolidated during the time after the 15M, saw these young people as a threat to the operation of the movement. It was not surprising, perhaps, that the young politicised people saw their involvement in this movement becoming increasingly difficult and quickly marginalised.

Conclusion. Beyond 15M: Power, Normalisation and Generational Conflict

Our exploration of the way in which power relations operate in both the PAH and White Tide provides us with new qualitative data for a better understanding about the unequal participation of (re)politicised young people within the post-15M groups in Lleida. We focussed on the divergences between different correlations of political capital at work in the PAH and the White Tide. While the PAH experienced some dramatic changes in the distribution of power after the founding 'leader' stepped down from the leadership position, attempts by young activists to change the way that the White Tide was operating were thwarted by the strong leadership of the older activists.

The fieldwork that we conducted permitted us to observe and examine the different relations that (re)politicised young people established in both movements. In the PAH, specific spaces were created to allow the participation of (re)politicised young people. This meant that over time they played a part in changing the strategic direction of the movement itself. However, in the White Tide movement, the model of political action and dynamics, which had been laid down by the older leadership, meant that young people could not get as much political traction. They felt that the White Tide was operating in the same way as 'old' institutionalised forms of politics.

The PAH and White Tide are political micro spaces where the generational struggle emerges in a very visible manner. In this sense, political discourses, the organisation and re-positioning of a range of internal groups of activists in these movements, together with the idea of a certain degree of 'normalisation,' appear to be fundamental to understanding the generational struggle at play in these movements. As Foucault states:

> Disciplinary normalization consists first of all in positing a model, an optimal model that is constructed in terms of a certain result, and the operation of disciplinary normalization consists in trying to get people, movements, and actions to conform to this model. (Foucault, 2006, p. 75)

In this sense, both the PAH and White Tide have actors and internal groups that seek 'political correctness' or 'good activism.' In the PAH, the various groups of activists exhibit the normalisation of the 'good activist' as the axis around which internal conflict revolves. The seizure of power by the young (re)politicised people in the PAH reveals the possibility of rebelling against the normalisation. That is clear when we see their reactions towards politically institutionalised, 'politically correct' or reformist forms of action. This process was not observed in White Tide due to the strong accumulation of political capital by older members with plenty of experience in reformist politics. Even though space was provided for young people to make their case in the assemblies of White Tide, there was no space for successful rebellion by them.

The social and economic crises that emerged in 2008 displayed an important fracture in contemporary institutional politics. In part, this is a consequence of the ways in which some young people are claiming more space for political action and engagement. Their claim for more direct involvement in decision making by citizens points to a significant generation gap. The generational gaps that appeared within post-15M political activism that we explored here can be seen as two different ways of conceiving political justification and legitimation, as well as the different understanding by each of the groups of what 'doing politics' is or, ultimately, what 'doing new politics' means.

As mentioned above, Bourdieu (2000) analyses internal conflicts in the political field, coming to a distinction between 'professionals' and 'profanes.' This distinction might also help us to understand the different kinds of politics at play in the PAH and White Tide. In these groups, we observed two different types of activism that struggled to establish their own understanding of mobilisation and their struggle (or lack of it). The rejection by the leadership of the White Tide of the (re)politicised young people looks like an entirely predictable response by what Bourdieu (2000) calls professional politicians. Equally, we can observe how the young radicals were profanes, opting for direct and politically 'incorrect' forms of struggle and direct mobilisation. Doubtless, there are other ways of making sense of this. However, what cannot be doubted is that the generational conflict and conflict in and between competing political actions and discourses that today characterise political activism in Lleida (Catalonia) are unlikely to go away.

Notes

1. Lleida is a city with 138,542 inhabitants (Instituto Nacional de Estadística [INE], 2016). It is one of four provincial capitals in Catalonia. Catalonia is one of the 17 autonomous communities in Spain. Autonomous communities are geopolitical entities akin to German Lander or states in the United States of America. There are political differences between Catalonia and the rest of Spain, which are worth highlighting. First, the *Partido Popular*, the conservative party in government in Spain since late 2011, has been relegated to sixth place in local Catalan elections. Second, a transversal pro-Catalan independence movement has gained strength since 2012. Third, there are strong anarchist roots in the political struggles that have taken place in Catalonia since the early 1920s. This has created a very particular understanding of protest and political organisation in social movements.
2. We refer to the movements and groups that emerged around the 15M (15 May) protests taking place across Spain from 2011 onwards, also called the 'Indignant Movement' ('*los Indignados*'). Mansilla (2015) introduced the concept of 'post-15M, to define this new stage of mobilisation. Young

people were the main protagonists in the camping out throughout Spain (as part of the movement), but they were not the only ones.
3. The analysis that follows is based on the application of ethnographical techniques for the drawing up of a monograph on political activism among young people in the city of Lleida. The fieldwork lasted over a year, starting in late-2014 and going on until mid-2016, when there was a progressive, although not definitive distancing from the field of study. This fieldwork is part of Eduard Ballesté Isern's doctoral thesis work, which has the provisional title 'Social movements, youth, power and politics in Lleida.'
4. This study is part of the research project GENIND (2013–2015). *The Indignant Generation. Space, Power and Culture in Youth Movements in 2011: A Transnational Perspective*. Ministry of Economy, Industry and Competitiveness (Spain). VI National Scientific Research, Development and Technological Innovation Plan. [CSO2012-34415].
5. Although the so-called Arab Springs had different trigger factors and took place within dictatorial power structures, the presence of young people from lower social classes without a political affiliation was a surprise for political analysts, who expected a political explosion led by the 'usual suspects,' that is: the Islamists and the defenders of human rights. What the young protagonists of the Tunis, Cairo and Sana uprisings share with their Western homologues is a lack of interest in politics in the years before the uprisings (Alwazir, 2012; Sánchez García, 2015).
6. The authors have analysed the different evolutions undergone by social movements, especially after their interlocution (or lack of it) with the State and the powers that be. Therefore, they talk about demobilisation (or process of "death" of the movement), institutionalisation (or assumption of some of their demands by the State mechanisms), and radicalisation (or increase in political demands), among other examples, such as commercialisation.
7. Other political groups also appeared, such as municipal election candidate lists based on the coming together of new, disparate left groups and the traditional left-wing parties.
8. All names of the interviewees have been changed to protect confidentiality.
9. Interview carried out on 9 May 2015.
10. Interview carried out on 9 May 2015.

References

Alwazir, A. Z. (2012, December). Youth inclusion in Yemen: A necessary element for success of political transition (Arab Reform Brief, No. 64). *Arab Reform Initiative*. Retrieved November 30, 2016, from http://www.arab-reform.net/en/node/452

Barth, F. (1969). *Ethnic groups and boundaries*. Oslo: Universitetsforlaget.
Bourdieu, P. (2000). *Poder, derecho y clases sociales* (A. García Inda, Trans.). Bilbao: Editorial Desclée de Brouwer.
Brubaker, R., & Cooper, F. (2000). Beyond identity. *Theory and Society, 29*(1), 1–47.
Castells, M. (2012). *Networks of outrage and hope: Social movements in the internet age*. Cambridge: Polity Press.
Colau, A., & Alemany, A. (2013). *¡Sí se puede! Crónica de una pequeña gran victoria*. Barcelona: Ediciones Destino.
della Porta, D., & Diani, M. (2006). *Social movements: An introduction*. Oxford: Blackwell.
Feixa, C., & Nofre, J. (2013). *#GeneraciónIndignada. Topías y utopías del 15M*. Lleida: Editorial Milenio.
Foucault, M. (2006). *Seguridad, territorio y población: Curso en el Collège de France: 1977–1978* (H. Pons, Trans.). Buenos Aires: Fondo de Cultura Económica.
Foucault, M. (2012). *Un diálogo sobre el poder y otras conversaciones* (M. Morey, Trans.). Madrid: Alianza Editorial.
GENIND. (2013–2015). *The Indignant Generation. Space, power and culture in youth movements in 2011: A transnational perspective*. VI National Scientific Research, Development and Technological Innovation Plan, Ministry of Economy, Industry and Competiveness, Spain. [CSO2012-34415].
Instituto Nacional de Estadística. (2016). Demografía y población. Retrieved from http://www.ine.es
Kriger, M. (2016). *La tercera invención de la juventud. Dinámicas de la politización juvenil en tiempos de la reconstrucción del Estado-Nación (Argentina, 2002–2015)*. Ciudad Autónoma de Buenos Aires: Grupo Editor Universitario.
Mansilla, J. A. (2015). Movimientos sociales y apropiaciones colectivas en la Barcelona post-15M: El papel de la Assemblea Social del Poblenou. *Etnográfica, 19*(1), 77–97. Retrieved November 30, 2016, from https://etnografica.revues.org/3909
Martí Puig, S. (2012). 15-M: The Indignados. In J. Byrne (Ed.), *The Occupy handbook*. London: Back Bay.
Matonti, F., & Poupeau, F. (2004). Le capital militant. Essai de définition. *Actes de la Recherche en Sciences Sociales, 155*, 4–11.
Navarrete, L. (2011). *Desmontando a ni-ni. Un estereotipo juvenil en tiempos de crisis*. Madrid: Injuve.
Rosanvallon, P. (2008). *Counter-democracy: Politics in an age of distrust* (A. Goldhammer, Trans.). Cambridge: Cambridge University Press.
Sánchez García, J. (2015). La revolución contra los jóvenes. Movimientos políticos juveniles y producciones discursivas en la insurrección egipcia. In J. M. Valenzuela (Coord.) (Ed.), *El sistema es antinosotros. Culturas, movimientos y resistencias juveniles*. México: Gedisa.

Subirats, J. (2015). Todo se mueve. Acción colectiva, acción conectiva. Movimientos, partidos e instituciones. *Revista Española de Sociología, 24,* 123–131. Retrieved November 29, 2016, from http://www.fes-sociologia.com/uploads/public/RES/09.pdf

Tugas, R. (2014). *Escac al poder. L'auge de l'esquerra alternativa.* Barcelona: Deu i onze editors.

Turner, V. (1986). *Del rito al teatro.* Bologna: Il Mulino.

Eduard Ballesté Isern is a PhD student at the University of Lleida, Catalonia, in the Department of Geography and Sociology. He is member of the Centre of Youth and Society Studies. His PhD examines social movements, youth and activism in Lleida after 15M. He works on youth involvement in politics and their relationship with social movements.

José Sánchez García is a Post-Doctoral researcher in the University of Lleida, Catalonia in the Centre of Youth and Society Studies. He holds a PhD in Social and Cultural Anthropology, and he works on youth religious music in Pakistanis collectives in Barcelona; gender identities in Gulf countries; youth political movements after 2011 in Spain and Egypt; and youth cultures in North Africa.

CHAPTER 19

New Modes of Youth Political Action and Democracy in the Americas: From the Chilean Spring to the Maple Spring in Quebec

Ricardo Peñafiel and Marie-Christine Doran

STUDENT PROTESTS IN THE AMERICAS

In the space of barely one year, the Americas experienced three major popular protest movements spearheaded by students. The first began in June 2011, in Chile, with a series of strikes and occupations at universities and secondary schools, leading into a six-month conflict, which spawned the largest social protest movement since the 1973 coup d'état (against Salvador Allende). A few months later, in February 2012, a movement that followed almost the same course as its 'southern twin' (Chile) erupted in Quebec (see Gallant, in this volume). Faced with the intransigence of governments refusing to

R. Peñafiel (✉)
Department of Political Science, Université du Québec à Montréal, Montreal, QC, Canada

M.-C. Doran
School of Political Studies, University of Ottawa, Ottawa, ON, Canada

© The Author(s) 2018
S. Pickard, J. Bessant (eds.), *Young People Re-Generating Politics in Times of Crises*, Palgrave Studies in Young People and Politics, DOI 10.1007/978-3-319-58250-4_19

recognise the representation of student organisations and the legitimacy of the street as a site of popular participation, these two conflicts in Chile and Quebec broadened and deepened, expanding beyond the strictly educational framework to encompass a broad spectrum of the general public in popular movements of transgressive contention (McAdam, Tarrow, & Tilly, 2001). Finally, to round off a year of student-led popular revolts, in May 2012, the "#*Yosoy132*" (I'm 132) movement erupted in Mexico to denounce the "mass manipulation" and collusion between politicians and giant media corporations; and to demand a "free, reasoned and informed" vote.

The main protagonists of these historically large actions were young people. This contrasts markedly with the findings of certain sociological studies on the political disaffection of young people (Baril, 2012; Fernández, 2000), the alleged narcissism and individualism of the so called 'Generation Y' (Twenge, 2014) and claims of declining social capital (Putnam, 1995; Sander & Putnam, 2010). Far from being apathetic or depoliticised, Chilean, Quebec and Mexican young people have refused to play the part (Amossy, 2010) of individuals investing in only their own future or of consumers of 'manufactured consent.' Instead, they succeeded in becoming unavoidable political actors stepping into a public space from where they were excluded. As such, their political participation is all the more significant because they had to fight smear campaigns and criminalisation of their actions (Dupuis-Déri, 2014; Véjar, 2012) by governments and medias, the general public and even part of the academic community.

Through a comparative analysis of the Chilean and Quebec cases with some references to the Mexican case, this chapter looks at how young people have been able to overcome the stigmas of violence, political apathy and individualism by using new information and communication technologies (NICT). Thus, they have created innovative forms of presence in the public space such as political flashmobs or spontaneous digital-based manifestations, including the use of friendly huge mascots that cuddle demonstrators to counteract the violent image of young people constructed by the media. Instead of resulting in the marginalisation of these movements, the criminalisation of students and the "disrespect" (Honneth, 2006) shown towards them by the State and media fuelled new forms of political subjectivation based on the sense of a "shared fundamental wrong" (*mise en commun d'un tort fondamental*) (Peñafiel, 2014; Rancière, 1995, pp. 41–68). Yet, even though these protest movements may appear to be solely reactions to neoliberal austerity measures in the midst of economic crisis, there main interest is to challenge the hegemony of restricted forms of representative government, as we shall see through the compared analysis of Chile.

In this chapter, we start by giving an analytical account of the Chilean and Maple Springs, in light of the ways governments and mass media have discredited student and young people's actions and proceeded to criminalise them both by discourses and legislative measures. The chapter then establishes and explains the inventive responses of students to this accusation of violence and the innovative use of new information and communication technologies (NICT) and add the Mexican example of the student-led pro-democracy movement "I'm 132" (*Yo soy 132*). Next the chapter addresses the 'struggle for democracy's meaning' and civil liberties at play between the students' actions and the declarations of governments, the latter defending a clearly restrictive view of representative democracy. The last part of the chapter contends that these struggles for the meaning and the innovative actions of the students defending their freedom of expression and non-violent features of their movements present characteristics of isonomy and a desire to fully participate in democratic deliberation and decision. This leads to the effects of these movements in terms of youth politics contribution to democracy.

Denigrating and Criminalising Youth Political Participation

The Chilean Case

At the beginning, it was nothing more than a very ordinary student strike. After having exhausted all possible legal recourse and redoubled their public denunciations, 6,000 students at the Central University of Chile (UCEN) declared an unlimited general strike on 4 April 2011 to denounce the takeover of their university by *Norte Sur S.A*. This group of private investors was profiting from education, even though such action is prohibited by the Organic Constitutional Law on Teaching (LOCE). This otherwise neoliberal law enacted under the Pinochet dictatorship to perpetuate (lock-in) the privatisation of higher education, nonetheless stipulates that private universities must remain non-profit institutions. The takeover of UCEN by private investors, in flagrant violation of the law, did not appear to disturb the Minister of Education of the time, Joaquín Lavín, who saw no more than a simple "conflict between individuals" in the situation.

This trivialisation of the violation of the law by the Minister of Education himself doubtlessly explains why this clause on the non-profit nature of educational institutions was circumvented by numerous universities—in which many left-wing and right-wing politicians have interests.

Starting with this first strike at UCEN, the general slogan "*no al lucro*" (no to profit) rapidly spread; by mid-April, all Chilean university students were mobilising around the calls issued by the Confederation of Students of Chile (*Confech*).[1] Instead of limiting themselves to a denunciation of the systematic violation of the LOCE, the movement broadened its demands to decry the commodification of education and to demand the democratisation of university management, increased public funding for higher education, and a series of measures aimed at fighting the "social segregation" reproduced and worsened by the education system.[2] The broadening of the conflict to the entire university sector reflected the systemic nature of the problem. The Minister of Education nevertheless persisted in disregarding the students, not considering them worthy interlocutors:

> They don't even have votes in ballot boxes, just cries in the street. No modern democracy debates these questions with students; these are important national debates on which we must confer in Congress. The question of education will be determined through extensive discussion in parliament. That is the place in which all visions must be brought forward and transversal agreements reached. (Joaquín Lavín, quoted in *La Tercera*, 28 June 2011)

This denial of students' status as counterparts and the government's refusal to recognise the street as a legitimate space for democratic expression pushed the struggle into increasingly higher levels of 'radicalism,' mass organising and creativity. By blocking the channels through which demands could be delivered, the government paradoxically enabled the expression of much deeper and more general criticisms, 'unspeakable' in an institutional framework of pacified conflict management.

Thus, on 1 June 2011, following *Confech*'s call to a "general strike and protest," university students were joined by secondary students and were supported by the National Public Service Union (ANEF), the Teaching College, as well as several rectors of so-called 'traditional' universities (preceding the dictatorship). By 3 June, there were 17 traditional universities on strike or occupied by students, camping there day and night and provided for by the population. Four days later, there were 20, while three new secondary schools joined six others who were already occupied. The following week, with more than 300 educational institutions on strike and occupied, protests surpassed 100,000 people in Santiago and 200,000 across the country (Véjar, 2012, p. 14). The number of schools and universities under occupation increased until it reached 1,556 on 28 July. The protests also grew, in numbers and frequency, mobilising hundreds of thousands of people, far beyond educational circles, on a quasi-weekly basis between June and November. They achieved historic records of 400,000 on 30 June, 500,000 on 21 August, 300,000 on 25 August, and 300,000 on 19 October 2011 (Véjar, 2012). Beyond the creativity and the diversification of forms of protest, which will be analysed below, the most striking aspect of the movement was the plethora of new sectors participating. These included the Unitary Confederation of Labor (CUT), teachers, public service workers, copper workers, and workers from many other unions, parents' associations, the mayors of some cities, *pobladores*[3] organisations, and more.

In addition to confronting the root of the crisis in Chilean education by demanding "free, quality, public education," the movement became what Ernesto Laclau (1996) called an "empty signifier" (Peñafiel, 2012). That is, it no longer solely reflected specifically student demands but 'signified' or federated a series of much broader demands and aspirations: for example, "fiscal reform"; "renationalisation of copper" and "nationalisation of natural resources"[4]; "binding popular plebiscites"; "Popular Constituent Assembly," recovery of memory and justice, etc. It is noteworthy that the three main claims of the movement became central themes of the 2014 campaign of President Michelle Bachelet, namely free higher education, as well as fiscal and Constitutional reform.[5]

Despite this tremendous popular success, the government's refusal to recognise the Chilean student movement was compounded by intense repression, including numerous cases of torture and human rights violation by security forces and a process of criminalisation of collective action that directly attacked the legitimacy of rights otherwise officially recognised by the Chilean democracy. As we will detail later in this chapter, "criminalisation of protest is a distinct and specific form of retrenching on acknowledged civil and political rights, rendering them synonymous to criminal behaviour that must be sanctioned legally and tolerates [abusive behaviour from state agents] towards citizens that are viewed as enemies in this new configuration where the struggle for the definition of democracy lies at heart" (Doran, 2017).

While legally recognised and historically confirmed by all governments that negotiated the ends of strikes with them before this moment, student associations in Chile have been treated as irrelevant and violent. However, this situation is certainly not unique to the Chilean case, as we will now see through a brief account of Quebec's Maple Spring, and references to Mexico's student movement '*Yo soy 132*.'

The Quebec Case

One might think that the criminalisation of collective action is unique to post-dictatorships like Chile. However, the same phenomenon occurred in one of the most stable liberal democracies in the world: Canada. It could even be argued that the repression was more massive in Quebec than in Chile. In similar conflicts, there were more than 3,500 arrests in Quebec (Lemonde, Bourbeau, Fortin, Joly, & Poisson, 2014) compared to 1,556 in Chile (Véjar, 2012). However, it would be unfair to draw such a conclusion insofar as the criminal justice systems of the two societies differ. In Chile, for example, 14,000 persons were taken in and questioned without being officially arrested. In any case, disproportionate repression was used against young people in both situations and, at least in Quebec, on an unprecedented scale. Numerous jurists and specialists believe the repression of the Maple Spring 2012 marked a turning point in the attitude of political authorities towards social mobilisation in Quebec (Lemonde et al., 2014; *Commission spéciale d'examen des événements du printemps 2012*, 2014; *Ligue des droits et libertés* et al., 2013). Political violence specialist Dupuis-Déri (2013) did not hesitate to rename the Maple Spring as the 'Truncheon Spring' (*Printemps de la matraque*).

The largest wave of mass arrests prior to this took place during the October crisis (1970), when Prime Minister Pierre Elliott Trudeau imposed the *War Measures Act* (Legislature of Canada, 1914) in the face of armed actions by the FLQ (*Front de libération du Québec*). The public order forces made 497 arrests. However, in a single night, on 23 May, with no terrorist threat or state of emergency to legitimise their action, the police arrested 518 people in Montreal and 176 in Quebec City, encircling them in a kettle (*souricière*) (Pickard, 2014). The majority of people arrested that night were not students but citizens protesting against the Law 12 (also known as Bill 78), which prohibited gatherings of more than 50 people. As in Chile, after several months of protests—including new, playful forms of demonstrations and the use of NICT (Peñafiel, 2016)—, the student strike movement broadened into a popular struggle. To adopt the slogans of the two movements: "A struggle for the entire society" (*La lucha es de la sociedad entera*); "Student strike, popular struggle!" (*La grève est étudiante, la lutte est populaire*).

At the beginning, however, the Quebec Spring was also no more than a simple student strike; something that Quebec had experienced dozens of times in the past without its ever having degenerated into a crisis. Student organisations opposed the 75% tuition increase—CAD$1,625 over five years—announced by the government. In accordance with practice dating back to the first student strikes in Quebec in the 1960s (Lacoursière, 2007) and also with the *Act respecting the accreditation and financing of students' associations* (Legislature of Québec, 1983), students pass strike resolutions in General Assemblies. Between 7 February and 5 March 2012, 123,000 students had a strike mandate. The more combative groups organised symbolic direct actions, such as blocking the Stock Exchange and banks, to raise public awareness about their struggle and denounce the social inequalities of the government decisions. However, the government firmly held to its refusal to negotiate, arguing that it had already taken its decision and that everyone had to pay their "fair share" for education and public finances (Richer, 2012).

On 22 March 2012, with more than 302,652 students on strike (Savard & Cyr, 2014, p. 67)—representing three quarters of the post-secondary students of Quebec—, they organised one of the largest political demonstrations in the history of Quebec, bringing almost 200,000 people onto the streets of Montreal (Lachapelle, 2012). Despite the historic scale of the demonstration and number of student organisations on strike, the government still refused to negotiate. It deployed two contradictory lines of argument: the first portrayed students as "spoiled kids" refusing to pay their fair share in an "investment" which would later earn them good salaries[6]; and the second sought to divide the movement by refusing to negotiate with the more radical CLASSE (acronym for *Coalition large de l'Association pour une solidarité syndicale étudiante* [Coalition of the association for student union solidarity], which amassed 50% of the students on strike), by accusing them of violence and intimidation.

It was not until April 2012, after 10 weeks of conflict, that the government made the first offers. These were considered insufficient by all the student organisations, which maintained their unlimited general strike. As students persisted, despite the slander and mass repression, a phenomenon of judicialization of the conflict emerged. Injunctions began to be mass-produced, especially by the head of the Quebec Superior Court, François Rolland. These injunctions denied the right of students of association and ordered an immediate return to class. Between 30 March and 18 May 2012, almost 50 injunctions or interim/safeguard orders were issued by Quebec's courts (Lemonde et al., 2014, p. 297). In reality, and despite the charges of contempt of court brought against some individuals, these injunctions could not be executed because of the solidarity of professors, students from other institutions, and civil society who organised pickets of hundreds of people in front of the targeted colleges and universities. However, this tactic helped increase the level of physical confrontation between the strikers and security forces and thus the image of violence, intimidation and illegality that the government sought to lend the strike. The government claimed that it was not a student strike, but an individual "boycott" which did not give participants any right to stop other students from going to their courses.

On this basis, on 18 May 2012, the Quebec National Assembly passed, 68 votes for and 48 against, *An Act to enable students to receive instruction from the postsecondary institutions they attend* (Legislature of Quebec, 2012), better known as Law 12, the "Special Law" (*la loi spéciale* or Bill 78). This 'emergency' law restricted gatherings to 50 people and prohibited rallies within 50 metres of educational institutions for one year. It also forced teachers to give their classes independently of the number of students present. Unions and student organisations were required to take all means to ensure that their members did not contravene its requirements, on pain of having their union dues suspended from a trimester for each day of infraction and fines of CAD$25,000 to $125,000 per day per organisation.

Far from dampening the movement (that had already multiplied its means of action by calling, via social networks, for daily night marches, festive and carnival actions, and diverse art projects), the adoption of the 'Special Law' (Law 12) generated a vast popular protest movement of '*casseroles*' (clanging on pots). The same day the law was passed, a Facebook event started by a college professor called on the public in the following terms:

> Every night, at 8pm, for 15 minutes, arm yourself with a pot or any other object capable of making noise and bang on it with all the rage this special law has created in you! / When the Chilean dictatorship restricted unlawful

assemblies to any gathering of more than four people, the Chileans used these means to express their rage. Let's take our inspiration from them! / **If you are against this special law, make some noise! / Pots of Quebec, unite!** (Bold characters are from the original).

By the following day, tens of neighbourhood groups gathered spontaneously, independent of the students, summoning other neighbours with the sounds of pots. The next day, there were hundreds of those street corners spontaneous protestors banging on their pots; and the day after, processions of tens of thousands of people got under way and moved through Montreal to merge with the student night marches which had been taking place without interruption since 24 April. In a less spectacular way, '*casserole*' protests were also held in tens of other cities in the province, as well as in Canada and the rest of the world in solidarity with the Quebec movement.

In the end, the government had to cancel the winter session in order to prevent the students from striking. Elections were called in order to "settle the issue" and evicted the governing Liberal Party on behalf of the main opposition party, the Quebecois Party (*Parti Québécois PQ*). The newly elected PQ government proceeded to repeal the *Special law 12* and replaced the initially planned increase of 75% over five years on education fees with a 3% increase per year. Yet, the student conflict did not occupy much of the political debate. Its effects were to be found elsewhere, in the questioning of the limits of democratic participation.

In sum, while being officially legally recognised by all governments, student associations in Chile and Quebec have in recent years been subjected to a process of criminalisation due to the supposed violence and illegitimacy of their actions. By these means, authorities and mass media have criminalised the exercise of fundamental rights such as the right of association, expression and assembly, and denied the status of legitimate interlocutor to those wishing to participate democratically in political deliberation and decision-making. Criminalisation of collective action (Seoane, 2003; Svampa, 2009) is a distinctive and specific form of undercutting well-established or acknowledged civil and political rights, rendering them synonymous with criminal behaviour that must be sanctioned by law. By reducing democracy to a purely formal concept (free elections and pluralism) and de-legitimising all claim-based social conflict, minimalist versions and narrow approaches to democracy open the door to the state's criminalisation of collective action and social movements. That is, they welcome measures rendering practices—hitherto considered peaceful and legitimate—illegal and illegitimate.

This process of criminalisation has been discussed a lot in the context of social protest against natural resource-based industry (Delgado Ramos, 2012, p. 78), where the civil rights of citizens are pitted against a very thriving economic system. Generally, literature on the criminalisation of social movements describes the penalisation of poor and marginalised people, which signals the emergence of the *penal state* as a core feature of the global expansion of neoliberalism and the urban marginality produced by the neoliberal government (Müller, 2012). Yet, these cases of student protest show that these are not the only social conflicts in which the state responds by criminalising protest. In fact, the use of criminalisation extends beyond specifically economic conflict to any kind of social protest that risks exposing the limitations placed on democracy (Doran, 2017; FIDH (*Fédération internationale des ligues des droits de l'Homme*), 2011).

Overcoming Stigmatisation and Appropriating the Public Sphere: Innovative Actions in Chile, Quebec and Mexico

In spite of the major difficulties related to criminalisation, student movements in Chile and Quebec alike have succeeded in creating innovative forms of expression and public participation in which young people have challenged representations of them as violent, presenting themselves as legitimate counterparts or political agonistic adversaries (Mouffe, 2002) in the conflict with the governments and its supporters. From mass demonstrations and occupations to Facebook events, from sectorial and social strikes to flash-mobs, from temporary blockades of bridges to *funas*[7] and *caceroleos*,[8] (pot clanging concert demonstrations), to protest songs (*cantos de protesta*) and graphic art, these young people from the two edges of the Americas have much in common. They used a colourful and diversified set of tools to create a space in the public sphere for themselves, by both inventing new repertoires of collective action and revisiting old ones. Putting forward objectives that are clearly political—being taken into account and able to share their visions in the public space—these movements proceeded to subvert the commercial and recreational limits of NICT (new information and communication technologies) to express their opposition: whether opposition to their exclusion from democratic deliberation or to laws that they had managed to reveal as 'unacceptable' when these impeded liberty of expression and manifestation. In the following section, we shall provide examples of these new communication strategies and of new repertoires of playful demonstrations used by both movements and assert their effects.

As we have seen, in Chile and Quebec, the student strike movements reached a scale in 2011–2012 that was unprecedented since the 1970s, involving national demonstrations of hundreds of thousands of people. To a large degree, this was due to their use of new social media (like Facebook and Twitter) to call for night marches and *caceroleos* as a protest against the arbitrary nature of the repression carried out by police forces. This included the sharing of videos to subvert the accusation of violence made against young people, as we can also see in the Mexican "*Yo soy 132*" (I'm 132) movement. This spontaneous and unprecedented movement shows a very innovative use of social media to counter-act the mass media versions of political actions taken by students.

In the Mexican well-known context of media concentration (Hallin, 2000), the movement began after Enrique Peña Nieto, the mass media's preferred presidential candidate, visited the *Universidad Iberoamericana*, an elite private university considered to be supportive of his candidacy. Peña Nieto, leader of the PRI 'Institutional Revolutionary Party' (*Partido de la Revolución Institucional*) and now President of Mexico, was driven out of the university by students shouting and holding banners stating that he had been responsible for the massive human rights violations perpetrated by the police and the army against a pacific demonstration of street flower merchants in the neighbouring community of Atenco. The students wanted to show that they would not be accomplices in the imposition of a president through manipulative political communication techniques trying to hide the use of State violence against citizens. After fleeing from the auditorium and hiding behind the curtains, Peña Nieto then summoned the media to claim that those who had chased him out were not students but "bullies" (*porros*), sympathisers of the leftist candidate AMLO (Andrés Manuel López Obrador) who had infiltrated and spoiled the meeting.

In response, that same night, an event organised by students via Facebook invited everyone present to display their student registration, testifying to their presence and agreement with the expulsion of the presidential candidate. The following day, 131 video-clips appeared, in which registered students were declaring their participation in the events and the repudiation of both Peña Nieto's past actions and of his manipulation of the media. At this point, someone had the idea of saying that, while he had not been present, he fully shared the students' anger against media manipulation of democracy, and that he "was" the 132nd participant. Following his example, thousands of other young people in Mexico and throughout the world joined the "I'm 132" (*Yo soy 132*) thus sparking the most important youth-led movements in favour of democracy since the tragic event of the Tlatelolco massacre, where several hundreds of students and young people had been killed by the Mexican police while demanding democratisation in Mexico on the eve of the 1968 Olympic Games.

In Quebec, the "Someone arrest me!" (*Arrêtez-moi quelqu'un!*) internet initiative (http://molotov.ca/realisations/arretez-moi-quelquun) is another good example of the subversive use of social media. In this case, 5,300 photo-messages 'applying' to be arrested were posted, stating that if innocent students defending the freedom of expression were to be taken in, they were willing to join the movement as citizens dedicated to democracy. These messages do not refer to specific students demands, but rather convey the importance of popular legitimacy opposed to the illegitimacy of the special law and of the assembly of representatives that voted for it, as we can observe in the following examples: "Charest (Prime Minister of Quebec) disobeys democracy, I disobey Law 78"; "I consider Law 78 illegitimate"; "Liberty is non-negotiable"; "Those who brought in Law 78 are the criminals"; "If the law is against the people, people will be outlaws"; "I am free, therefore I disobey"; "total contempt, global refusal."[9]

Within actions announced and organised by social media, the use of flash-mobs (Nicholson, 2005), was a very important form of social action used to subvert the stigmatisation of violence and rally support from other members of society by appearing in public spaces in unexpected and playful ways. Even though flash mobs were originally purely playful events where people gathered to have public pillow fights or other such recreational activities, the student movements in the Americas, as well as other movements soon began to use them to convey their political messages. Flash mobs aim to operate with an effect of pleasant surprise and to create in the general public an expectation for the next manifestation. Nevertheless, this playful and funny occupation of the public space states the right of students to do so and make obvious their efforts to be taken into consideration by authorities who try to exclude them by accusing them of being violent and carrying illegitimate claims.

The first of a long series of flash mobs was a choreographed scene from the videoclip of Michael Jackson's *Thriller*, acted out by Chilean students outside the presidential palace of Chile, *La Moneda*, in Santiago, on the first anniversary of the singer's death, to symbolise the "living-dead" state of Chilean education. This event attracted more than 7,000 people, in one of the largest flash-mobs since this kind of demonstration began worldwide. It was followed by a 1,800-hour relay race around *La Moneda*, and a series of other festive events based on a variety of famous characters such as Lady Gaga, super-heroes and Dragon Ball Z. Other collective actions included a *besotón* (kissing marathon), a die-in, "stripped naked for/by education," etc.

Very similar actions were used in Quebec; for example, a series of *maNufestations* involving people attending demonstrations naked, in order to attract attention, but also to present an image of vulnerability and demonstrate a refusal of social codes imposed through clothing.[10] Numerous night marches and biking manifestations involved the presence of funny giant stuffed animals (mascots) such as the '*Anarchopanda*,' a friendly giant panda who openly professed his political option in favour of direct and '*assembleist*' democracy. The presence of 'Rebel Banana' (*banane rebelle*) a giant banana dispensing hugs to passers-by, was also a big hit within the communicational strategy of students. Even though the intention was to subvert negative discourses against young people by making the actions fun and entertaining, they none-the-less highlighted serious and weighty issues: refusing 'austeritarian'[11] policies and proposing new ones based on the principle of free, quality, public education, and also global concerns such as climate change, fiscal reform, constitutional change, ethics in politics, etc.

The effects were quite surprising and succeeded in triggering the sympathy of otherwise disinterested sectors of the general public. In Chile, the effects went beyond that as the mass media were captivated and, rather than highlighting the supposed violence of demonstrations as was the standard practice, they were encouraged to acknowledge the good-humoured creativity of the surprising theatrical actions in their coverage of the student movement's flash-mobs.

In summary, faced with a government strategy of framing demonstrators as violent, or potentially violent and dangerous, thereby demonising and marginalising them, the young people involved in these protests actions succeeded in finding new ways of appearing in public space, despite efforts to push them out. In this way, they were able to create a "new public oppositional space" (Negt, 2007) where the foundations and limits of democracy were brought up to the public's attention and eventually discussed by sectors who usually are little interested in discussions around democracy.

As argued in the next section, this sparked an important struggle for the meaning (Laclau & Mouffe, 1985) of democracy, opposing surprisingly homogenous blocs in favour of purely representative and elective democracy to other views of political participation and deliberation. The core trend of the conflict was soon revolving around the idea of democracy itself. This, in turn, profoundly changed the political stage imposing new issues and new actors.

Antagonistic Conceptions of Participation and Democracy

The excessive repression and discrediting of these youth-led movements by presiding governments appear to be directly related to the willingness of the student movements to become political actors able to be taken into account and to participate in political deliberation and decision. The similarity of governmental discourses from Chile to Quebec reflect a common argumentative strategy to dismiss an adversary, more than the observation of specific acts of violence. In fact, what seems to have been considered "violent" is the student desire to participate politically outside prescribed institutional spaces.

As former Quebec Minister of Education, Lyne Beauchamp, declared at the National Assembly of Quebec, on 26 April 2012:

> We have a democratic system, we have a National Assembly of Quebec, we have elected representatives of the people because democracy is a way of settling our differences without violence in our society. It is the very principle of a democratic society. And, I repeat, it would not be worthy of a National Assembly and elected representatives of the people to yield to acts of violence, yield to intimidation, yield to civil disobedience which involves violence. (quoted in *Journal des débats de l'Assemblée nationale*, 26 April 2012)

As we saw earlier on, these declarations echo those of Chilean Minister of Education Joaquín Lavín, when he states that "No modern democracy debates these questions with students; these are important national debates on which we must confer in Congress" (quoted in *La Tercera*, 28 June 2011).

Moreover, many extracts from governmental speeches indicate clearly that the manifestations of political dissent within the student protests are to be excluded as un-democratic behaviour and considered to be violent. The case of the wearing of *le carré rouge*, a little red felt square worn by all supporters of the student movement, is very telling in this regard. As the most important symbol of a movement that soon rallied huge sectors of the general public, the little *carré rouge* was worn by many important artists and public personalities in Quebec. Without necessarily supporting the student's claims entirely, many people in the general public began to wear it to publicly dissent with governments and courts decisions to penalise students (Labrie, 2013). When prize-winning story-teller Fred Pellerin refused to claim his prize and appeared in the media wearing the *carré rouge*, Quebec Minister of Culture, Christine Saint-Pierre, declared: "[...] we know what the *carré rouge* means, it means intimidation and violence [...]" (quoted in Peñafiel, 2015b). The next day, during the Formula One Grand Prix in Montreal, all the people bearing the *carré rouge* were detained, searched and expelled from the event (*Le Devoir*, 11 June 2012).

The violence herein referred to by Minister Saint-Pierre in fact consisted solely of broken storefront windows. All of the other types of students' actions were actually perfectly legal: picket lines in front of universities that had voted the strike, temporary occupations of public offices such as the stock exchange building in Montreal, or road blockades to attract the government's attention after more than two months without any dialogue, all of the previous are disturbing yet not illegal or violent actions according to the legislation on Quebec. Thus, the discursive transformation of these practices into condemnable, violent and even terrorist practices by government's representatives show us how the criminalisation dynamic actually takes place.

Going further, the Chilean governmental discourse warned mobilised young people that their use of social conflict could lead to the return of authoritarianism. For example, Chilean President, Sebastián Piñera, faced with the fast expanding movement of strikes and social protest declared in August 2011:

> I am absolutely convinced that to make Chile a freer and more just country, more prosperous and with greater solidarity, the path of stone-throwing,

violence, and Molotov cocktails must not be taken [...] This path, we have known it in the past and it led us to a democratic rupture, to the loss of healthy conviviality, and many other consequences. (quoted in Emol.com, 18 August 2011)

In a Chilean society where the trauma of the past dictatorship are still vivid in the minds of many, this is a damning accusation (Doran, 2016, p. 219). Moreover, on the basis of claims that students were violent and dangerous, attempts were made by both governments to pass exceptional laws that would restrict individual and civil rights related to the right to dissent and protest. The official justification was that the civil rights had to be curtailed to better defend civil liberties. For example, as we saw earlier, Quebec's Bill 78 imposed extreme restrictions on the rights of association, expression and protest. Likewise, Montreal's P-6 bylaw (*By-law concerning the prevention of breaches of the peace, public order and safety, and the use of public property*, City of Montreal, 2001 (As amended by 12-024)), subordinated the right to protest to freedom of movement, prohibited the wearing of masks, and demanded that protesters provide their itinerary to the police. Chile's "Hinzpeter" bill (*Law to Strengthen Public Order*, debated in 2012), severely punishes actions like the occupation of official or private buildings, the blocking of traffic, being disrespectful towards the police, and wearing hoods or scarves covering the face.

While most of these bills or laws were rejected by Parliament, repealed by successor governments, or struck down by the courts, their immediate political impact was no less deadly for freedom. They lent the exercise of fundamental rights an appearance of illegitimacy and they unleashed repressive police techniques aimed at public intimidation, such as mass arrests and excessive use of crowd containment equipment and weapons. The practice of torture against arrested protesters in Chilean police stations was also documented by different organisations (*Comisión de Observadores de Derechos Humanos, Casa de Memoria José Domingo Cañas*, 2013; Human Rights Center of the Universidad Diego Portales' Faculty of Law, 2014).

Representing the public expression of positions contrary to the 'decisions' of elected officials as violence, these statements by Chilean and Quebec government officials assert a kind of decisionist legitimacy (Habermas, 1978): government decisions are legitimate, independently of their contents or the reaction of a large part of the public, as long as the government was elected and governs according to formal procedures.

Consequently, civil rights—such as freedom of expression, association and protest—may be limited, and even abolished or suspended, if part of the public takes it upon itself to pass judgement on the validity of a law (isonomy) or of a decision by elected representatives, while it has "no title to govern" (*sans titre à gouverner*) (Rancière, 2005).

However, the student movements succeeded in establishing themselves as interlocutors in the public arena, despite this denial of rights and this criminalisation. They did so through a process of political subjectivation that can be observed, in a striking parallel, in Chile between June and December 2011 and in Quebec between February and July 2012. In the face of government intransigence in refusing to recognise the representation of student organisations and the legitimacy of the strike and the street as a mode of popular participation, these two student conflicts, at opposite ends of the Americas, expanded beyond their strictly educational frameworks to transform into immense transgressive protest movements, which were 'radically' (at the roots) questioning the social and political order. While the relative success of the two movements differs—in Quebec, support for the student movement never surpassed 50% in the polls; while in Chile, support rose from 37% before the conflict to 80% at the end—they both share the capacity to mobilise and defeat attempts to de-legitimise and exclude them from public space. It is important to analyse this capacity, in order to understand the impact and nature of youth political participation in times of austerity.

Conclusion

Due to the State's exercise of "illegitimate," excessive, or arbitrary violence, partial struggles (such as student struggles)[12] are met with solidarity from wider audience one of the points of convergence being the defence of the right to dissent. The struggle waged by this new political force tends to form around the democratic principles underlying the frustrated sectorial demand, rather than around the demand as such (Corten, Huart, & Peñafiel, 2012). This demand becomes accessory or secondary and tends to be replaced by a series of other claims, no longer addressed to the state—which in any case, does not recognise them—but to all of society. For example, the "someone arrest me campaign" or the initiatives of the "*Yo soy 132—I'm 132*" movement in Mexico do not directly address the specific interests or demands of students. Rather, they contend the plea for an "authentic democracy." In the specific case of the

Mexican movement, its first public statements and actions denounced the "duopoly" of the two main television chains which, in collusion with political elites (especially of PAN and PRI),[13] manipulate public opinion and over-determine election results. In this case, as in the cases of the Chilean and Maple Springs examined in this chapter, a political subjectivation formed, born of an assertion of the principle of equality, which can certainly appear ephemeral and disappear after the effervescence of protests, but is no less enduring and fundamental in its principle; which reawakens and asserts itself through each of these *Plebeian Experiences* (Breaugh, 2013).

The student movements of the Americas succeeded in marking public space in the affected societies and in transforming charges of violence and political apathy levelled against young people through original strategies of communication. In doing this, these movements successfully exposed the impermeability of political systems and constructed spaces of expression, not only for students but for all citizens who wished to join in the democratic discussion.

In a context of economic and political crisis, marked by three decades of neoliberal policies in which many sectors are battling to save fragments of a social state in a permanent process of dismantlement, university students (and secondary students in Chile) showed that it was possible to resist a market concept of society and become political actors in and through conflict. In this regard, there are many differences between the Chilean and Quebec Springs. For example, while the student movement in Chile confronted a neoliberal system in place since the dictatorship, in Quebec the students were responding to austerity measures legitimised by the 2008 economic crisis and the public financial crisis generated by the ensuing recession. However, the two movements were practically identical in terms of the denial of recognition (Honneth, 2000) faced by student organisations. They came to be the favourite targets of government discourses of stigmatisation: as violent, as privileged, as spoiled kids refusing their "fair" share, and more. As such, their capacity to form movements allowing diverse sectors to converge must be measured against the specific difficulties that youth face in a world unwilling to accept them as legitimate speakers in public space (Joignant, 2007; Peñafiel, 2008). By challenging the criminalisation of collective action, the transgressive forms of public participation used by students in the cases studied here also show the limits of a strictly delegative form of democracy (O'Donnell, 1994), which reduces participation to the periodic exercise of universal suffrage.

The impact of these movements, which lasted well beyond the enactment of legislative changes responding to specific demands, can be assessed by the capacity they had to mobilise the support of societies invested in the defence of democratic principles, including the freedoms of expression, association and protest and, more broadly, the right to dissent These democratic principles were re-appropriated by all those who recognised themselves in the *interpellation* (Althusser, 1976) made by youth. Beyond sectorial demands, protest movements emerging from young people's initiatives cease to address the State—which in any case does not recognise them—and 'exercise' directly a 'full democracy' in which those excluded from public space can finally appear and express themselves. These movements thus lend society a reflexive insight on itself and on the very foundations of democracy. To paraphrase Rancière (1995), the moment when outcasts break into public space from which they have been excluded is the moment when the political breaks out, the social ceases to reproduce itself on its own naturalised bases and a reflexive and democratic debate on the foundations of the-being-together can be undertaken collectively.

Notes

1. Bringing together students from 25 so-called 'traditional' universities (preceding the dictatorship).
2. For the details of these demands, see the document *Convocatoria Movilización y Paro Nacional* (Call to mobilise and to a national strike) by Confech: http://movimientoestudiantil.cl/wp-content/uploads/2015/12/2011-05-CONVOCATORIA12MAYO.pdf. *For independent analyses of the segregational nature of the Chilean educational model*, see: Bellei, Contreras, and Valenzuela (2010), Berner and Bellei (2011), OECD (2011), and Pinedo Henriquez (2011).
3. Residents of working-class neighbourhoods and shantytowns.
4. Especially around the HidroAysen conflict, a protest movement against the construction of five hydroelectric stations in the south of Chile. This conflict, which began before the student strike movement began, continued and was strengthened when this space of pluri-sectorial protest opened.
5. However, the actual reforms enacted by President Bachelet diverge from the original intentions of the student movement: free education has been transformed into a grant reserved for the poorest students in an unchanged

private education system where profit is still a main trend. The fiscal reforms have been deemed much too modest and Constitutional reforms controlled by the Congress have been used by the government to try to deflect society's claim for popular constituent assemblies.
6. For example, then Minister of Education, Lyne Beauchamp, claimed in a television interview on Radio Canada, the state media, "The students want us to talk about their contribution by saying, 'I don't want my bill, send it to someone else.' To us, this will never be a good basis for discussion. University students must pay their fair share" (Radio Canada, 5 April 2012).
7. Chilean and Argentinian *funas* are direct actions, invented by organisations of the children of disappeared or tortured detainees. They are aimed at condemning the impunity of soldiers and collaborators with the Chilean and Argentinian dictatorial regimes. In Chile, the adoption of this practice by students might seem paradoxical insofar as it is used to denounce actions and declarations of public officials. However, this *funa* is no less significant, because it condemns as unacceptable attitudes presented as legal or legitimate.
8. *Caceroleos* are a form of displaying popular discontent (also called *cacerolazos* in Argentina and elsewhere), which simply consists of banging on pots. Similar to Europe's charivari or England's "rough music" (Thompson, 1972), this form of popular public expression was first used by the Chilean right-wing against Salvador Allende's Popular Unity government. A decade later, the pots changed allegiance and served to repudiate the military regime. In August 2011, after many weeks of student conflict, the *caceroleos* reappeared, recalling the time of the *Protestas* (national protest movement) against the dictatorship.
9. For a more detailed analysis, see Peñafiel (2015a).
10. Feminist author Martine Delvaux sees a relation to FEMEN's types of action and expands on this in "Les MaNUfestantes," *Revue À Bâbord*, 46, 2012, p. 27.
11. In French, the expression '*politiques austéritaires*' is used to describe both austerity politics and the authoritarian practices of repression and criminalisation that accompanied them in many cases.
12. These could very well be those of indigenous people, labourers, teachers, residents of a city threatened by a mega-project, citizens of a state outraged by a government decision, etc. For a socio-historic analysis of this type of spontaneous direct action, see Corten, Huart, and Peñafiel (2012).
13. Respectively, the National Action Party and the Institutional Revolutionary Party. It is important to clarify that the movement "*Yo soy 132—I'm 132*" is non-partisan and refuses to support the PRD (Democratic Revolution Party) or any other political formation.

References

Althusser, L. (1976). Idéologie et appareils idéologiques d'État. In *Positions (1964–1975)* (pp. 67–125). Paris: Les Éditions sociales.

Amossy, R. (2010). *La présentation de soi. Ethos et identité verbale*. Paris: Presses Universitaires de France (PUF).

Baril, G. (2012). *La diminution de la participation électorale des jeunes Québécois: Une recherche exploratoire de l'Institut du Nouveau Monde*. Québec: Directeur général des élections du Québec.

Bellei, C., Contreras, D., & Valenzuela, J. P. (Eds.). (2010). *Ecos de la revolución pingüina: Avances, debates y silencios en la reforma educacional*. Santiago: Pehuén Editores.

Berner, H., & Bellei, C. (2011). ¿Revolución o reforma? Anuncios, medidas y compromisos a la espera de la reforma educacional. *Política/Revista de Ciencia Política, 49*(2), 67–96.

Breaugh, M. (2013). *The plebeian experience: A discontinuous history of political freedom*. New York: Columbia University Press.

City of Montreal. (2001). By-law concerning the prevention of breaches of the peace, public order and safety, and the use of public property. R.B.C.M., chap. P-6. (As Amended by 12-024).

Comisión de observadores de Derechos Humanos [Human Rights Observers Commission] and Casa de Memoria José Domingo Cañas. (2013). *Human rights annual report 2013: Social protest, torture and other inhuman and cruel treatment: Impunity and the role of the state*. Retrieved January 15, 2017, from http://www.observadoresddhh.org/wp-content/uploads/2012/02/Informe-anual-2013.pdf

Commission spéciale d'examen des événements du Printemps 2012. (2014, March). *Rapport de la Commission spéciale d'examen des événements du Printemps 2012* [Report of the special commission of inquiry into the events of Spring 2012]. Retrieved January 14, 2017, from http://www.securitepublique.gouv.qc.ca/fileadmin/Documents/police/publications/rapport_CSEEP2012/rapport_CSEP2012.pdf

Coopérative Molotov communication. (2012). *Arrêtez-moi quelqu'un!* Retrieved January 18, 2017, from http://molotov.ca/realisations/arretez-moi-quelquun

Corten, A., Huart, C., & Peñafiel, R. (Eds.). (2012). *L'interpellation plébéienne en Amérique latine. Violence, actions directes et virage à gauche*. Paris and Montréal: Karthala/Presses de l'Université du Québec.

Delgado Ramos, G. C. (2012, January–February). Extractivismo minero, conflicto y resistencia social. *Realidad Económica, 265*, 60–84. Retrieved December 27, 2016, from http://pasc.ca/sites/pasc.ca/files/articles/ExtractivismoConflictoResistencia.pdf

Delvaux, M. (2012). Les maNUfestantes. À Bâbord! *Revue sociale et politque*, oct./nov., 46, 27–28.
Doran, M.-C. (2016). *Le Réveil démocratique du Chili. Une histoire politique de l'exigence de justice*. Paris: Karthala.
Doran, M.-C. (2017). Understanding the current criminalization of protest in Latin America: Beyond the obvious, a comparative analysis of Mexico and Chile. *Latin American Perspectives*. (forthcoming).
Dupuis-Déri, F. (2013). Printemps érable ou Printemps de la matraque? Profilage politique et répression sélective pendant la grève étudiante de 2012. In F. Dupuis-Déri (Ed.), *À qui la rue? Répression policière et mouvements sociaux* (pp. 198–241). Montréal: Écosociété.
Dupuis-Déri, F. (2014). Émergence de la notion de "profilage politique": Répression policière et mouvements sociaux au Québec. *Politique et Sociétés, 33*(3), 31–56.
Emol.com. (2011, August 18). *Piñera: "El camino de la violencia nos llevó al quiebre de la democracia"*. Retrieved January 10, 2017, from http://www.emol.com/noticias/nacional/2011/08/18/498480/pinera-el-camino-de-la-violencia-nos-llevo-al-quiebre-de-la-democracia.html
Fernández, G. (2000). Notas sobre la participación política de los jóvenes chilenos. In S. Balardini (Ed.), *La participación política y social de los jóvenes en el horizonte del nuevo siglo* (pp. 87–108). Buenos Aires: Consejo Latinoamericano de Ciencias Sociales (CLACSO).
FIDH (Fédération internationale des ligues des droits de l'Homme). (2011). *Rapport annuel 2011—L'obstination du témoignage*. Retrieved January 10, 2017, from http://www.fidh.org/IMG/pdf/obs_2011_fr-complet-2.pdf
Habermas, J. (1978). *Raison et légitimité. Problèmes de légitimation dans le capitalisme avancé*. Paris: Éditions Payot.
Hallin, D. (2000). Media, political power and democratization in Mexico. In J. Curran & M.-J. Park (Eds.), *De-westernizing media studies* (pp. 85–98). London and New York: Routledge.
Honneth, A. (2000). *La Lutte pour la reconnaissance*. Paris: Cerf.
Honneth, A. (2006). *La société du mépris. Vers une nouvelle théorie critique*. Paris: La Découverte.
Human Rights Center of the Universidad Diego Portales' Faculty of Law. (2014). *Annual report on human rights in Chile*. Retrieved January 18, 2017, from http://www.ombudsman.cl/pdf/informe-completo-ddhh-2014.pdf
Joignant, A. (2007). Compétence politique et bricolage. Les formes profanes du rapport au politique. *Revue française de science politique, 57*(6), 799–817.
Journal des débats de l'Assemblée nationale, 42(99), 26 April 2012. Retrieved January 18, 2017, from http://www.assnat.qc.ca/fr/travaux-parlementaires/assemblee-nationale/39-2/journal-debats/20120426/56955.html
Labrie, V. (2013). Les multiples vies du carré rouge. Plusieurs facettes, un même horizon. In J.-P. Boyer et al. (Eds.), *À force d'imagination. Affiches et artefacts du mouvement étudiant au Québec 1958–2013*. Montréal: Lux Editeur.

Lachapelle, J. (2012, April 21). Manif du 22 mars: Combien étaient-ils? *La Presse*. Retrieved January 18, 2017, from http://www.lapresse.ca/actualites/dossiers/conflit-etudiant/201204/21/01-4517612-manif-du-22-mars-combien-etaient-ils.php

Laclau, E. (1996). Why do empty signifiers matter to politics. In E. Laclau. *Emancipation(s)* (pp. 36–46). London: Verso.

Laclau, E., & Mouffe, C. (1985). *Hegemony and socialist strategy, towards a radical democratic politics*. London: Verso.

Lacoursière, B. (2007). *Le mouvement étudiant au Québec de 1983 à 2006*. Montréal: Sabotart.

La Tercera. (Araya, C.). (2011, June 28). Lavín anuncia recalendarización del año escolar en 200 colegios de Santiago. *La Tercera*. Retrieved January 3, 2017, from http://diario.latercera.com/2011/06/28/01/contenido/pais/31-74447-9-lavin-anuncia-recalendarizacion-del-ano-escolar-en-200-colegios-de-santiago.shtml

Le Devoir. (Nadeau, J.-F.). (2012, June 9). Le carré rouge de Fred Pellerin: 'Violence et intimidation,' affirme la ministre de la Culture. *Le Devoir*. Retrieved November 10, 2016, from http://www.ledevoir.com/culture/actualites-culturelles/352046/le-carre-rouge-de-fred-pellerin-violence-et-intimidation-affirme-la-ministre-de-la-culture

Legislature of Canada. (1914). *An Act to confer certain powers upon the Governor in Council and to amend the Immigration Act* [War Measure's Act]. [Assented to 22 August 1914]. Ottawa: King's Printer. (Repealed 21 July 1988)

Legislature of Quebec. (1983, June 23). *An Act respecting the accreditation and financing of students' associations*. 32nd Legislature, 4th Session, Québec.

Legislature of Quebec. (2012, May 18). *Bill n°78: An Act to enable students to receive instruction from the postsecondary institutions they attend*. 39th Legislature, 2nd Session, Québec. (Repealed 1 July 2013).

Lemonde, L., Bourbeau, A., Fortin, V., Joly, E., & Poisson, J. (2014). La répression judiciaire et législative durant la grève. In M. Ancelovici & F. Dupuis-Déri (Eds.), *Un Printemps rouge et noir. Regards croisés sur la grève étudiante de 2012* (pp. 295–326). Montréal: Écosociété.

Ligue des droits et libertés, Association des juristes progressistes et Association pour une solidarité syndicale étudiante. (2013). *Répression, discrimination et grève étudiante: Analyses et témoignages* [Report]. Retrieved January 10, 2017, from http://liguedesdroits.ca/wp-content/fichiers/rapport-2013-repression-discrimination-et-greve-etudiante.pdf

McAdam, D., Tarrow, S., & Tilly, C. (2001). *Dynamics of contention*. Cambridge: Cambridge University Press.

Mouffe, C. (2002). "La fin du politique" et le défi du populisme de droite. *Revue du MAUSS, 20*(2), 178–194.

Müller, M.-M. (2012, March). The rise of the penal state in Latin America. *Contemporary Justice Review, 15*(1), 57–76.

Negt, O. (2007). *L'espace public oppositionnel*. (Trad. A. Neumann). Paris: Payot.
Nicholson, J. A. (2005). Flash! mobs in the age of mobile connectivity. *Fibreculture Journal, 6.* (*Mobility, New Social Intensities and the Coordinates of Digital Networks*). Retrieved January 10, 2017, from http://citeseerx.ist.psu.edu/viewdoc/download?doi=10.1.1.566.6906&rep=rep1&type=pdf
O'Donnell, G. (1994). Delegative democracy. *Journal of Democracy, 5*(1), 55–69.
OECD. (2011). *Education at a glance 2011: OECD indicators*. OECD Publishing. Retrieved November 10, 2016, from http://dx.doi.org/10.1787/eag-2011-en
Peñafiel, R. (2008). Le Rôle politique des imaginaires sociaux. Quelques enjeux théoriques autour de leur conceptualisation. *Politique et Sociétés, 27*(1), 99–128.
Peñafiel, R. (2012). Le 'Printemps chilien' et la radicalisation de l'action collective contestataire en Amérique latine. *Lien social et politiques, 68,* 121–140.
Peñafiel, R. (2014). Récits et subjectivations politiques intersectionnelles transversales. L'exemple des actions collectives transgressives en Amérique latine. *Politique et sociétés, 33*(1), 15–40.
Peñafiel, R. (2015a). Le Sens des casseroles. Charivaris, *cacerolazos* et création d'espaces publics transgressifs dans et par le bruit. *Cahiers des imaginaires, 8*(11), 9–28.
Peñafiel, R. (2015b). La criminalisation de la participation citoyenne par des conceptions consensualistes de la démocratie participative. *Revue québécoise de droit international* [Special Issue: *L'État de droit en Amérique latine et au Canada*], 247–271.
Peñafiel, R. (2016). Minorisation médiatique et stratégies communicationnelles des groupes stigmatisés: Analyse comparée des "Printemps" chilien (2011) et québécois (2012). In Writers' collective L'Esprit libre (Ed.), *(In)visibilités médiatiques* (pp. 81–93). Montréal: Revue L'Esprit libre.
Pickard, S. (2014). Keep them kettled! Protesting and policing and anti-social behaviour in Britain. In S. Pickard (Ed.), *Anti-social behaviour in Britain. Victorian and contemporary perspectives* (pp. 77–91). Basingstoke: Palgrave Macmillan.
Pinedo Henriquez, C. (2011). Educación en Chile: ¿Inclusión o exclusión? *Tejuelo, 12,* 47–79.
Putnam, R. D. (1995). Bowling alone: America's declining social capital. *Journal of Democracy, 6*(1), 65–78.
Radio-Canada. (2012, April 5). *Québec élargit son programme de prêts étudiants aux familles de la classe moyenne*. Retrieved January 5, 2017, from http://ici.radio-canada.ca/nouvelle/556516/greve-etudiante-jeudi
Rancière, J. (1995). *La Mésentente. Politique et Philosophie*. Paris: Galilée.
Rancière, J. (2005). *La Haine de la démocratie*. Paris: La Fabrique.

Richer, J. (2012, March 11). Les Québécois doivent payer leur juste part, dit Bachand. *La Presse*. Retrieved January 18, 2017, from http://www.lapresse.ca/actualites/politique/politique-quebecoise/201203/11/01-4504470-les-quebecois-doivent-payer-leur-juste-part-dit-bachand.php

Sander, T. H., & Putnam, R. D. (2010). Still bowling alone? The post-9/11 split. *Journal of Democracy, 21*(1), 9–16.

Savard, A., & Cyr, M.-A. (2014). La rue contre l'État. Action et mobilisations étudiantes en 2012. In M. Ancelovici & F. Dupuis-Déri (Eds.), *Un Printemps rouge et noir. Regards croisés sur la grève étudiante de 2012* (pp. 59–86). Montréal: Écosociété.

Seoane, J. (Ed.). (2003). *Movimientos sociales y conflicto en América Latin*. Buenos Aires: Consejo Latinoamericano de Ciencias Sociales (CLACSO).

Svampa, M. (2009). Mouvements sociaux, matrices sociopolitiques et nouveaux contextes en Amérique latine. *Problèmes d'Amérique latine, 4*(74), 113–136.

Thompson, E. P. (1972). "Rough music": Le Charivari anglais. *Annales E.S.C., 27*(2), 285–312.

Twenge, J. M. (2014). *Generation me: Why today's young Americans are more confident, assertive, entitled—And more miserable than ever before* (Rev. and Updated ed.). New York: Simon & Schuster.

Véjar, P. (Ed.). (2012). *Informe RADDE: Criminalización de la movilización estudiantil en Chile en el año 2011*. Santiago: Asociación Chilena pro Naciones Unidas/Foro por el Derecho a la Educación. Retrieved January 14, 2017, from http://educacionparatodos.cl/wp-content/uploads/2015/10/Informe-RADDE-2013.pdf

Ricardo Peñafiel is Associate Professor at the Department of Political Science of the University of Quebec in Montreal and researcher in GRIPAL (Research Group on Political Imaginaries in Latin America). His current work focuses on populism, and the criminalisation of social movements, as a communicational phenomenon and an ideological struggle around democracy and violence.

Marie-Christine Doran is Associate Professor at the School of Political Studies, University of Ottawa, Canada, and Researcher at the International Panel on Exiting Violence (IPEV, Paris) and GRIPAL. Her current work focuses on criminalisation of protest, political violence, religion and politics, as well as human rights from below and her latest book features the Chilean case.

CHAPTER 20

Youth Participation in Eastern Europe in the Age of Austerity

Marko Kovacic and Danijela Dolenec

INTRODUCTION

Since the 2008 global financial crisis, a number of countries of the European Union (EU) have adopted austerity policies. Austerity, the neoliberal doctrine that promotes cutting public spending in order to restore competitiveness (Blyth, 2013, p. 12), is often framed by policy-makers as 'common sense' and as the only rational policy response in the given circumstances. Furthermore, austerity is often explained with reductionist arguments by its proponents, without seeking to understand its impact on different groups. The human cost of austerity policies was largely invisible (McKee, Karanikolos, Belcher, & Stuckler, 2012) until recently, due to a lack of reliable data. Despite the growing political economy literature on the negative effects of austerity on various aspects of society, there are still gaps to be filled in regard to the impact of austerity measures. One of these

---

M. Kovacic (✉)
Department of Public Policy and Political Sociology, Institute for Social Research in Zagreb, Zagreb, Croatia

D. Dolenec
Department of Political Sciences, University of Zagreb, Zagreb, Croatia

© The Author(s) 2018
S. Pickard, J. Bessant (eds.), *Young People Re-Generating Politics in Times of Crises*, Palgrave Studies in Young People and Politics, DOI 10.1007/978-3-319-58250-4_20

gaps is the impact of austerity policies on patterns of political participation among young people, which we address in this chapter.

Many countries in the EU, and particularly those of Eastern Europe, today face unusually high rates of youth unemployment. According to Eurostat (2016e), the EU average for unemployment among young people aged 15–30 peaked in 2013 at 23.8 per cent. This trend is accompanied by declining involvement of young people in conventional forms of political participation, such as voting in parliamentary elections (Ilišin, Bouillet, Gvozdanović, & Potočnik, 2013). However, it is important not to make generalisations because significant differences exist among EU member states.[1] For instance, the United Kingdom has experienced rising rates of electoral participation among young people (see Pickard, in this volume; 2018). Similarly, though democracy across Europe is facing a crisis of representation, evidenced through increasing disconnect between citizens and political parties (Mair, 2013)—contemporary research reveals significant differences between the political behaviour of older and younger generations (Dalton, 2011). Following these broad trends, we start from the assumption that both the global financial crisis and the subsequent repertoire of austerity policies have affected European societies unevenly, with differences particularly pronounced along the lines of core-periphery (Epstein, 2014; Hanzl-Weiss & Landesmann, 2013; Jacoby, 2014; Vachudova, 2014). Populations of Southern and Eastern Europe have been worse hit by austerity measures, in contrast to European states, Germany and Austria, where these impacts have been less pronounced. Taking this on board, we analyse how this dynamic relates to youth political participation. Many empirical studies focus on youth participation in Western Europe (Gaiser, De Rijke, & Spannring, 2010; Grasso, 2016; Pickard, 2018; Sloam, 2007) and Southern Europe (Hooghe, 2012; Lima & Artiles, 2013; Morciano, Scardigno, Manuti, & Pastore, 2014), while there are only a few studies of Eastern Europe (Kovacheva, 2000).

Firstly, we argue that austerity policies have aggravated social welfare by increasing the proportion of young people who remain living with their parents late into their twenties. Secondly, we argue that their prolonged economic dependence thwarts their bid to attain relative autonomy (Garrido & Requena, 1996), and that this is reflected in their modes of political participation. In other words, we explore the interaction between the economic dependence of young people and type of their political participation. Therefore, our main research objective is to explore how austerity policies, mediated through a prolonged life in the parental home, affect the patterns and repertoires of youth political activism and participation. A deferred process of gaining autonomy arguably suppresses innovation and creativity among young people, which are important for their political participation (Siurala, 2000). We argue that prolonged reliance on the family might lead to 'infantilisation,' marked by political apathy and non-participation, or it might lead to an increase in contentious political action. This chapter explores patterns of youth participation in Europe by relying on dependency theory (see below), which postulates a core-periphery dynamic among EU member states. In order to relate the varied impact of austerity between the core and the periphery of Europe to differences in youth political participation, we analyse indicators of economic and social effects of austerity policies in the EU, focusing in particular on countries of Eastern Europe. Coupled with that, we use International Social Science Programme (ISSP) survey data to contrast features of youth political participation in the EU core and its Eastern periphery.

The chapter proceeds as follows. In the first section, we present key arguments regarding effects of austerity policies, their differentiated impact across the core and periphery of Europe, and related expectations regarding youth political participation. In the second section, we outline our comparative analysis of the impact of austerity by examining several indicators for the 28 member states of the EU. In the third section, we analyse ISSP (2014) survey data for 14 countries of Western and Eastern Europe, exploring features of youth conventional and unconventional political participation and relating them to effects of austerity measures. In the final section, we summarise our findings and discuss their implications.

Theoretical Framework

Earlier literature on political participation in Europe stressed the difference between Western democracies on the one hand, and post-Communist countries on the other. Since the global financial crisis of 2008, political economic analyses have emphasised the core-periphery divide within Europe, characterised by strong economic performance of the North-western core, and a variety of economic deficiencies in both the Southern and Eastern peripheries. Though the process of European integration is premised on the idea that all member states/countries will converge towards the liberal democratic model of development (Green Cowles & Smith, 2000), a growing body of literature has shown that European economies have instead clustered into distinctive varieties of capitalism (e.g., Bohle & Greskovits, 2012; King, 2007; Nölke & Vliegenthart, 2009). Eastern European countries have developed into liberal economies, characterised by the unhappy marriage of declining welfare standards and liberalised economies that depend on foreign investment (Bohle & Greskovits, 2012).

Core-periphery models, which emerged from dependence theory and the global political economy approach in the 1970s, help explain some features of contemporary social and economic inequalities, and "the dynamics of underdevelopment and regional inequalities on the global level" (Naustdalslid, 1977, p. 203). In Wallerstein's original formulation, the world system encapsulates countries of Africa, South America, and parts of Asia (periphery) being economically dependent on North America and Western Europe (core). Developed in opposition to modernisation theory, which assumed that all countries were moving along a linear path towards the 'superior' development model of the United States, dependency theory emphasised the fact that poor and wealthy countries are part of the same whole, global capitalist system, rather than similar entities at different stages of development. More importantly, this literature argued that underdevelopment in the periphery was the direct result of development in the centre.

The 2008 global financial crisis drew attention to diverging trajectories among EU member states, aspects of dependency theory have re-emerged in contemporary analysis. Authors such as Schweiger and Magone (2014), de la Porte and Pochet (2014), and Busch, Hermann, Hinrichs, and Schulten (2013) argue that the global financial crisis and the subsequent Eurozone sovereign debt crisis, together with the existing democratic deficit of the EU, have accentuated the internal divisions within the EU. According to Schweiger and Magone (2014, p. 259), the EU is divided "between the Eurozone core group and differentiated peripheries amongst the outsiders." This raises the issue of whether, and in what way, the distinct features of political economies of the EU's core and periphery impact the political participation of young people.

Within the core-periphery dynamic, we understand the global financial crisis of 2008 as aggravating already existing differences among EU member states, given that they represent a logical extension of the long-term trend of increasing economic liberalism in the EU. Neoliberal economic policies were taken up by the EU in its reforms during the 1990s (Judt, 2009). For Hall (2012), the guiding principle of the EU, which used to be "peace for Europe," was reformulated by the Single European Act (1987) into "prosperity for everyone via the Single Market." The criteria in the Treaty of Maastricht on European Union (1992) and The Stability and Growth Pact (1998) effectively closed a number of policy options available for pursuing social objectives (Esping-Andersen, 2002; Green Cowles & Smith, 2000). As a result, the EU's policy prescriptions after the 1990s started to resemble increasingly those of international financial organisations such as the International Monetary Fund (IMF) and the World Bank (Guillén & Palier, 2004). In a deliberate emulation of the model of development in the United States, the Washington consensus on deregulation, the minimal State and low taxation travelled to Europe (Judt, 2009).

Austerity as a concept stands for economic measures implemented by national governments with the aim of reducing public expenditure and controlling public sector debt. Ostensibly, their principal aim is to restore the trust of financial markets and investors, thereby restoring competitiveness, but their principal effects have been on the social fabric of European states. As several analyses show (e.g., Blyth, 2013; Busch et al., 2013), in the attempt to consolidate public finances, austerity measures created negative consequences for the European social model. This resulted in significant cuts in welfare in Greece, Hungary, Italy, Portugal and elsewhere, jeopardising the "very foundations of social and economic development" (Lehndorff, 2012, p. 15). In contrast, Western European countries like Austria, France, Germany, and Sweden were performing much better (Lehndorff, 2012).

Figure 20.1 shows levels of investment into social protection for a selection of European states, in order to illustrate some of the dynamic described above. The annual data, ranging between 2005 and 2013, has been selected so as to capture changes in the level of social protection before and after the financial crisis of 2008. Furthermore, Fig. 20.1 reveals considerable differences among member states of the EU with respect to overall levels of social welfare. While in Denmark the total level of expenditure on social protection per inhabitant ranges between EUR 11,500 and EUR 15,000, in Bulgaria the range is between EUR 450 and EUR 1000. Figure 20.1 also shows that while the core European countries reacted to the economic crisis by substantially increasing investment into social protection, the same cannot be said of the peripheral states. Peripheral members of the EU both entered the crisis with much lower levels of social protection, and they have not been able to substantially increase it since 2008. In the case of Hungary for instance, the levels of investment in social protection per inhabitant are actually lower post-2008.

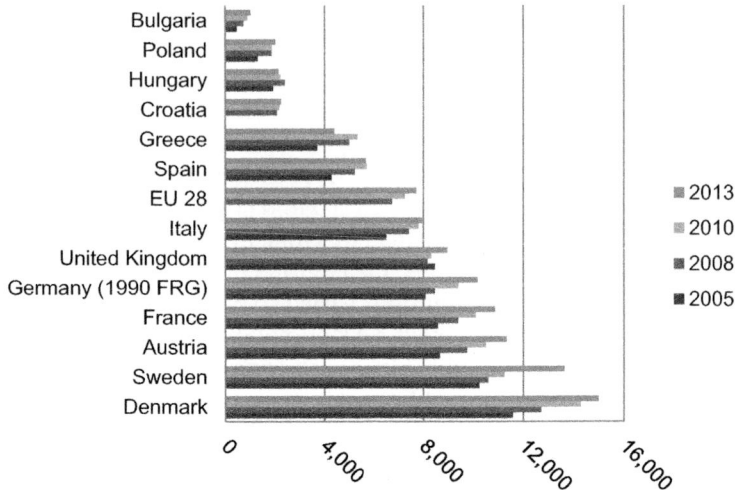

Fig. 20.1 Total expenditure on social protection, per inhabitant (in Euros), Europe. Source: Eurostat (2016a) 'Expenditure on social protection, 2003–13'

In brief, austerity measures implemented post-2008 emphasised already existing differences regarding social protection among core and peripheral states of the EU. Austerity measures have had a stronger impact in peripheral regions of Europe, with consequences for various social groups. In this chapter, we focus on young people, and in particular on the possible effects of austerity on youth participation in Eastern Europe. Young people are expected to be particularly vulnerable because their quest for identity and social integration is occurring in unstable and risky circumstances of democratic transition where societal and political spheres change drastically (France, 2007; Furlong & Cartmel, 1997).

The political and social experiences of young people shape their political identity and actions as adults. Thus, it is important to explore the political actions of young people because their social and political behaviour may reveal important features of the social and political reality of our future (Kimberlee, 2002; Mannheim, 1970; Pickard, 2018). Given the severe effects of austerity policies that we describe, analysts are now talking of a "lost generation" (International Labour Organization [ILO], 2012). We expect this phenomenon to be particularly pertinent for young people in the periphery of Europe, where they are encountering the so-called double transition (Ule, 1988). In the post-socialist context, young people's transition from childhood to adulthood takes place in a changing context of countries undergoing political and economic transformation into liberal democracies (Ilišin et al., 2013). Furthermore, key life events such as marriage or parenthood are being postponed, especially in Southern and Eastern Europe (Ilišin et al., 2013). This phenomenon of "extended youth," which is characteristic of Mediterranean countries, means that integration of young people into society is being prolonged (Ule, 1988). Arguably, austerity policies, and in particular high levels of unemployment among youth in the European peripheries have further aggravated youth dependence on their parents. How does this prolonged dependence translate into patterns and repertoires of political activism and participation?

Research on Southern European countries shows that high youth unemployment rates push young people into a state of frustration, caused primarily by the lack of available jobs in the labour market, in response to which they initiate various contentious activities (Cairns, de Almeida Alves, Alexandre, & Correia, 2016; Williamson, 2014). Given this finding, we analyse whether similar patterns are observable in Eastern European countries.

As is the case with general political participation, investigating empirically youth political participation includes activities aimed at "attempting to influence the activity of government and the selection of officials, trying to affect the values and preferences which guide the political decision-making process, and seeking to include new issues on the agenda" (Morales, 2009, p. 57). Political participation is closely related to democratic and economic performance of a country, and, as Dalton (1988) argues, the success of democracy is measured by the extent of citizens' participation in the decision-making process. In addition, Putnam (2000) claims that consolidated democracies have higher conventional political participation rates, due to more developed democratic political culture.

In order to avoid conceptual stretching (Sartori, 1970) and to avoid making the study of political participation is "a study of everything" (Van Deth, 2001, p. 2), in this chapter, youth political participation is understood as attempts of young people to influence the decision-making process and put their issues on the political agenda (Kovacheva, 2005). Barnes and Kaase's (1979) differentiate between conventional and unconventional political participation, and this was later elaborated by Inglehart (1990). This is a distinction between *elite-directed activities* (voting, party membership, union membership), as opposed to *elite directing activities* (political discussion, participation in new social movements and protest activities).

Building on their argument, Grasso (2016, p. 17) operationalises conventional political participation in terms of voting, contacting a politician, donating money, joining a party, doing unpaid voluntary work for a political party, while unconventional political participation is captured by indicators such as signing a petition, joining a boycott, joining an environmental organisation, attending a demonstration and occupying public spaces. Taking this into account, a vast number of recent empirical studies focusing on young people confirm that they incline more towards unconventional political participation (Dalton, 2011; Grasso, 2016; Ilišin et al., 2013). As Kovacheva points out, research on young people in principle deals with three fundamental forms of political participation: "involvement in institutional politics (elections, campaigns and membership); protest activities (demonstrations and new social movements); and civic engagement (associative life, community participation, voluntary work)" (2005, p. 25). However, despite these recent discussions, very limited empirical research exists regarding unconventional youth participation due to measurement problems and the bias in self-reporting (Amnå & Ekman, 2014; Dalton, 2011; Kovacheva, 2005).

What About Us? Empirical Evidence from the Eastern Europe Periphery

In this section, we explore the relationship between the effects of austerity and political participation of young people in core and peripheral European states. Following similar analyses (Busch et al., 2013; Müller, 2014), austerity measures are operationalised into four indicators: unemployment rate, social expenditure on the Gross Domestic Product (GDP), risk of poverty and material deprivation. In addition, given our focus on young people, we include two more indicators: youth unemployment rate and the average age when young people leave their parental home. All data shown in Table 20.1 are for the year 2014 and retrieved from Eurostat, apart from the "social expenditure of the GDP" indicator, which was retrieved from the Organisation for Economic Co-operation and Development (OECD) database. In the following section, we present this data and the main findings, then relate the effects of austerity measures to patterns of young people's political participation. Information

Table 20.1 Austerity in the core and peripheral EU member states, 2014

Country	Unemployment (%)	Social expenditure (% of GDP)	Risk of poverty (%)	Material deprivation (%)	Youth unemployment (%)	Youth leaving home (average age)
Periphery						
Bulgaria	11.4	n.a.	40.1	33.1	23.8	29.1
Croatia	17.3	n.a.	29.3	13.9	45.5	31.0
Cyprus	16.1	n.a.	27.4	15.3	36.0	28.4
Czech Republic	6.1	19.1	14.8	6.7	15.9	26.7
Estonia	7.4	16.0	26.0	6.2	15.0	24.2
Greece	26.5	26.1	36.0	21.5	52.4	29.3
Hungary	7.7	21.4	31.8	24.0	20.4	27.7
Italy	12.7	29.0	28.3	11.6	42.7	30.1
Latvia	10.8	14.2	32.7	19.2	19.6	28.0
Lithuania	10.7	n.a.	27.3	13.6	19.3	26.1
Malta	5.8	n.a.	23.8	10.2	11.7	30.6
Poland	9.0	19.5	24.7	10.4	23.9	28.3
Portugal	14.1	24.5	24.7	10.6	34.7	28.8
Romania	6.8	n.a.	40.3	26.3	24.0	28.5
Slovakia	13.2	17.4	18.4	9.9	29.7	30.8
Slovenia	9.7	21.5	0.4	6.6	20.2	28.6
Spain	24.5	26.1	29.2	7.1	53.2	29.1
Periphery, average	**12.34**	**21.35**	**26.78**	**14.48**	**28.71**	**28.55**
Core						
Austria	5.6	27.9	19.2	4.0	10.3	25.4
Belgium	8.5	29.2	21.6	5.9	23.2	25.1
Denmark	6.6	29.0	17.9	3.2	12.6	21.2
Finland	8.2	30.0	17.3	2.8	20.5	21.9
France	10.3	31.9	18.5	6.7	24.2	23.7
Germany	5.0	24.9	20.6	5.0	7.7	23.8
Ireland	11.3	19.2	27.6	8.4	23.9	25.8
Luxembourg	6.0	23.0	19.0	1.4	22.3	26.7
Netherlands	7.4	n.a.	16.5	3.2	12.7	23.6
Sweden	7.9	27.1	16.9	0.7	22.9	20.9
United Kingdom	6.1	21.6	24.1	7.3	16.9	24.3
Core, average	**7.53**	**26.38**	**19.93**	**4.41**	**17.93**	**23.85**

Sources: OECD (2016) and Eurostat (2016b, 2016c, 2016d, 2016e, 2016f, 2016g)

on patterns of young people's political participation are obtained from the International Social Science Programme (ISSP) programme, the 2014 module on citizenship.

Core EU countries are characterised by higher overall economic development in contrast to Eastern and Southern Europe, regions most severely hit by austerity measures. In that sense, austerity measures may be seen as amplifying already strong core-periphery differences within Europe. Table 20.1 shows that core EU countries are performing better on all selected indicators. For instance, material deprivation, an indicator capturing the extent to which people have access to goods necessary for a decent life, is three times higher in the periphery than in the core of Europe. In addition, peripheral countries are marked by comparatively higher risk of poverty rates, demonstrating aggravated social welfare in the aftermath of austerity.

Regarding young people, Table 20.1 shows that those from peripheral Europe leave their parents' home later (average age is 28.5 years) in comparison to their peers from the West (average age 23.85 years). Though we know that cultural factors play a role here as well (Ule & Kuhar, 2008; Wallace & Kovatcheva, 1998), when analysed together with the social impact of austerity, the average age of young people leaving home does seem to be related primarily to economic factors. Furthermore, youth unemployment is substantially lower in the core, where the average rate is 17.93%, while the average youth unemployment rate in the EU periphery is 28.71%. This is in line with other studies, which have established that peripheral European counties have higher rates of youth unemployment (O'Reilly et al., 2015). Along the same lines, Table 20.1 shows that general unemployment levels are almost double in the periphery when compared to the core of Europe.

These findings suggest that life prospects of young people in the periphery of Europe are considerably more adverse than those of the core countries. In the following sections, we explore the possible relationships that austerity has had on patterns of conventional and unconventional youth political participation, focusing particularly on Eastern Europe.

We cluster political participation into two categories, using Grasso's (2016) conceptualisation of conventional and unconventional participation (see also Pickard, 2018). Unconventional political participation is captured by relying on the following survey items: signing a petition, boycotting certain products, taking part in protests, contacting the media, choosing products for political or environmental reasons, and expressing political views on the internet. Our measurement of conventional political participation includes the following survey items: voting in an election, contacting a politician, attending a political meeting or rally, donating money, and being a member of a party. In addition, young people are defined based on the mode value of national definitions of youth for the EU-28 countries (Eapyouth, 2015), that is, as the age group between 18 and 30.

Table 20.2 shows data on conventional participation among young people for countries of the core and of the Eastern periphery. Our selection of countries classified as core and Eastern periphery is based on countries that participated in the International Social Science Programme (ISSP) survey. The first two columns in Table 20.2 show percentages of young people who agree with the statement that voting is elections was important,

Table 20.2 Conventional youth participation, EU member states, 2014

	Voting in elections (%)		Contacting politician (%)	Rally participation (%)	Donations to politicians (%)	Party membership (%)
	Not important	Important				
Austria	5.4	35.65	14.8	19	40.4	6.2
Belgium	8.75	35.15	10.1	19.1	54.6	4.5
Denmark	3.9	41.05	10.7	28.2	54.9	4
Finland	12.35	30.8	6.8	17.3	38.3	3.2
France	4.3	40.95	7.5	20.7	43.7	2.4
UK	8.9	34.9	8.8	9.8	44.2	9.8
Sweden	2.2	41.3	17	29.8	53.8	5.3
Core	**6.54**	**37.11**	**10.81**	**20.56**	**47.12**	**5.1**
Croatia	11.15	33.35	5.7	8.2	26.4	9.5
Czech Republic	11.7	32.05	12.1	23.4	16.6	2.1
Hungary	9	34.2	2.6	6	3.5	2.5
Lithuania	5.4	39.25	7.7	13.4	38.7	6.5
Poland	7.4	35	3.2	7.8	20.2	1.2
Slovakia	14.85	27.05	5	6.2	6.3	n.a.
Slovenia	17.2	68.9	12.1	12	26.5	4.3
Eastern Europe	**10.92**	**38.54**	**6.9**	**11**	**19.74**	**4.35**
χ^2 (1;2)		2.52	2.629	1.097	34.644	1.64
p		0.110	0.000	0.000	0.000	0.200

Source: International Social Science Programme (ISSP). (2014). *Citizenship*. Retrieved from http://zacat.gesis.org/webview/index.jsp?object=http://zacat.gesis.org/obj/fStudy/ZA6670

while the remaining columns in Table 20.2 show the percentage of young people who report participating in the given activity, such as contacting a politician or being member of a political party. The last two rows show results of chi square test, used to establish whether there was a statistically significant difference in youth conventional participation rates between the two regions.

Table 20.2 shows that core countries are marked by higher rates of youth conventional participation in comparison to peripheral countries; in other words, in the Eastern periphery, fewer young people use available options for influencing decision-making process within the democratic system. Regarding regional differences, results of the chi square test suggest that for two dimensions—voting in elections and party membership—differences among youth in the core and in the Eastern periphery are not statistically significant. In the case of the remaining three dimensions—contacting a politician, rally participation and donation to a politician—statistically significant differences exist between young people in the core and in the periphery, with young people in the core showing much higher levels of activity. The low percentage regarding "donating funds to politicians" in Eastern Europe might be related to limited financial and material resources available to young people in these countries.

Next, we look at unconventional modes of youth political participation, shown in Table 20.3. The first two columns in Table 20.3 show the percentage of young people who agree that choosing products for political or environmental reasons is important, while the remaining five columns show the percentage of young people who stated that they participated in a certain activity.

As was the case with conventional political participation, data from Table 20.3 show that young people in the Eastern periphery are marked by significantly lower levels of unconventional political participation. Comparing regional averages between young people in the core and in the periphery of Europe shows substantial differences. While for instance 27.94% of young people in the core of Europe report participation in protests, only 12.1% of those in the Eastern periphery report this type of participation. What is particularly interesting is the indicator "choosing products for political and environmental reasons." Despite ubiquitous public debates on environmental issues and strong arguments about the necessity for new modes of understanding and acting towards natural environment, this message resonates with only 19% of young people in Eastern Europe. Chi square test results reveal statistically significant

Table 20.3 Unconventional youth political participation, EU member states, 2014

	Choosing products for political or environmental reasons (%)		Signing petitions (%)	Boycott (%)	Contacting media (%)	Participating in protests (%)	Expressing views on internet (%)
	Not Important	Important					
Austria	14.1	30.6	57.5	54.2	11.8	25.9	25.1
Belgium	18.2	23.15	69.9	36.5	8.2	27.8	21.7
Denmark	15.45	23.4	65	46.7	9	32.4	31.6
Finland	24.4	26.25	48.9	51.3	10.1	8.3	22.8
France	14.65	24.35	72.1	48.3	4.2	49.2	21.2
Sweden	7.65	37.5	75.5	70.8	10.8	33.3	40.2
UK	17.1	22.95	50.8	32.1	7.3	18.7	21.2
Core	**15.93**	**26.89**	**62.81**	**48.56**	**8.77**	**27.94**	**26.26**
Croatia	14.7	22	48.1	13.6	3.9	6.2	16.2
Czech Republic	20.9	20.9	54.8	25.7	11.8	13.3	27
Hungary	11.15	18.7	4.7	4.4	0.9	5.1	4.3
Lithuania	26.2	14.45	28.3	12.3	3.1	9.4	12.5
Poland	23.1	18	18.6	13.4	2.7	7.9	12.3
Slovakia	20.9	15.8	43.8	12.7	3.8	11.2	14.4
Slovenia	14.65	25.45	24.5	33.3	9.4	31.6	24.4
Eastern Europe	**18.8**	**19.33**	**31.83**	**16.49**	**5.1**	**12.1**	**15.87**
χ^2		41.56	3.02	37.07	37.229	1.858	47.364
p		0.000	0.000	0.000	0.000	0.000	0.000

Source: International Social Science Programme (ISSP). (2014). *Citizenship*. Retrieved from http://zacat.gesis.org/webview/index.jsp?object=http://zacat.gesis.org/obj/fStudy/ZA6670

differences between the two regions on all the presented indicators. This strengthens the finding that young people in the core are more active in unconventional modes of political participation. For example, they are keener to choose products for political or environmental reasons, express their views on various internet platforms, or to contact the media in order to address injustices.

Taken together, results on patterns of young people's political participation in conventional and unconventional activities distinguish young people in the core from those in the Eastern periphery of Europe. These findings are in line with studies that have shown the levels of political competence among young people to be lower in Eastern compared to Western Europe (Spajic-Vrkas & Cehulic, 2016). Furthermore, young people in Eastern Europe have lower levels of participation in unconventional compared to conventional modes of participation, suggesting their lower overall contentious potential. In contrast to findings from Southern Europe, where research showed significant levels of contentious activities and young people's participation in general (Cairns et al., 2016; Hooghe, 2012; Williamson, 2014), young people in Eastern Europe generally withhold from political participation, and in particular from unconventional modes of political participation.

Conclusion

In this chapter, we explored ways in which austerity policies have influenced patterns of youth political participation among the core and peripheral EU countries, focusing in particular on features of youth political participation in Eastern Europe. Our analysis showed that, despite the negative effects of austerity policies across Europe, their affect was stronger in the EU peripheries. Higher levels of exposure to risk of poverty and material deprivation, coupled with higher levels of general and youth unemployment were in our analysis related to statistically significant differences in the levels of youth political participation between the European core and its Eastern periphery. Young people on the periphery, instead of using their creativity and innovation to explore both conventional and unconventional modes of political participation, tend to refrain from all participation, and this seems particularly true for young people in Eastern Europe.

While severe socioeconomic conditions, which were further aggravated by austerity measures, resulted in the rise of unconventional political participation activities among youth in Southern Europe, the same has not been the case in Eastern Europe. On the contrary, our findings suggest a political passivity that cuts across the distinction between conventional and unconventional modes of political participation. When analysed together with lower levels of political interest, knowledge and trust (see Henn, Weinstein, & Hodgkinson, 2007), a rather gloomy picture emerges of young people's political potential in Europe's Eastern periphery. This finding has clear implications for democratic prospects of countries of Eastern Europe, some of which are currently exhibiting signs of the right-wing populism and authoritarian tendencies, for instance Hungary and

Poland. Our analysis also suggests that democratisation studies must rely more substantively on insights from political economy in order to explain features of political participation.

Finally, given that our findings suggest an interesting distinction between the Southern and Eastern peripheries when it comes to young people's involvement in contentious action. In future work, we would like to focus on systematically outlining the various features of young peoples' political participation in Southern and Eastern Europe, and rely on a broader array of empirical sources apart from international surveys. This should enable us to more confidently assess the cross-regional variance of young peoples' potential for contentious action, and the many features that may help explain it.

NOTE

1. Western European countries (**the core**): Austria, Belgium, Denmark, Finland, France, United Kingdom and Sweden; Eastern European countries (**the periphery**): Croatia, Czech Republic, Hungary, Lithuania, Poland, Slovakia and Slovenia.

REFERENCES

Amnå, E., & Ekman, J. (2014). Standby citizens: Diverse faces of political passivity. *European Political Science Review*, 6(2), 261–281.

Barnes, S., & Kaase, M. (Eds.). (1979). *Political action: Mass participation in five Western democracies.* Beverly Hills, CA: Sage Publications.

Blyth, M. (2013). *Austerity: The history of a dangerous idea.* Oxford: Oxford University Press.

Bohle, D., & Greskovits, B. (2012). *Capitalist diversity on Europe's periphery.* Ithaca, NY: Cornell University Press.

Busch, K., Hermann, C., Hinrichs, K., & Schulten, T. (2013). Euro crisis, austerity policy and the European social model. How crisis policies in Southern Europe threaten the EU's social dimension. *Friedrich-Ebert Stiftung*. Retrieved October 26, 2016, from http://library.fes.de/pdf-files/id/ipa/09656.pdf

Cairns, D., de Almeida Alves, N., Alexandre, A., & Correia, A. (2016). *Youth unemployment and job precariousness: Political participation in a neo-liberal era.* Basingstoke: Palgrave Macmillan.

Dalton, R. (1988). *Citizen politics in Western Democracies. Public opinion and political parties in the United States, Great Britain, West Germany, and France.* Chatham, NJ: Chatham House Publishers.

Dalton, R. (2011). Youth and participation beyond elections. In R. Dalton (Ed.), *Engaging youth in politics: Debating democracy's future* (pp. 112–131). New York and Amsterdam: International Debate Education Association.

de la Porte, C., & Pochet, P. (2014). Boundaries of welfare between the EU and member states during the "great recession". *Perspectives on European Politics and Society, 15*(3), 281–292.

Eapyouth. (2015). *Definition of youth according to age limits*. Retrieved November 27, 2016, from http://eapyouth.eu/sites/default/files/documents/request_4_age_limit.pdf

Epstein, R. (2014). Overcoming "economic backwardness" in the European Union. *JCMS: Journal of Common Market Studies, 52*(1), 17–34.

Esping-Andersen, G. (2002). *Why we need a new welfare state*. Oxford: Oxford University Press.

Eurostat. (2016a). *Expenditure on social protection, 2003–13*. Retrieved October 28, 2016, from http://ec.europa.eu/eurostat/statistics-explained/index.php/File:Expenditure_on_social_protection,_2003–13_(%25_of_GDP)_YB16.png

Eurostat. (2016b). *People at risk at poverty*. Retrieved October 30, 2016, from http://ec.europa.eu/eurostat/tgm/table.do?tab=table&init=1&language=en&pcode=t2020_50&plugin=1

Eurostat. (2016c). *Unemployment rate*. Retrieved October 30, 2016, from http://ec.europa.eu/eurostat/tgm/table.do?tab=table&init=1&language=en&pcode=tipsun20&plugin=1

Eurostat. (2016d). *Material deprivation*. Retrieved October 30, 2016, from http://ec.europa.eu/eurostat/statistics-explained/index.php/File:Severe_material_deprivation_rates,_2012-15_(early_data)_-_%25_of_population_update.png

Eurostat. (2016e). *Youth unemployment*. Retrieved October 30, 2016, from http://ec.europa.eu/eurostat/statistics-explained/index.php/File:Table_1_Youth_unemployment,_2015Q4_(%25).png

Eurostat. (2016f). *Youth leaving home—Average age*. Retrieved October 30, 2016, from http://ec.europa.eu/eurostat/statistics-explained/index.php/Being_young_in_Europe_today_-_family_and_society

Eurostat. (2016g). *Government gross debt*. Retrieved October 30, 2016, from http://ec.europa.eu/eurostat/statistics-explained/index.php/File:Public_balance_and_general_government_debt,_2012–2015_(%25_of_GDP)_YB16_III.png

France, A. (2007). *Understanding youth in late modernity*. Maidenhead: McGraw-Hill/Open University Press.

Furlong, A., & Cartmel, F. (1997). Risk and uncertainty in the youth transition. *Young: The Nordic Journal of Youth Research, 5*(1), 3–20.

Gaiser, W., De Rijke, J., & Spannring, R. (2010). Youth and political participation. Empirical results for Germany within a European context. *Young, 18*(4), 427–450.

Garrido, L., & Requena, M. (1996). *La emancipación de los jóvenes en España*. Madrid: Instituto de la Juventud (Ministerio de Trabajo y Asuntos Sociales).

Grasso, M. T. (2016). *Generations, political participation and social change in Western Europe*. London: Routledge.

Green Cowles, M., & Smith, M. (2000). *The state of the European Union. Risks, reform, resistance, and revival* (Vol. 5). Oxford: Oxford University Press.

Guillén, A., & Palier, B. (2004). Introduction: Does Europe matter? Accession to EU and social policy developments in recent and new member states. *Journal of European Social Policy, 14*(3), 203–209.

Hall, P. (2012, October 18). *Trouble in the Eurozone: Views on the once and future crisis*. Director's Seminar, Minda de Ginzburg Center for European Studies, Harvard University, Cambridge, MA. Retrieved November 22, 2016, from https://www.youtube.com/watch?v=vwWTMdTlRq0

Hanzl-Weiss, D., & Landesmann, M. (2013). *Structural adjustment and unit labour cost developments in Europe's periphery: Patterns before and during the crisis*. Retrieved November 22, 2016, from http://wiiw.ac.at/structural-adjustment-and-unit-labour-cost-developments-in-europe-s-periphery-patterns-before-and-during-the-crisis-p-2986.html

Henn, M., Weinstein, M., & Hodgkinson, S. (2007). Social capital and political participation: Understanding the dynamics of young people's political disengagement in contemporary Britain. *Social Policy and Society, 6*(4), 467–479.

Hooghe, M. (2012). Taking to the streets: Economic crises and youth protest in Europe. *Harvard International Review, 34*(2), 34–38.

Ilišin, V., Bouillet, D., Gvozdanović, A., & Potočnik, D. (2013). *Mladi u vremenu krize*. Zagreb: IDIZ i Friedrich Ebert Stiftung.

Inglehart, R. (1990). *Culture shift in advanced industrial society*. Princeton: Princeton University Press.

International Labour Organization (ILO). (2012). *World of work report 2012: Better jobs for a better economy*. Retrieved November 22, 2016, from https://www.cliclavoro.gov.it/Moduli%20e%20Documenti/world_of_work_report_2012.pdf

International Social Science Programme (ISSP). (2014). *Citizenship*. Retrieved October 22, 2016, from http://zacat.gesis.org/webview/index.jsp?object=http://zacat.gesis.org/obj/fStudy/ZA6670

Jacoby, W. (2014). The politics of the Eurozone crisis: Two puzzles behind the German consensus. *German Politics Society, 32*(2), 70–85.

Judt, T. (2009, February 12). What is living and what is dead in social democracy? *The New York Review of Books, 56*(2). Retrieved from http://www.nybooks.com/articles/2009/12/17/what-is-living-and-what-is-dead-in-social-democrac/

Kimberlee, R. (2002). Why don't British young people vote at general elections? *Journal of Youth Studies, 5*(1), 85–98.

King, L. (2007). Central European capitalism in comparative perspective. In B. Hancké, M. Rhodes, & M. Thatcher (Eds.), *Beyond varieties of capitalism: Conflict, contradictions, and complementarities in the European economy* (pp. 307–327).

Kovacheva, S. (2000). *Keys to youth participation in Eastern Europe*. Strasbourg: Council of Europe Publishing.

Kovacheva, S. (2005). Will youth rejuvenate the patterns of political participation? In J. Forbig (Ed.), *Revisiting youth political participation* (pp. 19–29). Strasbourg: Council of Europe Publishing.

Lehndorff, S. (2012). *A triumph of failed ideas: European models of capitalism in the crisis*. Brussels: European Trade Union Institute.

Lima, M., & Artiles, A. (2013). Youth voice(s) in EU countries and social movements in Southern Europe. *Transfer: European Review of Labour and Research, 19*(3), 345–364.

Mair, P. (2013). *Ruling the void: The hollowing of Western democracy*. London: Verso.

Mannheim, K. (1970). The problem of generations. *Psychoanalytic Review, 57*(3), 163–195.

McKee, M., Karanikolos, M., Belcher, P., & Stuckler, D. (2012). Austerity: A failed experiment on the people of Europe. *Clinical Medicine, 12*(4), 346–350.

Morales, L. (2009). *Joining political organisations: Institutions, mobilisation and participation in Western democracies*. Colchester: European Consortium for Political Research Press.

Morciano, D., Scardigno, A. F., Manuti, A., & Pastore, S. (2014). An evaluation study of youth participation in youth work: A case study in Southern Italy. *Educational Research for Policy and Practice, 13*(1), 81–100.

Müller, G. (2014). Fiscal austerity and the multiplier in times of crisis. *German Economic Review, 15*(2), 243–258.

Naustdalslid, J. (1977). A multi-level approach to the study of center-periphery systems and socio-economic change. *Journal of Peace Research, 14*(3), 203–222.

Nölke, A., & Vliegenthart, A. (2009). Enlarging the varieties of capitalism: The emergence of dependent market economies in East Central Europe. *World Politics, 6*(4), 670–702.

Organisation for Economic Co-operation and Development (OECD). (2016). *Social expenditure of the GDP*. Retrieved October 30, 2016, from https://stats.oecd.org/Index.aspx?DataSetCode=SOCX_AGG#

O'Reilly, J., Eichhorst, W., Gábos, A., Hadjivassiliou, K., Lain, D., Leschke, J., et al. (2015). Five characteristics of youth unemployment in Europe. *Sage Open, 5*(1), 1–19. Retrieved October 22, 2016, from https://iris.unitn.it/retrieve/handle/11572/118356/28725/O%27Reilly%20et%20al.%202015_SAGE%20Open.full.pdf

Pickard, S. (2018). *Politics, protest and young people. Political participation and dissent in Britain in the 21st century.* London: Palgrave Macmillan. [forthcoming]
Putnam, R. (2000). *Bowling alone: America's declining social capital.* New York: Simon & Schuster.
Sartori, G. (1970). Concept misformation in comparative politics. *American Political Science Review, 64*(4), 1033–1053.
Schweiger, C., & Magone, J. M. (2014). Differentiated integration and cleavage in the EU under crisis conditions. *Perspectives on European Politics and Society, 15*(3), 259–265.
Single European Act. (1987). *Amending treaty establishing the European economic community, 25 March 1957.* Retrieved January 18, 2017, from http://eur-lex.europa.eu/legal-content/EN/TXT/?uri=URISERV%3Axy0027
Siurala, L. (2000). *Changing forms of youth participation.* Paper presented at the round table on New Forms of Youth Participation, Biel, Switzerland. Retrieved November 29, 2016, from www.coe.fr/youth/research/participation
Sloam, J. (2007). Rebooting democracy: Youth participation in politics in the UK. *Parliamentary Affairs, 60*(4), 548–567.
Spajic-Vrkas, V., & Cehulic, M. (2016). Istraživanje građanskog odgoja i obrazovanja—Višerazinski pregled. In M. Kovačić & M. Horvat (Eds.), *Od podanika do građana: Razvoj građanske kompetencije mladih* (pp. 153–186). Zagreb: Institut za društvena istraživanja i GONG.
The Stability and Growth Pact. (1998). *Resolution of the amsterdam European council on the stability and growth pact.* Retrieved January 22, 2017, from http://eur-lex.europa.eu/legal-content/EN/TXT/?qid=1412156825485&uri=URISERV:l25021
Treaty of Maastricht on European Union. (1992). Retrieved January 17, 2017, from http://eur-lex.europa.eu/legal-content/EN/TXT/?uri=uriserv%3Axy0026
Ule, M. (1988). *Mladina in ideologija.* Ljubljana: Delavska enotnost.
Ule, M., & Kuhar, M. (2008). Orientations of young adults in Slovenia toward the family formation. *Young, 16*(2), 153–183.
Vachudova, M. A. (2014). EU leverage and national interests in the balkans: The puzzles of enlargement ten years on. *JCMS: Journal of Common Market Studies, 52*(1), 122–138.
Van Deth, J. (2001, April 6–11). *Studying political participation: Towards a theory of everything?* Joint Sessions of Workshops, European Consortium for Political Research, Grenoble, France.
Wallace, C., & Kovatcheva, S. (1998). *Youth in society: The construction and deconstruction of youth in East and West Europe.* Basingstoke: Palgrave Macmillan.
Williamson, H. (2014). Radicalisation to retreat: Responses of the young to austerity Europe. *International Journal of Adolescence and Youth, 19*(1), 5–18.

Marko Kovacic is a Research Assistant in Public Policy and Political Sociology at the Institute for Social Research in Zagreb, Croatia, where he studies youth political participation, youth work and civic education. His academic background is in political science and public policy.

Danijela Dolenec is Assistant Professor at University of Zagreb, Croatia, researching comparative politics of post-socialism, contentious politics and social science methodology. She published *Democratic Institutions and Authoritarian Rule in Southeast Europe* (ECPR, 2013) and currently leads the research project *Disobedient Democracy*.

Index[1]

NUMBERS & SYMBOLS
#FeesMustFall (#FMF), 21, 24, 28, 30, 33–5
#JezWeCan, 120–1
#MomentumGrassroots, 124–6
#PayBacktheMoney, 29
#RhodesMustFall (#RMF), 9, 21, 24, 28, 30–5
#SaveHongKong, 100
#*Yosoy132*, 350, 351, 354, 359, 360, 365, 368n13
4Chan, 10, 99–101, 103–6, 109, 110, 110n4, 143, 144
15M, 13, 102, 333–46
38 Degrees, 183
99 percent, 121
1033 program, 47–9, 50–2, 54n14, 54n15

A
active citizenship, 221, 266
activism, 8, 9, 11, 13, 19, 21, 28, 30, 31, 41–54, 59–74, 81, 86, 88, 98, 99, 101, 109, 110, 133n9, 143, 164, 182–3, 185, 187–9, 191, 206, 227, 237, 240, 242, 247, 256, 259, 263–6, 274, 299, 301, 303–5, 323, 333–46, 377, 381
activist artwork, 85
activist biographies, 187
activist reading a book, 202
affordable housing, 116, 181, 238
Africa, 2, 5, 6, 15, 19–36, 59–74, 81, 378
African Americans, 46, 47, 54n12, 54n15, 140, 143–5, 148, 150, 300, 304–6
African National Congress Youth League (ANCYL), 25–8
agency, 2, 7–8, 10, 27, 68, 255
agnostic democracy, 315–32
agonism, 153
alienation (political), 27, 144, 162, 174, 179, 218, 233, 235, 256, 277, 279, 281, 282, 325
alternative facts, 140

[1] Note: Page numbers with "n" denote notes.

alternative lessons, 285
alternative news, 149
altruism, 153, 222
Amnesty International, 71, 84
Anarchopanda, 15, 361
anarchy/anarchists, 15, 84, 87, 90, 102, 149, 285, 337, 340, 345n1
ANCYL. *See* African National Congress Youth League (ANCYL)
anger, 14, 35, 88, 143, 151–3, 299, 326, 360
Anglin, Andrew, 143–5, 148–51, 155–6n7
Anonymous, 100–1, 105, 106, 109, 110n3, 143, 148
antagonism, 78, 152, 153, 279, 289
anti-apartheid, 19, 23, 27
anti-austerity, 120, 123, 257, 290n2, 290n3, 317
anti-capitalist, 199, 208, 334, 342
anti-colonialism, 23
anti-establishment, 340
anti-fracking, 123
anti-politics, 132
anti-racism, 287
anti-radicalisation, 11, 162, 164, 167–8
anti-social behaviour, 324
anti-terrorism, 164
anti-war, 120, 189
apathy (political), 7, 13, 27, 80, 179, 202, 233, 235, 247, 257, 277, 290, 316–18, 350, 366, 377
Arab Spring, 206, 335, 346n5
arbitrary arrest, 6
Argentina, 368n8
arrêtez-moi quelqu'un, 360
arson, 35
art engagé, 85
artwork/art, 10, 50, 85–7, 91, 171, 277, 356, 358
Asia, 2, 15, 97–110, 233–48, 378

asymmetrical power relations, 109
austerity, 5, 13, 14, 78, 80, 89, 116, 120, 123, 140, 142, 180–2, 190, 212n5, 217–22, 227, 228, 234, 244–7, 255–8, 266, 268n1, 273, 276, 281, 291n5, 307, 317, 318, 320, 323, 335, 341, 350, 365, 366, 368n11, 375–89

  measures, 78, 80, 89, 123, 142, 217, 218, 246, 256, 276, 291, 318, 335, 341, 350, 366, 375–7, 379, 380, 382, 384, 388

  policies, 5, 13, 14, 116, 140, 180, 181, 255, 257, 258, 268n1, 281, 291n5, 375–7, 380, 381, 388

  regimes, 5
Australia, 2, 5–7, 11, 15, 101, 110n3, 155n4, 164, 166, 169, 180, 217–28, 236
Australian Youth Forum (AYF), 221
Austria, 141, 155n4, 376, 379, 380, 383, 385, 387, 389n1
authoritarianism, 3, 11, 144, 363
autonomy, 8, 11, 83, 108, 201, 204, 205, 209, 210, 236, 240, 242, 261, 263, 265, 275, 284, 285, 308, 311, 376, 377

B

bailout, 5, 276
ballot box(es), 318, 352
banane rebelle, 361
banking crisis, 4, 5, 237, 242
bankruptcy, 5, 276
barricades, 107, 206, 208
Beck, Ulrich, 61, 80, 235, 278
Beijing, 99, 234
Belgium, 161, 383, 385, 387, 389n1

belonging, 65, 67, 123, 151, 153, 174, 236, 333, 338
BES. *See* British Election Study (BES)
besotón, 361
Bessant, Judith, 99, 124, 139–56, 219, 223, 237, 277, 289, 290
big oganising, 125
bird watching, 67
Bite the Ballot, 184
Black Consciousness, 31
Black Lives Matter, 6, 305, 306
Black Panthers, 305
black youth, 30, 32, 220, 300
blockades, 358, 363
blog, 45, 46, 53, 79, 85, 146, 170, 171, 173, 241, 288
Bologna, 12, 253, 258–60, 263, 266
Born-Free generation, 23, 36n2
Bourdieu, Pierre, 279, 323, 337, 345
boycotting, 184, 189, 236, 356, 382
boycotting a product, 86, 182, 384
Breitbart, 148, 149
Brexit, 6, 127, 139
Britain. *See* UK
British Election Study (BES), 132n1
British Social Attitudes surveys, 188
British Youth Council, 184
Bulgaria, 268n5, 379, 380, 383
bulletproof vests, 50
business leaders, 14
bypassing mainstream/conventional/traditional media, 8, 11–14, 48, 60, 61, 63, 69, 78, 80, 101, 103, 104, 110, 115, 120, 132, 140, 147, 148, 153, 179, 181–3, 185, 187, 191, 193, 202, 205, 218–20, 225, 226, 236, 242, 256, 257, 267, 274, 275, 277, 278, 283, 284, 289, 316, 335, 341, 376, 377, 381, 382, 384–8

C
California, 9, 41–54, 297–311
camps, 62, 63, 123, 148, 192, 242, 336
Canada, 77–91, 180, 349–68
canteens (popular), 260–2, 264, 265
carré rouge, 363
Cartmel, Fred, 235, 236, 282, 380
casseroles, 356
Catalan, 337, 345n1
Catalonia, 13, 333–46
cause-based politics, 82, 219, 236
cause-orientated politics, 236
Central America, 2, 15, 349–68
centri sociali, 259, 260
Change.org, 183
chat rooms, 104, 106
Chile, 6, 349–68
China, 6, 97, 105–7, 234, 242, 246
Chinese Communist Party, 97
citizenship, 8, 11, 12, 62, 79, 181, 192, 217–28, 266, 267, 322, 381, 384
Citizenship Studies, 316
clean ups, 59, 65, 70
clicktivism, 184, 189, 193
climate change, 5, 71, 155n5, 361
collaborative individualization, 266
collective action, 12, 13, 237, 257, 265, 266, 278, 289, 306, 353, 354, 357, 358, 361, 366
communal meals, 15, 208, 209
communism, 105, 337
communities, 4, 10, 12, 15, 44, 45, 47, 49, 54n15, 62, 63, 68, 70, 71, 79, 84, 104, 123, 125, 126, 130, 131, 144, 150, 152, 153, 164, 166, 187, 189, 199, 208, 220–4, 234–6, 238, 258, 265, 273, 282, 285, 297, 298, 300, 301, 304–11, 317, 321, 322, 324, 325, 337, 350, 359, 382

community building, 7, 8, 11, 197–294
Community Rights Campaign (CRC), 43, 44, 46, 47, 54n12
community work, 300, 309
concerts, 81, 85, 125, 279, 358
conditional participation, 256
confrontation, 64, 69, 72, 343, 356
conservation, 68, 71, 72
conservatism, 6, 11, 155n6, 211n2
conspiracy theories, 140
consumerism, 5, 11, 63, 184, 203, 205, 209, 210, 235, 310
contacting a politician, 182, 382, 385, 386
conventional politics, 61, 69, 132, 193, 202, 236, 275, 278, 283, 284
cooperatives, 257
Corbynistas, 10, 115–34
Corbynites, 120
Corbyn, Jeremy, 116, 118–23, 125–32, 132n4, 133n5–8, 134n11
corruption, 14, 29
costumes, 50
counter-conduct, 11, 199–212
counter movement, 13, 105
counter-terrorism, 162, 164, 165
CRC. *See* Community Rights Campaign (CRC)
creativity, 78, 86, 126, 202, 204, 210, 274, 288, 352, 353, 361, 377, 388
credit, 4, 5, 223
criminalization, 4, 9, 13, 42, 44–6, 48, 53, 219, 298, 300–3, 306, 308, 311, 350, 353, 354, 357, 358, 363, 365, 366, 368n11
criminal justice reform, 13, 298, 299, 307

crisis
  in banking, 237, 242
  in constitutional affairs, 2
  of democracy, 1, 6, 10, 97–110, 310
  in the environment, 2, 9, 60, 64
  in finance, 4
  in politics, 10, 20, 62, 366
Croatia, 383, 385, 387, 389n1
cultural associations, 227
currency crisis, 5
cyber-activism, 109
cycling, 88
cynicism, 89, 179, 193, 210
Cyprus, 383
Czech Republic, 383, 385, 387, 389n1

D
Daily Stormer (the), 141, 143–6, 148–53
Dalton, Russell, 182, 189, 192, 376, 381, 382
damaging property, 184
debt, 2, 3, 5, 180, 223, 268n1, 276, 378, 379
decolonisation, 31
democracy, 1, 3, 6, 11, 13, 14, 20, 21, 23, 26, 77, 78, 89, 91, 97–110, 115, 117, 123, 126, 140, 143, 181, 184, 192, 217–28, 246, 247, 273, 275, 277, 285, 289, 291n5, 315–28, 335, 349–68, 376, 377, 381
democratic capitalism, 318
democratic participation, 77, 79, 117, 316, 357
demonstrations, 15, 30, 50, 51, 68, 79, 81, 84, 85, 88, 91, 183, 185, 188–91, 205, 236, 237, 287, 334, 336, 338, 342, 343, 354, 355, 358, 359, 361, 382

Denmark, 141, 379, 383, 385, 387, 389n1
dependence/dependency, 25, 238, 255, 261, 376–8, 381
depoliticization, 193, 274, 280, 308, 309, 350
deregulation, 3, 4, 218, 254, 255, 268n3, 379
die-ins, 305
digital media, 10, 146–8, 153
digital technologies, 103, 116, 121, 125, 126, 131, 146–8, 184
direct action, 153, 236, 246, 306, 334, 355, 368n7, 368n12
direct democracy, 123, 126, 140
direct volunteering, 222
disaffection, 256, 275, 343, 350
discrimination, 22, 31, 36n1, 82, 263
disempowerment, 273, 277
disenfranchisement, 316
disengagement (political), 61–3, 247, 317
disillusionment, 234, 317
displaying a badge, 183, 185, 191
dissent, 4, 26, 62, 79, 152, 199, 201–2, 205, 363–5, 367
distributed denial of service attacks, 100, 106, 149
documentary videos, 86
donating to a cause/party, 182, 183, 191, 382, 385

E
Eastern Europe, 14, 375–89
ecological footprint, 86
economic crisis, 4, 5, 11, 29, 116, 155n6, 179, 180, 190, 237, 259, 275, 317, 344, 350, 366, 379
Economic Freedom Fighters (EFF), 9, 21, 23, 24, 28–35
economic growth, 5, 14

economic hardship, 257
EDL. *See* English Defence League (EDL)
education, 2–4, 14, 24, 25, 33, 52, 53n1, 53n2, 54n6, 63, 64, 68–70, 74n3, 91n1, 116, 125, 187, 192, 218, 220, 225, 236, 245, 255, 273, 298, 303, 328n2, 351–3, 355, 357, 361, 367n5
EFF. *See* Economic Freedom Fighters (EFF)
elections, 6, 8, 26, 36n1, 61, 68, 69, 79, 84, 89, 115, 117–20, 122, 124, 126–8, 130–2, 132n1, 132n2, 139–42, 144, 145, 155n4, 182, 183, 191, 211n2, 217, 244, 248n3, 256, 277, 284, 286, 290n2, 316, 317, 326, 337, 339, 345n1, 346n7, 357, 366, 376, 382, 385, 386
electoral participation, 77, 376
electoral register/roll, 118, 127, 217
electoral turnout, 77, 89, 132n1
elites, 3, 14, 29, 34, 80, 140, 152, 190, 205, 234, 256, 276, 323, 335, 359, 366
emailing, 121, 125
emotions, 42, 50, 110, 140–3, 151–4, 207, 210, 274, 321, 325
empowering activities, 125
empowerment, 153, 262, 301
engagement, 7, 11–13, 20, 27, 30, 32, 35, 59, 61, 63, 73, 74, 81, 84, 86, 89, 99, 122, 129, 144, 153, 165, 169, 171, 173, 182, 184, 193, 219, 220, 224, 235, 236, 240–2, 244, 247, 248, 253, 254, 256–9, 262, 263, 265, 266, 274, 277, 278, 287, 289, 317, 320–1, 323, 325, 327, 344, 382
England, 315–28. *See also* United Kingdom

English Defence League (EDL), 141–3, 237
enthusiasm, 102, 116, 121, 122, 124, 126, 131, 223, 242
entrepreneurial self, 226
entryism, 10, 130
entryists, 128, 130
environment (the), 66–8, 70, 73, 83, 225, 302
environmental activism, 9, 59–74
environmental clubs, 59, 60, 64–73
environmentalism, 9, 15, 60–73
environmental responsibility, 27, 67–9, 87
Estonia, 383
ethical consumerism, 184
ethnography, 9, 12, 13, 41–54, 143, 238, 253–68, 274, 309, 334, 335, 340, 346n3
EU. *See* European Union (EU)
Europe, 2, 11, 15, 116, 124, 141, 144, 154n1, 179–93, 218, 219, 237
European Union (EU), 6, 14, 127, 154n2, 185, 268n1, 276, 290n2, 290n3, 291n5, 316, 375–80, 383–5, 387, 388
evictions, 71, 335, 338, 339
e-volunteering, 220, 224
exclusion, 13, 33, 173, 181, 209, 222, 228, 241, 273, 275, 358
extended youth, 239, 381
extremism, 6, 10, 131, 162–4, 166, 168, 172

F
Facebook, 52, 79, 101, 104–6, 125, 146, 150, 169–71, 183, 189, 191, 263, 356, 358, 359
fake news, 148
false consciousness, 20, 21
family-based morality, 206
family-based politics, 11, 201
Fanonian moment, 20, 35, 36
Farage, Nigel, 6, 139
Femen, 368n10
finance, 4, 5, 29, 355, 379
financial house, 5
Finland, 383, 385, 387, 389n1
Five Star movement, 187
flashmobs, 350
folk devils, 166
France, 2, 6, 140, 141, 154n2, 155n3, 155n4, 155n6, 161, 179, 185, 268n5, 275, 379, 383, 385, 387, 389n1
franchise, 163, 182, 240
freedom of association, 365
freedom of the press, 6, 163
freedom of speech, 6, 106, 148, 285
free legal advice, 257
free medical services, 257
funas, 358, 368n7
Furlong, Andy, vi, 3, 61, 189, 235, 236, 282, 380

G
gang culture, 238
gap years, 224
gender, 21, 22, 32, 81, 140, 192, 200, 284, 300
generational inequalities, 2, 266
generation differences, 182, 187, 188, 190
generations, 1, 20, 33, 79, 99, 116, 120, 132, 146, 169, 187–90, 193, 235, 236, 240, 242, 255, 257, 264, 268, 280, 281, 287, 288, 318, 324, 327, 334, 345, 376
Germany, 5, 6, 140–2, 154n2, 161, 179, 185, 268n5, 275, 376, 379, 383

Gezi Resistance, 11, 199–212
Gezi Spirit, 11, 201, 206–11
GFC. *See* Global Financial Crisis (GFC)
Glasgow, 237–9, 241–7
Global Financial Crisis (GFC), 5, 9, 12, 21, 23–5, 24, 28, 35, 116, 180, 217, 218, 233, 253–7, 261, 263, 264, 266, 268n1, 268n3, 273, 375–8
globalization, 61, 64, 82, 155n6, 234, 237, 327
global politics, 139, 378
global warming, 5, 71, 361
global 'war on terror,' 4
governance, 5, 10, 14, 68, 226, 276, 310, 311, 319
graduates, 3, 7, 63–6, 69, 81, 201, 260, 281
graffiti, 86, 202, 204, 206, 209, 210, 334
grassroots organizations/ members, 10, 13, 115–34, 240, 242, 259, 267, 298–301, 308
Great Recession (the), 4
Greece, 5, 12, 179, 185, 273–91, 379, 383
Green Party/Greens, 115, 128, 189
green politics, 339
G20 summit, 82

H

Habermas, Jürgen, 99, 103–5, 107, 109, 110, 364
habitus, 12, 274, 279, 285, 286, 288–90, 342
hacktivism, 144, 148, 149
health issues, 341
Henn, Matt, 77, 235, 236, 388
hetero-politics, 12, 273–5
higher education, 3, 33, 53n1, 116, 218, 351–3

high school students, 34, 42, 44, 45, 48, 49, 53, 54n7, 54n15, 302, 303
hip-hop, 84, 85, 87
homeless, 71, 259–66, 268n7, 280
home ownership, 190
homophobia, 210, 226
Hong Kong, 6, 10, 12, 97–110, 233–48
Hong Kong Golden, 10, 99–101, 103–7, 109, 110
horizontal, 68, 123, 131, 341
housing, 2, 128, 155n6, 233, 238, 243, 244, 255, 257, 259, 260, 264, 316, 321, 335, 339, 340
housing occupations, 257
humanitarian crisis, 4, 140
humanitarian disaster, 4
human rights, 14, 71, 74n2, 82, 83, 225, 346n5, 353, 359
humour, 11, 163, 168, 171–4, 206
Hungary, 379, 380, 383, 385, 387, 388, 389n1
hybrid identities, 60, 61, 66, 71–3
hyper-consumerism, 206

I

Identitarian movement, 141
identities, 6, 11, 34, 35, 60–2, 64–7, 71–3, 74, 105, 108–10, 168–70, 173, 184, 189, 201, 209, 211n4, 235, 237, 244, 247, 275, 289, 306, 320, 328, 340, 380
illegal graffiti, 86
imagination/imaginative, 7, 9, 28, 33, 73, 121, 143, 166
IMF. *See* International Monetary Fund (IMF)
immigrants/immigration, 91, 91n1, 140, 142, 143, 149, 154n2, 155n4, 155n6, 166, 234, 237, 263, 280, 286
impoverishment, 275

inclusiveness, 11, 201, 207–10
indebtedness, 275, 289
Indignados, 79, 276, 334, 336, 339, 341, 345n2, 346n4
individual autonomy, 209, 210
Individual Electoral Registration (IER), 127
individualism, 210, 265, 275, 282, 289, 350
Indonesia, 62
Indyref, 12, 233–48
inequalities, 4, 5, 9, 14, 20–5, 34, 35, 82, 83, 181, 190–2, 193, 221, 227, 234, 236, 237, 246, 266, 279, 284, 297, 301, 307, 324, 355, 378
infantilisation, 377
injustices, 7, 9, 14, 61, 72, 82–3, 152, 167, 298, 299, 303, 325, 326, 387
innovation, 4, 268n4, 377, 388
insecurity, 3, 181, 254, 275, 289
Instagram, 52, 125
intergenerational inequality, 2
International Monetary Fund (IMF), 60, 276, 291n5, 379
International Social Science Programme (ISSP), 79, 377, 384, 385
internet, 28, 30, 99, 103–6, 121, 124, 144, 146, 149, 169, 170, 189, 205, 280, 302, 303, 360, 385, 387
internet trolls, 105
interns, 218, 221
internships, 218, 221
Ireland, 171, 383
Islam, 155n5, 155n7, 166, 170, 171, 211n2
isolation, 11, 279, 305, 307, 309
isolationism, 6
isonomy, 14, 351, 365
ISSP. *See* International Social Science Programme (ISSP)

issue-based politics, 219
Istanbul, 15, 199, 203, 208
Italy, 12, 141, 179, 185, 187, 253–68, 379, 383

J

JDP. *See* Justice and Development Party (JDP)
Jihadi, 172
job insecurity, 255, 276
joining a political party, 182, 382
Jones, Owen, 3, 116, 121, 123, 316
journalism, 14, 280, 288
justice, 2, 3, 43, 78, 80, 82–3, 110, 120, 153, 154, 164, 226, 235, 238, 239, 247, 297–304, 307, 309, 310, 323–6, 353, 354
Justice and Development Party (JDP), 11, 199–201, 203–5, 209–11, 211n2, 212n5
justice reform, 299

K

Kenya, 9, 15, 59–61, 63, 71, 73
kettle/kettling, 354

L

labelling, 165, 169
labour market, 3, 4, 24, 61, 180, 218, 221, 222, 237, 247, 254, 255, 268n3, 381
land degradation, 71
Latvia, 383
law enforcement, 42–4, 297, 302, 304, 306
Lebanon, 62
legitimacy, 1, 85, 88, 90, 103, 140, 153, 180, 184, 323, 350, 353, 360, 364, 365
leisure, 7, 169, 234, 237, 238

Lesbian, Gay, Bisexual, Transgender and Queer (LGBTQ), 199, 208, 210, 211n3
liberalism, 2, 103, 378
Libya, 4
life politics, 236, 281
lifestyle choices, 78, 86, 87
lifestyle politics, 184, 189
Lithuania, 141, 383, 385, 387, 389
Lleida, 13, 333–46
local saving groups, 257
Los Angeles, 9, 15, 41–54, 297, 303, 306
low-paid work, 218
Luxembourg, 383

M

mainstream media, 7, 86, 140, 142, 144, 173, 202
Malaysia, 6
Malik, Shiv, 2, 116
Malta, 383
Manning, Nathan, 7
maNufestations, 15, 361
Maple Spring, 13, 349–68
marches, 34, 84, 88, 206, 305, 306, 356, 357, 359, 361
marginalisation, 24, 27, 63, 316, 350
Marsh, David, 79, 102, 110n3, 180, 184, 189, 235, 236, 277
mass arrests, 354, 364
mass demonstrations, 358
mass media, 162, 235, 351, 357, 359, 361
meals (communal), 208, 209
media coverage, 212n6, 217
me generation, 1
Member of Parliament (MP), 118, 120, 128–31, 132n4, 133n9, 183–4, 188
meme, 106, 145, 150
mental illness, 321

Mexico, 13, 350, 354, 358–62, 365
Middle East, 219
migrants, 259–61, 263, 264, 268n7
Militant Tendancy, 128–9
Millennial generation, 169
mobilization, 7, 31, 33, 68, 89, 121, 193, 200–2, 238, 247, 281, 283, 286, 306, 339, 343, 345, 345n2, 354
Momentum, 10, 115–34
money donation, 182, 183, 185, 191, 382, 385
Montreal, 81, 82, 354, 355, 357, 363, 364
moral panics, 169
Mouffe, Chantal, 152–4, 276, 278, 358, 362
movementists, 10, 115–34
Movimento Cinque Stelle (Five Star movement), 187
MP. *See* Member of Parliament (MP)
Muslims, 7, 11, 140, 144, 155n5, 161–74, 199, 208, 275
mutual help, 12, 267
Myanmar, 6

N

National Campaign against Fees and Cuts (NCAFC), 123
National Citizenship Service (NCS), 316
National Curriculum, 316
National Health Service (NHS), 125, 127, 326
nationalism, 4, 6, 143, 234, 237, 241, 248n2
nationalist political parties, 140, 141, 244
National Voter Registration Day (#NVRD), 184
nature lovers, 62

NCAFC. *See* National Campaign against Fees and Cuts (NCAFC)
NICT. *See* New communication and information technologies (NICT)
NCS. *See* National Citizenship Service (NCS)
NEET. *See* not in education, employment or training (NEET)
neighbourhood tours, 302
neoliberalism, 3, 9, 60, 61, 68, 78, 89, 90, 116, 226, 276, 308, 311, 315, 318–20, 358
Netherlands (the), 6, 155n3, 155n6
network cultures, 148
New communication and information technologies (NICT), 350, 351, 358
New Labour, 120–2, 132n5
new social movements, 60, 181, 382
New York Police Department (NYPD), 304
New Zealand, 180
NGO. *See* non-governmental organisation (NGO)
NHS. *See* National Health Service (NHS)
non-governmental organisation (NGO), 62, 84, 275, 280
non-violent resistance, 202
Norris, Pippa, 77, 192, 322
not-for-profit sector, 219, 225
not in education, employment or training (NEET), 255
NYPD. *See* New York Police Department (NYPD)

O

occupations, 98, 99, 102, 133n6, 183–5, 190, 191, 203, 211n1, 237, 240, 257, 264, 287, 335, 339–41, 349, 352, 353, 358, 360, 363, 364

Occupy, 79, 102, 106, 109, 121, 133n9, 190, 203, 210, 246
Occupy Central, 97–100, 106, 107
Occupy London, 123, 181
Occupy Wall Street, 99, 156n8, 335
OECD. *See* Organisation for Economic Cooperative Development (OECD)
One Member One Vote (OMOV), 118, 129
online activism, 11, 99, 101, 182, 183, 185, 187, 191, 206
openness, 11, 188, 201, 207–10
Organisation for Economic Cooperative Development (OECD), 290n1, 382

P

pacifist resistance, 340
PAH. *See Plataforma de Afectadospor las Hipotecas* (PAH)
pamphlets, 85, 149
parliamentary expenses scandal, 242
Parliamentary Labour Party (PLP), 117, 126, 131
participatory citizenship, 316
Partispace, 12, 258
part-time work, 3, 218
party membership, 61, 115–19, 122, 124, 128, 130–2, 132n2, 132n3, 141–4, 146, 181–3, 185, 187, 191, 235, 240, 244, 247, 248n2, 256, 277, 291n5, 381, 382, 385
PaTH. *See* Prepare, Trial, Hire (PaTH)
Penguin Media, 205
People's Republic of China (PRC), 97, 98, 107
personality, 120, 121, 363
pessimism, 243, 257, 280
petitioning, 183, 187, 236
petitions, 306, 323

petition signing, 79, 84, 182, 326, 382, 384, 387
Pickard, Sarah, 1–15, 61, 79, 80, 88, 89, 99, 101, 115–34, 148, 182, 184, 189, 219, 240, 242, 256, 277, 316, 318, 354, 376, 380, 384
pickets, 356, 363
Plataforma de Afectadospor las Hipotecas (PAH), 334–6, 338–45
PLP. *See* Parliamentary Labour Party (PLP)
Podemos, 336
Poland, 141, 155n6, 179, 186, 187, 380, 383, 385, 387, 389, 389n1
police violence, 48, 205, 211n1, 297, 304, 305
police/policing, 2, 13, 15, 41–54, 297–311
political agency, 2, 7–8, 10, 27, 68, 255
political alienation, 27, 256, 277, 281, 282
political apathy, 13, 247, 316–18, 350, 366, 377
political autonomy, 8, 242, 308
political capital, 341, 343, 344
political consumerism, 11
political correctness, 140, 319, 344
political disengagement, 61–3, 247, 317
political dissatisfaction, 192, 309
political emotion, 151–4
political graffiti, 85
political institutions, 102, 202, 219, 223, 227, 236, 256, 327, 338
political legitimacy, 1, 103, 140, 180, 184
political meetings, 385
political party membership. *See* party membership

political socialisation, 83, 123, 142, 148
political subjectivities, 11, 200–2, 209, 210
pop-up phone banks, 125
popular canteens, 260–2, 264, 265
populism, 4, 10, 35, 132, 139–56, 234, 388
populist parties, 139, 140, 187, 268n1
Portugal, 379, 383
Positive for Youth, 316
post-material values, 189, 192
post-truth politics, 140
poverty, 5, 6, 51, 83, 168, 180, 238, 276, 290n1, 305, 382–4, 388
poverty line, 218
PRC. *See* People's Republic of China (PRC)
precarious employment, 181, 190
precarious labour market, 222
precarity, 3, 74, 273, 275, 289, 318, 327
prejudice, 2, 7, 62, 166, 173
Prepare, Trial, Hire (PaTH), 218
press conferences, 306
Pride Parade, 208
pro-democracy movement, 97–9, 108, 109, 234, 351
productivity, 5, 180
professional environmentalists, 60, 66, 68, 69
property damaging, 184
protest, 5, 9, 10, 12–14, 20, 22, 25, 28–31, 33–5, 50, 63–5, 68, 72, 78, 80, 81, 84, 85, 87, 88, 90, 98–100, 109, 123, 133n9, 144, 149, 181, 184, 188–90, 199, 200, 202, 205, 206, 208–10, 211n1, 219, 234, 240, 242, 243, 247, 257, 276, 297–9, 303, 305–9, 311, 321, 326–8, 333,

334, 336, 345n1, 345n2, 349, 350, 353, 356–9, 361, 363–7, 367n4, 368n8, 382, 384, 386, 387
public forums, 206
public opinion, 103, 109, 340, 366
public services, 2, 70, 221, 261, 320, 336, 353
public spending cuts, 3, 5, 375
punks, 84, 86

Q
Quebec, 9, 10, 15, 77–91, 349–68
queer communities, 199, 209, 210

R
race relations, 6
racists/racism, 6, 83, 143, 145, 161, 166–9, 173, 174, 263, 287
radical(s), 32, 34, 35, 118, 123, 155n6, 163, 164, 169–71, 193, 244, 247, 289, 319, 334, 340, 342, 343, 345, 355
radicalisation, 11, 161–74, 346n6
Rainbow Nation, 9, 19–36
rallies, 81, 121, 125, 147, 150, 154n2, 234, 306, 356
Rancière, Jacques, 278, 350, 365, 367
RASH. *See* red anarchist skin heads (RASH)
reading a book out loud, 202
Reboiseurs du monde, 84
recession, 5, 25, 218, 261, 266, 276, 366
recycling, 234
red anarchist skin heads (RASH), 84
red dress woman dressed in, 15, 201, 202
referendum, 6, 127, 139, 145, 234, 238, 240–7, 281, 282, 290n3, 291n5, 316

refugees, 4, 140, 260, 280, 282
religion(s), 4, 6, 21, 161–74, 200, 283
renewal, 203, 317
representative democracy, 14, 78, 89, 335, 351
repression, 285, 340, 353–5, 359, 362
resistance, 11, 12, 65, 69, 84, 85, 88, 90, 108, 163, 168, 171, 173, 174, 199–211, 244, 247, 266, 273, 275, 279, 323–6, 340
re-tweeting, 150
right-wing parties, 319
riots, 79, 89, 309, 326
ritual(s), 208
Rhodes statue, 30–2
Romania, 383
Russia, 6

S
Sanders, Bernie, 6, 131
SAPA. *See* South Africa Press Association (SAPA)
schools, 9, 13, 15, 34, 41–57, 220, 222, 223, 238, 240, 241, 247, 297–314, 325, 349, 353
school curriculum, 223, 303, 305
school-to-prison pipeline, 300–2
Scotland, 12, 233–48
Scottish National Party (SNP), 115, 240, 241, 244, 248n2
searching for political information online, 182
self-actualisation, 61, 69, 236
self-determination, 234, 235, 237, 239, 242–4, 246, 247, 262, 265, 267
self-empowerment, 12, 262, 265, 267
self-help, 264, 265
self-management, 85, 257–9, 267, 284
self-organising, 207

sharing political information online, 182, 183, 191
short films, 86
signature gathering, 306
signing a petition, 84, 182, 326, 382, 384
silencing, 11, 201, 205, 206
Singapore, 170
sit-ins, 149, 183, 184, 191, 306
skinhead(s), 84, 86
Sloam, James, 189, 190, 235, 254, 256, 318, 326, 376
slogan(s), 29, 36n4, 108, 204, 208, 209, 333, 352, 355
Slovakia, 383, 385, 387, 389n1
Slovenia, 141, 383, 385, 387, 389n1
Snapchat, 125
SNP. *See* Scottish National Party (SNP)
social action, 152, 224, 236, 360
social change, 12, 23, 53, 73, 193, 225, 237, 267, 308, 309
social dislocation, 12
social engagement, 258, 266
social enterprise, 12, 219, 220, 224–6, 227
social entrepreneurs, 220, 225, 226
social exclusion, 173, 181
social fragmentation, 236
social inequalities, 5, 14, 234, 355
socialism, 123, 151
Socialist Workers Party (SWP), 128
social media, 7, 9–11, 21, 29–31, 35, 52, 53, 79, 116, 117, 120, 121, 124–6, 128, 129, 140, 146, 151, 168–70, 184, 189, 193, 202, 205, 206, 240, 241, 247, 322, 326, 359, 360
social movement(s), 6, 21, 28, 30, 31, 35, 42, 45, 60, 81, 88, 95–196, 254, 281, 282, 299, 305, 334, 336, 337, 345n1, 346n6, 357, 358, 382

social progress, 309
social welfare, 25, 63, 66, 163, 166, 254, 298, 376, 379, 384
solidarity, 12, 30, 32, 51, 82–4, 126, 150, 189, 208, 253–68, 275, 280, 282, 285, 317, 318, 325, 340, 355–7, 363, 365
SONA. *See* State of the Nation Address (SONA)
songs, 19, 85, 106, 208, 358
South Africa, 5, 6, 20–36, 36n1, 36n2, 36n4, 36n5
South Africa Press Association (SAPA), 29
South America, 2, 15, 349–68, 378
Southern Europe, 376, 381, 384, 388
Spain, 5, 102, 140, 161, 179, 186, 187, 334, 345n1, 345n2, 380, 383
squares, 98, 181, 281, 283, 334, 341, 363, 386
SRC. *See* Student Representative Council (SRC)
SSA. *See* Statistics South Africa (SSA)
stand-by citizens, 256
starting a political group, 183, 191
State (the), 34, 60, 66, 70, 78, 80, 85, 86, 88–91, 298, 299, 306, 346n6, 350, 365, 367
State of the Nation Address (SONA), 29
state violence, 273, 356
Statistics South Africa (SSA), 24, 25, 35
stereotype(s), 1, 166, 168, 169, 171, 173, 174, 226
Stormers, 10, 139–56
storytelling, 306
street marches, 206
strikes, 98, 128, 183, 185, 191, 349, 351–6, 358, 359, 363, 365, 367n4

student(s), 7, 14, 19–39, 41–57, 59–76, 80, 81, 83, 84, 98, 102, 116, 127, 134n12, 201, 223, 237, 238, 240, 242–4, 246, 259, 260, 274, 279, 281, 284, 287, 288, 297–313, 349–73
student movements, 17–94, 353, 354, 358, 360–3, 365, 366, 367n5
Student Representative Council (SRC), 33
student unions, 63–5, 68, 69, 73, 74n1, 74n2, 355
surveillance, 11, 43, 91, 161, 166, 167, 169, 205, 300
sustainability, 267
swearword workshop, 210
Sweden, 179, 186, 268n5, 379, 380, 383, 385, 387, 389n1
SWP. *See* Socialist Workers Party (SWP)
symbols, 32, 85, 182, 210, 363
Syria, 4, 128, 140
SYRIZA, 280, 282, 290n2, 291n5

T
Tahrir Square, 99
Taksim Square, 212n6
taxpayers, 5, 29
teaching to immigrants, 280
technology, 4, 28, 61, 126, 144, 146–8, 153, 167, 180, 184
tech-savvy, 122, 146
terrorism, 11, 142, 161–7, 169
threat(s), 4, 5, 11, 13, 14, 48, 100, 140, 142, 162, 165, 166, 168, 219, 242, 276, 289, 317, 323, 327, 328, 339, 343, 354
time-banks, 224
Trade Union and Socialist Coalition (TUSC), 128

trade unions, 79, 118, 123, 237, 248n3, 268n1, 334, 342
traditional politics, 69, 73, 116, 117, 130, 132, 219, 334, 335, 341
transgression, 319, 326–8
tree planting, 59, 65, 67, 71, 72
trending on Twitter, 121, 150
trolling/trolls, 105, 140, 144, 146, 148, 149
Trotskyists, 128, 129
truancy, 41, 44–6, 53n2, 306
Trump, Donald, 6, 125, 139, 144, 145, 149
Truncheon Spring, 354
tuition fees, 3, 7, 33, 116, 123, 237, 244, 316
tuitions, 80, 355
Tumblr, 125
Turkey, 6, 11, 199–212, 268n5
TUSC. *See* Trade Union and Socialist Coalition (TUSC)
tweeting, 125, 204, 306
Twitter, 79, 98, 105, 121, 125, 146, 148, 150, 169, 189, 287, 359

U
UCEN. *See* Central University of Chile (UCEN)
UK. *See* United Kingdom (UK)
UKIP. *See* United Kingdom Independence Party (UKIP)
Ukraine, 4
ultra-nationalist parties, 140
ultra-right, 6, 10, 139–42, 144, 146, 148, 150–3, 154
Umbrella Revolution, 98, 99
unconventional politics, 11, 190, 289, 377, 381, 382, 384, 386, 388
underemployment, 3, 246, 273
underground protest, 10, 78, 87, 88, 90

underground resistance, 84
UNICEF. *See* United Nations International Children's Fund (UNICEF)
United Kingdom (UK), 6, 10, 97, 115–37, 154n2, 161, 170, 179, 180, 184, 186–8, 218, 221, 224, 233–48, 248n3, 268n5, 275, 315–28, 376, 380, 385, 387, 389n1
United Kingdom Independence Party (UKIP), 6, 115, 139, 237
United Nations International Children's Fund (UNICEF), 290n1
United States (US), 2, 4–6, 9, 12, 13, 41–54, 63, 100, 102, 131, 133n6, 139, 143, 144, 163, 165, 170, 236, 297–311, 345n1, 378, 379
universal suffrage, 98, 234, 239, 240, 367
university tuition fees. *See* tuition fees
unpaid work, 221, 223
unrest, 35, 162, 166, 219, 276, 339
urban gardening, 257
user-generated data, 170
using violence, 91n5, 185, 191, 205, 359

V

vandalism, 35
veganism, 86
victimhood, 148
victimization, 11, 162, 167
video streaming, 206
violence, 13, 21, 34, 48, 49, 51, 88, 89, 151, 163, 164, 166, 167, 183, 185, 191, 205, 211n1, 273, 297, 304, 305, 323, 324, 340, 350, 351, 354–7, 359–66

viral (to go), 151
visiting political website, 183
volunteering, 12, 182, 219–24, 225–7, 236, 257, 265
Volunteering Australia, 220, 222, 227
volunteers, 125, 129, 220–4, 227, 280
volunteer tourists, 224
voter registration, 127, 316
voting, 8, 61, 79, 90, 115, 118, 131, 132, 181, 182, 184, 187, 217, 241, 242, 247, 277, 286, 319, 376, 381, 382, 385, 386. *See also* elections
Vromen, Ariadne, 110n3, 223, 236
vulnerable suffrage, 24

W

war on terror, 4, 162
wearing campaign/political symbols, 182, 309
Westminster, 117, 234, 241, 242, 244, 248n3
WhatsApp, 106
White Tide, 334–6, 341–5
Williamson, Howard, 218, 381, 388
woman in red dress (the), 15, 201, 202
Wong, Joshua, 244
Work for the Dole, 218, 222
working collaboratively, 221
World Bank, 60, 379

X

xenophobia, 21

Y

YCC. *See* Youth Citizenship Commission (YCC)
Yo Soy, 132, 351, 354, 359, 360

YOTP. *See* Youth Organizer Training Program (YOTP)
Young Lords, 304
young people's voices, 204, 316, 321, 322
Youngspiration, 244
Youth Citizenship Commission (YCC), 316, 321
youth culture, 211n4, 299
Youth Organizer Training Program (YOTP), 45, 49, 50, 54n7, 54n15
Youth Parliament, 184, 316, 321
youth policy, 87, 116
youth provision, 316
youth service provision, 116, 316, 317
youth services, 2, 13, 116, 316–18, 320, 322, 325, 327, 328, 328n1, 328n3
youth support networks, 218
youth underemployment, 3, 273
youth unemployment, 3, 9, 21, 25, 34, 35, 142, 245, 254, 255, 273, 290n1, 376, 381–4, 388
youth waithood, 61
youth work, 13, 14, 315–28
youth workers, 322, 327
YouTube, 79, 124, 125, 146–8, 169

Z

zero-hours contracts, 245
zero tolerance, 9, 42–4, 46, 47, 52, 53, 53n4, 300